I AM THAT I AM

I AM THAT I AM

Prabhuji

I AM THAT I AM
by Prabhuji

First edition

Printed in Round Top, New York, United States

Published by Prabhuji Mission
Website: prabhuji.net

Avadhutashram
PO Box 900
Cairo, NY, 12413
USA

Painting on the cover by Prabhuji:
"I am that I am"
Acrylic on canvas, New York
Canvas Size: 12"x16"

Library of Congress Control Number: 2024917337
ISBN-13: 978-1-945894-78-7

Contents

Preface 1
Introduction 5

Article 1: Here I am, I am here 9
Article 2: Solitude: to be one with the Whole 25
Article 3: Waiting for the unknowable 39
Article 4: Here and now 45
Article 5: A duet of one 55
Article 6: The parable of the inner palace 73
Article 7: Being and non-being in the Garden of Eden 105
Article 8: On the quest for meaning 127
Article 9: The reflection of unity 155
Article 10: *Mitzvot*: symbols of the return 181
Article 11: The recognition of consciousness 203
Article 12: The voice of silence 239
Article 13: Hassidism: living in grace 251
Article 14: A fire is burning here! 265
Article 15: The turkey-prince: shedding the garments of illusion 275
Article 16: Unity and human expression - *Tanya* Chapter 20 293
Article 17: Unity and divine expression - *Tanya* Chapter 21 313
Article 18: The Retroprogressive journey of *teshuvah* 329

About Prabhuji 397
The term Prabhuji by H.G. Swami Ramananda 409
The term *avadhūta* 411
About the Prabhuji Mission 421
About the Avadhutashram 423
The Path of Retroprogressive Alignment 425
Prabhuji today 427

ॐ अज्ञानतिमिरान्धस्य ज्ञानाञ्जनशलाकया ।
चक्षुरुन्मीलितं येन तस्मै श्रीगुरवे नमः ॥

oṁ ajñāna-timirāndhasya
jñānāñjana-śalākayā
cakṣur unmīlitaṁ yena
tasmai śrī-gurave namaḥ

Salutations unto that holy Guru who, applying the ointment [medicine] of [spiritual] knowledge, removes the darkness of ignorance of the blinded [unenlightened] and opens their eyes.

This book is dedicated, with deep gratitude and eternal respect, to the holy lotus feet of my beloved masters His Divine Grace Bhakti-kavi Atulānanda Ācārya Mahārāja (Gurudeva) and His Divine Grace Avadhūta Śrī Brahmānanda Bābājī Mahārāja (Guru Mahārāja).

Preface

The story of my life is an odyssey from what I believed myself to be to what I truly am… an inner and outer pilgrimage. A journey from the personal to the universal, from the partial to the whole, from the illusory to the real, from the apparent to the true. A wandering flight from the human to the divine.

Everything that awakens at dawn rests at dusk; every lit flame eventually extinguishes. Only what begins, ends; only what starts, finishes. But what dwells in the present is neither born nor dies, for that which lacks a beginning never perishes.

As a simple autobiographer and narrator of significant experiences, I share my intimate story with others. My story is not public but profoundly private and intimate. It does not belong to the turmoil of social life, but is a sigh kept in the most hidden depths of the soul.

I am a disciple of seers, enlightened beings, shadows of the universe who are nobody and walk in death. I am just a whim or perhaps a joke from the heavens and the only mistake of my beloved spiritual masters. I was initiated in my spiritual childhood by the moonlight, which showed me its light and shared its being with me. My muse was a seagull that loved to fly more than anything else in life.

In love with the impossible, I traversed the universe, obsessed with the brilliance of a star. I traveled countless paths, following the traces and vestiges of those with the vision to decipher the hidden. Like the ocean that longs for water, I sought my home within my own house.

I do not claim to be a guide, coach, teacher, instructor, educator, psychologist, enlightener, pedagogue, evangelist, rabbi, *posek halacha*, healer, therapist, satsangist, psychic, leader, medium, savior, guru, or authority of any kind, whether spiritual or material. I allow myself the audacity and daring to represent nothing and no one but myself. I am only a traveler whom you can ask for directions. With pleasure,

I point you to a place where everything calms upon arrival... beyond the sun and the stars, your desires and longings, time and space, concepts and conclusions, and beyond all that you believe you are or imagine you will be.

I paint sighs, hopes, silences, aspirations, and melancholies, inner landscapes, and sunsets of the soul. I am a painter of the indescribable, inexpressible, and indefinable, and unconfessable of our depths... or maybe I just write colors and paint words. Aware of the abyss that separates revelation and works, I live in a frustrated attempt to faithfully express the mystery of the spirit.

Since childhood, little windows of paper captivated my attention; through them, I visited places, met people, and made friends. Those tiny mandalas were my true elementary school, high school, and college. Like skilled teachers, these *yantras* have guided me through contemplation, attention, concentration, observation, and meditation.

Like a physician studies the human body, or a lawyer studies laws, I have dedicated my entire life to the study of myself. I can say with certainty that I know what resides and lives in this heart.

My purpose is not to persuade others. It is not my intention to convince anyone of anything. I do not offer theology or philosophy, nor do I preach or teach, I simply think out loud. The echo of these words may lead you to the infinite space of peace, silence, love, existence, consciousness, and absolute bliss.

Do not search for me. Search for yourself. You do not need me or anyone else, because the only thing that really matters is you. What you yearn for lies within you, as what you are, here and now.

I am not a merchant of rehashed information, nor do I intend to do business with my spirituality. I do not teach beliefs or philosophies. I only speak about what I see and just share what I know.

Avoid fame, for true glory is not based on public opinion but on what you really are. What matters is not what others think of you, but your own appreciation of who you are.

Choose bliss over success, life over reputation, and wisdom over information. If you succeed, you will know not only admiration but also true envy. Jealousy is mediocrity's tribute to talent and an open acceptance of one's own inferiority.

I advise you to fly freely and never be afraid of making mistakes. Learn the art of transforming your mistakes into lessons. Never blame others for your faults: remember that taking complete responsibility for your life is a sign of maturity. Flying teaches you that what matters is not touching the sky but having the courage to spread your wings. The higher you rise, the more graciously small and insignificant the world will seem. As you walk, sooner or later you will understand that every search begins and ends in you.

Your unconditional well-wisher,
Prabhuji

Introduction

The semantic roots of the term *religion* come from the Latin word *religare*, which evokes the idea of "reunion or reconnection." This concept was adopted by early Christian theorists and theologians such as Servius, Lactantius, and Saint Augustine and later explored by contemporary thinkers. It symbolizes a journey of return, not to a distant entity, but toward the intrinsic essence of the human being. It is not a preliminary meeting, but a *teshuvah*, a Hebrew term that means "return to the origin." This process symbolizes a return to our primordial source, a response to the disconnection caused by the maelstrom of material achievements. In this context, religion is interpreted as an effort to reconnect with our own authenticity.

Our unceasing quest for reconnection is rooted in a primal fear of the unknown. Human beings use their beliefs as shields to protect themselves from the fear of uncertainty and avoid directly facing their own doubts. Many find sanctuary for the soul in doctrines and dogmas, bastions of certainty and stability amid a vast and incomprehensible cosmos. Although common in all religious traditions, these practices often foster division instead of unity since they confuse faith with superstition. Adhering to pre-established dogmas constrains the mind and limits freedom for exploring and understanding.

In a state of freedom, approaching Truth or the Divine is not achieved through imposed beliefs but through deep, individual inquiry. Beliefs often construct a preconceived image of the Divine, which restricts our ability to perceive. Human creations, such as rituals and dogmas, are mere manifestations of thought. Created by thought, these manifestations cannot be intrinsically sacred. Understanding what is truly sacred is attained when we rid ourselves of fear and pain. Then, authentic love emerges, imbued with innate wisdom, leading the mind to a state of total serenity. In this profound silence, the sacred reveals itself in its purest and most essential form.

The essence of religion is not found in our current mental state, fraught with fears and projections, but in the expansion of our consciousness when breaking free from the psychological traps that we ourselves have created. True spirituality is manifested in communion with others, transcending divisions of doctrine or dogma. Compassion and genuine love emerge in the exploration beyond that which is conventional.

Religion is an adventure toward self-knowledge and self-transformation, a path of reunion with our original source and the rediscovery of our inherent oneness with totality. In this journey of inner transformation, the ego dissolves, allowing a deep and unbreakable connection with our essential being. Then, a fresh and calm consciousness emerges, receptive to the changes and dualities of life.

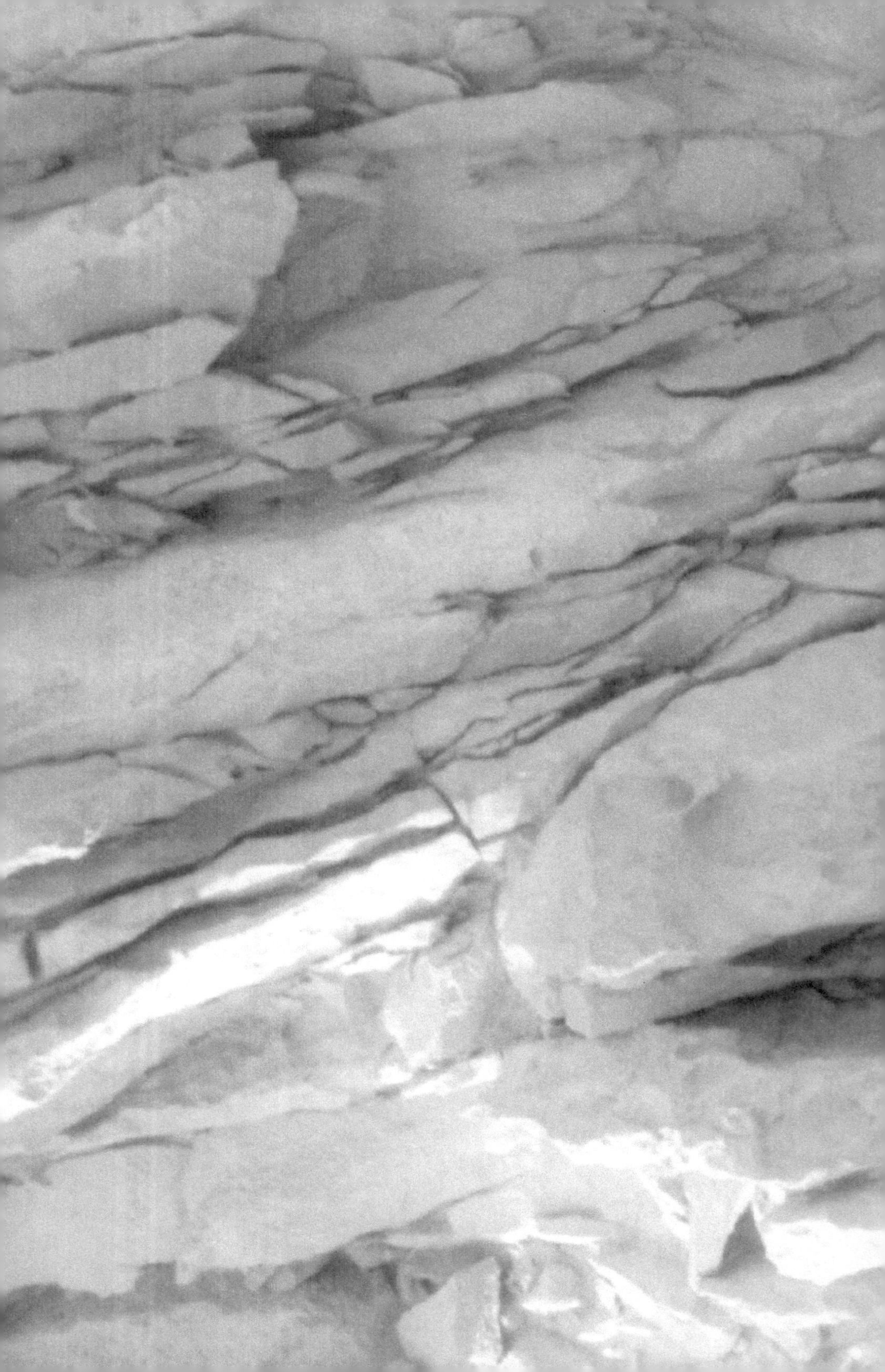

ARTICLE 1

HERE I AM, I AM HERE

Human beings do not live based on their own experience, but by following the inherited conception that defines them as independent entities. This interpretation, passed down through generations as unquestionable, leads us to conclude that we are isolated from others and from our origin. Granting more authority to this version than to our direct experience gives rise to human suffering.

If you have never been to Afghanistan, any ideas you have about how Afghans live are not real but are based on your belief in the information provided by the media. Similarly, your self-perception is mostly made up of beliefs that come from others. These are concepts that you remember or forget depending on your moods and circumstances. Whatever is mutable, transient, or temporary cannot be our reality.

We do not perceive our reality. We perceive ideas that come from other people we do not know, such as foreigners, strangers, and outsiders. We tend to define ourselves according to others' opinions. Our parents began designing our personality by giving us a name and a role in the family. The conditioning process is reinforced in school, college, the workplace, and so on. My father thought I was smart, and my mother that I was too skinny. My high school classmates thought I danced well but was bad at studying. My colleagues thought of me as a nice guy, but very quiet. Based on our ups and downs, successes and failures, we build our ego, which is not our creation, but society's.

To maintain the idea of being someone, we must strategically decorate our image to present to ourselves and others. We identify with this fabricated image and display it publicly. We send a doll, made in our supposed likeness, to live for us in society. Inquiry into our reality focuses on the roots of this image.

Whatever we think or believe about the universe, others, and ourselves is based on perceptions, sensations, emotions, and thoughts. Therefore, mental activity alters our perception of reality. Our conditioning modifies our experience of life. Neither the mind, body, nor the universe are as they seem to us. We are not even what we think we are. Due to the mutability of the content of experience, reality seems temporary to us. Reality cannot be mutable. What we really are does not vary but resides constantly in and within us as what we are. Understanding this fact is a cordial invitation to the reality that, while not objective, is the very essence of all experience.

We are not a sensation, feeling, or perception. Nor are we the opinions of our parents, siblings, relatives, friends, colleagues, neighbors, or enemies. Clinging to their descriptions of us prevents us from recognizing our authenticity, which transcends all ideas, beliefs, and stories. We should not rebel against the opinion of others but detach ourselves from our mental version. Actually, this interpretation does not affect who we are, it only prevents us from recognizing our own beingness.

> הוּא הָיָה אוֹמֵר: "אִם אֵין אֲנִי לִי, מִי לִי. וּכְשֶׁאֲנִי לְעַצְמִי, מָה אֲנִי. וְאִם לֹא עַכְשָׁיו, אֵימָתָי".
>
> (פרקי אבות א', י"ד)
>
> He [Hillel the elder] used to say: "If I am not for myself, who is for me? But if I am for myself, what am I? And if not now, then when?"
>
> (*Pirkei Avot*, 1.14)

The wise master Hillel teaches me that if I do not define myself, no one will. If I do not delimit myself, no one will limit me. If I do not interpret myself, I will remain as nobody. Without conceptualizing myself, I am a shadow of existence. In my authenticity, I am just a presence and nothing more.

The more we recognize that we cannot find the proper definition, the closer we get to the answer. Conscious inquiry begins by noticing that our reality cannot be verbalized, conceptualized, or defined because it lacks objective existence. It is at that moment that questions such as "Where am I?" or "Who am I?" direct us to the very essence of our personality and the foundation of egoic identification. The more we relinquish the belief of being an object, that is to say, "something" or "someone," the deeper we delve into the exploration of the foundations of our existence.

The retroprogressive process

My teachings are based on doubt; I do not preach faith in something but doubt in everything and everyone. Belief stagnates; doubt catalyzes. Questioning is a sign of growth and evolution. My message neither exalts beliefs nor condemns doubts. It invites you to delve into your doubts fearlessly, until you exhaust them and then jump to the other side. At the beginning, you will doubt your beliefs, preconceived ideas, traditions, views, and conventions. Then there will be doubts about your own existence and what you believe or think you are. At some point, doubts will arise about the "doubter," the separate "I" who does the doubting.

Self-exploration is about investigating the source and origin of our own existence. It is an exploration into the very roots of what we call "I."

> רַבִּי אֶלְעָזָר אוֹמֵר: "[...] וְדַע מַה שֶּׁתָּשִׁיב לְאֶפִּיקוֹרוֹס".
>
> (פרקי אבות ב', י"ד)
>
> Rabbi El'azar said: "[...] And know what to respond to Epicurus."
>
> (*Pirkei Avot*, 2.14)

Rabbi Elazar advises us to know how we respond to others, in other words, to investigate and question our reactions to society. For example, the concept "I" is what we use the most to communicate with others. Every human being consists of a collection of desires, ambitions, dreams, concepts, and beliefs that, like satellites, revolve around the concept "I." With this word, we express our desires: I want this or I want that; our nationality: I am Dutch, I am Chilean, I am American; our beliefs: I am Christian, I am Muslim, I am Hindu, I am secular, I am an atheist. Although we may define ourselves in different ways, the idea of "I" will always be present. Yet few wonder what the term "I" refers to. Many of our shared convictions deserve to be questioned. Investigating the idea "I," the thought "I," and the feeling "I," creates a conducive situation for recognizing consciousness.

Self-inquiry in the form of questions such as "where am I?" or "who am I?" directs attention to a source and origin where there is no object or entity. The realization of consciousness consists in the recognition of the undefinable self. In the reunion of beingness with itself, the inconceivable is revealed to be our eternal essence.

וַיִּשְׁמְעוּ אֶת קוֹל ה' אֱלֹהִים מִתְהַלֵּךְ בַּגָּן לְרוּחַ הַיּוֹם וַיִּתְחַבֵּא הָאָדָם וְאִשְׁתּוֹ מִפְּנֵי
ה' אֱלֹהִים בְּתוֹךְ עֵץ הַגָּן:
וַיִּקְרָא ה' אֱלֹהִים אֶל הָאָדָם וַיֹּאמֶר לוֹ אַיֶּכָּה:

(בראשית ג', ח'–ט')

And they heard the voice of the Lord God moving about in the garden in the breeze of the day; and the man and his wife hid from the presence of the Lord God amongst the trees of the garden. And the Lord God called unto the man, and said unto him: "*ayeka?*" (where are you?).

(Genesis, 3:8–9)

It is revealing to ponder why God, being omniscient, asks Adam about his whereabouts. This interaction should not be interpreted literally; rather, it is a didactic tool. Through this question, God does not seek literal answers but facilitates meditative self-inquiry. The omniscient God did not ask Adam where he was in order to find him, but to offer him merciful guidance. Where is that "I" your whole life revolves around? *Ayeka* (איכה), or "where are you?" is a question asking us to define ourselves. Abraham, Jacob, and Samuel replied *hineni* (הנני), or "here am I." This answer to the divine call is the realization of consciousness.

וַיְהִי אַחַר הַדְּבָרִים הָאֵלֶּה וְהָאֱלֹהִים נִסָּה אֶת אַבְרָהָם וַיֹּאמֶר אֵלָיו אַבְרָהָם וַיֹּאמֶר
הִנֵּנִי:

(בראשית כ"ב, א')

> And it came to pass after these things, that God tested Abraham, and He said to him, "Abraham," and he said, "*hineni*" (here am I).
>
> (Genesis, 22:1)
>
> וַיֹּאמֶר אֵלַי מַלְאַךְ הָאֱלֹהִים בַּחֲלוֹם יַעֲקֹב וָאֹמַר הִנֵּנִי:
> (בראשית ל"א, י"א)
>
> And the angel of God said to me in the dream, "Jacob!" and I said, "*hineni*" (here am I).
>
> (Genesis, 31:11)
>
> וַיֹּאמֶר אֱלֹהִים לְיִשְׂרָאֵל בְּמַרְאֹת הַלַּיְלָה וַיֹּאמֶר יַעֲקֹב יַעֲקֹב וַיֹּאמֶר הִנֵּנִי:
> (בראשית מ"ו, ב')
>
> And God spoke unto Israel in the visions of the night, and said, "Jacob, Jacob," and he said, "*hineni*" (Here am I).
>
> (Genesis, 46:2)
>
> וַיִּקְרָא ה' אֶל־שְׁמוּאֵל וַיֹּאמֶר הִנֵּנִי:
> (שמואל א' ג', ד')
>
> And the Lord called Samuel; and he said, "*hineni*" (Here am I).
>
> (1 Samuel, 3:4)

Characters such as Abraham, Jacob, and Samuel are role models that recognize consciousness and identify "I." This teaches us that the essential search is within, toward the realization of the self. Through their testimony, they indicate consciousness, *hineh* (here), and presence, *ani* (I am).

We often believe that our existence is defined by our physical location: a country, a city, a street, even a body or a mind. Yet if we are ignorant of our true essence and identity, it is impossible to determine where we are really "located." In the scriptures, the notion of *hineni*, or "here I am," is more than a statement of physical presence; it is a recognition of consciousness. Thus, the question "where are you?" is intrinsically parallel to "who are you?" It is not a matter of defining our location in physical space, but of recognizing that we are the epicenter of totality. Martin Heidegger called this *Dasein* or "being there." *Da* in German is "here" or "there." *Dasein* is "being here," that is, the "here of being."

"וַיִּפְגַּע בַּמָּקוֹם" (בראשית כ"ח, י"א), רַב הוּנָא בְּשֵׁם רַבִּי אַמֵּי אָמַר: "מִפְּנֵי מָה מְכַנִּין שְׁמוֹ שֶׁל הַקָּדוֹשׁ־בָּרוּךְ־הוּא וְקוֹרְאִין אוֹתוֹ מָקוֹם? שֶׁהוּא מְקוֹמוֹ שֶׁל עוֹלָם וְאֵין עוֹלָמוֹ מְקוֹמוֹ, מִן מַה דִּכְתִיב: 'הִנֵּה מָקוֹם אִתִּי' (שמות ל"ג, כ"א), הֱוֵי הַקָּדוֹשׁ־בָּרוּךְ־הוּא מְקוֹמוֹ שֶׁל עוֹלָם וְאֵין עוֹלָמוֹ מְקוֹמוֹ". אָמַר רַבִּי יִצְחָק: "כְּתִיב: 'מְעֹנָה אֱלֹהֵי קֶדֶם' (דברים ל"ג, כ"ז), אֵין אָנוּ יוֹדְעִים אִם הַקָּדוֹשׁ־בָּרוּךְ־הוּא מְעוֹנוֹ שֶׁל עוֹלָמוֹ וְאִם עוֹלָמוֹ מְעוֹנוֹ, מִן מַה דִּכְתִיב (תהילים צ', א'): 'ה' מָעוֹן אַתָּה', הֱוֵי הַקָּדוֹשׁ־בָּרוּךְ־הוּא מְעוֹנוֹ שֶׁל עוֹלָמוֹ וְאֵין עוֹלָמוֹ מְעוֹנוֹ".

(בראשית רבה, ס"ח)

"And he reached the place" (Genesis, 28:11). Rabbi Huna says, in the name of Rabbi Ami: "Why do we substitute the name of the Holy Blessed One and we call Him 'Place'? For He is the Place of the world, yet His world is not His place. We learn it from the verse: 'Behold, there is a place with Me.' (Exodus, 33:21). From here we learn that the Holy Blessed One is the place of the world, yet His world is not His place." Rabbi Yitzḥak said: "It is written: 'The dwelling, ancient God' (Deuteronomy, 33:27). From this verse alone we cannot determine whether the Holy Blessed One is the dwelling of the world or if the world is the dwelling of the Holy One. However, from the verse: 'O Lord, You are a dwelling' (Psalms, 90:1), we learn that the Holy Blessed One is the dwelling of the world, yet His world is not His dwelling."

(*Bereshit Rabbah*, 68)

It is not consciousness that resides in each of us. Instead, we reside in consciousness. We abide and live in the indivisible God, the One without a second. In the disidentification from the body–mind complex and the recognition of consciousness, the experience of being is no longer limited by the boundaries of a specific place. Our authentic nature does not reside in a particular geographical location. It is not the I-subject that seeks consciousness, but consciousness that seeks itself. Consciousness is not a quality that can be possessed to varying degrees, nor a place where we reside, but what we are, that is, beingness itself. In fact, we are not merely another experience that occurs within consciousness; rather, we are the consciousness within which all experience unfolds. Everything that happens does not happen to me – it happens in me.

> וַיָּבֹא הַמֶּלֶךְ דָּוִד וַיֵּשֶׁב לִפְנֵי ה' וַיֹּאמֶר מִי אָנֹכִי ה' אֱלֹהִים וּמִי בֵיתִי כִּי הֲבִאֹתַנִי עַד־הֲלֹם:
>
> (שמואל ב' ז', י"ח)
>
> And the king David went in and sat before the Lord; and he said: "Who am I, O Lord God, and what is my family, that You have brought me thus far?"
>
> (2 Samuel, 7:18)

I am a doctor, a lawyer, Raymond, Rose, Chilean, Hindu, Catholic, Protestant, religious, secular, atheist, tall, short, young, old, married, or single. As long as we offer conventional answers, we will remain unsatisfied. All these answers are related to the periphery and not the center. They are superficial; they are not vital. Clearly, the only authoritative definition of yourself is your own. If the inquiry is clear and direct, the answer will be vivid and authentic.

We often define ourselves by our activities. But our personality does not always satisfy us or faithfully represent us. We seek positive answers and run away from negative ones. "But if I am for my own self [only], what am I?" (וכשאני לעצמי, מה אני?). What am I when I am the only one who observes observation or is aware of consciousness? The questions "where am I?" and "who am I?" are addressed to you and ask you to define yourself according to your own experience. It is perhaps the first time that you are the sole authority for answering this question from your direct vision.

As strange as it may seem, the beginner's answer to the question "who are you?" is the most real. A bewildered expression is more authentic than an intellectual conceptualization that we develop after years of study, courses, and books.

Our authentic essence cannot be a definition because we can always inquire about the one who is aware of that definition. When reaching any conceptualization, we must look toward the one who is conscious of it, the definer or conceptualizer. The time will come when we give up the search for a conceptualization because objective nature is temporary, it begins and ends. What is real in us must be eternal and immutable. All identifications are ephemeral; they appear and disappear. Only consciousness remains constantly present.

לְעוֹלָם יְהֵא אָדָם יְרֵא שָׁמַיִם בַּסֵּתֶר וּבַגָּלוּי וּמוֹדֶה עַל הָאֱמֶת וְדוֹבֵר אֱמֶת בִּלְבָבוֹ וְיַשְׁכֵּם וְיֹאמַר: "רִבּוֹן כָּל הָעוֹלָמִים וַאֲדוֹנֵי הָאֲדוֹנִים, לֹא עַל צִדְקוֹתֵינוּ אֲנַחְנוּ מַפִּילִים תַּחֲנוּנֵינוּ לְפָנֶיךָ כִּי עַל רַחֲמֶיךָ הָרַבִּים, מָה אָנוּ מֶה חַיֵּינוּ מֶה חַסְדֵּנוּ, מַה צִּדְקוֹתֵינוּ, מַה יְּשׁוּעָתֵנוּ, מַה כֹּחֵנוּ מַה גְּבוּרָתֵנוּ, מַה נֹּאמַר לְפָנֶיךָ ה' אֱלֹהֵינוּ וֵאלֹהֵי אֲבוֹתֵינוּ הֲלֹא כָּל הַגִּבּוֹרִים כְּאַיִן לְפָנֶיךָ וְאַנְשֵׁי הַשֵּׁם כְּלֹא הָיוּ וַחֲכָמִים כִּבְלִי מַדָּע וּנְבוֹנִים כִּבְלִי הַשְׂכֵּל כִּי רוֹב מַעֲשֵׂיהֶם תֹּהוּ וִימֵי חַיֵּיהֶם הֶבֶל לְפָנֶיךָ, וּמוֹתַר הָאָדָם מִן הַבְּהֵמָה אָיִן כִּי הַכֹּל הָבֶל".

(סידור התפילה, תפילת שחרית)

A person should always be God-fearing in private and in public, acknowledging the truth, and speaking the truth within his heart, and arising early, he should proclaim: "Master of all worlds and Lord of all lords! Not in the merit of our righteousness do we cast our supplications before You, but in the merit of Your abundant mercy. What are we? What is our life? What is our kindness? What is our righteousness? What is our salvation? What is our strength? What is our might? What can we say before You, O Lord, our God and the God of our forefathers? Are not all the mighty like nothing before You? The famous as if they never existed? The wise as if devoid of wisdom? And the perceptive as if devoid of intelligence? For most of their deeds are futile, and the days of their life are like a vanishing mist before you. The preeminence of man over the beast is nonexistent, for all is like a vanishing mist."

(*Siddur, Daily morning prayer, Shaḥarit*)

The end of the search is the revelation of consciousness, not as an identification but as what we really are.

Regardless of what others believe, the question "where am I?" will lead us to where we are. No matter how they define us, the question "who am I?" will continue to point to the essence. Reality can be neither a belief nor a definition because it is the source of all ideas. What we truly are cannot be verbalized because it is the very origin of words.

Verbalization only indicates the road to take, but it cannot replace what has been pointed out. No matter what the definition is, the reality of what we are always resides at its foundation.

Self-realization

Nothing is easier than realizing our true nature. There is no reason to postpone it even for a moment. All procrastination is just another mental strategy.

וְאִם לֹא עַכְשָׁיו, אֵימָתָי.

(פרקי אבות א', י"ד)

And if not now, then when?

(*Pirkei Avot*, 1.14)

If we observe our mental activity, we will notice that we give too much importance to interpreting experience. We obey the conditioned content of experience as if it were the highest authority. When we stop identifying with that content, only silence remains, which allows the recognition of our reality.

Every idea about who we are comes from the past. Our "I" originates from what is known. To explore our reality, it is imperative to observe. From observation, we situate ourselves in the now.

Existence knows no other moment other than the present. Yesterday is known through memory and tomorrow through imagination. Our reality is what we are now, which is the only moment to reencounter our authentic nature.

Although it may seem to us that the main obstacle to recognizing consciousness is distance, it is in fact closeness. Its intimacy is such that consciousness is the most obvious of all experiences. However, we replace reality with a narrative, which distorts our vision. This comic strip is an interpretation that assumes authority over perception. Yet, reality is closer than that interpretation, than any word, emotion, or idea, and even than our own heart:

> כִּי־קָרוֹב אֵלֶיךָ הַדָּבָר מְאֹד בְּפִיךָ וּבִלְבָבְךָ לַעֲשֹׂתוֹ׃
>
> (דברים ל', י"ד)
>
> Rather, the thing is very close to you; it is in your mouth and in your heart, so that you can fulfill it.
>
> (Deuteronomy, 30:14)

Consciousness is closer to us than any experience. This verse says "very" (מאד) because no matter how close we are to our authentic nature, we can always be closer, until all distance disappears, and we realize consciousness as our own knowingness.

Like dreams, whatever is false and illusory is temporary. It comes and goes. Our identifications are transient; they arise and disappear like waves in the sea. On the other hand, what is real is immutable and unalterable. Consciousness does not share the same fate as the mind and body. Our conscious presence has no beginning and no end, no birth and no death. What we truly are has always existed and will always exist. Our authenticity was, is, and will be before birth, during life, and eternally after death.

> וְהוּא הָיָה וְהוּא הֹוֶה, וְהוּא יִהְיֶה בְּתִפְאָרָה.
>
> (סידור התפילה, פיוט "אדון עולם")

And he who was, and he who is, and he who shall remain in splendor.

(*Siddur*, "*Adon Olam*" *Piyyut*)

In the *Song of Moses,* we find the following verses:

כִּי שֵׁם ה' אֶקְרָא   הָבוּ גֹדֶל לֵאלֹהֵינוּ׃
הַצּוּר תָּמִים פָּעֳלוֹ   כִּי כָל־דְּרָכָיו מִשְׁפָּט
אֵל אֱמוּנָה וְאֵין עָוֶל   צַדִּיק וְיָשָׁר הוּא׃

(דברים ל"ב, ג'–ד')

For when I proclaim the name of the Lord;
Give glory to our God!
The Rock!—His deeds are perfect,
For all His ways are just;
A faithful God, never unjust.
Righteous and just is He.

(Deuteronomy, 32:3–4)

The holy *Zohar* comments on these words from Moses:

אָמַר רִבִּי חִיָּיא: "הַאי קְרָא אוֹלִיפְנָא מִנֵּיהּ חָכְמְתָא עִלָּאָה, וְהָכִי הוּא. אֲבָל סֵיפֵיהּ דִּקְרָא, מְקַשֵּׁר קִשְׁרָא דִּמְהֵימְנוּתָא, בְּמַאי דִּכְתִיב: 'הוּא'. כְּמָה דְּאַתְּ אָמֵר: 'צַדִּיק וְיָשָׁר הוּא' (דברים ל"ב, ד'). כְּלוֹמַר הוּא כֹּלָּא. הוּא חַד בְּלָא פֵּרוּדָא. דְּאִי תֵּימָא כָּל הָנֵי סַגִּיאִין אִנּוּן, חָזַר וְאָמַר: 'הוּא', כֻּלְּהוּ סַלְּקִין וּמִתְקַשְּׁרָן וּמִתְאַחֲדָן בְּחַד. וְכֹלָּא, הוּא הָיָה, וְהוּא הוֹוֶה, וְהוּא יְהֵא. וְהוּא חַד. בְּרִיךְ שְׁמֵיהּ לְעָלַם וּלְעָלְמֵי עָלְמִין. עַד כֵּן מִתְקַטְּרִין מִלִּין, וּמִתְאַחֲדִין מִלִּין קַדִּישִׁין, דִּשְׁמָא דְקוּדְשָׁא־בְּרִיךְ־הוּא".

(ספר הזוהר, האזינו, ח')

Rabbi Ḥiya said, "From this verse, we have learned celestial wisdom, and it is so. Yet, the end of the verse connects the knot of faith by writing the word *hu* (meaning 'He'), as it is written: 'Righteous and just is He,' (Deuteronomy, 32:4) which means **He** is everything, **He** is one without division. For should you think that all these [attributes mentioned in the verse] are many; therefore, it says again: *hu* (He), as they all arise, connect, and join into one. And He is everything; He was, He is, and He will be. And He is one. Blessed is His name forever and ever. Hence, things are connected, and the holy matters [i.e., attributes] of the name of the Holy One, Blessed be He, are joined."

(*Zohar*, "*Ha'azinu*," 8)

When we perceive the moon and the stars, we conclude that they are distant. But if we observe with attention, we will see that every perception, no matter how distant it may seem to us, is experienced in exactly the same place as our thoughts and innermost emotions. Although we may think we hear sounds in the distance, we perceive them as close as our thoughts, ideas, or feelings. All experiences, whether visual, auditory, olfactory, or tactile, occur deep within us. Only the mental interpretation of these experiences convinces us that perceptions occur at a distance.

When touching a bottle with our eyes closed, we perceive a certain texture. This perception does not occur in the bottle or in the hand, but deep within us. It does not testify to the existence of an external bottle, but rather is just an experience perceived with the same intimacy as thoughts, emotions, and sensations. We consider ourselves to be bodies that contain a fragment of consciousness capable of perceiving external objective diversity. But in reality, the mind, the body, and the universe happen within us, not the other way around. If our interior were a place, that place would simply be another experience that occurs in pure knowingness. There is no place where consciousness is absent:

לֵית אֲתַר פָּנוּי מִנֵּיהּ, כְּנִשְׁמְתָא דְּאִשְׁתַּכְּחַת בְּכָל אֵבֶר וְאֵבֶר דְּגוּפָא.
(תיקוני הזוהר, קכ"ב, ב')

There is no place devoid of Him, just as the soul is present in each and every limb of the body.

(*Tikkunei HaZohar*, 122b)

Although we believe we know a diversity of objects, in fact we only know knowingness itself. We have never known anyone or anything. Such knowingness does not occur in a specific place, because every corner is included in knowingness.

The mind fractures pure knowingness into an apparent subject–knower and an object–known. Thought is a modulation of knowing. It is capable of presenting unity as a duality of two distant phenomena. However, this is a fantasy, a mental mirage that is devoid of reality. There is only knowingness, which is one and the same with our beingness.

Knowingness is indivisible; it does not possess fragments or portions, nor does it allow for separate objects or entities. There is no part of knowingness that is closer or more distant. The presence that knows is knowingness itself. There is only one indivisible flow of knowingness, knowing itself uninterruptedly.

אֶחָד וְאֵין יָחִיד כְּיִחוּדוֹ, נֶעְלָם וְגַם אֵין סוֹף לְאַחְדּוּתוֹ.
(סידור התפילה, פיוט "יגדל אלוהים חי")

He is One, and there is no unity like His Oneness,
inscrutable and infinitive is His unity.
(*Siddur*, "*Yigdal Elohim Ḥai*," *Piyyut*)

Here I am, because "here" is not the place where I am, but what I am. Life is just one long path of learning, from here to here. Every idea or belief about you comes and goes, just as the ocean's waves arise and disappear. All definitions are false; being without definitions is the only reality. Do not fight definitions, but instead, allow them to disappear on their own. And be what remains. Be that which neither comes nor goes. Enjoy the bliss of really being... of being the Self.

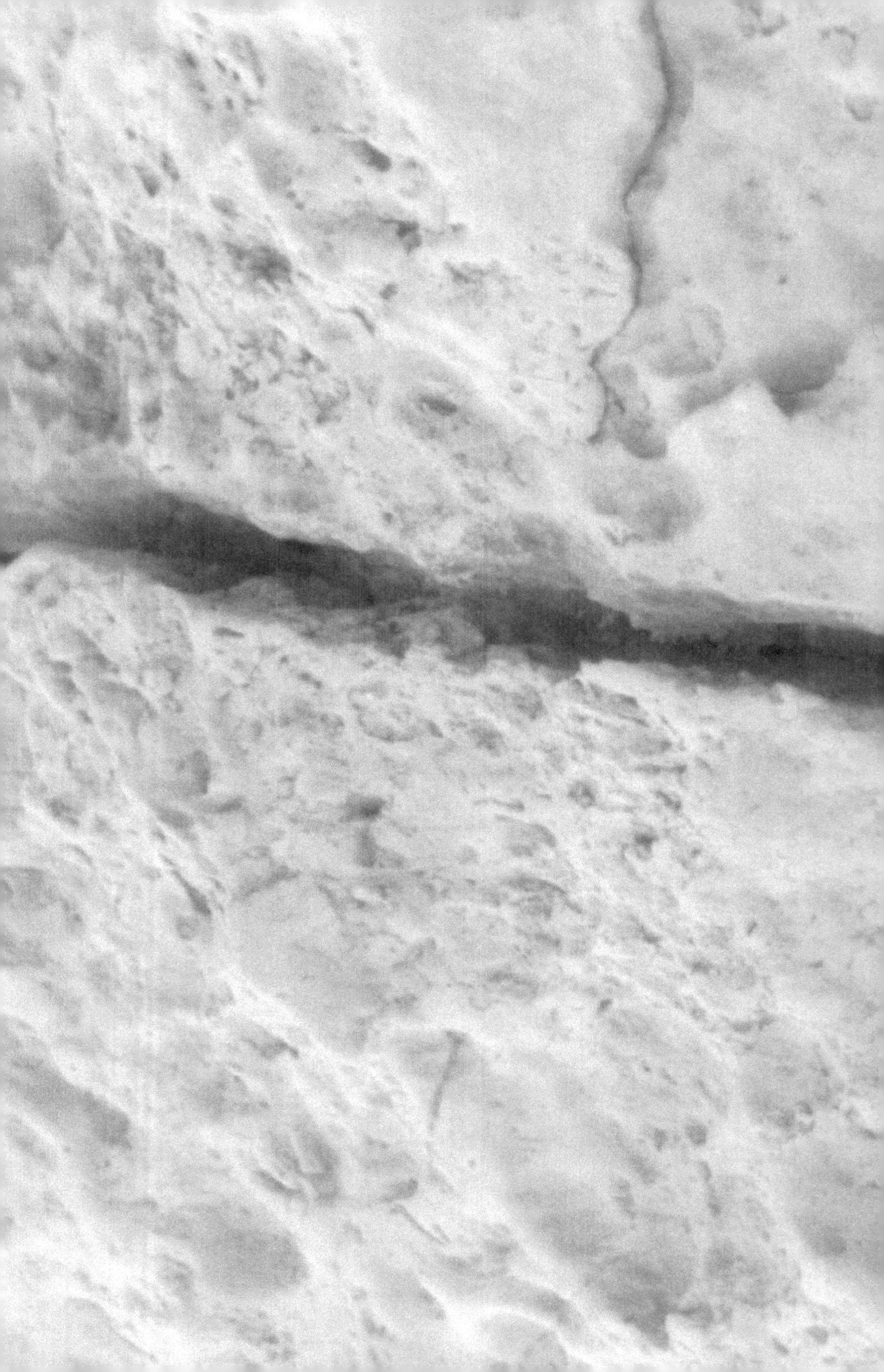

ARTICLE 2

SOLITUDE: TO BE ONE WITH THE WHOLE

Question:

I have studied many different meditation techniques. I would like to know what meditation is and what techniques you teach.

Answer:

Strange as it may seem, I do not teach meditation techniques. The "methods of meditation" taught nowadays are merely relaxation techniques. They may be beneficial for lowering blood pressure or alleviating depression, but they are not real paths to liberation. Many people want to learn how to meditate, but no one can teach them because meditation does not involve activity of any kind. Repeating mantras or visualizing sacred letters is not meditating; it is removing obstacles to create the proper conditions for meditation to happen. Meditation is not an action but an event: it happens, it occurs, it takes place. Therefore, instead of learning to meditate we need to know how to keep ourselves unoccupied and just observe. As we cultivate inactivity and observation, we create the proper situation for meditation to occur.

> חֲסִידִים הָרִאשׁוֹנִים הָיוּ שׁוֹהִים שָׁעָה אַחַת וּמִתְפַּלְּלִים, כְּדֵי שֶׁיְּכַוְּנוּ אֶת לִבָּם לַמָּקוֹם.
>
> (משנה, ברכות, ה', א')
>
> The pious men of old used to wait one hour and then pray so that they would direct their heart to the "Place" [the Divine].
>
> (*Mishnah*, "*Berachot*," 5.1)

Observation is the only means to disidentify or separate ourselves from our mental conditioning. When we assume the role of "doers," we identify with the body, mind, and emotions. To distance ourselves from this identification, it is essential to adopt the attitude of a vigilant witness. To observe is to seek absolute solitude, seclusion, or isolation, which is called *hitbodedut* in Hebrew. To observe is to isolate ourselves from the objective world that we believe we perceive through our senses and distance ourselves from everything we own, believe, think, and feel, in order to be what we really are. Respect or awe toward God is called *yir'ah* (יראה) in Hebrew. This term contains the same letters as the word *re'iyah* (ראיה), or "vision." That is, vision leads to having respect for God and being in awe of God.

רוֹצֶה ה' אֶת־יְרֵאָיו אֶת־הַמְיַחֲלִים לְחַסְדּוֹ:

(תהילים, קמ"ז, י"א)

The Lord desires those who are in awe of Him, those that wait for His mercy.

(Psalms, 147:11)

Meditation can be external or internal: the former is a preparation for the latter and entails ceasing to identify with the physical body. For this purpose, it is necessary to contemplate the body: observe our hands, physical sensations, and so on. In the East, many practices have been developed to direct attention to the body such as yoga, tai chi, and tea ceremonies, among others.

וּמִבְּשָׂרִי אֶחֱזֶה אֱלוֹהַּ:

(איוב י"ט, כ"ו)

And from my flesh shall I see God.

(Job, 19:26)

As the observer of your physical shape, you can continue to breathe while contemplating the air entering your nostrils. Note the difference between the cooler air that you inhale and the warmer air that you exhale. Do not control your breathing, just watch it. Instead of being the one who breathes, be a distant witness to the respiratory process and allow it to happen by itself.

שֹׁרֶשׁ הַכֹּל – הִתְבּוֹדְדוּת. כִּי הוּא עִנְיָן נִשְׂגָּב, גָּדוֹל וָרָם לִזְכּוֹת לְסֵדֶר קְדֻשָּׁה. וְאִתְּנַח סִימָנָא מֵרַבְּוָתָא קַדְמָאֵי (וְהֵנַּח סִימָן לְכָךְ מֵרַבּוֹתֵינוּ הָרִאשׁוֹנִים): "בַּד קֹדֶשׁ יִלְבָּשׁ" (ויקרא ט"ז, ד'), הַכַּוָּנָה "בַּד", שֶׁהוּא מִתְבּוֹדֵד – אָז "קֹדֶשׁ יִלְבָּשׁ". (החיד"א , עבודת הקודש, ציפורן שמיר, נ"א)

The root of everything is *hitbodedut*, (seclusion). It is a sublime, immense, and elevated matter [to be mastered] for the sake of holiness. And our ancient masters gave us a sign regarding this: "He shall put on the holy linen (*Baad Kodesh Yilbash*)" (Leviticus, 16:4) [in Hebrew, the word *baad* means "linen" and is composed of the two letters: *beit* (ב) and *dalet* (ד), which also form the root of the word *hitbodedut*, meaning "seclusion"]. The meaning is: "when he isolates himself (*baad*), then he shall be clothed in holiness (*kodesh yilbash*)."

(The Ḥida, *Avodat HaKodesh*, "*Zipporen Shamir*," 51)

Next, observe the mind. Repeating God's names is unnecessary. No mental activity, however sacred or spiritual it may seem, can be called as meditation. Meditation begins when one stops being the doer to become a fearless witness. Observe the flow of thoughts, do not analyze them nor repress them; only watch them without the intervention of the mind. To the extent that you remain alert, mental movement naturally decreases.

וְכֵן הִתְבּוֹנֵן [יַעֲקֹב] בְּכָל דָּבָר וְעַל יְדֵי זֶה הִגִּיעַ תְּחִלָּה לִבְחִינַת יִרְאָה תַּתָּאָה בִּשְׁלֵמוּת. וּמְרֻמָּז בַּפָּסוּק "וַיִּקַּח מֵאַבְנֵי הַמָּקוֹם וַיָּשֶׂם מְרַאֲשֹׁתָיו" (בראשית כ"ח, י"א) רָאשֵׁי תֵּבוֹת גִּימַטְרִיָּא צ"א, מִסְפַּר שְׁנֵי שֵׁמוֹת ה-ו-י-ה, א-ד-נ-י, בְּחִינַת "וַה' בְּהֵיכַל קָדְשׁוֹ" (חבקוק ב', כ') שֶׁנִּסְתַּכֵּל בְּכָל דָּבָר אֵיךְ שֶׁבְּכָל דָּבָר נִבְרָא יֵשׁ בְּחִינַת "ה' בְּהֵיכַל קָדְשׁוֹ", שֶׁנִּמְשָׁךְ עַל יְדֵי כ"ב אוֹתִיּוֹת הַתּוֹרָה כַּנַּ"ל.

(רבי אברהם דב מאבריטש, בת־עין, בראשית, ויצא)

And so [Jacob] observed everything and thus initially reached the state of complete *yir'ah tata'ah*, or "lower awe," and this is hinted at in the verse: "And he took from the stones of the place and he put them beneath his head" (Genesis, 28:11) (*Vayikaḥ Me'avney Hamakom Vayasem Merashotav*), where the numeric value of the first letters M.H.V.M adds up to 91, which equals to the total numeric value of two of God's names: H-V-Y-H and A-D-O-N-A-I, which are the two aspects indicated in the verse: "And the Lord [the aspect of H-V-Y-H] is in His holy temple [the aspect of A-D-O-N-

A-I]" (Habakkuk, 2:20). So, he [Jacob], observed that in all manifested things there exists the aspect of "the Lord is in His holy temple" which is brought about by the 22 letters of the Torah, as mentioned before.

(Rabbi Avraham Dov of Avritch,
Bat Ayin, "*Bereshit*," "*Vayetze*")

Next, watch your emotional activity. This may seem difficult at first, since emotions are more subtle. Finally, observe the feeling called "I." By observing it, you shall realize that it is only an idea that claims ownership over every thought, emotion, sensation, or perception. When that "I," or *ani* in Hebrew, is observed, it reveals itself to be nothing, or *ain*. Observe the observer, the meditator; only then shall you achieve absolute solitude: freedom from everything and everyone, even from yourself. In this state, you will stop being what you thought you were and become what you have always been.

וְגַם בְּכַמָּה חִבּוּרִים מֵהָרִאשׁוֹנִים נִמְצָא שֶׁהַהִתְבּוֹדְדוּת וְהַפְּרִישׁוּת וְהַדְּבֵקוּת הָיוּ נוֹהֲגִים בָּהּ חֲסִידֵי יִשְׂרָאֵל, הַיְנוּ שֶׁבִּהְיוֹתָם לְבַדָּם מַפְרִישִׁים מִדַּעְתָּם עִנְיְנֵי הָעוֹלָם וּמְקַשְּׁרִים מַחְשְׁבוֹתָם עִם אֲדוֹן הַכֹּל, וְכָךְ לִמֵּד מהרר"י הַמְקֻבָּל הַנִּזְכָּר, שֶׁזֶּה מוֹעִיל לַנֶּפֶשׁ שִׁבְעָתַיִם מֵהַלִּמּוּד, וּלְפִי כֹּחַ וִיכֹלֶת הָאָדָם יִפְרֹשׁ וְיִתְבּוֹדֵד יוֹם אֶחָד בְּשָׁבוּעַ אוֹ יוֹם אֶחָד בַּחֲמִשָּׁה עָשָׂר יוֹם אוֹ יוֹם אֶחָד בְּחֹדֶשׁ, וְלֹא יִפְחֹת מִזֶּה. וְהָרמב"ן ז"ל כָּתַב עַל פָּסוּק שֶׁנֶּאֱמַר בְּיַעֲקֹב אָבִינוּ: "קוּם עֲלֵה בֵית־אֵל וְשֶׁב־שָׁם" (בראשית ל"ה, א'), מַאי 'וְשֶׁב שָׁם'? כְּמוֹ "בְּשׁוּבָה וָנַחַת תִּוָּשֵׁעוּן" (ישעיהו ל', ט"ו). הַיְנוּ שֶׁיָּכִין דַּעְתּוֹ בְּיִשּׁוּב הַדַּעַת עִמּוֹ יִתְבָּרַךְ. וְזוֹ הִיא שֶׁשָּׁנִינוּ: "חֲסִידִים הָרִאשׁוֹנִים הָיוּ שׁוֹהִים שָׁעָה אַחַת וּמִתְפַּלְּלִים כְּדֵי שֶׁיְּכַוְּנוּ לִבָּם לַמָּקוֹם" (משנה, ברכות ה', א'). וּפֵרְשׁוּ הַמְפָרְשִׁים דְּרוֹצֶה לוֹמַר שֶׁהָיוּ מְפַנִּים דַּעְתָּם מֵעִנְיְנֵי הָעוֹלָם וּמְקַשְּׁרִים דַּעְתָּם לַאֲדוֹן הַכֹּל יִתְבָּרַךְ בְּמוֹרָא וּבְאַהֲבָה. הֲרֵי תֵּשַׁע שָׁעוֹת שֶׁהָיוּ בְּטֵלִים מִלִּמּוּדָם לִמְלֶאכֶת הַהִתְבּוֹדְדוּת וְהַדְּבֵקוּת וּמְדַמִּים אוֹר שְׁכִינָה שֶׁעַל רָאשֵׁיהֶם כְּאִלּוּ מִתְפַּשֵּׁט סְבִיבָם וְהֵם בְּתוֹךְ הָאוֹר יוֹשְׁבִים, וְכֵן מָצָאתִי בַּקּוּנְטְרֵס הַיָּשָׁן שֶׁל הַפְּרוּשִׁים הָרִאשׁוֹנִים: "וְאָז הֵם רוֹעֲדִים בַּטֶּבַע וּשְׂמֵחִים עַל אוֹתָהּ רְעָדָה כַּדָּבָר שֶׁנֶּאֱמַר 'עִבְדוּ אֶת ה' בְּיִרְאָה וְגִילוּ בִּרְעָדָה' (תהילים ב', י"א)" וְכִדְפֵרֵשׁ רַבֵּנוּ נִסִּים.

(ספר החרדים, רבי אלעזר אזכרי, ממקובלי צפת במאה ה-16, במצוות התשובה, פרק ד')

In some of the compositions by the ancients, we find that seclusion, isolation, and devotion were practiced by the pious of Israel. The meaning is that when alone, they would isolate their thoughts from any worldly matter and connect them with the Lord of all. And thus Mahari, the renowned Kabbalist, taught that it is seven times more beneficial for the soul than to study. According to one's power and ability, one should get secluded for a day once a week, every fifteen days, or every month, but not less than that. And the Ramban, of blessed memory, wrote about the verse which had been said about Jacob, our Father: "Arise and go up to Bethel and abide there" (Genesis, 35:1). What does "abide (*shev*) there" mean? It is like [the verse]: "With tranquility (*shuvah*) and restfulness shall you be saved" (Isaiah, 30:15), meaning one should prepare himself with peace of mind to be with Him [the Lord], Blessed be He. And this is what we learn in the *Mishnah* (*Berachot*, 5.1): "The pious men of old used to wait one hour before praying so that they would direct their heart toward HaMakom (The Place, a reference to God)." And the commentators explained that he [the sage who spoke the *Mishnah*] wanted to say that they used to empty their minds of all worldly matters and connect it to the Blessed Lord of all in awe and love. That is, it was nine hours [daily] that they were idle from their studies and dedicating themselves to the seclusion work (*hitbodedut*) and devotion (*dvekut*) and visualizing the light of *Shechinah* (God's feminine aspect), which surrounded their heads, as though spreading all around them so that they sit inside the light. I also found it in the old manuscript of the first recluses: "And then they naturally trembled and were happy about this trembling, as it is written: 'Serve the Lord with awe, and rejoice with trembling' (Psalms, 2:11)", and as Rabeinu Nissim explained this verse.

(Rabbi El'azar Azkari, From the 16th century Kabbalists of Safed, *Sefer Ḥaredim*, "*BeMitzvat HaTeshuvah*", chapter 4)

Observation leads to greater clarity. For example, the experience of religious Jews when putting on *tefillin* (phylacteries) can be extraordinary, as long as it is not performed mechanically as an ordinary activity. Only with a meditative attitude will they be able to perceive the holiness of *tefillin*. What matters is not executing a precept, or *mitzvah*, but how it is done. If precepts are fulfilled as an obligation, whatever is happening inside is ignored. The *mitzvah* (precept) brings us closer (*tzavta*) to sanity. The process of meditation leads to the revelation of our authentic nature as an integral part of the Whole, of God.

אַיֶּכָּה. הַמְבַקֵּשׁ לָדַעַת מְקוֹם הַמְבֻקָּשׁ יֹאמַר – "אֵיפֹה הוּא?": "אֵיפֹה הֵם רוֹעִים" (בראשית ל"ו, ט"ז), "אֵיפֹה שְׁמוּאֵל וְדָוִד" (שמואל א', י"ט, כ"ב), "אֵיפֹה לִקַּטְתְּ הַיּוֹם" (רות ב', י"ט), אֲבָל הַשּׁוֹאֵל – "אַיֵּה הוּא?", אֵינוֹ כִּי אִם מַתְמִיהַּ שֶׁלֹּא מְצָאוֹ בִּמְקוֹמוֹ הָרָגִיל. כְּמוֹ "רוֹאָיו יֹאמְרוּ אַיּוֹ" (איוב כ', ז'), "אַיֵּה חֲסָדֶיךָ הָרִאשֹׁנִים" (תהילים פ"ט, נ'), "אַיֵּה שָׂרָה אִשְׁתֶּךָ" (בראשית י"ח, ט') כְּלוֹמַר מַדּוּעַ אֵינֶנָּה פֹּה עִמְּךָ, וְכֵן כָּאן: "אַיֶּכָּה"? פֵּרוּשׁוֹ: מַדּוּעַ נֶחְבֵּאתָ וְאֵינְךָ בִּמְקוֹמְךָ הָרָגִיל... וְאָמְרוּ (סנהדרין, ל"ח, ב'): "אַיֶּכָּה – לְאָן נָטָה לִבְּךָ?", וּכְפֵרוּשׁ הגר"א: "אַיֶּכָּה, הִתְבּוֹנֵן בְּעַצְמְךָ – אֵיךְ נָפַלְתָּ מִמַּעֲלָתְךָ? אַיֵּה מַדְרֵגָתְךָ?"

(הכתב והקבלה, פרשת בראשית, פרק ג' פסוק ט')

Ayeka. (Where are you?) One who wants to know the location of somebody would say: *eifoh hu?* ("where is he?"). [*eifoh* is a Hebrew word for "where?"] as: *eifoh hem ro'im?* ("where are they pasturing?") (Genesis, 36:16); "*eifoh Shmuel ve David*" ("where are Samuel and David?") (1 Samuel, 19:22); and "*eifoh likatet hayom*" ("where did you glean today?") (Ruth, 2:19)]. But one who asks *ayeh* [another way to ask "where?"] is only wondering why something or someone could not be found in their regular place, as "*ro'av yomru ayyo*" ["Those who have seen him will say, 'where is he?'" (Job, 20:7)]; "*ayeh ḥasadeicha harishonim*" ["where is your initial mercy?" (Psalms, 89:50)]; or "*ayeh Sarah ishtecha*" ["where is your wife, Sarah?" (Genesis, 18:9)]. That is to say, why she is not present here with you? Likewise, here "*ayeka?*" means "why are you hiding and not in your regular place?" And it was said *ayeka – le'an natah libcha?* ["where are you – toward what has your heart turned?" (*Sanhedrin*, 38b)]. As the Vilna Ga'on explained: "*Ayeka*, observe yourself; how did you fall off your high level? Where is your original high position?".

(*HaKtav VeHakabbalah*, *Bereshit*, 3.9)

There are those who fulfill religious precepts but completely ignore their inner world. They practice out of obligation, driven by the egoic phenomenon. These religious, extremely religious, and even tremendously religious egos perform their duties in darkness. No matter how much they practice, they do not experience true inner transformation. This is how the prophet Isaiah describes those who are totally disconnected from their inner selves.

וְהָרְשָׁעִים כַּיָּם נִגְרָשׁ כִּי הַשְׁקֵט לֹא יוּכָל וַיִּגְרְשׁוּ מֵימָיו רֶפֶשׁ וָטִיט:

(ישעיהו נ"ז, כ')

But the wicked are like the troubled sea, for it cannot rest and its waters cast up dirt and mud.

(Isaiah, 57:20)

He compares these people to an ocean that swells and raises mud from the bottom. Turbulence covers underwater beauty. Likewise, the waves of our mental agitation prevent us from paying attention to the depths of the inner universe.

Just as a person who does not properly grasp external reality is considered demented, those who ignore inner reality are also insane. Unfortunately, most of humanity suffers from inner autism. Someone who only has information about external reality cannot perceive the true power of the *mitzvah*. If our attitude is meditative, we fulfill precepts as an individuality and not as an ego. Meditation is the evaporation of ego and the blossoming as individuality. It entails revealing our true nature. It makes us aware that we are an exhalation from the very depths of existence: a part whose only reason for being is service to the Whole.

וַאֲנִי נִבְרֵאתִי לְשַׁמֵּשׁ אֶת קוֹנִי.

(משנה, קידושין ד', י"ד)

And I was created to serve my owner (Lord).

(*Mishnah*, "*Kiddushin*," 4.14)

[...] הַהִתְבּוֹדְדוּת הִיא אַחַת הַנִּכְבָּדוֹת שֶׁבֵּין הַמִּדּוֹת הַתְּרוּמִיּוֹת, וְהִיא דַּרְכָּם שֶׁל גְּדוֹלֵי הַצַּדִּיקִים וּבְאֶמְצָעוּתָהּ הִגִּיעוּ הַנְּבִיאִים לִידֵי הִתְגַּלּוּת. וְהִיא נֶחֱלֶקֶת לְהִתְבּוֹדְדוּת חִיצוֹנִית וּלְהִתְבּוֹדְדוּת פְּנִימִית. וְכַוָּנַת הַהִתְבּוֹדְדוּת הַחִיצוֹנִית הִיא הַשָּׂגַת הַהִתְבּוֹדְדוּת הַפְּנִימִית שֶׁהִיא הַמַּדְרֵגָה הָעֶלְיוֹנָה בְּסֻלָּם הַהִתְגַּלּוּת וְלֹא עוֹד אֶלָּא שֶׁהִיא הַהִתְגַּלּוּת עַצְמָהּ! [...] וְאַחַר כָּךְ תֵּאֵר אֵיךְ זָלְגוּ מֵעֵינֵיהֶם הַדְּמָעוֹת כְּמַעְיָן הַמִּתְגַּבֵּר וְנִמְשַׁךְ מִמֶּנּוּ נַחַל שֶׁאֶפְשָׁר לִצְלֹחַ אוֹתוֹ כְּנַחַל מַיִם, וְזֶהוּ מַאֲמָרוֹ: "עֹבְרֵי בְּעֵמֶק הַבָּכָא מַעְיָן יְשִׁיתוּהוּ" (תהילים פ"ה, ז'). וְאֵי זֶה תֵּאוּר הַדְּבָרִים כַּהֲוָיָתָם אֶלָּא לְשׁוֹן הַפְלָגָה הַמְתָאֶרֶת אֶת רֹב הַבֶּכֶה. וּבְכִיָּה זוֹ שְׁנֵי טְעָמִים לָהּ. הָאֶחָד הוּא הַצַּעַר עַל תְּקוּפַת הַחַיִּים שֶׁחָלְפָה וְעוֹד תַּחֲלֹף בְּלֹא אוֹתוֹ עֹנֶג שֶׁהֵם מִתְמַכְּרִים לוֹ; וְהַשֵּׁנִי הוּא הִתְרַגְּשׁוּת חֲזָקָה עַל שֶׁהִשִּׂיגוּ מְבֻקָּשָׁם, כְּמוֹ שֶׁבּוֹכֶה הָאוֹהֵב שֶׁהָיָה נָתוּק שָׁנִים רַבּוֹת מֵעַל אֲהוּבַת לִבּוֹ וְסוֹף־סוֹף זָכָה לְהִתְאַחֵד עִמָּהּ.

(רבי אברהם בן הרמב"ם, ספר המספיק לעובדי השם, פרק ההתבודדות)

Seclusion (*hitbodedut*) is among the most respectable noble qualities. It is the path of the greatest saints and through which prophets attained revelation. It is divided into external and internal seclusion. Of which the purpose of external seclusion is to lead to inner seclusion, which is the highest step in the ladder of revelation, and, moreover, is revelation itself! [...] and later is described how tears flowed from their eyes [of saints who practice seclusion] like an overflowing fountain from which a river that can be crossed emerges, as stated, "Passing through the Valley of Weeping (*Bacha*), they made it a place of springs" (Psalms, 84:7), this is not a realistic description but an exaggeration to describe the extent of the crying. This crying has two reasons: One is the sorrow for time that has passed and will pass without this addictive joy, and the other is extreme excitement because what they requested was granted, in the same way, that a lover who was away from his beloved one for many years cries when he finally reunites with her.

(Rabbi Avraham, son of Maimonides, *Sefer HaMaspik Le'Ovdey Hashem*, "*Seclusion*")

In the book of Exodus, we read about the revelation of the burning bush. To introduce this event, the Torah tells us that Moses was a shepherd, and this occurred while he was leading his sheep to graze:

וּמֹשֶׁה הָיָה רֹעֶה אֶת־צֹאן יִתְרוֹ חֹתְנוֹ כֹּהֵן מִדְיָן וַיִּנְהַג אֶת־הַצֹּאן אַחַר הַמִּדְבָּר וַיָּבֹא אֶל־הַר הָאֱלֹהִים חֹרֵבָה:

(שמות ג', א')

And Moses grazed the flock of Jethro, his father-in-law, the priest of Midian, and he led the flock by way of the wilderness and he came to the mountain of God, to Ḥorev.

(Exodus, 3:1)

Some commentators explain the significance of mentioning Moses' occupation due to the secluded life that shepherds lead.

וְגַם הָעִיּוּן צָרִיךְ הִתְבּוֹדְדוּת בַּשָּׂדֶה [...] וְעוֹד שֶׁנָּהַג הַצֹּאן אֶל מָקוֹם קָדוֹשׁ לְשֶׁיָּבוֹא לוֹ שֶׁפַע אֱלֹהִי וְזֶהוּ שֶׁנֶּאֱמַר: "וַיָּבֹא אֶל הַר הָאֱלֹהִים חֹרֵבָה" – לְמָקוֹם חָרֵב שֶׁאֵין שָׁם בְּנֵי־אָדָם שֶׁיַּטְרִידוּ עִיּוּנוֹ.

(רבי יצחק קארו, תולדות יצחק על התורה, שמות ג', א')

Meditation requires solitude in the fields[...] and moreover, he [Moses] lead the herd to a holy place so he can receive divine abundance there. This is what the verse says: "And he came to the mountain of God, to Ḥorev." [Ḥorev, the name of the mountain shares root with *ḥarev*, which means "desert" or "dry and empty place"], to a desert place, vacant from people, who can disturb his meditation.

(Rabbi Isaac Karo, *Toldot Yitzḥak* on the Torah, Exodus, 3:1)

Rabbi Shlomo Ephraim Luntschitz, in his famous commentary *Kli Yakar* on the Torah, also comments on this verse:

אֲבָל מִכָּל־מָקוֹם הֻצְרַךְ לְהוֹדִיעַ שֶׁהָיָה רוֹעֶה כִּי רֹב הַנְּבִיאִים בָּאוּ לִידֵי נְבוּאָה מִתּוֹךְ הָרְעִיָּה כִּי הַנְּבוּאָה צְרִיכָה הִתְבּוֹדְדוּת וְעַל־יְדֵי שֶׁיִּרְאֶה הַשָּׁמַיִם מַעֲשֵׂה יְדֵי אֱלֹהִים כְּמוֹ שֶׁכָּתוּב (תהילים ח', ד'): "כִּי אֶרְאֶה שָׁמֶיךָ מַעֲשֵׂי אֶצְבְּעֹתֶיךָ" וְגוֹ'. כִּי עַל־יְדֵי זֶה תִּהְיֶה כָּל מַחְשַׁבְתּוֹ בִּמְצִיאַת הַשֵּׁם יִתְבָּרַךְ עַד אֲשֶׁר יֵעָרֶה עָלָיו מִמָּרוֹם רוּחַ ה', מָה שֶׁאֵינוֹ מָצוּי כָּל כָּךְ בְּיוֹשֵׁב בְּבֵיתוֹ אוֹ בְעוֹשֶׂה אֵיזוֹ מְלָאכָה אַחֶרֶת בַּשָּׂדֶה, זוּלַת הָרוֹעֶה הַיּוֹשֵׁב פָּנוּי בְּרוֹב הַזְּמַנִּים.

(כלי יקר על התורה, שמות ג', א')

However, it was necessary to inform that he [Moses] was a shepherd, because most of the prophets came to prophecy from being shepherds, as prophecy require solitude, and watching the sky, God's creation, as written in Psalms, 8:4: "When I see Your heavens, the work of Your fingers", will bring him to a complete absorption in the search for the Lord Blessed be He, until the spirit of God will be bestowed on him. This is not so common with people who sit at home or are busy with any other field work, but it is common with the shepherds who mostly sit unoccupied.

(*Kli Yakar* on the Torah, Exodus, 3:1)

Some of the most important *Mussar* books such as the *Mesilat Yesharim*, or "The path of the upright," and the *Ḥovot HaLevavot*, or "*The duties of the hearts*," mention *hitbodedut*, or "seclusion" as an important component of spiritual life:

וְיָקָר מִן הַכֹּל הוּא הַהִתְבּוֹדְדוּת, כִּי כְּמוֹ שֶׁמֵּסִיר מֵעֵינָיו עִנְיְנֵי הָעוֹלָם כֵּן מַעֲבִיר חֶמְדָּתָם מִלִּבּוֹ, וּכְבָר הִזְכִּיר דָּוִד הַמֶּלֶךְ עָלָיו הַשָּׁלוֹם בִּשְׁבָח הַהִתְבּוֹדְדוּת וְאָמַר: (תהילים נ"ה, ז'–ח') "מִי יִתֶּן לִּי אֵבֶר כַּיּוֹנָה" וְגוֹ' "הִנֵּה אַרְחִיק נְדֹד אָלִין בַּמִּדְבָּר סֶלָה". וְהַנְּבִיאִים אֵלִיָּהוּ וֶאֱלִישָׁע, מָצָאנוּ הֱיוֹתָם מְיַחֲדִים מְקוֹמָם אֶל הֶהָרִים מִפְּנֵי הִתְבּוֹדְדוּתָם. וְהַחֲכָמִים הַחֲסִידִים הָרִאשׁוֹנִים ז"ל הָלְכוּ בְּעִקְּבוֹתֵיהֶם, כִּי מָצְאוּ

לָהֶם זֶה הָאֶמְצָעִי הַיּוֹתֵר מוּכָן לִקְנוֹת שְׁלֵמוּת הַפְּרִישׁוּת, לְמַעַן אֲשֶׁר לֹא יְבִיאוּם הַבְלֵי חַבְרֵיהֶם לְהַהְבִּיל גַּם הֵם כְּמוֹתָם.
(רמח"ל, מסילת ישרים, ט"ו)

More important than anything else is solitude. Because when one removes worldly matters from before one's eyes, one also removes lust for them from one's heart. King David, peace be unto him, praised solitude saying (Psalms, 55:7–8): "Oh, that I had wings like a dove! [...]; yes, I would wander far away; I would lodge in the wilderness forever." And we find that the prophets Elijah and Elisha would set their dwelling place in the mountains due to their practice of solitude. And the early pious sages, of blessed memory, followed in their footsteps, for they found solitude to be the best path to acquire perfection in separation, so that the vanities of their neighbors would not lead them to become vain like them.
(Ramḥal, *The path of the upright*, 15)

וְכַאֲשֶׁר תֶּחֱזַק הַכָּרָתוֹ בֵּאלֹהִים יוֹתֵר מִזֶּה וְיֵדַע הָעִנְיָן הַמְכֻוָּן אֵלָיו בִּבְרִיאָתוֹ וִיצִיאָתוֹ אֶל הָעוֹלָם הַזֶּה הַכָּלֶה וְיַכִּיר מַעֲלַת הָעוֹלָם הָאַחֵר הַקַּיָּם יִמְאַס בָּעוֹלָם הַזֶּה וּבְסִבּוֹתָיו וְיִמָּסֵר בְּמַחְשַׁבְתּוֹ וּבְנַפְשׁוֹ וְגוּפוֹ אֶל הָאֱלֹהִים יִתְבָּרַךְ וְיִשְׁתַּעְשֵׁעַ בְּזָכְרוֹ בִּבְדִידוּת וְיִשְׁתּוֹמֵם מִבִּלְתִּי הַמַּחְשָׁבָה בִּגְדֻלָּתוֹ. וְאִם יִהְיֶה בְּמַקְהֵלוֹת לֹא יִתְאַוֶּה כִּי אִם לִרְצוֹנוֹ וְלֹא יִכְסֹף כִּי אִם לִפְגִיעָתוֹ וְתַטְרִידֵהוּ שִׂמְחָתוֹ בְּאַהֲבָתוֹ מִשִּׂמְחַת אַנְשֵׁי הָעוֹלָם בָּעוֹלָם וְשִׂמְחַת אַנְשֵׁי הָעוֹלָם הַבָּא בָּעוֹלָם הַבָּא. וְזֹאת הָעֶלְיוֹנָה שֶׁבְּמַדְרֵגוֹת הַבּוֹטְחִים מֵהַנְּבִיאִים וַחֲסִידִים וּסְגֻלַּת הָאֱלֹהִים הַזַּכִּים וְהוּא מַה שֶּׁאָמַר הַכָּתוּב (ישעיהו כ"ו, ח'): "אַף אֹרַח מִשְׁפָּטֶיךָ ה' קִוִּינוּךָ לְשִׁמְךָ וּלְזִכְרְךָ תַּאֲוַת נָפֶשׁ", וְאָמַר: "צָמְאָה נַפְשִׁי לֵאלֹהִים לְאֵל חָי (תהילים מ"ב, ג')".
(רבנו בחיי אבן פקודה, חובות הלבבות, שער הבטחון, פרק ז')

When one's recognition of God strengthens more than this, and he understands the true intent why he was created and brought to this fleeting world, and he recognizes the exaltedness of the eternal, next world, he will detest this world, and its means. With mind, soul, and body, he will surrender himself to the blessed Almighty, and delight in remembering Him in solitude. He will feel desolate when he is not [capable of] meditating on His greatness. If he is among a crowd of people, he will long for nothing else than to do His will and yearn only to come near to Him. His joy in his love of God will distract him from the pleasures worldly people have in this world, and even from the joy of souls in the next world. This is the highest of the levels of those who trust in God, reached by the prophets, pious ones, and treasured, pure men of God, and this is what the verse refers to in saying "Even [for] the way of Your judgments, O Lord, have we hoped for You; for Your Name and for Your remembrance is the desire of [our] soul directed." (Isaiah, 26:8), and "my soul thirsts to the Almighty, the living God; [when shall I come and appear before God?]" (*Tehilim*, 42:3).

(Rabeinu Bahya ibn Paquda, *The Duties of the Hearts*, Fourth treatise "*Trust*," chapter 7)

Question: Dear Prabhuji, why is meditation called *hitbodedut*, or "seclusion" in Hebrew? What is the relationship between loneliness and meditation?

Answer: It is called *hitbodedut* because it leads to a state in which not even the idea called "I" accompanies you. From the egoic perspective, you say, "I am." But in meditation, the self reveals itself as nothingness, or ain. This is absolute solitude, because nothing is perceived as being separate from your being. You realize yourself as beingness, the very essence of everything that exists. In this absolute solitude, you find that all humans, flowers, seas, and stars are part of you, not separate objects. In solitude, you find everything and everyone; you find God. Only then do you understand the true meaning of *ein od milevado*, or "there is no more than only Him." It is God's aloneness (*levad*), not yours. Your loneliness (*levadi*) comes from lacking the "other." Divine aloneness (levado) is born out of fullness. It is a solitude in which nothing and no one is lacking: it is our blessed, authentic nature.

——— ARTICLE 3 ———

WAITING FOR THE UNKNOWABLE

Question:

In my meditation practice, sometimes I feel that I can sit and humbly wait in silence for the rest of my life. At other times, I feel that waiting is a waste of time and I just want to get up. Dear Prabhuji, is this impatience due to my lack of trust?

Answer:

The demand of our heart confirms the presence of egoic volition. We resist because we think we know what the process entails. When events do not meet our expectations, we become impatient, frustrated, and eventually disinterested. When we lose enthusiasm, we return to the meaningless routine of mundane life, in search of trivial pleasures.

While we wait, we begin to doubt that we will ever be blessed with enlightenment. Egoic demands prevent us from seeing that what we are waiting for has already happened. However, to realize this, it is essential to be humble and have no expectations.

Expectations pose a significant obstacle to meditation because they are a sign of pride and reflect the arrogance of wanting to impose our own designs upon life. Our desire to manipulate existence is like a drop of water trying to control the ocean.

The heavens are closed to prayers with a demanding spirit. For our prayers to be heard, they should be filled with gratitude. Since the mind is an accumulation of unfulfilled desires, demands are embedded in thoughts. It is unrealistic to expect sincere gratitude from the mind.

Unlike a hunter stalking prey, our meditative waiting should be free of expectations. We should wait just for the sake of waiting, not focused on what we are waiting for. If we wait for something or someone, whether material or spiritual, it will only be another mental projection, a repetition of what we already know. If we can define what we are waiting for, it will necessarily be only a projection of our past. While meditating, let us wait to be graced with the unknowable, or knowingness itself, which knows all experience.

If we are waiting for an idea of enlightenment or God, it is like looking for the canvas inside a painting. The painting unfolds on the canvas, but the canvas itself cannot be found in the image. Any idea that we expect, whether enlightenment or God, will merely be a mental creation. No matter what is our idea of reality, it will always be just that, an idea.

The moment the recognition of consciousness occurs, you will realize that it is unlike anything you ever expected. We are always awakening to the unexpected. You will be surprised that no master or sacred book has managed to describe it. They have only given guidelines and indications, like fingers pointing to the moon, but a finger is not the moon. You too will face insurmountable difficulties in trying to explain what is happening to you. So many have tried and failed: Abraham, Moses, the Ba'al Shem Tov, the Buddha, Lao Tzu, Śaṅkara, Chaitanya, and many others.

> וְדָבָר זֶה אֵין כֹּחַ בַּפֶּה לְאָמְרוֹ וְלֹא בָּאֹזֶן לְשָׁמְעוֹ וְלֹא בְּלֵב הָאָדָם לְהַכִּירוֹ עַל בֻּרְיוֹ.
> (רמב"ם, משנה תורה, ספר המדע, הלכות יסודי התורה, ב', י')

> And this subject, the mouth has no power to express it, nor the ear to perceive it, nor can the human heart fully understand with clarity.
>
> (Rambam, *Mishneh Torah*, "*Sefer HaMadda*," "*Foundations of the Torah*," 2.10)

The unknowable cannot be described or verbalized. Therefore, meditating is waiting, but without knowing anything about what we are waiting for. It is waiting patiently and without demands, without knowing for what or whom.

> אֲבָל מִי שֶׁחוֹשֵׁק לִהְיוֹת מֶרְכָּבָה לוֹ יִתְבָּרַךְ [לְהַשֵּׁם יִתְבָּרַךְ] עַל־יְדֵי הַתּוֹרָה הוּא דָּבָר גָּדוֹל, וְזֶהוּ "דָּבָר גָּדוֹל מַעֲשֵׂה מֶרְכָּבָה" (סוכה, כ"ח, א'), רָצָה לוֹמַר לַעֲשׂוֹת עַצְמוֹ מֶרְכָּבָה לְהַשֵּׁם יִתְבָּרַךְ עַל־יְדֵי הַתּוֹרָה.
> (בעל שם טוב, כתר שם טוב, חלק ראשון, קע"ד)

> But one who desires to be a chariot for Him, Blessed be He [the Blessed Lord], through the Torah is a great thing, and the act of the chariot is a great thing, that is, to make oneself a chariot for the blessed Lord through the Torah.
>
> (Ba'al Shem Tov, *Keter Shem Tov*, part one, 174)

A chariot is a horse-drawn vehicle. It is a means of transportation and a material object, so it has no will of its own. The driver decides when to go and when to stop. If the driver wishes, it will travel long distances and if not, it will remain stationary as long as necessary. While waiting, the chariot has no expectations or demands whatsoever.

Many people have great ambitions in life to become entrepreneurs, politicians, experts, or professionals. However, the Ba'al Shem Tov refers to something truly wonderful: the aspiration to surrender to the Whole and to be a simple chariot guided by existence. Genuine meditation is a waiting with the tranquility of those who have placed their will in the hands of God.

Meditating means silently waiting like the chariot, not knowing what the driver's plans are. Without expectations, divine waiting empties us of all that is known. That same patient waiting is the means to manifest what is real and authentic within us.

> אֲנִי מַאֲמִין בֶּאֱמוּנָה שְׁלֵמָה בְּבִיאַת הַמָּשִׁיחַ, וְאַף עַל פִּי שֶׁיִּתְמַהְמֵהַּ, עִם כָּל זֶה אֲחַכֶּה לּוֹ בְּכָל יוֹם שֶׁיָּבוֹא.
>
> (סידור התפילה, י"ג העיקרים, עיקר י"ב)

> I believe with complete faith in the coming of the Messiah, and although he may tarry, nevertheless, I wait for him to come every day.
>
> (*Siddur*, "*Thirteen Principles*," principle 12)

—— ARTICLE 4 ——

HERE AND NOW

Most humans live in the temporary, striving for the atemporal. They dwell in the relative while seeking the absolute. Clearly, it is impossible to access atemporality through temporality. However, to appreciate timelessness, we must first understand what time is.

Many believe that time flows like a river: what was is the past, what is occurring now is the present, and what will happen is the future. This might be true if we remained still while time was in constant motion. But in fact, we evolve from childhood to adolescence, from adolescence to youth, then to maturity. This leads some thinkers to postulate that time is immutable while we change. They would say that the river remains static, and we perceive it flowing because we walk along its bank. Yet, despite various proposed hypotheses, very few truly understand the nature of time.

The popular belief says that time flows from yesterday to tomorrow. We perceive time as a sequence of events. The present turns into the past and the future constantly becomes the present. Now is the precise instant when the future becomes the past. The mind conceives the present moment as a line that marks the end of yesterday and the beginning of tomorrow, the end of what was and the beginning of what will be.

The mind attempts to segment temporality into moments; however, the duration of each instant becomes incalculable. Their flow is so swift that moments seem to appear and disappear simultaneously. It is impossible to refer to temporality as separate fragments because it is a continuous flow.

When referring to time, we should consider its two aspects: chronological and psychological. Chronological time guides our daily activities. Calendars and clocks provide conventions that define seconds, hours, days, months, years, and centuries. Yet time has no physical properties that can be measured. What calendars and clocks actually measure is the duration that separates two natural events, such as daily or annual changes in the position of the Earth relative to the Sun. Various methods of measuring time have been developed throughout history. Today, the most accurate way to measure time is with atomic clocks, which define the duration of a second based on atomic resonance frequencies.

Psychological time, on the other hand, is how we perceive time. For example, the chronological yesterday is on the calendar, while the psychological yesterday is in our memories and recollections. The chronological tomorrow belongs to the clock, whereas the psychological tomorrow resides in our hopes, ambitions, expectations, and dreams. Humans' entire lives take place in their memory. Their mind is the product of the past, while the now is merely a corridor to the future. Their psychological life is based on time, for without time, thinking is impossible.

Time creates duality by providing the illusion that the contents of empirical reality flow from yesterday to tomorrow. Time seems to fracture the monistic nature of the now, creating an apparent separation between the contents of the past and the future. Every day, we awaken to a reality seemingly similar to the one we left behind the night before. We conclude that the same contents have sustained their attributes and that they will remain similar in the future. Our perception of time arises from the dualistic mental interpretation of the contents of the temporal flow.

It is intriguing to explore whether time, as we conceive it, is real and whether it exists independently of the mind. In truth, time is a result of thought, for without mental activity, it cannot exist. This is evidenced by the state of deep, dreamless sleep. In the absence of objects and thoughts, time disappears. Indeed, time is merely memory interacting with the present and projecting itself as the future. Our tomorrow is nothing more than our yesterday projected onto the screen of the mind.

It is impossible to conceive the duration of an instant because it is completely subjective and does not obey any principle. To investigate the nature of the now in depth, we must separate it from yesterday and tomorrow, from all nostalgia and hope. Isolating the now reveals the inexistence of a chronological present. An instant is not a fraction of time but a dividing line between past and future, between what was and what will be. At that timeless point, all events freeze because time needs a duration or a space to move. The now is devoid of all activity, even mental and emotional activity.

Our conceptualization of the present as a unit of time is illusory. What we consider the passage of time is merely an imaginary mental creation. Of course, I am not suggesting discarding chronological time or eliminating clocks and calendars. If we did so, we would be late for work, and our children would miss the school bus. I propose renouncing all belief in the existence of any other time besides the present. Then, the now vanishes as a fraction of time to reveal itself as consciousness itself.

To place ourselves in the now is to leap into the timeless, into transcendental eternity. We will be surprised to discover that the concept of the present moment as a fraction of time is imaginary. By abandoning the idea of any other instant except the now, the present transcends the dimension of time to reveal itself as our reality. Yesterday precedes the now and tomorrow follows it. If we remain in what exists between the two, we will be situated in our authentic nature.

Similarly, the limiting idea that we are located in a geographical place is illusory. The concept of spatiality replaces the non-dual nature of the here with an apparent difference between the contents of here and there. To explore the true essence of the here, I suggest the same approach we followed with the now. Let us isolate the here by renouncing every thought about the existence of any other place. Let us relinquish the here and abandon all belief in the there.

Even if we think of our future goals or remember the most remote past, the experience of that moment always occurs now. No matter how far in the future or in the past that moment is, we will experience it as now. Likewise, if we think of distant places like Tokyo, Delhi, another planet or galaxy, at the moment when that place is our direct experience, we are always here.

Every instant in time, as well as every place in space, is unfailingly experienced as here and now. The future cannot be experienced until it arrives to the now; hence, its existence depends entirely on the now. Likewise, an imaginary place cannot be experienced unless it is here; therefore, it borrows its apparent existence from the here. Time and space exist as mental concepts and can only be real if they are experienced. Since they can only be experienced here and now, they depend on the here and now to exist. All places, in their most pristine nakedness, are contained in the here, just as all moments are contained in the now. The only substantiality of the here and now is consciousness. Both the here and the now, as well as space and time, have no other reality than our own essence.

Therefore, here and now are doors leading to *eternal and infinite absolute consciousness*. By *eternal*, I do not mean in the temporal sense that includes all years, but in the sense of timelessness. By *infinite*, I do not mean in the geographical sense encompassing all places but transcending the concept of space. By *absolute consciousness*, I do not mean a level of consciousness superior to all others, but in the sense that it contains all levels of consciousness.

As we focus on the here, it disappears as a geographical place to reveal itself as consciousness; it evaporates as a spatial dimension to reveal itself as the essence of what we really are. By dwelling within the here and now, we place ourselves in the reality of what we are. Situating ourselves in the here and now consists of the profound realization that both time and space are mere mental creations or imaginations, while consciousness is the absolute reality. Since we can only exist here and now, whatever level of consciousness we are at, it will always be absolute consciousness.

Consciousness hides itself by disappearing into an objective reality called *'olam*, which means "world" in Hebrew. It comes from the root 'a.l.m (ע.ל.מ), which contains both the concept of place and the idea of time: *le'olam* means "forever" and *me'olam* means "since always." The term *he'elem* is derived from *'olam* and means "disappearance or concealment"; therefore, *'olam*, or "objective reality," is not a positive creation that *aggregates* or *creates* something, but the opposite. Objective reality is the concealment of consciousness. Therefore, consciousness becomes the universe by concealing itself, which allows becoming without exchanging. Consciousness achieves its objectification through its self-concealment or voluntary withdrawal. God, called in Hebrew *Alufo Shel 'Olam*, or "The Lord of the world," hides in you, as you.

אֶת־הַכֹּל עָשָׂה יָפֶה בְעִתּוֹ גַּם אֶת־הָעֹלָם נָתַן בְּלִבָּם מִבְּלִי אֲשֶׁר לֹא־יִמְצָא הָאָדָם
אֶת־הַמַּעֲשֶׂה אֲשֶׁר־עָשָׂה הָאֱלֹהִים מֵרֹאשׁ וְעַד־סוֹף׃

(קהלת ג', י"א)

> [God] has made everything to pass precisely in its time, and He also set in their heart the *'olam* [can be translated as "world, eternity, or concealment"] so that no one can fathom the work which God had done from beginning to end.
>
> (Ecclesiastes, 3:11)

Midrash Rabbah on this verse says:

> "אֶת־הַכֹּל עָשָׂה יָפֶה בְעִתּוֹ גַּם אֶת־הָעֹלָם נָתַן בְּלִבָּם" (קהלת ג', י"א). [...] אָמַר רַבִּי אַחְוָה בְּרֵיהּ דְּרַבִּי זֵירָא: "הָעֹלָם – הָעֳלַם מֵהֶם שֵׁם הַמְפֹרָשׁ". [...] וְאָמַר רַבִּי טַרְפוֹן: "פַּעַם אַחַת שָׁמַעְתִּי וְנָפַלְתִּי עַל פָּנַי". הַקְּרוֹבִים שֶׁכְּשֶׁהֵם שׁוֹמְעִין אוֹתוֹ, נוֹפְלִים עַל פְּנֵיהֶם וְאוֹמְרִים: "בָּרוּךְ שֵׁם כְּבוֹד מַלְכוּתוֹ לְעוֹלָם וָעֶד". אֵלּוּ וָאֵלּוּ לֹא הָיוּ זָזִין מִשָּׁם עַד שָׁעָה שֶׁנִּתְעַלֵּם מֵהֶם, שֶׁנֶּאֱמַר: "זֶה שְּׁמִי לְעֹלָם" (שמות ג', ט"ו), לְעַלֵּם כְּתִיב. וְכָל כָּךְ לָמָּה? "מִבְּלִי אֲשֶׁר לֹא יִמְצָא הָאָדָם אֶת הַמַּעֲשֶׂה אֲשֶׁר עָשָׂה הָאֱלֹהִים מֵרֹאשׁ וְעַד סוֹף". (קהלת ג', י"א).
>
> (קהלת רבה ג', י"א)

> He made everything beautiful, in its time. Also, the world (*ha'olam*) [can also read "of what is hidden"], He placed in their heart (Ecclesiastes, 3:11). [...] Rabbi Aḥva, son of Rabbi Zeira, said: "The world (*ha'olam*)—the explicit name was concealed (*ho'alam*) from them." [...] And Rabbi Tarfon said: "One time I heard it [the name] and I fell on my face. Those nearby, when they hear it, fall on their faces, and say: 'Blessed be the name of His glorious kingdom for ever and ever.' These and those would not move from there until the time when it was forgotten (*shenit'alem*) from them, as it is stated: 'This is My name forever (*le'olam*)' (Exodus, 3:15), it is written: *le'alem* [the word *le'olam* is written without a vowel, so it can be read as *le'alem,* which means "to hide"]. Why? 'so that no one can fathom the work which God had done from beginning to end' (Ecclesiastes, 3:11)."
>
> (*Kohalat Rabbah*, 3.11)

Absolute reality hides behind illusions such as time and space but is revealed by transcending them in the now and here.

אָמַר רַבִּי בּוּן: "מַאי דִּכְתִיב: 'מֵעוֹלָם נִסַּכְתִּי מֵרֹאשׁ מִקַּדְמֵי אָרֶץ' (משלי ח', כ"ג), מַאי מֵעוֹלָם? שֶׁצָּרִיךְ לְהַעְלִימוֹ מִכְּלֵי עָלְמָא. דִּכְתִיב: 'גַּם אֶת הָעֹלָם נָתַן בְּלִבָּם' (קהלת ג', י"א), אַל תִּקְרָא 'הָעוֹלָם' אֶלָּא 'הֶעְלֵם'.

(ספר הבהיר, סימן י')

Rabbi Boon said: "What is the meaning of the verse: 'I was set up from everlasting (*me'olam*), from the beginning, before ever the earth was' (Proverbs, 8:23). Why *me'olam*? Because He needs to conceal it from everybody. As it is written: 'He also set in their heart the '*olam*' (Ecclesiastes, 3:11), do not read *ha'olam* (world), but *he'elem* (concealment)."

(*Sefer HaBahir*, 10)

הִנֵּה בְּרִבּוּי הַהִשְׁתַּלְשְׁלוּת נִתְהַוָּה מִזֶּה צִמְצוּם גָּמוּר וְהֶעְלֵם גָּדוֹל שֶׁנִּתְעַלֵּם בְּחִינַת כֹּחַ הָאֱלֹהִי הַמְחַיֶּה אֶת הָעוֹלָם וְנִתְלַבֵּשׁ בִּלְבוּשִׁים רַבִּים וַעֲצוּמִים, כִּי עוֹלָם הוּא מִלְּשׁוֹן הֶעְלֵם כַּנּוֹדָע.

(אדמו"ר הזקן, ליקוטי תורה, פרשת שלח, ב', ד')

And with the advancement of the emanation, there was a complete contraction and great concealment, in which the quality of divine power, which vitalizes the world, concealed itself and clothed itself with many great garments, as it is well-known that the word *'olam* conveys also *he'elem*.

(The Alter Rebbe, *Likkutei Torah*, "*Shlach*," 2.4)

Since time and space are mental constructs, their apparent existence is contingent upon thought. Consciousness does not know time and space because it knows only itself. Knowing knows nothing outside of knowing. However, the apparent objective reality composed of thoughts, sensations, and perceptions is supported by consciousness. Just as the diversity of a dream cannot exist without the waking state, an imaginary reality cannot be known apart from knowing.

Although we are conscious presence, we imagine ourselves to be separate entities residing within a body observing an objective multiplicity. This imagination can arise only because consciousness of consciousness exists. The egoic phenomenon is illusory, but it appears to exist because it relies on consciousness. Mind, time, and space are mere temporary appearances, while our knowingness is perpetually present, knowing its own knowing. Time and space possess no independent existence; only knowingness truly exists.

Many people ask if there is any way to eliminate the illusion of time and space. This illusion will persist as long as we believe in the existence of the one who asks and wishes to eliminate them. Believing that something or someone exists outside the here and now sustains the dream of a temporal existence. Time and space should not be eliminated because they consist only of appearances, which derive their reality from consciousness. The here and now are always available to us, wide-open doors to access our authentic nature.

Bliss is not experienced in time; it is the timeless within the now. In a state of great joy, only the present exists. The mind turns on after a happy experience, records it as a memory, and then tries to reproduce it. Time is both acquisition and letting go; by letting go of it, the mind in fact obtains and accumulates. From this post-experiential intervention, the mind creates time, since recalling a memory always follows the original experience. Time seems to stop while experiencing bliss but, in fact, time has always been static. What stops is not time but the mind. Like two sides of the same coin, the mind and time appear and disappear together, because when the mind stops, time stops. Upon reaching the deepest mental stillness, time ceases to exist.

The waves contained in the sea are water. Likewise, the experiences contained in time and space are consciousness. Just as no bubble, wave, sea, or ocean can exist without water, no thought, emotion, sensation, or perception can exist without consciousness. Therefore, consciousness is the container of everything and, in turn, is contained in everything. Just as water is the foundation of every bubble and wave, consciousness is the foundation of every experience. Because consciousness shares the same substance as everything and everyone, everything and everyone is essentially consciousness.

Obviously, any technique to control the mind within the temporal context cannot lead to timeless awareness. The recognition of consciousness is not an event that takes place in time because it can only be recognized in the absence of time and space. Just as it is easier to see the bottom of a lake when its waters are still, consciousness becomes evident when mental activity quiets down. Bliss is not a future goal; it reigns when we relax into the timeless state of now. Meditation is just surrendering to the eternal now and the infinite here.

To situate oneself in the here and now means realizing that they encompass absolutely everything and everyone and, in turn, are contained in the deepest intimacy of everything and everyone. Remaining in the here and now reveals to us the ultimate reality, in which cognitive movement ceases to oscillate between subject and object, between memory and imagined future, and to establish itself in non-duality. More than a moment or a place, the here and now are a presence that is conscious of itself. The here and now are simply the obviousness of being.

—— ARTICLE 5 ——

A DUET OF ONE

וְקָרָא זֶה אֶל־זֶה וְאָמַר קָדוֹשׁ קָדוֹשׁ קָדוֹשׁ ה' צְבָאוֹת מְלֹא כָל־הָאָרֶץ כְּבוֹדוֹ:
(ישעיהו ו', ג')

And one [*ze*, or "this one"] called to the other [*ze*, or "this one"] and said, "Holy, Holy, Holy is the Lord of Hosts; the whole earth is full of His glory."

(Isaiah, 6:3)

In the presence of all that fills the whole earth, we can only exclaim, "Holy, Holy, Holy." Amid a presumed duality, **this one** calls **this one**, in a duet of one. Looking around, we perceive only perception. There is awareness that everything and everyone is composed of the same substance as consciousness. Whether we look, listen, feel, taste, or smell, only observation is observed by the only one capable of observing.

Trees, houses, people, mountains, and flowers are perceived, but since we have never perceived anything independent of perception, we cannot be certain of their existence. As we have never known of the existence of a house or mountain separate from knowing, it is impossible to be certain that these exist independently. There is only complete certainty of the existence of perception or consciousness.

If a mosquito could exist separated from perception, we would know that we perceived a real and existing mosquito. But as long as what is perceived does not have an existence of its own, we lack any evidence that it exists outside of consciousness. In our own experience, we do not know the universe; we only know the knowing itself. Truly, the perception of perception is the only certainty.

וְהִנֵּה כְּתִיב: "וְקָרָא זֶה אֶל זֶה" (ישעיהו ו', ג'). שֶׁבְּחִינַת "זֶה" קוֹרֵא וּמַמְשִׁיךְ בְּחִינַת "זֶה", הַיְנוּ מָה שֶׁהקב"ה נִקְרָא "זֶה" וְכוּ', וְהָעִנְיָן הוּא דְּהִנֵּה כְּתִיב "זֶה סֵפֶר תּוֹלְדֹת אָדָם" (בראשית ה', א') – שֶׁקָּאֵי עַל הַשְּׁבָטִים שֶׁהָיוּ י"ב כְּמִנְיַן "זֶה", וְנִקְרָא "תּוֹלְדוֹת אָדָם" לְפִי שֶׁשִּׁפְרֵיהּ דְּיַעֲקֹב הוּא מֵעֵין שְׁפְרֵיהּ דְּאָדָם קַדְמָאָה, וְהֵם בְּחִינַת מֶרְכַּבְתָּא תַּתָּאָה י"ב בָּקָר שֶׁהֵם בְּחִינַת הַחַיּוֹת וְהָאוֹפַנִּים שֶׁהֵם תָּמִיד בִּתְשׁוּקָה וְרִשְׁפֵּי אֵשׁ לִבָּטֵל וְלִכָּלֵל בְּאוֹר אֵין־סוֹף לְהַמְשִׁיךְ בְּחִינַת הוי' שֶׁנִּקְרָא "זֶה", וְלָכֵן נִקְרָאִים גַּם כֵּן בְּשֵׁם "זֶה" לְפִי שֶׁעִקַּר תְּשׁוּקָתָם

לְהַמְשִׁיךְ בְּחִינַת "זֶה" וְכוּ', וּכְמוֹ שֶׁכָּתוּב: "וְקָרָא זֶה אֶל זֶה" וְכוּ' "קָדוֹשׁ קָדוֹשׁ קָדוֹשׁ ה'".

(אדמו"ר מהר"ש, תורת שמואל, תרכ"ז , מאמרים, דודי לי ואני לו, רכ"ז)

And it is written "*vekara ze el ze*," "And the one [angel] (*ze*, or 'this one') called to the other [angel] (*ze*, or 'this one')" (Isaiah, 6:3), meaning that the aspect of "This" in one calls and effluxes the aspect of "This" in the other, for The Holy One, Blessed be He, is called "This," and so on. The idea is that we see that in the verse "This (*ze*) is the record of the generations of Adam" (Genesis, 5:1) which refers to the tribes of Israel (the sons of Jacob and their descendants), which were 12 and that is the numerical value of the word *ze* , זה (the letter ז=7 + the letter ה=5). The tribes are called "the generations of Adam" because the beauty of Jacob resembles the beauty of Adam. They are, in essence, the 12 animals (cattle) pulling the lower chariot (*merkavah*), which are parallel to the holy animals and animated wheels (2 types of angels that are pulling the higher chariot), that are always burning in flames of desire to be nullified and to be included in the unlimited light, to efflux the aspect of ה-ו-י-ה (The holy name of God that [literally] means "being"), which is called *ze* and, therefore, they are also named *ze*, for their main desire is to efflux the aspect of *ze*, etc. As it is written: "And one (*ze*, or "this one') called to the other (*ze*, or "this one") and said: Holy, holy, holy, is the Lord of hosts…"

(Admor Maharash, *Torat Shemu'el*, Year of 627, "*Ma'amarim*," "*Dodi Li Va'Ani Lo*," 227)

Looking around, we do not see multiplicity but the One without a second; only perception is perceived; only knowing is known. Wherever the gaze is directed, no objects are seen, but only seeing itself is seen; there is only consciousness of consciousness itself. This One is both the perceiver and what is perceived. Reality is the celebration of conscious presence. When we realize ourselves as this, we stop believing we are subjects perceiving objects. Then, the glory of God that fills the whole universe is recognized.

יָבֹא זֶה וִיקַבֵּל זֹאת מִזֶּה לְעַם זוּ. יָבוֹא זֶה – זֶה מֹשֶׁה. דִּכְתִיב:"כִּי זֶה מֹשֶׁה הָאִישׁ" (שמות ל"ב, א'). וִיקַבֵּל זֹאת – זוֹ הַתּוֹרָה דִּכְתִיב: "וְזֹאת הַתּוֹרָה אֲשֶׁר שָׂם מֹשֶׁה" (דברים ד', מ"ד). מִזֶּה – זֶה הקב"ה. דִּכְתִיב: "זֶה אֵלִי וְאַנְוֵהוּ" (שמות ט"ו, ב'). לְעַם זוּ – אֵלּוּ יִשְׂרָאֵל שֶׁנֶּאֱמַר "עַם זוּ קָנִיתָ" (שמות ט"ו, ט"ז).
(תלמוד בבלי, מנחות נ"ג, ב')

"Let **this** one come and receive **this** from **this** one for **this** people." It is explained:
"Let **this** one come" is referring to Moses, as written about him: "For **this** man Moses" (Exodus, 32:1).
"And receive **this**" is referring to the Torah, as it is written: "And **this** is the Torah which Moses set [before the children of Israel]" (Deuteronomy, 4:44).
"From **this** one" is referring to the Holy One, Blessed be He, as it is written: "**This** is my God and I will exalt Him" (Exodus, 15:2).
"For **this** people" refers to the Israelites, as it is stated about them: "**This** people that You have acquired" (Exodus, 15:16).

(*Babylonian Talmud*, "*Menaḥot*," 53b)

When we come to realize our true nature, we cease to see ourselves as separate observers of the world around us. Instead, we become aware of the divine presence that permeates the entire universe. Our authentic nature is the timeless, formless essence in which all distinctions fade away. The only constant reality is the pure, limitless, and infinite consciousness. The Upanishadic scriptures call this totality Brahman, or *pūrṇam*, while it indicates the apparent separation between the perceiver and the perceived with the words *idaṁ* (this) and *adaḥ* (that). This is stated in the invocation of the *Īśāvāsya Upanishad*:

ॐ पूर्णमदः पूर्णमिदं पूर्णात् पूर्णमुदच्यते ।
पूर्णस्य पूर्णमादाय पूर्णमेवावशिष्यते ॥
ॐ शान्तिः शान्तिः शान्तिः ॥

oṁ pūrṇam adaḥ pūrṇam idaṁ
pūrṇāt pūrṇam udacyate
pūrṇasya pūrṇam ādāya
pūrṇam evāvaśiṣyate
oṁ śāntiḥ śāntiḥ śāntiḥ

> That (*adaḥ*) is the Whole, this (*idaṁ*) is the Whole; from that Whole, this Whole is manifested. When this Whole is extracted, that Whole is still the Whole. *Oṁ* peace, peace, peace.
>
> (*Īśāvāsya Upanishad*, invocation)

We typically use the word *that* for something distant or beyond our immediate reach, while "this" is used for what is near or close. Philosophically, the term *adaḥ* can be interpreted as the transcendent aspect of God, whereas *idaṁ* represents His immanent aspect.

In the Bhagavad Gita, Lord Kṛṣṇa uses the term *idaṁ* to refer to the physical body as the field:

इदं शरीरं कौन्तेय क्षेत्रमित्यभिधीयते ।
एतद्यो वेत्ति तं प्राहुः क्षेत्रज्ञ इति तद्विदः ॥

idaṁ śarīraṁ kaunteya
kṣetram ity abhidhīyate
etad yo vetti taṁ prāhuḥ
kṣetra-jña iti tad-vidaḥ

> O, son of Kuntī, this body is called the field, and whoever knows it is called the knower of the field.
>
> (Bhagavad Gita, 13.2)

Idaṁ is used to denote what we usually see as objective, concrete, and perceivable. This is confirmed in the first mantra of the *Īśāvāsya Upanishad*, which refers to the objective foundation as *idaṁ*: *Oṁ īśāvāsyam idaṁ sarvaṁ*. Therefore, if *idaṁ* denotes objectivity or the manifested, then *adaḥ* refers to the unmanifested subjectivity. As the *Bṛhad-āraṇyaka Upanishad* states:

द्वे वाव ब्रह्मणो रूपे मूर्तं चैवामूर्तं च मर्त्यं चामृतं च स्थितं च यच्च सच्च त्यच्च ॥

dve vāva brahmaṇo rūpe mūrtaṁ caivāmūrtaṁ ca martyaṁ cāmṛtaṁ ca sthitaṁ ca yac ca sac ca tyac ca.

There are two different forms of Brahman, the gross and the subtle, the mortal and the immortal, the limited and the unlimited, the definite and the indefinite.

(*Bṛhad-āraṇyaka Upanishad*, 2.3.1)

Adaḥ refers to the unknowable or unmanifested, while *idaṁ* designates what is immediately perceivable—our empirical, manifest reality. *Adaḥ* means "that," alluding to what is distant, remote, or beyond immediate perception. However, this distance is not physical but cognitive. By eliminating the notion of distance, "that" becomes "this." When the separation between us and the remote is removed, *adaḥ* transforms into *idaṁ*.

The information humans have about themselves is mostly superficial, limited to their names, nationalities, professions, and other such identifiers. Even for those with deeper knowledge of themselves, it is often at most psychological. In truth, humans live in ignorance of their true nature, and do not even know what they do not know. This ignorance creates a cognitive distance between what we believe we are and what we truly are. Overcoming this distance ultimately means awakening to our authentic identity as unlimited Brahman.

This verse asserts that the totality is both "that" and "this," which seem to be two mutually exclusive statements. Claiming that totality is "that" seems to exclude the objectual, leaving it outside the totality. Likewise, claiming that totality is "this" seems to omit subjectivity as an essential part of wholeness. If *adaḥ* and *idaṁ* are considered separately, they present an incomplete totality, which is untenable. A correct understanding of the text is achieved only when it is read from the perspective of totality or *pūrṇam*.

Existence seems to present itself in two dimensions: subjective and objective. Outside of subject and object, there is no third option. By declaring that *adaḥ* and *idaṁ* are *pūrṇam*, the Upanishad emphatically states that only *pūrṇam* is real. The text could have simply said that the totality includes everything, but the sage chose not to omit or ignore our differentiated, dual, and relative experience. Our ordinary perception is distinguished by the difference between the observer, the subject, and the observed, the object. In this dual experience, we do not see ourselves as part of the observed, *idaṁ*. However, according to the Upanishad, the essence of both the observer and the observed is the same: *pūrṇam* or "unlimited totality." This message is echoed in Zen Buddhism in the *Heart Sūtra*:

> **इह शारिपुत्र रूपंशून्यता शून्यतैव रूपंरूपान्न पृथक्शून्यता शून्यतया न पृथग्रूपं यद्रूपंसा शून्यता य शून्यता तद्रूपम् । एवमेव वेदना संज्ञा संस्कार विज्ञानम् ।**
>
> *iha śāriputra rūpaṁ śūnyatā śūnyataiva rūpaṁ*
> *rūpān na pṛthak śūnyatā śūnyatayā na pṛthag rūpaṁ*
> *yad rūpaṁ sā śūnyatā ya śūnyatā tad rūpam. evam eva vedanā-saṁjñā saṁskāra-vijñānam.*
>
> Listen, Śāriputra, form is emptiness, and emptiness is form. Form is nothing but emptiness, emptiness is nothing but form. The same is true for feelings, perceptions, mental formations, and consciousness.
>
> (*Heart Sūtra*)

The Vedantic message holds that the relationship between subject and object is inclusive, contrasting with our everyday perception, which completely separates them. In our ordinary experience, by excluding what is observed, individuals perceive themselves as incomplete. This partial and illusory perception is the root of a deep sense of dissatisfaction. Totality cannot be enclosed or defined by a specific form. Any shape, be it physical, material, astral, ethereal, or spiritual, means that there are limits. A silhouette without a distinction between an inside and an outside makes no sense as a form. From our relative and partial perspective, we perceive ourselves as confined in a limited world that is distinct from us. We perceive the limitation of an objective world separate from the perceiver. This experience of difference between subject and object contradicts the Upanishads' assertion that the essence of both the observer and the observed is *pūrṇam*. Diversity, by its very nature, implies limitation. As long as we consider ourselves limited and incomplete, we will continue striving to escape this feeling and seek completeness through means that only provide temporary satisfaction. The dissatisfaction that accompanies human beings stems from this limited self-perception.

The search for pleasure, enjoyment, and happiness is deeply intertwined with this sense of limitation. According to Vedanta, this search is futile, since in essence, we are eternally unlimited. Although our true nature is infinite totality, the Upanishad acknowledges our dualistic experience through terms like "that" and "this." *Adaḥ* alludes to the subjectivity that seems distinct from the observed, while *idaṁ* refers to objectivity, which appears different from the observer and shows differences between objects. Although they seem to be subjectivity and objectivity, *pūrṇam* encompasses everything. Vedanta rejects the absolute reality of the dual experience but does not discredit the experience itself. The ancient sages did not deny the subject–object relationship but its absolute reality, accepting it as a relative experience.

If the dual experience of objects were accepted as part of *pūrṇam*, then *pūrṇam* would be limited to an undifferentiated subjective experience. Such an experience would be sought as an escape from duality, which would apparently lack *pūrṇam*. However, *mokṣa*, or "liberation," cannot result from an escape, since such a liberation would simply be a reaction to the illusion and, therefore, part of it. Enlightenment is not like alcohol or drugs; it cannot be reduced to an experience, however pleasurable, because all experience is limited, relative, and temporary.

Vedanta does not reject the dual experience of subject and object but denies the conclusion that we are something separate from what we perceive. Duality is an experience, not reality itself. The human illusion lies not in experiencing duality but in believing that this experience is the Truth. If we dream of studying medicine, we will not have a diploma when we wake up. If we dream of winning the lottery, our bank account balance will not be changed when we open our eyes in the morning. During a dream, experiences seem real, but upon waking, we understand that it was all just a dream.

The Vedantic negation of our dualistic perception of reality is not based on faith but on *śruti* as *pramāṇa*. The revealed scriptures have more than theological and mythological value; they are also a valid means of acquiring knowledge. *Pramāṇas* give us access to information from the empirical world. Just as the eyes perceive colors and the ears sound, the revealed scriptures are the means of attaining knowledge of ultimate reality. The Upanishadic statements, when heard from a truly realized master, are an effective means of obtaining valid knowledge about our true nature.

According to Aristotle, the material cause refers to the means used in the process of creation, while the efficient cause is the creating agent. Take a painting, for example: the canvas and pigments are the material cause, while the painter is the efficient cause. This leads us to two fundamental questions about the universe: what is its material cause, known as *upādāna-kāraṇa*, and what is its efficient cause, or *nimitta-kāraṇa*? The Upanishads assert that Brahman is the material cause of the universe.

> यतो वा इमानि भूतानि जायन्ते । येन जातानि जीवन्ति । यत्प्रयन्त्यभिसंविशन्ति ।
> तद्विजिज्ञासस्व । तद्ब्रह्मेति ।
>
> *yato vā imāni bhūtāni jāyante. yena jātāni jīvanti. yat prayanty abhisaṁviśanti. tad vijijñāsasva. tad brahmeti.*
>
> Seek to know that from which all beings here are born; having been born, by which they remain alive; and into which, on departing, they enter. That is Brahman.
>
> (*Taittirīya Upanishad*, 3.1.1)

In Vedanta, Brahman is the efficient cause. However, the scriptures do not explicitly indicate this. Since the existence of more than one unlimited totality is impossible, an unlimited material cause necessarily excludes the possibility of a second unlimited efficient cause. The Upanishad establishes that both subjectivity and objectivity are *pūrṇam* or Brahman, and therefore, they share the same material and efficient cause. As effects of a single cause, subject and object are essentially identical. If an efficient cause were required, the creator God of the universe would be only a part of the totality or *pūrṇam*.

The dreaming experience also shares a single material and efficient cause. The dreamer is both: the substance as well as the creator of the dream. Dreaming is a dual experience in which a relationship between subject and object is established. However, the diversity we observe in the dream is illusory, since the substance of all objects and characters is identical to the dreamer. In the dream, we are both the observer and the observed, both subject and object. Similarly, in the first part of the mantra, we can say that both the efficient cause and the material cause are *pūrṇam* or Brahman. Just as in the case of the dreamer, *pūrṇam* dissolves any apparent difference between subjectivity and objectivity. The Upanishad's assertion that totality is "this" and "that" eliminates the apparent difference between subject and object that we experience.

The first line of the mantra says: *Oṁ pūrṇam adaḥ pūrṇam idaṁ*, which means "That (*adaḥ*) is the Whole, this (*idaṁ*) is the Whole." The second line continues: *pūrṇāt* (from the totality) *pūrṇam*, (the totality) *udacyate* (originates). This phrasing suggests an apparent cause-and-effect relationship between the formless *pūrṇam* (*adaḥ*, mentioned first) and the *pūrṇam* with form (*idaṁ*, mentioned second). Thus, *pūrṇāt pūrṇam udacyate* translates as "from that Whole, this Whole manifests." This section of the mantra alludes to creation, whose reality, according to Vedanta, is *mithyā*, or "illusory," like a mirage in the desert, where reality is not absolute but merely empirical and phenomenal. Similarly, the non-existent snake (this) seems to manifest from the existing rope (that).

In our daily experience, we observe that an effect usually produces a change in its corresponding cause. For example, making wooden furniture involves altering trees. Similarly, buying a house or a car means a reduced bank balance. However, this mantra seems to defy conventional logic. According to the mantra *pūrṇasya pūrṇam ādāya pūrṇam evāvaśiṣyate*, "when this Whole is extracted, that Whole remains the Whole." The phenomenal world, immediately accessible to our senses (this), is a projection onto consciousness (that). Ultimate reality, like a rope misperceived as a snake, neither diminishes nor increases with the appearance or disappearance of this illusion. The Absolute is not affected by changes on the relative plane.

We generally assume that in any cause–effect relationship, the cause experiences a change and generates the effect. In contrast, Brahman remains immutable but is also the cause of the entire universe. Its apparent change can be compared to the process that gold undergoes in making jewelry. The essence of gold, mined and melted down, is unchanged when it is transformed into a bracelet, a pair of earrings, or a ring. Similarly, it is possible to create a universe from *pūrṇam* without it being truly affected.

Pūrṇāt pūrṇam udacyate. The omission of *adaḥ* and *idaṁ* in this mantra clearly indicates that only *pūrṇam* truly exists. Just as clay does not change when used to make pots or vases, *pūrṇam* remains immutable even though objective diversity (*idaṁ*) arises from it. Distinguishing between cause and effect is not an easy task. It would be wrong to say that a ceramic pot is an effect of clay. The pot is not entirely different from the clay; in fact, it is still clay. Making the pot does not produce two separate entities, the pot and the clay. Although we see a pot, the clay has not disappeared. The pot and the clay are not two essentially different realities. This example illustrates that in the empirical realm, the effect is not completely distinct from its material cause. By understanding that the effect is a manifestation of its cause, we can accept that both are, in essence, one and the same. Similarly, although we perceive a diversity of names and forms through our senses, ultimately, everything is *pūrṇam*.

This *śloka* of the *Catuḥ-ślokī-bhāgavatam* declares:

अहमेवासमेवाग्रे नान्यद्यत्सदसत्परम् ।
पश्चादहं यदेतच्च योऽवशिष्येत सोऽस्म्यहम् ॥

aham evāsam evāgre
nānyad yat sad-asat param
paścād ahaṁ yad etac ca
yo 'vaśiṣyeta so 'smy aham

> Before creation, I alone existed, there was nothing superior or different from me in the form of real (*sat*) or unreal objects (*asat*), which are illusions. Also, after [creation] began, I was all that existed. Once this [creation] ends, I will be all that remains.
>
> (*Śrīmad-bhāgavatam*, 2.9.33)

If we extract the objective from the subjective or unite them, all that remains is totality. If we remove *idaṁ pūrṇam*, the objectivity, from *adaḥ pūrṇam*, the subjectivity, or combine them, all that remains is *pūrṇam*. Although gold takes the form of a ring or a bracelet, it is still gold. Even if we melt the ring down, it is still gold.

Pūrṇam or Brahman is immutable. Many believe that to attain consciousness, the world and its diversity must disappear. However, to appreciate its fabric there is no need to destroy the shirt. Perception of the clay does not require destroying the pot. Similarly, we do not need to eliminate the dual experience, or the phenomenal world, in order to experience *pūrṇam*. It is possible to perceive the gold even when looking at bracelets, chains, earrings, and rings. Gold jewelry will never be anything other than gold. The Upanishad uses terms like adding and subtracting to illustrate that nothing affects Brahman. By giving the unlimited Brahman a name and form, nothing is added or taken away from it. Similarly, by removing creation, *pūrṇam* remains completely unaltered.

What can be negated is not real. Reality, by definition, cannot be negated. All objects lack reality because they can be negated in both time and space. All differences in the objective dimension are illusory. The objective world has no real independent existence. Since it is superimposed on Brahman, its existence depends entirely on *pūrṇam*. If we examine any object, we will discover that it is only a name and form, reducible to another substance. This substance, in turn, is a name and form reducible to micro-substances. Hence everything that can be objectified lacks an ultimate definition and its own reality. Objectivity consists of names and forms in a constant process of mutation, limited by space and time, and its reality is sustained by Brahman. By observing different objects, we can perceive the lack of real differences. They are simply limited, reducible, and negatable names and forms and their differences dissolve in Brahman. Since they have no true substantiality, there are no different objects. Regarding the efficient cause, I would say that creation cannot be adequately understood as an act separate from the creator. Humans, in their daily lives, generate effects from their activities because they believe they are subjects distinct from their actions. However, an action of the totality cannot be considered independent, since the totality includes everything. If nothing exists outside of *pūrṇam*, it encompasses both itself and its actions.

When we extract a portion of something, the source naturally diminishes proportionally to what is extracted. Following this logic, we might think that if God is the origin of the universe, God should have diminished after creating it. However, the Upanishad tells us that God did not diminish after creating the universe. It is impossible to subtract anything from the unlimited totality. If the totality encompassed everything, we would need a space free of it to place what is extracted, which is impossible.

In our relative understanding, we assume that the effect reduces the substance of its cause. This view is based on the law of cause and effect that prevails in our dual reality of subject and object. According to the Upanishad, if we subtract something from the totality, the totality does not diminish. Therefore, the emanation of the universe has caused no reduction in the totality. In unlimited totality, all action lacks an effect separate from its cause, as if nothing had ever occurred. In our relative and dual dimension, what we do is not the same as what we are; our activities modify our personality. But on the absolute level, there is no difference between God's existence and actions.

Activity and action, though similar, are not identical. Action does not have an existence separate from being. In contrast, activity binds and enslaves us through its reactions or effects. We can only see ourselves as active if our activity is distinct from what we are. However, if action is intrinsic to our being, then we can consider ourselves inactive. This type of action does not enslave or limit us because it is not something we do but what we are. It is not an activity separate from us but our very essence. The law of cause and effect only makes sense on the dual plane, with the notions of subject and object. The deep interdependence in the universe does not allow the existence of a cause separate from its effect. If we see the universe holistically, as an organism, we cannot accept that one of its parts functions independently. Like a river flowing toward the ocean, we flow through our actions until they dissipate, leaving only the ocean of consciousness. Similarly, instead of activity, only the immutable Being remains. What is called *yoga*, or 'union,' refers to the integration of being and doing. In our dual and relative reality, experience is often marked by conflict and disintegration. We strive to complete our inner world through sensory contact with the empirical world we perceive. The existence of this objective reality depends on our sensory perception. However, God's activity is not the result of what an actor or creator does. In this sense, God's creative activity cannot be considered activity in the conventional sense. In the Bhagavad Gita, Kṛṣṇa clearly states:

चातुर्वर्ण्यं मया सृष्टं गुणकर्मविभागशः ।
तस्य कर्तारमपि मां विद्ध्यकर्तारमव्ययम् ॥

cātur-varṇyaṁ mayā sṛṣṭaṁ
guṇa-karma-vibhāgaśaḥ
tasya kartāram api māṁ
viddhy akartāram avyayam

The four-fold caste system has been created by me according to the differentiation of qualities and actions. Though I am the author, know me as non-doer and eternal.

(Bhagavad Gita, 4.13)

God and His action are inseparable. Although He created everything, in reality, God has never performed any action. The unlimited totality manifests as the universe without diminishing God's content. The idea of a creation originating in a creator is based on the cause-and-effect relationship. However, this law is irrelevant in the absence of factors like space and time, which are consequences of creation and therefore subsequent to it. Therefore, they cannot affect God. If we understand that the principle of cause and effect does not apply to God, it is absurd to conceive of creation as an effect and God as its cause. God is *sarva-kāraṇa-kāraṇam*, 'the primary cause of all causes,' without really being the cause of anything. Although God is often considered the source of the universe, in reality, nothing has ever happened because God has never created anything. God, the immutable totality, remains the same as before creating the world. For many, it is difficult to understand that the universe, as we perceive it, has never really been created. This is especially hard to accept when we look around and see a variety of tangible objects like chairs, tables, trees, and people. We can see and touch these solid objects. However, when observing a tree with a powerful microscope, the tree no longer appears solid, but reveals itself to be a collection of atoms. With an even more powerful microscope, we see even smaller particles that are very different from atoms. The tree disappears and becomes inconceivable quantum spaces. Thus, we understand that there has never been a tree in itself. Instead, our vision and physical conditions have shown us something solid based on these microparticles.

What we call a "tree" has not been created; rather, it is the result of our way of perceiving a sea of particles. Our perception can vary, becoming more subtle or gross. Similarly, the universe has not been created as we perceive it. We perceive reality according to what our senses reveal to us. The form of the tree does not really exist as such; it is a construction of what our senses allow us to capture. That is why the Rig Veda states:

एकं सद्विप्रा बहुधा वदन्ति ।

ekaṁ sad viprā bahudhā vadanti

Poets, sages, and masters call the one Being by different names.
(Rig Veda, 1.164.46)

And the *Śrīmad-bhāgavatam* points out:

वदन्ति तत्तत्त्वविदस्तत्त्वं यज्ज्ञानमद्वयम् ।
ब्रह्मेति परमात्मेति भगवानिति शब्द्यते ॥

vadanti tat tattva-vidas
tattvaṁ yaj jñānam advayam
brahmeti paramātmeti
bhagavān iti śabdyate

The sages who have realized the Absolute, the non-dual knowledge, refer to it as Brahman, Paramātmā or Bhagavān.
(*Śrīmad-bhāgavatam*, 1.2.11)

After eating or sleeping well, we experience a sense of satisfaction or fullness. However, this satisfaction is not absolute, it is relative and temporary. The next day we will feel hungry and tired again. This experience of happiness or satisfaction is transient. The realization of our original fullness is only possible by awakening to the consciousness that subject and object, observer and observed, are in essence, the same. The difference we perceive between them is merely apparent. Illusorily, we isolate ourselves from life by identifying with an idea called "I." We observe the world from within a sack of flesh and bones with walls of skin, through the windows of the senses, and with the filter of the mind that evaluates what is perceived. We believe that what we perceive is entirely different from that which perceives. We even assume that the mind–body complex is the perceiver. Everything we consider perceivable through our senses is *idaṁ*, or what we call "manifested" or "material." However, the reality of the observer is no greater than that of the observed, since both share the same essence: Brahman. The moment we understand that the observer and the observed, the subject and the object, are one, they immediately transform into the observed. The subject–object duality only fades away by simultaneously recognizing their unified reality. The scriptures, acting as *pramāṇa*, teach us that this difference is merely apparent, revealing the true unity. The mantra encapsulates the Vedantic vision in its entirety. Mistakenly, we believe that the subject has a reality superior to the objects it perceives. However, the reality on which the observer is based is no more significant than that of the objects observed. As subjects perceiving empirical reality, we are no more real than what we perceive. Our true essence is unlimited consciousness, or *pūrṇam*. Both the observer and the observed share the same essence: consciousness. The apparent duality between subject and object is only a projection onto *pūrṇam*, which remains unaltered. Waves, moisture, and tsunamis do not affect the essential substance of water. The diversity of phenomenal reality has no true substance and is only a superimposition on reality. Our true nature is the unchanging and formless reality where every difference dissolves. The only enduring reality is pure, unlimited, and infinite consciousness, Brahman or *pūrṇam*.

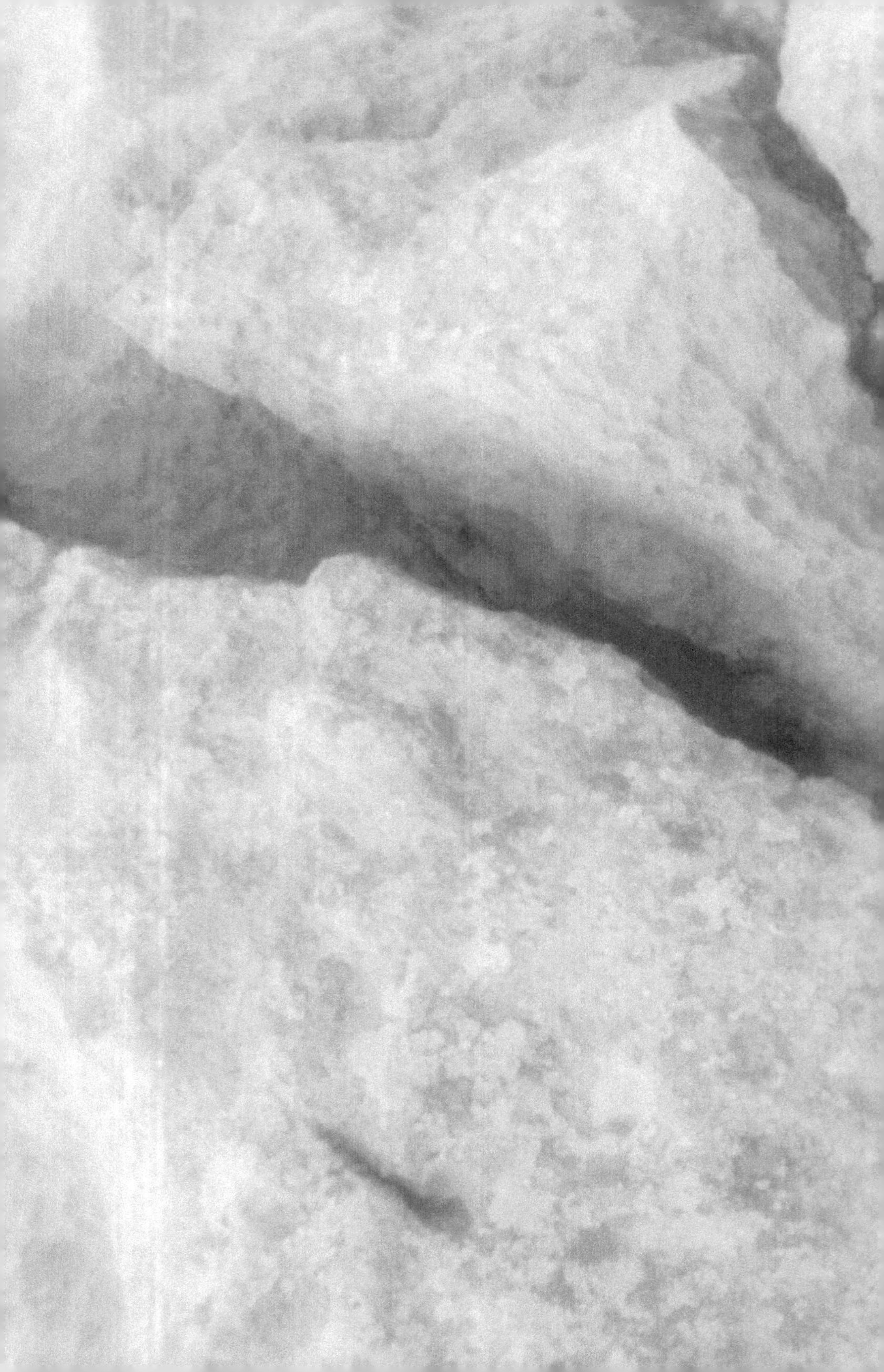

ARTICLE 6

THE PARABLE OF THE INNER PALACE

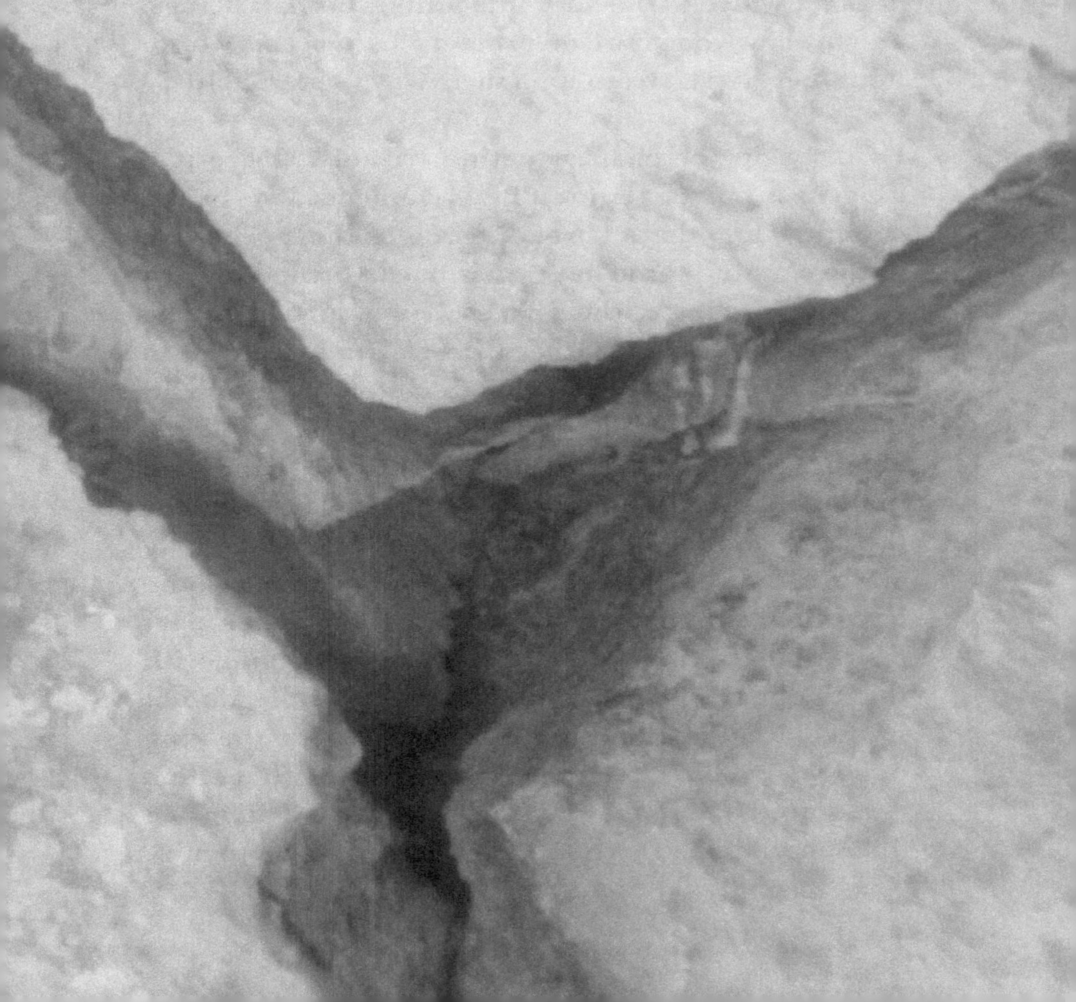

Rambam (1135–1204 CE) is considered one of the greatest Jewish enlightened masters of all time. He is also called Maimonides, Moses ben Maimon, and referred to as "The Great Eagle." His tombstone reads, "From Moses to Moses, there has never been anyone as great as Moses." Here I discuss a chapter of his famous book *Guide for the Perplexed*.

This current chapter, that we bring now, does not include any matter that has not been dealt with in the previous chapters. It is a kind of *hatimah* (conclusion or signature) and at the same time, it will explain how those who achieved true knowledge of God worship Him; and it will guide you how to get to that work, or *avodah*, which is the supreme aim of human beings, and to show you how God protects them in this world, until they depart from it on their way to eternal life.

I will begin the chapter with a parable. There is a king in a palace. Some of his subjects live in the country and others abroad. Some of those who live in the country some have their backs turned toward the king's palace, their faces being turned in the opposite direction. Others desire and zealous to enter the palace to visit the abode of the king and meet him personally, but they have not yet been able to even see the facade. Of those, some have managed to reach it and go around it, searching for the front door. Of these, some have entered the gate and walk through the hallways, and of those, some have finally managed to penetrate the inner part of the palace and they are in the same room with the king in his palace. But even these people, do not immediately upon entering the palace, see the king or spoken to him, because once inside, another effort is required before they can stand before the king, at a distance, or close by, hear his words or speak to him.

And now I want to clarify for you the meaning of the parable. The subjects who are abroad are people without religion, who have not inquired for themselves nor received by tradition, such as the Turks who are wandering in the North and the Kushites that go around in the South, and those who dwell among us and are like them. I regard them as irrational beings and not as humans; they are below mankind but above monkeys, for they have the form and figure of humans and certain mental faculties superior to those of the apes.

Those who are in the country, with their backs turned to the king's palace, are those who have religion, beliefs, and ideas, but hold on to false doctrines, which they either adopted by great mistakes made in their own self-inquiry, or received from others who misled them. Because they are going in the wrong direction, the more they walk, the farther they get from the king's palace. They are worse than the first class, so much so that under certain circumstances, it may be necessary to sacrifice them in order to abolish their doctrines, so that they will not divert others.

Those who desire to reach the palace and get inside, though they never managed to see it, are the crowd of the religious people. , i.e. those who observe the divine commandments but are ignorant.

Those who arrive at the palace but wander about it are the great scholars of religion. They believe in true principles they received through tradition, and learn practical worship and rituals, but do not investigate the roots of the Torah or explore with the intention of verifying their faith.

Those who undertook to deepen their investigation of religious principles have come into the hallways. Clearly, these can also be divided into different ranks. Those who have exemplary proof of everything that can be proved with an exemplary proof, and who has ascertained in divine matters to the extent that it is possible, everything that may be ascertained. And who has come close to certainty in those matters in which one can only come close to it—he has come to be with the king in the inner parts of his mansion.

My son, know that as long as you are engaged in studying the mathematical sciences and logic, you are one of those who circle the palace searching for the gate. Thus, our sages figuratively use the phrase: "Ben-zoma is still outside." When you understand physics, you have entered the hall; and when, after completing the study of natural philosophy, you master metaphysics, you have entered the innermost court, and you are with the king in the same palace. You have attained the level of the wise men. They, however, are of different levels of perfection.

But those who direct their thought toward the attainment of perfection in metaphysics, turning completely toward God, emptying their thought of all objectivity (והוא מפנה מחשבתו מזולתו**), who employ all their cognitive activities to the investigation of reality, to perceive from it the divine and to realize it existentially, in every way possible, they are the ones who enter the palace of the king at the level of prophets.**

(*Guide for the perplexed*, part 3, chapter 51)

This is one of the last chapters of his book. The Rambam begins by noting that he does not intend to add anything new that has not been mentioned in previous chapters, only to summarize the book. He compares this chapter to an artist's signature on the canvas, done after the painting is finished. This signature-chapter expresses something intimate, characteristic, and unique of his individuality. The Rambam refers here to a very special topic he calls *avodah*, "labor or work." After explaining the precepts and intellectual understanding, he believes it is the right moment to refer to the culmination of human life, enlightenment, or prophecy.

Below, we will elaborate on each section.

זֶה הַפֶּרֶק אֲשֶׁר נִזְכָּרֵהוּ עַתָּה, אֵינוֹ כּוֹלֵל תּוֹסֶפֶת עִנְיָן עַל מָה שֶׁכָּלְלוּ אוֹתוֹ פִּרְקֵי זֶה הַמַּאֲמָר, וְאֵינוֹ רַק כִּדְמוּת חֲתִימָה, עִם בֵּאוּר עֲבוֹדַת מַשִּׂיג הָאֲמִתִּיּוֹת הַמְיֻחָדוֹת בַּשֵּׁם יִתְעַלֶּה אַחַר הַשָּׂגָתוֹ, אֵי זֶה דָּבָר הוּא, וְהֵישִׁירוֹ לְהַגִּיעַ אֶל הָעֲבוֹדָה הַהִיא אֲשֶׁר הִיא הַתַּכְלִית אֲשֶׁר יַגִּיעַ אֵלֶיהָ הָאָדָם וְהוֹדִיעוֹ אֵיךְ תִּהְיֶה הַהַשְׁגָּחָה בּוֹ בָּעוֹלָם הַזֶּה עַד שֶׁיֵּעָתֵק אֶל צְרוֹר הַחַיִּים.

This current chapter, that we bring now, does not include any matter that has not been dealt with in the previous chapters. It is a kind of *hatimah* (conclusion or signature) and at the same time, it will explain how those who achieved true knowledge of God worship Him; and it will guide you how to get to that work, or *avodah*, which is the supreme aim of human beings, and to show you how God protects them in this world, until they depart from it on their way to eternal life.

The brilliant master uses a metaphor to describe the proximity of different types of human beings to the transcendental.

וַאֲנִי פּוֹתֵחַ הַדְּבָרִים בְּזֶה הַפֶּרֶק בְּמָשָׁל שֶׁאֶשָּׂאֵהוּ לְךָ, וְאוֹמַר, כִּי הַמֶּלֶךְ הוּא בְּהֵיכָלוֹ וַאֲנָשָׁיו כֻּלָּם, קְצָתָם אַנְשֵׁי הַמְּדִינָה וּקְצָתָם חוּץ לַמְּדִינָה, וְאֵלּוּ אֲשֶׁר בַּמְּדִינָה, מֵהֶם מִי שֶׁאֲחוֹרָיו אֶל בֵּית הַמֶּלֶךְ וּמְגַמַּת פָּנָיו בְּדֶרֶךְ אַחֶרֶת, וּמֵהֶם מִי שֶׁרוֹצֶה לָלֶכֶת אֶל בֵּית הַמֶּלֶךְ וּמְגַמָּתוֹ אֵלָיו, וּמְבַקֵּשׁ לְבַקֵּר בְּהֵיכָלוֹ וְלַעֲמֹד לְפָנָיו,

אֶלָּא שֶׁעַד הַיּוֹם לֹא רָאָה פְּנֵי חוֹמַת הַבַּיִת כְּלָל. מִן הָרוֹצִים לָבֹא אֶל הַבַּיִת, מֵהֶם שֶׁהִגִּיעַ אֵלָיו וְהוּא מִתְהַלֵּךְ סְבִיבוֹ מְבַקֵּשׁ לִמְצֹא הַשַּׁעַר, וּמֵהֶם מִי שֶׁנִּכְנַס בַּשַּׁעַר וְהוּא הוֹלֵךְ בַּפְּרוֹזְדוֹר, וּמֵהֶם מִי שֶׁהִגִּיעַ עַד שֶׁנִּכְנַס אֶל תּוֹךְ הַבַּיִת וְהוּא עִם הַמֶּלֶךְ בְּמָקוֹם אֶחָד שֶׁהוּא בֵּית הַמֶּלֶךְ, וְלֹא בְּהַגִּיעוֹ אֶל תּוֹךְ הַבַּיִת יִרְאֶה הַמֶּלֶךְ אוֹ יְדַבֵּר עִמּוֹ, אֲבָל אַחַר הַגִּיעוֹ אֶל תּוֹךְ הַבַּיִת אִי־אֶפְשָׁר לוֹ מִבִּלְתִּי שֶׁיִּשְׁתַּדֵּל הִשְׁתַּדְּלוּת אַחֶרֶת, וְאָז יַעֲמֹד לִפְנֵי הַמֶּלֶךְ וְיִרְאֵהוּ מֵרָחוֹק אוֹ מִקָּרוֹב, אוֹ יִשְׁמַע דְּבַר הַמֶּלֶךְ אוֹ יְדַבֵּר עִמּוֹ.

I will begin the chapter with a parable. There is a king in a palace. Some of his subjects live in the country and others abroad. Some of those who live in the country some have their backs turned toward the king's palace, their faces being turned in the opposite direction. Others desire and zealous to enter the palace to visit the abode of the king and meet him personally, but they have not yet been able to even see the facade. Of those, some have managed to reach it and go around it, searching for the front door. Of these, some have entered the gate and walk through the hallways, and of those, some have finally managed to penetrate the inner part of the palace and they are in the same room with the king in his palace. But even these people, do not immediately upon entering the palace, see the king or spoken to him, because once inside, another effort is required before they can stand before the king, at a distance, or close by, hear his words or speak to him.

Clearly, the king in the metaphor refers to the King of kings or to God, ultimate reality, or consciousness. Below, The Rambam explains the parable in detail:

וְהִנְנִי מְפָרֵשׁ לְךָ זֶה הַמָּשָׁל אֲשֶׁר חִדַּשְׁתִּי לְךָ, וְאוֹמַר, אָמְנָם אֲשֶׁר הֵם חוּץ לַמְּדִינָה, הֵם כָּל אִישׁ מִבְּנֵי אָדָם שֶׁאֵין לוֹ אֱמוּנַת דָּת, לֹא מִדֶּרֶךְ עִיּוּן וְלֹא מִדֶּרֶךְ קַבָּלָה, כִּקְצוֹת התור"ך הַמְשׁוֹטְטִים בְּצָפוֹן, וְהַכּוּשִׁיִּים וְהַמְשׁוֹטְטִים בַּדָּרוֹם, וְהַדּוֹמִים לָהֶם מֵאֲשֶׁר אִתָּנוּ בָּאַקְלִימִים הָאֵלֶּה, וְדִין אֵלּוּ כְּדִין בַּעֲלֵי חַיִּים שֶׁאֵינָם מְדַבְּרִים

וְאֵינָם אֶצְלִי בְּמַדְרֵגַת בְּנֵי אָדָם, וּמַדְרֵגָתָם בַּנִּמְצָאוֹת לְמַטָּה מִמַּדְרֵגַת הָאָדָם וּלְמַעְלָה מִמַּדְרֵגַת הַקּוֹף, אַחַר שֶׁהִגִּיעַ לָהֶם תְּמוּנַת הָאָדָם וְתָאֳרוֹ וְהַכָּרָה יוֹתֵר מֵהַכָּרַת הַקּוֹף.

And now I want to clarify for you the meaning of the parable. The subjects who are abroad are people without religion, who have not inquired for themselves nor received by tradition, such as the Turks who are wandering in the North and the Kushites that go around in the South, and those who dwell among us and are like them. I regard them as irrational beings and not as humans; they are below mankind but above monkeys, for they have the form and figure of humans and certain mental faculties superior to those of the apes.

Observing human society today, we notice that most people have a purely materialistic conception of life. From such a perspective, I perceive myself as a subject enclosed within a body that observes an external objective multiplicity. Such a life is no more than a journey from cradle to grave. Not really living, it is just surviving. As the well-known American Protestant clergyman Douglas Horton (1891–1968) said: "Materialism is the only form of distraction from true bliss."

The life of beings who are far from the divine and themselves is focused on simply running after superficial necessities. They live concerned solely with increasing the basic pleasures of eating, sleeping, mating, and protecting themselves. They identify exclusively with their physical appearance. In the analogy, these are the subjects who do not reside within the king's territory but live in distant lands. Still, they are considered subjects of the king because the distance between them and God is God. Nothing can conceal God except God Himself. These human beings move only on the surface and lack aspiration for what is deep within. The Torah describes this state as a double concealment:

וְאָנֹכִי הַסְתֵּר אַסְתִּיר פָּנַי בַּיּוֹם הַהוּא [...]
(דברים ל"א, י"ח)

And I will hide, I will surely hide my face on that day [...]
(Deuteronomy, 31:18)

These beings suffer from double concealment because they have a problem and they do not know they have one. In addition to living in illusion, they have not realized they do. Materialistic people enjoy technological advancements and the benefits they bring but suffer because they have neglected their inner lives. **"The subjects who are abroad"** (אשר הם חוץ למדינה) go through the world without souls; they live far from God, the Truth, life, and themselves.

Life has a superficial aspect and a deep one: matter is the outside; spirit is the inside. They comprise a harmonic unit. Materialism is born of the exaggerated emphasis on the superficial aspect. This imbalance is disharmonious, dissonant, and conflictive.

וַאֲשֶׁר הֵם בַּמְדִינָה אֶלָּא שֶׁאֲחוֹרֵיהֶם אֶל בֵּית הַמֶּלֶךְ, הֵם בַּעֲלֵי אֱמוּנָה וְעִיּוּן, אֶלָּא שֶׁעָלוּ בְּיָדָם דֵּעוֹת בִּלְתִּי אֲמִתִּיּוֹת, אִם מִטָּעוּת גְּדוֹלָה שֶׁנָּפַל בְּיָדָם בְּעֵת עִיּוּנָם, אוֹ שֶׁקִּבְּלוּ מִמִּי שֶׁהִטְעָם, וְהֵם לְעוֹלָם, מִפְּנֵי הַדֵּעוֹת הָהֵם, כָּל אֲשֶׁר יֵלְכוּ יוֹסִיפוּ רֹחַק מִבֵּית הַמֶּלֶךְ, וְאֵלּוּ יוֹתֵר רָעִים מִן הָרִאשׁוֹנִים הַרְבֵּה, וְאֵלּוּ הֵם אֲשֶׁר יָבִיא הַצֹּרֶךְ בִּקְצַת הָעִתִּים לְהָרְגָם וְלִמְחוֹת זֵכֶר דֵּעוֹתָם שֶׁלֹּא יַתְעוּ זוּלָתָם.

Those who are in the country, with their backs turned to the king's palace, are those who have religion, beliefs, and ideas, but hold on to false doctrines, which they either adopted by great mistakes made in their own self-inquiry, or received from others who misled them. Because they are going in the wrong direction, the more they walk, the farther they get from the king's palace. They are worse than the first class, so much so that under certain circumstances, it may be necessary to sacrifice them in order to abolish their doctrines, so that they will not divert others.

There are those who live within the kingdom but turn their backs on the king. These are the masses who, while considering themselves "spiritual," walk in the wrong direction. They have read or heard insufficient information and partially understood truths can do more harm than ignorance. They believe that they are advancing by reading books or websites, following practices invented by pseudo-masters, or attending lectures, courses, or retreats. Despite their efforts, they only manage to move farther from the path.

Rambam's words sound more relevant today than ever before. Nowadays, spirituality has become a profitable business. Many are now consumers for an industry of self-growth seminars, meditation courses, tantra, hatha yoga, crystals, chakras, tarot, *śaktipāta*, Kabbalah, and so on. Professional satsangists have emerged, who publicly present themselves as enlightened. They travel around with their wandering circus, putting on a grotesque pseudo-spiritual show.

Others confuse paths of liberation with psychology and promote their business with attractive slogans such as "achieve inner peace," "attain happiness," "instant enlightenment," "*śaktipāta* for awakening," and so on. The guides, instructors, and teachers of these methods are simply merchants in search of buyers. They publish books to increase the clientele of their centers. Their students are clients and consumers, not disciples.

The main spiritual businesses, or perversions of spirituality, revolve around self-help, new age, shamanism, and magic. Although presented as paths for holistic development, their only intention is to stimulate the masses to improve their personal performance in today's competitive society. New age is a general label for the range of spiritual merchandise that ranges from the old Spiritism to alternative healing. Magic covers astrologers, clairvoyants, psychics, and fortune tellers. New Kabbalah businesses present a laughable version of ancient Hebrew wisdom and new ones appear every day.

This industry is a manifestation of a totally perverted spirituality. Ancient disciplines such as hatha yoga have been deformed in the West, both in spirit and method. Although all instructors deny it, what was originally a psychophysiological and spiritual path has been transformed into a purely physical practice. Instead of preparing for spiritual evolution, hatha yoga is practiced to improve one's figure, lose weight, gain flexibility, or reduce stress. Meditation has changed from being a gateway to true nature into a practice to relax, lower blood pressure, overcome depression, and reduce insomnia.

After only a few years of practice, hatha yoga apprentices become teachers; they in turn rush to open training courses for new instructors. The motives behind these activities are mostly financial. In ancient times, the prerequisites for a disciple to receive spiritual training from a master were compassion, austerity, and surrender. Now, the only requirement to be a yoga teacher is money.

As in any industry, spiritual businesses are governed by the rules inherent in all commercial competition. Most teachers are far from living up to the merchandise they sell. A great multitude live with their backs to the Truth, with well-documented ignorance. In Rambam's parable, these people are far below the first group who live abroad. They are dangerous because they confuse others by spreading the wrong attitude toward spiritual life. Instead of aspiring to know the king, many are busy constructing their own thrones.

וְהָרוֹצִים לָבֹא אֶל בֵּית הַמֶּלֶךְ וּלְהִכָּנֵס אֶצְלוֹ אֶלָּא שֶׁלֹּא רָאוּ בֵּית הַמֶּלֶךְ כְּלָל, הֵם
הֲמוֹן אַנְשֵׁי הַתּוֹרָה רָצָה לוֹמַר עַמֵּי הָאָרֶץ הָעוֹסְקִים בַּמִּצְווֹת.

Those who desire to reach the palace and get inside, though they never managed to see it, are the crowd of the religious people. , i.e. those who observe the divine commandments but are ignorant.

This third group includes followers and believers of institutionalized religions and religious "isms." These eternal practitioners are in every religious organization. The Rambam considers those who only deal with commandments and precepts to be simple, faithful believers, who are ignorant and incapable of embracing discipleship.

These followers lack self-confidence so they choose to depend on an external authority. Instead of being liberated with the help of the sacred scriptures and their teachings, they become slaves to them. They live through a kind of psychological slavery, subjugated by books, myths, and guides. Stagnant in spiritual practices, they do not stop to assess their goals and aspirations. Alongside their blind leaders, they comprise the sad phenomenon of institutionalized belief. They are like the shepherds Nietzsche detests:

> Zealously and with shouting they drove their herd along their path, as if there were only one path to the future! Indeed, these shepherds, too, still belonged among the sheep!
>
> (Friedrich Nietzsche, *Thus spoke Zarathustra*, "*On Priests*")

These followers are aggressive toward others or themselves because they persist in evading all responsibility for their lives. This way, they can blame religion for their failures and weaknesses. Among followers, we find those who attack gurus: first they put their masters on a pedestal, only to later demonize them. Fanatical followers operate under the law of the pendulum, first idealizing and then demonizing. They are like those who idealized Jesus, to later crucify him, and finally build a religious framework around him.

Followers' outward passion conceals that they do not experience what they preach; this passion is only based on dogmatic beliefs. Their outer veneer of faith hides that they go about the world with empty hands, because they have never seen the king's abode, even from a distance. Followers promote institutionalized religion because their need is more social than spiritual. They are completely unlike disciples, who are beings of peace and love. Disciples evolve and develop; followers are stuck in fanaticism.

Although The Rambam made important contributions to the *halachah*, or "Jewish legal system," he did not see religion as only tradition or ritual. He clearly says that the observance of precepts, rules, and regulations alone does not ensure an awakening on the level of consciousness. An exaggerated emphasis on ritualism can certainly affect the essence of a living religious experience.

וְהַמַּגִּיעִים אֶל הַבַּיִת הַהוֹלְכִים סְבִיבוֹ, הֵם הַתַּלְמוּדִיִּים אֲשֶׁר הֵם מַאֲמִינִים דֵּעוֹת אֲמִתִּיּוֹת מִדֶּרֶךְ קַבָּלָה, וְלוֹמְדִים מַעֲשֵׂה הָעֲבוֹדוֹת, וְלֹא הִרְגִּילוּ בְּעִיּוּן שָׁרְשֵׁי הַתּוֹרָה וְלֹא חָקְרוּ כְּלָל לְאַמֵּת אֱמוּנָה.

Those who arrive at the palace but wander about it are the great scholars of religion. They believe in true principles they received through tradition, and learn practical worship and rituals, but do not investigate the roots of the Torah or explore with the intention of verifying their faith.

While it is true that religion is a single phenomenon, human beings respond to it based on their level of consciousness. Religion can be divided into three main types: instinctive, intellectual, and sublime.

Instinctive religion is the most primitive. Its followers believe in a capricious god and the human capacity to manipulate divine will. They use ritualism, magic, and superstition to gain benefits. They make offerings to appease their gods, believing that if the gods are pleased, they will grant a good harvest or material wealth; if not, the gods will unleash natural disasters such as earthquakes or floods.

We cannot yet say that this level has been completely overcome. Even nowadays, there are individuals who harbor these religious beliefs. Primitive religion is instinctual and if human beings continue to perceive the world instinctively, we will continue to see this approach to religion. Their level of consciousness must develop further to overcome these archaic spiritual manifestations.

The next level is intellectual religion, which transcends superstition in favor of theology. Within this category, there are the "great scholars of religion" described by The Rambam: the scholars, doctors, and leaders of organized religion who are as blind as the multitude of followers that they guide. Such religions rely solely on theoretical information and exert power over the masses through rules and regulations.

Each "ism" has its own theology, which includes logical conclusions about God's desires, intentions, and plans as well as detailed explanations about creation, the soul, sin, heaven, and hell. This second type of religion is the product of human thoughts about the Divine. Unlike the magic of the instinctual type, the intellectual type comprises ideas, concepts, conclusions, and words about the Truth. It features long lists of laws and prohibitions but lacks direct transcendental experience. Hence this category includes organized and institutionalized religion. Among its main characteristics are proselytism, preaching, evangelizing, propaganda, and advertising. Their efforts to convince others hint at their own insecurity about what they preach, since their message is based on theologies that do not come from a genuine experience of Truth.

Authentic religion is the highest level and the most refined religious expression. More than a belief, it is a quality of the soul. It is born from direct experience and therefore transcends traditions, organizations, and theologies. It does not strive to evangelize, but rather to share an experience. It emphasizes peace, love, compassion, and bliss, rather than intimidating its followers with sin, condemnation, and hell.

"... do not investigate the roots of the Torah or explore with the intention of verifying their faith." The information offered by religious scholars lacks existential value. Their sermons do not nourish us, because like junk food, they lack any nutritional benefits. The good memory of these scholars helps them better document their own ignorance. They explain what they do not know and they describe what they have never seen. They do not pass on direct experience to their followers but deliver second-hand theoretical information borrowed from others. They have nothing but words to offer to their congregations.

Such leaders and their followers wander around the walls of the king's abode, floating on the surface of existence. Their lives unfold in the shadows of the surface, never venturing into the depths of their inner selves. The leaders of organized religions have not evaluated their own messages and intentions. Although their traditional dress, theologies, beliefs, and scriptures may vary, in essence they are exactly the same. They are variations of the same phenomenon, distinguished only by seemingly different terms and rituals. Some say that all religions share the same essence and lead to the same end. But in the case of organized religion, there is no doubt that all religious "isms" are identical and lead nowhere.

It is strange that the titles of these religious leaders, such as "His Divine Grace," "His Holiness," or "The great *tzadik* or *ga'on*" are much longer than the name of the one who they claim to represent:

God. They strive more to memorize verses and *ślokas* than to understand their true meaning. They believe that adding sheep to the flock of their organizations is a most auspicious task. In fact, this work of evangelization and preaching only contributes to spreading ignorance. Sacred literature is not understood by memorizing it, but by experiencing what it describes. Knowledge obtained only from books is not spiritual, since wisdom only originates in the awakening of consciousness.

While it is true that, out of His infinite love, God created man in God's own image and likeness, human beings also created gods in their own image and likeness: out of their selfishness, loneliness, misery, pride, and fear. Humanity has invented countless rituals, ceremonies, traditions, dogmas, myths, and beliefs, which are taught and practiced in churches, mosques, temples, and synagogues. The motivation has been to escape fear, create a sense of security, gain comfort, and alleviate uncertainty. Once humanity convinced itself these spiritual consolations were meaningful, it clung to them and labeled them "sacred." However, insecurity and fear can only be overcome through acceptance, not consolation; through observation, not belief.

Clearly, an invented god is profane. Organized dogmatism has transformed religion into self-hypnosis. Unless one transcends this conditioning, with the fear and suffering that this brings, it is impossible to perceive something divine. Revealing what is real and recognizing consciousness is only possible by closely observing our conditioning, beliefs, and conclusions. Without going beyond this conditioning, there is no peace, only an idea of peace; without reaching peace, it is impossible to caress the sacred.

Our invented beliefs imprison us in an unlocked cell. If we do not leave, it is because we are attached to the sense of security and comfort that they give us. Many religious people hold on to their beliefs out of fear of the unknown. They try to flee from the insecurity in their hearts. They confuse true religion with traditions, beliefs, rituals, ceremonies, and dogmas that restrain their freedom and stupefy their minds.

Clearly, if we are not free, it is impossible to observe and access the Truth. If our search emanates from what we have been indoctrinated with, we are not seeking the Truth, but rather ideas and beliefs. The paradox is that our beliefs prevent our search for the Truth. Our religiosity with its god-ideas, keep us from what is real. They direct us toward the pursuit of our imaginary beliefs and not of the Truth. Blinded by what we believe to be, we cannot discover what really is.

The Rambam continues by referring to the parable:

> אֵלֶּה שֶׁהֶעֱמִיקוּ לְעַיֵּן בְּעֶקְרוֹנוֹת הַדָּת נִכְנְסוּ לַפְּרוֹזְדוֹר. הָאֲנָשִׁים שָׁם לְלֹא סָפֵק בְּדַרְגוֹת שׁוֹנוֹת. מִי שֶׁיֵּשׁ לוֹ הוֹכָחָה מוֹפְתִית לְכָל מָה שֶׁהוּכַח בְּהוֹכָחָה מוֹפְתִית וְיוֹדֵעַ יְדִיעָה וַדָּאִית אֶת כָּל מַה שֶּׁאֶפְשָׁר לָדַעַת יְדִיעָה וַדָּאִית מֵהַדְּבָרִים הָאֱלוֹהִיִּים, וְהוּא קָרוֹב לְוַדָּאוּת בְּמָה שֶׁבּוֹ אֶפְשָׁר רַק לְהִתְקָרֵב לְוַדָּאוּת – הוּא עִם הַמֶּלֶךְ בְּתוֹךְ הַבַּיִת.

> **Those who undertook to deepen their investigation of religious principles have come into the hallways. Clearly, these can also be divided into different ranks. Those who have exemplary proof of everything that can be proved with an exemplary proof, and who has ascertained in divine matters to the extent that that is possible, everything that may be ascertained. And who has come close to certainty in those matters in which one can only come close to it—he has come to be with the king in the inner parts of his mansion.**

Only true seekers have access to the inner palace. An authentic search for ultimate reality is not born out of childish curiosity. It is much more than an interest in reading books, going on a retreat, or attending lectures. It goes beyond taking a few courses and rushing to teach. As I mentioned above, religious followers cling to their beliefs for comfort and to escape their fears, while true seekers are willing to give up everything for Truth. As David says, when he was in the wilderness:

אֱלֹהִים אֵלִי אַתָּה אֲשַׁחֲרֶךָּ צָמְאָה לְךָ נַפְשִׁי כָּמַהּ לְךָ בְשָׂרִי בְּאֶרֶץ־צִיָּה וְעָיֵף בְּלִי־מָיִם:

(תהילים ס"ג, ב')

God, You are my God; I search for You, my soul thirsts for You, my body yearns for You, as a parched and thirsty land that has no water.

(Psalms, 63:2)

Many years ago in India, an elderly swami told me the following story. I think it illustrates this idea well:

A young disciple approached his spiritual master and offered his humble reverences. After a few moments of respectful silence, he said,

—"Beloved Master, I perform my spiritual practices daily, but nothing happens. I would like to know what I need in order to realize God."

The wise old man told him:

—"Follow me and I will show you what you need in order to realize God."

They went to a nearby river and the master went into the water. Then, he called his disciple:

—"Come, I will show you what you need in order to realize God."

The young disciple entered the river full of expectations. When he reached a certain depth, the master pushed his shoulders and submerged him. The disciple tried to free himself, but the master held him firmly under the water. After a few moments, which seemed like an eternity to the young disciple, the master released him. When the disciple regained his breath, the master asked him:

—"When you were under the water, what was your main desire?"

Without hesitating, the young disciple replied:

—"Only one thing: to breathe. I only wanted air…"

The guru asked:

—"In that moment, wouldn't you have preferred money, fame, a family, wealth, power, pleasures, sweets, ice cream, or cakes?"

The disciple answered sharply:

—"No sir, I only needed to breathe, I wanted air and nothing else..."

Then the spiritual master said:

—"That is what you need for enlightenment. When your desire for God is as intense as your desire for air while you were under the water, when God is your only aspiration day and night, then you will undoubtedly realize God."

In our generation, entertainment plays a major role in our lives. Most people are looking for new and more sophisticated distractions on televisions, computers, or cell phones. Many confuse spiritual searching for another kind of recreation or hobby. In our consumer society, many have made spiritual life a job or business. Meditation retreats are offered in luxurious hotels, yoga courses in exotic locations, and tai chi weekends at summer vacation spots. It is hard to distinguish whether this merchandise is knowledge or tourism.

The quality of our search will depend on the motivation that impels us to follow the path of the soul. If we want entertainment, fun, income, or friends, our spiritual search will be limited to receiving information but not undergoing true transformation.

For many, religious life is just another mask. Their efforts to transcend the ego are a disguise. Only an investigation that stems from a vital need will not cease until reality is revealed. Only an existential search can lead to the Light.

An exploration based on logic alone will be fruitless. Like the sophists, we would be able to argue for or against any postulate. On the other hand, sincere seekers, intuiting the transcendental, ask themselves, like Unamuno in his book *The Tragic Feeling of Life*, "Is it only true what is rational? Is there not a reality that is unavailable to reason and perhaps contrary to it?"

As long as we cannot transcend the mental level—saturated with ideas, concepts, conclusions, rational theories, and logical hypotheses—we will only establish schools of thought. If the demand for truth is insufficient, it gives rise to new philosophical doctrines. Only an authentic thirst for Truth will lead to a revealing vision of reality that transcends thought.

There is so much loneliness, pain, and misery in the world, that under the name of Truth, we venture to annihilate our suffering. However, such truth will only be the opposite of pain. Seeking bliss out of our misery is like marrying out of fear of being alone: it cannot be a sincere aspiration for Truth. It is a continuation of our pursuit of money, fame, sex, and relief. In fact, disguised as seekers, we are only trying to solve problems and escape difficulties. Seeking Truth in the hope of solving our problems is an evasive act, lacking true understanding and awareness. While we are busy escaping, we cannot find anything real.

Meditatively attentive, situated in the present, Truth will reveal itself in every action. For example, the yoga of action, or karma yoga, teaches that Truth or God is not sought through action, but in action itself. *Pirkei Avot* tells us that the reward for a *mitzvah* (precept) is the *mitzvah* itself. Because actions performed with a solution-focused attitude lack understanding and value; they are only a means to rewards or results. We believe that by serving, meditating, or loving we will reach the Truth. However, love, service, and meditation lose all their value when we turn them into a means to an end.

The mystery of the unknown is not sought in the same way that we seek money, fame, or sex. The mind cannot search for anything unknown to it. It can only aspire for what it can project, based on what it already knows. In trying to think of God, we will necessarily be dealing with a mental projection created by our traditions and conditioning. Thinking about the Truth is a cultural inheritance of our society. Truth does not accept objectification and, therefore, it cannot be sought or found; once found, it loses its vitality.

In this life, consciousness is the only thing impossible to define, yet impossible to ignore. As egoic entities, we are illusions. False entities cannot pursue what is real or authentic. Truth can be revealed in an instant free of memory and the past. We cannot search for, achieve, reach, or know Truth: we can only be it. Truth cannot be pursued, only found. It reveals itself when searching stops. By stopping to pursue our mental projections of Truth, we realize that we are enlightened. Suddenly, we realize that we are what we aspired to be. This is expressed by Master Kokuan:

> Mediocrity is gone. The mind is clear of limitations. I seek no state of enlightenment. Neither do I remain where no enlightenment exists. Since I linger in neither condition, eyes cannot see me. If hundreds of birds covered my path with flowers, such praise would be meaningless.
>
> (*The Ten Bulls of Zen, verse 8*)

Obviously, we cannot find the Truth by searching for it, but if we do not seek, we will never find. Rather than recommend intellectual philosophical research, I suggest inquiring into the nature of inquiry itself.

Many confuse withdrawal for the inner quest to be extreme egoism. However, it should be noted that, in examining our own consciousness, we are not inquiring into the personal but into the universal, because the inquiry itself is the evaporation of all difference. With observation, the walls that demarcate our supposedly independent personality collapse. Clearly, what is intuited beyond mental domains cannot be defined with words. However, we should not be frustrated by the limitations of words, because it may be that the unspeakable is just what we are looking for.

"Those who undertook to deepen their investigation of religious principles have come into the hallways." The Rambam talks about those who fulfill their religious obligations and their leaders who know the sacred books. Abiding by the religious precepts of *halachah* is not enough to enter the hallways. It is essential to question the principles of religion and bookish knowledge. The etymological meaning of the term *religion* is "to reconnect" or "to bond again." Religion is not only a collection of rituals, ceremonies, and dogmas but an inner experience; it is to gather our scattered energies in order to focus them on the Truth.

To explore the very principles of religion, we must investigate the investigator. This is a call to evaluate what it means to be religious. In order to recognize a religious being, it is important to clearly explore the motives that drive different minds. Of course, each mind develops its own motivations: sex, honor, fame, respect, or riches. The mind is memory and conditioning that we have received from past generations. This includes culture, dogmas, beliefs, tradition, and so on. The mind is not a solid object but an activity: thoughts, hopes, aspirations, longings, ambitions, pretensions, greed, and desires. If we try to understand what a religious being is through our conditioned mind, we will get incomplete answers. A religious mind can only be understood from the perception of mental activity itself.

Obviously, it is impossible to conduct a real investigation if there is no freedom. A mind overloaded with dogmas and conclusions lacks the clarity necessary to observe. A Muslim mind will see life based on the Koran. A Christian mind will see life based on the New Testament and the message of the apostles. A mind conditioned by tradition and culture, whether Jewish, Buddhist, Hindu, or Jain, cannot freely observe mental activity. If we project our mental content, the observation will be tarnished by beliefs and traditions.

To distinguish what is apparent from what is real, we must distance ourselves from our popes, bishops, rabbis, gurus, and their interpretations of sacred books. To discover the illusory, we need a total absence of religious, ideological, and cultural attachments. Only then will it be possible to uncover what the human mind has invented in the name of religion to flee from its fears, desires, confusions, insecurities, and sufferings. Fearful, confused, and insecure beings who only want pleasure cannot really be religious. They do not seek Truth, but to avoid fear and escape pain. Those who seek pleasure do not pursue the divine and sacred; they are eager for sensory pleasures. Such beings lose their religious quality because these aspirations nourish the egoic phenomenon.

Of course, there is nothing wrong with enjoying what life offers here and now, like a sunrise or a sunset by the sea. It is the effort to repeat pleasurable experiences that snatch away our religious quality. In order to access our true religious nature, we must transcend suffering and distress.

Human beings do not know how to get rid of suffering. Their pain inevitably leads them to run from fear and pursue pleasure.

Organized religion has tried to solve this problem by promising paradise after death. However, suffering is part of human nature; it is not a private or personal experience. Instead, we need to identify how the pain of humanity expresses itself in us. It is a matter of recognizing it as a collective experience, since, without recognizing it, it is impossible to realize the religious nature.

Likewise, we must identify fear, not as a personal experience, but as a human phenomenon. Observing, we will notice that time is the origin of fear and, therefore, of mental activity. We mistakenly seek the cause of our pain in order to eliminate it. But if we focus on the specific reason for our fear, violence, or suffering, we reinforce the egoic phenomenon and observation loses clarity. We have been taught that we must face, reject, or control fear and suffering by identifying its causes and try to eliminate them. But if we destroy one cause, the solution will be temporary, and suffering will return. Only by putting aside the reasons and observing suffering itself will we realize that it is not something different from us. Observation reveals to us that the experience is not different from the experiencer; the observed is not different from the observer.

Only by transcending fear can we have a clear vision. Then, we realize that the pursuit of pleasure or enjoyment has no relation whatsoever with love. We will understand that meditation cannot be to escape something or pursue a goal. Only by investigating will we realize the limitations of a conditioned mind and awaken to an observation that surpasses thought. By exploring, we will identify the mental limitations and observation beyond thought will emerge.

When we delve into the principles of religion, we enter the inner corridors of the king's palace, that is, to the corridors within us.

וְהַכֹּהֲנִים וְהָעָם הָעוֹמְדִים בָּעֲזָרָה, כְּשֶׁהָיוּ שׁוֹמְעִים שֵׁם הַמְפֹרָשׁ שֶׁהוּא יוֹצֵא מִפִּי כֹּהֵן גָּדוֹל, הָיוּ כּוֹרְעִים וּמִשְׁתַּחֲוִים וְנוֹפְלִים עַל פְּנֵיהֶם, וְאוֹמְרִים: "בָּרוּךְ שֵׁם כְּבוֹד מַלְכוּתוֹ לְעוֹלָם וָעֶד".

(משנה, יומא, ו', ב')

> And the priests and the people who stood in the Temple courtyard, when they heard the Explicit Name issuing forth from the mouth of the High Priest, would bow down, prostrate themselves, fall on their faces (*pneihem*), and say: "Blessed is the name of the glory of His kingdom forever and ever."
>
> (*Mishnah*, "*Yoma*," 6.2)

The Hebrew word *panim* (פָּנִים), or "face," according to the sages of antiquity, is interchangeable with *pnim* (פְּנִים), or "interior." Thus, "they fall on their faces" also means "they fall on their inner faces" (ונופלים על פניהם – *venoflim al pneihem*). Similarly, meditation is about dropping into the depths of our inner self, as explained by the Alter Rebbe in *Likutei Amarim*, also called *Tanya*:

> "לְךָ אָמַר לִבִּי בַּקְשׁוּ פָנָי" (תהילים כ"ז, ח'). פֵּרוּשׁ: בַּקְשׁוּ פְּנִימִית הַלֵּב.
> (ספר התניא, חלק ד', אגרת הקודש, ד')

> My heart said on your behalf: "Seek my face (*panai*)," (Psalms, 27:8) The meaning of it is: "Seek the interiors (*pnimiyut*) of the heart.
>
> (*Tanya*, part 4, "*Iggeret HaKodesh*," 4)

Meditation is not about doing something, but just allowing ourselves to drop into the depths of our inner self. The verse uses the plural *pneihem*, or "interiors," because each one of us has different families and histories, that is, our own corridors. However, the same harbor awaits us all.

In the objective world of names and forms, we value what is taught, learned, and memorized, because on the phenomenal plane, the only way to know something is by acquiring information. However, on the inner plane, only our own direct experience has value. Religion is our inner world; therefore, it is impossible to teach it. We can learn certain words and memorize prayers, but it is impossible to teach or learn how to pray. Teaching or studying religion is as absurd as teaching to love. Praying, worshipping, or meditating are ways of loving. God is the unknown, so it is impossible to access God through known rituals and theologies. Religion is not a doctrine or discipline but a search. A complete transformation is necessary to penetrate religion. A mind that is a warehouse of dogmas, traditions and beliefs must be converted into a tranquil lake that reflects the full moon of Truth.

"Those who undertook to deepen their investigation of religious principles have come into the hallways. Clearly, these can also be divided into different ranks. Those who have exemplary proof of everything that can be proved with an exemplary proof, and who has ascertained in divine matters..." The confusion between knowledge and wisdom has been a great misfortune for humankind. Knowledge can be acquired from teachers, books, retreats, courses, and lectures, but wisdom is a revelation. Knowledge comes from thought, while wisdom is born from consciousness. Knowledge informs, whereas wisdom transforms.

Knowledge brings anxiety because the mind is insatiable and always seeks to accumulate and hoard. Wisdom, on the other hand, brings peace and contentment. The ego fills with pride for accumulating knowledge until it becomes insufferable; it gets fat, expands, and inflates like a balloon, but always suffers because this world has many needles. On the contrary, wisdom threatens the very existence of the egoic phenomenon. Knowledge is from the mind; wisdom is from consciousness. Knowledge is related to memory and, therefore, it is past; it consists of stored information and is confined within the framework of time. Wisdom belongs to the now, to the present; it corresponds to eternity.

Through knowledge we become aware of differences, but through wisdom we awaken to the undivided reality. Knowledge disintegrates, separates, and divides, while wisdom leads to the One without a second. Knowledge helps us understand, while wisdom gives us access to the reality that transcends all understanding. For the knowledgeable, matter and spirit are totally different. For the wise, matter is the external aspect of spirit and spirit is the inner heart of matter.

Knowledge that is disconnected from wisdom limits us. It leads us to new technologies, but not to the wisdom to use them properly. We know about atomic energy, but we have used it to create bombs. Another sad example is the internet, a great fruit of knowledge in a world devoid of wisdom. Knowledge can be necessary, but it can also be dangerous if it is put at the service of greed or pride. The proper place of knowledge is to serve as a basis for developing wisdom. Knowledge is necessary and beneficial in phenomenal reality but is an obstacle if we apply it to our inner world. Human beings have been trapped in this cycle for a long time, which limits their freedom. The Rambam says we must study everything that is possible to understand, but he makes it clear that our capacity for understanding has a limit. To discover the eternal, we must be liberated of all knowledge.

וְדַע בְּנִי שֶׁאַתָּה כָּל עוֹד שֶׁתִּתְעַסֵּק בַּחָכְמוֹת הַלִּמּוּדִיּוֹת וּבִמְלֶאכֶת הַהִגָּיוֹן, אַתָּה מִכַּת הַמִּתְהַלְּכִים סְבִיב הַבַּיִת לְבַקֵּשׁ הַשַּׁעַר, כְּמוֹ שֶׁאָמְרוּ רַבּוֹתֵינוּ זִכְרוֹנָם לִבְרָכָה עַל צַד הַמָּשָׁל, עֲדַיִן בֶּן זוֹמָא מִבַּחוּץ, וּכְשֶׁתָּבִין הָעִנְיָנִים הַטִּבְעִיִּים, כְּבָר נִכְנַסְתָּ בִּפְרוֹזְדוֹר הַבַּיִת, וּכְשֶׁתַּשְׁלִים הַטִּבְעִיּוֹת וְתָבִין הָאֱלֹהִיּוֹת, כְּבָר נִכְנַסְתָּ עִם הַמֶּלֶךְ אֶל הֶחָצֵר הַפְּנִימִית וְאַתָּה עִמּוֹ בְּבַיִת אֶחָד, וְזֹאת הִיא מַדְרֵגַת הַחֲכָמִים, וְהֵם חֲלוּקֵי הַשְּׁלֵמוּת.

My son, know that as long as you are engaged in studying the mathematical sciences and logic, you are one of those who circle the palace searching for the gate. Thus, our sages figuratively use the phrase: "Ben-zoma is still outside." When you understand physics, you have entered the hall; and when, after completing the study of natural philosophy, you master metaphysics, you have entered the innermost court, and you are with the king in the same palace. You have attained the level of the wise men. They, however, are of different levels of perfection.

With an inclusive attitude, Rambam speaks in universal terms. His teachings are not limited to a particular nation, race, group, or religious institution. For him, the entrance to the king's house is not reserved for a certain group; it is open to all humanity. Enlightenment does not belong to an exclusive spiritual club. For example, we see that in his famous *Mishneh Torah*, in *Sefer HaMadda* (*The book of knowledge*), he refers to enlightenment as follows:

מִיסוֹדֵי הַדָּת לֵידַע שֶׁהָאֵל מְנַבֵּא אֶת בְּנֵי הָאָדָם.
(משנה תורה, ספר המדע, הלכות יסודי התורה, ז', א')

It is from the foundations of religion to acknowledge that God bestows prophecy upon human beings.
(*Mishneh Torah*, "*Sefer HaMadda*,"
"*Foundations of the Torah*," 7.1)

Access to self-realization is not determined by our beliefs, but our spiritual potential. Even among those who have managed to enter the king's abode, we see different levels. According to The Rambam, what is possible to understand is limited. Only those who transcend intellectual comprehension can enter.

The term *metaphysics* comes from Greek and means "beyond the physical." This is the branch of philosophy that deals with the fundamental principles of our reality. It is focused on clarifying the basis of our understanding of the universe such as identity, existence, being, time, and space. For Immanuel Kant, metaphysical statements constitute *a priori* synthetic judgments that are beyond all human sensory experience. For him, metaphysics is an inevitable necessity of the human being. Arthur Schopenhauer referred to human beings as "metaphysical animals."

The human mind is part of the physical. Therefore, all our made-up beliefs are not part of metaphysics. We can also see Rambam's opinion by examining his *Treatise on Resurrection*:

רָאִינוּ שֶׁאֵין מִן הַדִּין לְכַוֵּן לְמָה שֶׁנִּרְצֵהוּ, כְּלוֹמַר לְבָאֵר וּלְקָרֵב סְעִפֵּי הַדָּת, וּלְהַנִּיחַ שָׁרָשָׁיו נֶעֱזָבִים, שֶׁלֹּא אֲבָאֲרֵם וְלֹא אַיְשִׁיר אֶל אֲמִתָּתָם. וְכָל שֶׁכֵּן שֶׁכְּבָר פָּגַשְׁנוּ אָדָם שֶׁהָיָה נֶחְשָׁב מֵחַכְמֵי יִשְׂרָאֵל, וְחַי ה', יוֹדֵעַ הָיָה דֶּרֶךְ הֲלָכָה, וְנָשָׂא וְנָתַן בְּמִלְחַמְתָּהּ שֶׁל תּוֹרָה כְּפִי מַחְשַׁבְתּוֹ מִנְּעוּרָיו, וְהוּא הָיָה מְסֻפָּק אִם ה' גֶּשֶׁם בַּעַל

עַיִן וְיָד וָרֶגֶל וּבְנֵי מֵעַיִם, כְּמוֹ שֶׁבָּא בַּפְּסוּקִים, אוֹ אֵינוֹ גּוּף[...] רָאִינוּ שֶׁצָּרִיךְ לָנוּ לְבָאֵר בְּחִבּוּרֵינוּ הַתַּלְמוּדִיִּים עִקָּרִים תּוֹרִיִּים עַל צַד הַסִּפּוּר, לֹא עַל צַד הָבִיא רְאָיָה, כִּי הֲבָאַת הָרְאָיָה עַל הַשָּׁרָשִׁים הָהֵם צְרִיכָה לִמְהִירוּת בְּחָכְמוֹת רַבּוֹת, לֹא יָדְעוּ הַתַּלְמוּדִיִּים דָּבָר מֵהֶן, כְּמוֹ שֶׁבֵּאַרְנוּ בְּ'מוֹרֶה הַנְּבוֹכִים', וּבָחַרְנוּ לִהְיוֹת הָאֲמִתּוֹת מְקֻבָּלוֹת אֵצֶל הֶהָמוֹן לְפָחוֹת.

(רמב"ם, איגרת תחיית־המתים)

We have realized that it would not be proper to aim at what we initially wanted, that is, to clarify and make the details of religion (the *mitzvot*) accessible, while leaving its roots unexplained, without pointing to their truth. Especially, when we have already encountered a person who was considered one of the wise men of Israel, and, may God be my witness, he was well-versed in the ways of *halachah*, and studied the Torah according to his concepts since youth. And he had the doubt whether God is material, possessing eyes, hands, feet, and intestines, as appears in the verses, or whether He is incorporeal. So, we realized that we must explain in our Talmudic writings the fundamental Torah principles in a [simple] narrative way, not by providing proofs, because bringing proofs for those roots require expertise in many disciplines of which Talmudists know nothing, as we explained in the *Guide of the Perplexed*. Therefore, we prefer that the truths will be, at least, acceptable by the masses.

(Rambam, *Iggeret Teḥiyat HaMetim*)

Those who live focused only on physical reality wander around the palace without coming near the center. In order to enter the royal abode, we have to penetrate deep within ourselves. Metaphysics is indispensable for awakening and understanding that the foundation of objective reality is consciousness. Moving only in superficial objectuality, we shall never know silence, peace, and love. If we are only conscious of the outward dual appearance of life, we will remain unaware of our true identity.

"When you understand physics, you have entered the hall; and when, after completing the study of natural philosophy,

you master metaphysics, you have entered the innermost court, and you are with the king in the same palace. You have attained the level of the wise men. They, however, are of different levels of perfection." Access to the inner garden of the king transcends both the physical and metaphysical. It leads to enlightenment. From our sensory experience, we perceive ourselves to be confined beings, as forms in space and time. Observing ourselves through a mind and senses, we believe we are limited creatures. Our illusory self-perception awakens a sense of lack. This is the source of our deep bitterness and desperate efforts to avoid it. As we awaken to the reality of who we are, the divisions at the macrocosmic and microcosmic levels, between matter and spirit, fall away. A single nature is revealed behind an apparent and temporary reality.

אֲבָל מִי שֶׁהֶעֱסִיק מַחְשַׁבְתּוֹ אַחַר שְׁלֵמוּתוֹ בָּאֱלוֹהִיּוֹת, וְנָטָה כֻּלּוֹ אֶל ה' יִתְרוֹמָם וְיִתְהַדָּר, וְהוּא מְפַנֶּה מַחְשַׁבְתּוֹ מִזּוּלָתוֹ, וְשָׂם כָּל פְּעֻלּוֹת שִׂכְלוֹ בַּחֲקִירַת הַנִּמְצָאִים כְּדֵי לִלְמֹד מֵהֶם עָלָיו, שֶׁיֵּדַע הַנְהָגָתוֹ אוֹתָם בְּאֵיזֶה אֹפֶן אֶפְשָׁרִית לִהְיוֹת, הֲרֵי אֵלֶּה הֵם אֲשֶׁר נִמְשְׁלוּ בְּמוֹשַׁב הַמֶּלֶךְ, וְזוֹ הִיא דַּרְגַּת הַנְּבִיאִים.

But those who direct their thought toward the attainment of perfection in metaphysics, turning completely toward God, emptying their thought of all objectivity (והוא מפנה מחשבתו מזולתו), who employ all their cognitive activities to the investigation of reality, to perceive from it the divine and to realize it existentially, in every way possible, they are the ones who enter the palace of the king at the level of prophets.

Any metaphysical study reveals the need to transcend thought. Without going beyond the mind, recognizing pure consciousness is impossible. Through the study of physics and metaphysics, we raise intellectual capacity to its maximum. Overcoming thought means rising above the mind, not lowering ourselves below it. Once we study everything that can be studied, we can leave the mental cage. Only when we reach the edge of the cliff will there be no alternative other than spreading our wings and flying. A story I heard from a *sādhu*, a Hindu saint, in Rishikesh, illustrates this point:

A king received a fine gift of two precious falcons. The monarch delivered both creatures to a falconry to be trained.

After some time, the master of the falconry informed the king that one of the falcons was flying majestically in the heights, but the other had not moved from its branch since arriving. The monarch commanded that various experts from his kingdom be called to see if they could find a solution, however, none of them were able to make the bird fly.

The king called for some of his wisest counselors; his frustration was great when he saw that no one could make the bird leave its branch and fly.

One of his advisers told him that perhaps the best thing to do would be to find someone more accustomed to a life in contact with nature to solve a problem like this.

The king gave the order to search in his kingdom for a farmer who might be able to do something about it.

One morning the king was amazed to see through his window that both falcons were flying very high, and immediately said: -

—"Who has accomplished this?"

—"A farmer, your majesty."

The monarch ordered:

—"Bring me this hero immediately."

The simple farmer was brought in the presence of the king, who thanked him for his efforts and asked him:

—"So my good man, could you tell me how you were able to convince that falcon to fly?"

To which the farmer replied:

—"I simply took out my tools and cut off the branch on which the falcon was standing, Your Majesty."

If we cut the two remaining branches, physical and metaphysical knowledge, this will leave us no alternative but to fly.

Metaphysical knowledge helps us see that the mind, instead of perceiving reality, projects its content upon it. It paints reality with its own colors. The mind does not perceive the world as it is, but as it appears to the mind. Instead of being the means to perceive reality, the mind and senses filter reality. Rather than enabling us to access reality, they distort it. We do not perceive things as they are, but according to our programming.

"But those who direct their thought toward the attainment of perfection in metaphysics..." Deep metaphysical understanding leaves us on the threshold of meditation. Meditation means directing ourselves completely toward the Truth. It consists of observing without the mind intervening. Meditation is not a method or technique but simply observing what is, as it is.

"... Emptying their thought of all objectivity..." The Rambam is obviously not referring to the act of thinking. The intellectual faculties have already been exhausted, taking them to their maximum. By "all cognitive activity," The Rambam refers to the cognitive faculty as a whole, including attention, which is the active aspect of consciousness that must be directed toward the investigation of the objective diversity that surrounds us (הנמצאים).

Our perception of the world unfolds within a dual framework of subject–object. We see ourselves as observers of a diversity of objects. We understand empirical reality as something totally alien and essentially different from what we are. We think of reality in terms of what we possess or lack and not what we are. The world of names and forms is shown as a separate phenomenon, disconnected from us as subjects. However, the Torah describes an absolute reality beyond the apparent duality, a reality where only the One exists, the pure infinite consciousness, God: *Ein od milvado,* "There is no more than only Him."

Recognizing consciousness means transcending the fractured reality of subject and object. Only by observing do we empty ourselves of what is objective. We go beyond an object when we create distance between us as subject and the object. Bodily identification is overcome by observing our physical sensations, paying attention to our back, feet, facial muscles, hands, and so forth. Then, we observe our breathing. You, as an observer, take your breath as the observed object. Watch the air that enters the nostrils. Notice the difference between the cooler air that you inhale and the warmer air that you exhale. Do not control your breathing, just pay attention to it, observe it attentively. Instead of actively breathing, allow breathing to occur on its own accord; be a distant witness of the process. After a few months of observing the breath, you can continue by observing thoughts. Simply observe your mental activity without analyzing or repressing it. The Rambam explains it as follows: **"...employ all their cognitive activities to the investigation of reality, to perceive from it the divine and to realize it existentially ..."**

Gradually, you will realize that thoughts, ideas, concepts, and conclusions are observed objects. Do not make distinctions between sacred or profane thoughts, elevated or degraded, interesting or simple. Minimize the importance of the quantity or quality of mental fluctuation. Just stand by as the witness of the mind and its activity. Then, try to observe your emotional activity. At first, it may be a little more difficult because of the subtlety of emotions. However, you will soon discover that they belong to objective reality. As you go into the king's abode, you will find the main object, the doer of your actions, the thinker of thoughts, the feeler of your emotions: the ego, or as Vedanta calls it, *ahaṅkāra,* "the doer." The ego is the impostor who has taken over the place of the monarch, pretending to be the king. Do not fight or resist, just watch it closely. By observing it carefully, you will realize that this "I" is nothing more than a thought, idea, emotion, or feeling. Just watch the one who attributes to itself what happens: the "I," in Hebrew is called *ani*, a word that has same letters as *ain,* or "nothing."

Only then will you have realized solitude. In this solitude, observe the observer and discover the ultimate reality of all realities: pure and crystalline consciousness. When consciousness is aware of itself, the relative platform completely collapses. The totality of the world is decomposed, dismantled, and demolished. It is a state in which the observer, while observing, is simultaneously what is observed. When the cognitive ability focuses on cognition itself, attention is placed on attention itself, consciousness is aware of itself, and observation observes itself, then the experience of *Echad ve yachid*, or the "One without second," occurs. The observer is simultaneously observed and yet the observer and the observed do not cease to be the observer and the observed.

During the observation process, just look without expecting anything. Free yourself from all expectations. We all know what it means to observe. Throughout our lives, we have observed places, flowers, trees, animals, objects, and people. It is not necessary to explain observation in detail; just apply this natural capacity to your inner reality. Focus it on the mind and feelings without judging or reacting. Over time, observation stabilizes. Ultimately, what remains is observation with nothing to observe; observing is its intrinsic nature. In its solitude, observation observes itself. Consciousness becomes self-aware or conscious of itself. The ultimate reality or the divine background of existence is revealed in its absolute purity. Recognizing consciousness is realizing that you are the King. This is the experience of the prophets, or what we call "enlightenment." I can assure you that what follows is truly amazing, and extraordinary.

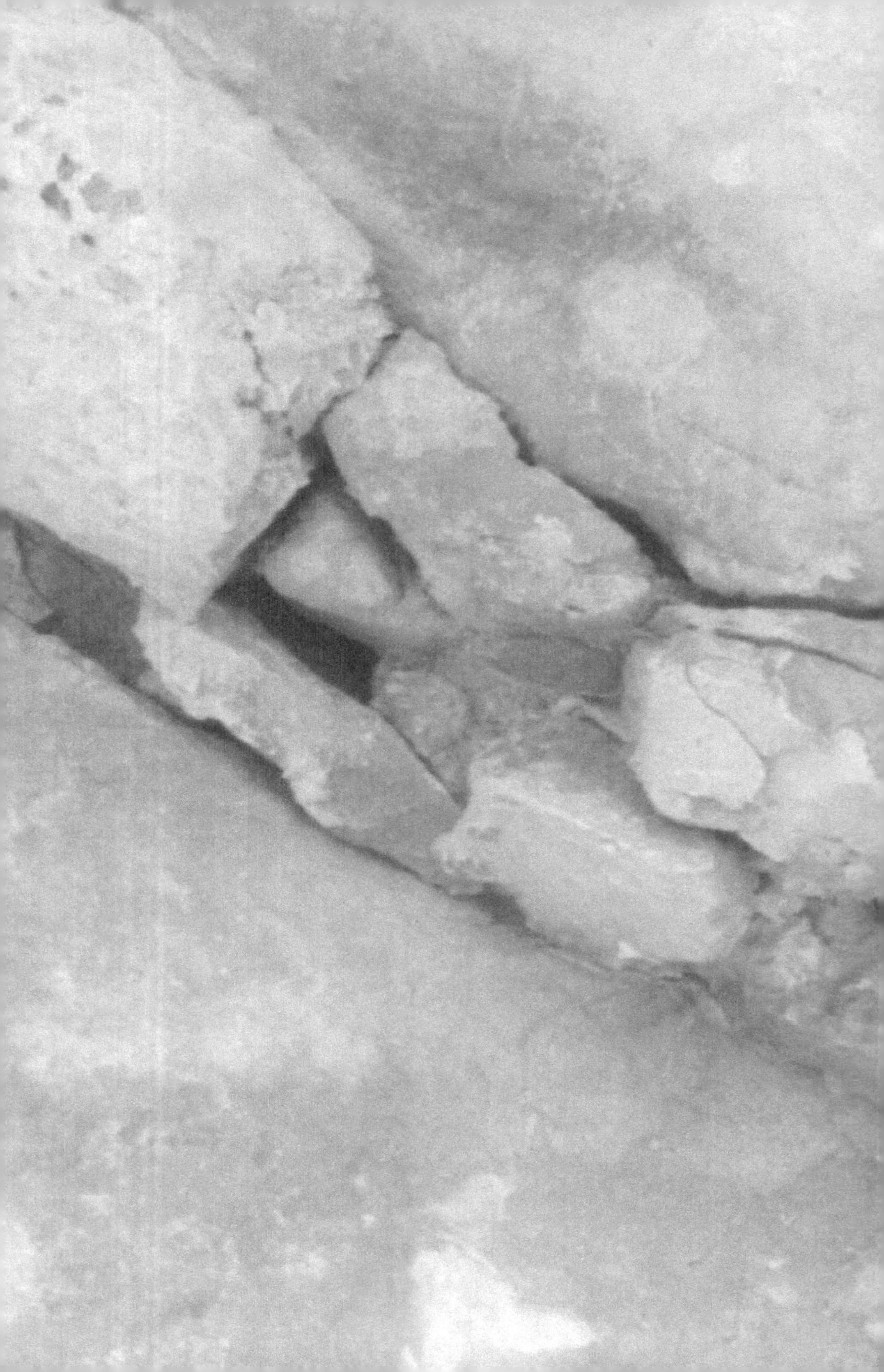

—— ARTICLE 7 ——

BEING AND NON-BEING IN THE GARDEN OF EDEN

וּמֵעֵץ הַדַּעַת טוֹב וָרָע לֹא תֹאכַל מִמֶּנּוּ כִּי בְּיוֹם אֲכָלְךָ מִמֶּנּוּ מוֹת תָּמוּת:
(בראשית ב', י"ז)

But of the Tree of Knowledge of Good and Evil you shall not eat of it, for on the day that you eat thereof, you shall surely die.

(Genesis, 2:17)

The term *original sin*, or *ancestral sin*, comes from Christian doctrine. It asserts that sin arose when the first humans, Adam and Eve, disobeyed God and ate the forbidden fruit from the Tree of Knowledge of Good and Evil.

וְהַנָּחָשׁ הָיָה עָרוּם מִכֹּל חַיַּת הַשָּׂדֶה אֲשֶׁר עָשָׂה ה' אֱלֹהִים וַיֹּאמֶר אֶל־הָאִשָּׁה אַף כִּי אָמַר אֱלֹהִים לֹא תֹאכְלוּ מִכֹּל עֵץ הַגָּן:
וַתֹּאמֶר הָאִשָּׁה אֶל הַנָּחָשׁ מִפְּרִי עֵץ־הַגָּן נֹאכֵל:
וּמִפְּרִי הָעֵץ אֲשֶׁר בְּתוֹךְ־הַגָּן אָמַר אֱלֹהִים לֹא תֹאכְלוּ מִמֶּנּוּ וְלֹא תִגְּעוּ בּוֹ פֶּן תְּמֻתוּן:
וַיֹּאמֶר הַנָּחָשׁ אֶל הָאִשָּׁה לֹא־מוֹת תְּמֻתוּן:
כִּי יֹדֵעַ אֱלֹהִים כִּי בְּיוֹם אֲכָלְכֶם מִמֶּנּוּ וְנִפְקְחוּ עֵינֵיכֶם וִהְיִיתֶם כֵּאלֹהִים יֹדְעֵי טוֹב וָרָע:
וַתֵּרֶא הָאִשָּׁה כִּי טוֹב הָעֵץ לְמַאֲכָל וְכִי תַאֲוָה הוּא לָעֵינַיִם וְנֶחְמָד הָעֵץ לְהַשְׂכִּיל וַתִּקַּח מִפִּרְיוֹ וַתֹּאכַל וַתִּתֵּן גַּם־לְאִישָׁהּ עִמָּהּ וַיֹּאכַל:
וַתִּפָּקַחְנָה עֵינֵי שְׁנֵיהֶם וַיֵּדְעוּ כִּי עֵירֻמִּם הֵם וַיִּתְפְּרוּ עֲלֵה תְאֵנָה וַיַּעֲשׂוּ לָהֶם חֲגֹרֹת:
(בראשית ג', א'–ז')

Now the serpent was cunning, more than all the beasts of the field that the Lord God had made, and it said to the woman: "Did God indeed say, 'You shall not eat of any of the trees of the garden'?"

And the woman said to the serpent: "Of the fruit of the trees of the garden we may eat.

But of the fruit of the tree that is in the midst of the garden, God said, 'You shall not eat of it, and you shall not touch it, lest you die'."

> And the serpent said to the woman, "You will surely not die, for God knows that on the day that you eat thereof, your eyes will be opened, and you will be like God, knowing good and evil."
>
> And the woman saw that the tree was good for food and that it was a delight to the eyes, and the tree was desirable to make one wise; so she took of its fruit, and she ate, and gave also to her husband with her, and he ate.
>
> And the eyes of both of them were opened, and they noticed that they were naked, and they sewed fig leaves and made themselves girdles.
>
> (Genesis, 3:1–7)

The first couple enjoyed original holiness before consuming the forbidden fruit. Their insubordination subjected humanity to the captivity of sin because, like a genetic disease, the deprivation of original holiness is passed on from one generation to the next. The Catechism of the Catholic Church explains:

> Through his sin, Adam, as the first man, lost the original holiness and righteousness he had received from God, not only for himself but for all humans.
>
> Adam and Eve transmitted human nature to their descendants, wounded by their first sin and hence deprived of original holiness and righteousness. This deprivation is called "original sin."
>
> As a result of the original sin, human nature was weakened in its powers, subject to ignorance, suffering, and the domination of death, and inclined to sin (an inclination called "concupiscence").
>
> ("Catechism of the Catholic Church," part 1, section 2, chapter 1, "Original Sin")

If Adam and Eve had not consumed the fruit of knowledge, human beings would not have the capacity to discern between good and evil. After consuming it, they became aware of their nakedness and chose to cover themselves. Many treat this narrative as allegorical, but it is undeniable that humans possess such discernment and, therefore, they bear personal responsibility for their actions.

> To be sure, sin was in the world before the law was given, but sin is not charged against anyone's account where there is no law. Nevertheless, death reigned from the time of Adam to the time of Moses, even over those who did not sin by breaking a command, as did Adam, who is a pattern of the one to come. But the gift is not like the trespass. For if the many died by the trespass of the one man, how much more did God's grace and the gift that came by the grace of the one man, Jesus Christ, overflow to the many! Nor can the gift of God be compared with the result of one man's sin: The judgment followed one sin and brought condemnation, but the gift followed many trespasses and brought justification. For if, by the trespass of the one man, death reigned through that one man, how much more will those who receive God's abundant provision of grace and of the gift of righteousness reign in life through the one man, Jesus Christ!
>
> Consequently, just as one trespass resulted in condemnation for all people, so also one righteous act resulted in justification and life for all people. For just as through the disobedience of the one man the many were made sinners, so also through the obedience of the one man the many will be made righteous. The law was brought in so that the trespass might increase. But where sin increased, grace increased all the more, so that, just as sin reigned in death, so also grace might reign through righteousness to bring eternal life through Jesus Christ our Lord.
>
> (Romans, 5:13–21)

The term *free will* comes from the Latin *liberum arbitrium*, which denotes the capacity to choose between good and evil. However, humans do not choose from a stance of existential neutrality. Each separate "I" comprises a set of drives that compel individuals to make decisions and steer them away from their aversions. Indeed, there is no singular entity within the mind or the body orchestrating our actions. Countless physiological processes occur within us without our conscious awareness. Our organs execute thousands of biochemical reactions per second and our metabolism continually strives to maintain homeostasis. Given that we control a mere fraction of these myriad activities, it is ludicrous to think of ourselves as controlling our bodies and minds. Only out of ignorance do many claim to have control over their thoughts or actions.

Everyone yearns for peace and happiness, yet, paradoxically, it is mental activity that fosters discomfort and dissatisfaction. If we truly governed our thoughts, we would choose to think that no matter what happens, everything is perfectly fine. If so, no incident could disturb our tranquility or bliss, and we would hear statements such as: "I was robbed of a thousand dollars, but everything's perfect"; "My boss threatened to fire me, but I think that's great"; "My daughter is sick, but that's excellent." These phrases would be commonplace if humans could dominate their mental activities, halt negative thoughts, and prevent situations from disturbing their earthly paradise. Yet, the reality is that thought control is unattainable.

Consider thirst, for example, which arises involuntarily and triggers the idea to head to the refrigerator to look for a drink. We neither govern the onset of thirst nor the thoughts that propel us to quench it. We can talk about karma or destiny, but it is undeniable that we encounter what existence lays before us; we receive what life delivers.

Our desires depend on our social, family, genetic, and environmental conditioning. Evidently, we lack control over these inclinations. Preferences for vanilla ice cream, chocolate, or Coca-Cola, or disinterest in alcohol or drugs, are outcomes of classical or operant conditioning. If predisposed to cigarettes or coffee, we can only superficially suppress consumption; it is impossible to dictate our cravings or to master our sensations, thoughts, preferences, and inclinations.

Arthur Schopenhauer categorized objects into four classes: empirical, abstract, mathematical, and the "I." According to the fourfold root of the principle of sufficient reason, objects are subject to laws that make them be what they are and not otherwise: (1) empirical objects adhere to the law of causality, (2) abstract objects to the laws of logic, (3) mathematical objects to the law of consistency, for instance, triangles have three angles and circles are round, and (4) the "I" to the law of character. Humans react to the world according to their inherent character, which conditions individual responses. Our inclinations and preferences inevitably shape our interactions with the world.

Free will is a fallacious concept suggesting that individuals can act entirely as they wish and desire anything. Researcher Mark Hallett asserts, "Free will does exists, but it's a perception, not a power or a driving force. People experience free will. They have the sense they are free. The more you scrutinize it, the more you realize you don't have it."

Schopenhauer, in his essay *On the freedom of the will*, contended that while humans can do what they want, they cannot desire what they want. Albert Einstein later echoed these sentiments. After considering the insights of Sigmund Freud and Friedrich Nietzsche, it is naïve to assume that decisions stem from existential neutrality. Apostle Paul deliberated on this in his letter to the Romans:

> What shall we say, then? Is the law sinful? Certainly not! Nevertheless, I would not have known what sin was had it not been for the law. For I would not have known what coveting really was if the law had not said, "You shall not covet." But sin, seizing the opportunity afforded by the commandment, produced in me every kind of coveting. For apart from the law, sin was dead. Once I was alive apart from the law; but when the commandment came, sin sprang to life and I died. I found that the very commandment that was intended to bring life actually brought death. For sin, seizing

> the opportunity afforded by the commandment, deceived me, and through the commandment put me to death.
> So then, the law is holy, and the commandment is holy, righteous, and good. Did that which is good, then, become death to me? By no means! Nevertheless, in order that sin might be recognized as sin, it used what is good to bring about my death, so that through the commandment sin might become utterly sinful. We know that the law is spiritual; but I am unspiritual, sold as a slave to sin. I do not understand what I do. For what I want to do I do not do, but what I hate I do. And if I do what I do not want to do, I agree that the law is good. As it is, it is no longer I myself who do it, but it is sin living in me. For I know that good itself does not dwell in me, that is, in my sinful nature. For I have the desire to do what is good, but I cannot carry it out. For I do not do the good I want to do, but the evil I do not want to do—this I keep on doing. Now if I do what I do not want to do, it is no longer I who do it, but it is sin living in me that does it.
>
> (Romans, 7:7–20)

Paul states, "As it is, it is no longer I myself who do it, but it is sin living in me." In truth, no independent entity is accountable for such inclinations and behaviors. There is no separate "I" to blame for preferences and actions deemed sinful.

Some argue that my views justify antisocial or even criminal behaviors. This critique stems from a misunderstanding. All antisocial and criminal acts are products of conditioning. Only by acknowledging this can we prevent such behavior.

Unaligned activities stem from the belief that we are responsible for our actions. Destructive and antisocial behaviors emanate from the illusory "I." These become inconceivable when we stop believing we are independent personalities controlling a mind and a body.

What humanity inherited from Adam was not sin itself but the concept of a sinful entity—an allegory for the emergence of the egoic phenomenon. By consuming the forbidden fruit, the notion of an entity accountable for its actions emerged. Every action originating from the egoic phenomenon carries the seed of sin. Even ostensibly positive behaviors are intrinsically sinful if they arise from an ego-doer. That is why Shneur Zalman of Liadi advises us to hate the sin but love the sinner, since sin is the action that arises from an idea of separation and independence.

> וְגַם הַמְקֹרָבִים אֵלָיו וְהוֹכִיחָם וְלֹא שָׁבוּ מֵעֲוֹנוֹתֵיהֶם, שֶׁמִּצְוָה לִשְׂנֹאתָם, מִצְוָה לְאָהֳבָם גַּם כֵּן, וּשְׁתֵּיהֶן הֵן אֱמֶת: שִׂנְאָה מִצַּד הָרַע שֶׁבָּהֶם, וְאַהֲבָה מִצַּד בְּחִינַת הַטּוֹב הַגָּנוּז שֶׁבָּהֶם, שֶׁהוּא נִיצוֹץ אֱלֹהוּת שֶׁבְּתוֹכָם הַמְחַיֶּה נַפְשָׁם הָאֱלֹהִית.
> (ספר התניא, ליקוטי אמרים, פרק ל"ב)
>
> Furthermore, even those whom one is enjoined to hate—for they are close to him, and he has rebuked them, but they still have not repented of their sins—one is obligated to love them too. And both the love and the hatred are truthful [since] the hatred is on account of the evil within them, while the love is on account of the good hidden in them, which is the divine spark within them that animates their divine soul.
>
> (*Tanya*, chapter 32)

Sinful activity may be detested, but divine consciousness is worthy only of love.

> וַתִּפָּקַחְנָה עֵינֵי שְׁנֵיהֶם וַיֵּדְעוּ כִּי עֵירֻמִּם הֵם וַיִּתְפְּרוּ עֲלֵה תְאֵנָה וַיַּעֲשׂוּ לָהֶם חֲגֹרֹת:
> (בראשית ג', ז')
>
> And the eyes of both of them opened, and they noticed that they were naked, and they sewed fig leaves and made themselves girdles.
>
> (Genesis, 3:7)

This allegory denotes a shift in consciousness that led humans to cover their nakedness or what is, as it is. In our nakedness, we do not harm anyone through antisocial behavior because we are aligned. Our original state is to be one and the same with the flow of wholeness. Like a river flowing toward the ocean, you are drawn toward the Whole. You do not arrive as a solitary swimmer struggling against the current, but floating, completely relaxed within God's will. You disappear as a separate entity and surrender to the river of life that takes you to the oceanic ideal of consciousness.

Creation from a philosophical perspective

Understanding the notion of creation from a philosophical perspective is essential. Creation is related to the good since God, after creating, says:

> וַיַּרְא אֱלֹהִים אֶת־כָּל־אֲשֶׁר עָשָׂה וְהִנֵּה־טוֹב מְאֹד [...]
>
> (בראשית א', ל"א)
>
> And God saw all that He had made, and behold, it was very good [...].
>
> (Genesis, 1:31)

Creation is intrinsically linked to Being, which is, in turn, directly linked to goodness. In other words, everything that God has created is an entity that possesses existence and, by having existence, is inherently good. This relationship indicates that goodness is a fundamental quality of all that exists, since its mere existence is a manifestation of the divine creative act. Thus, both creation and Being are sources of goodness; they are both attributes derived from God. Although God has created everything with goodness, humans, in exercising freedom, have opted for non-being instead of Being, thus perverting good and transforming it into evil. In other words, humans have emptied Being of its fullness, or *pleroma*.

> וַתֵּרֶא הָאִשָּׁה כִּי טוֹב הָעֵץ לְמַאֲכָל וְכִי תַאֲוָה־הוּא לָעֵינַיִם וְנֶחְמָד הָעֵץ לְהַשְׂכִּיל וַתִּקַּח מִפִּרְיוֹ וַתֹּאכַל וַתִּתֵּן גַּם־לְאִישָׁהּ עִמָּהּ וַיֹּאכַל:
>
> (בראשית ג', ו')

> And the woman saw that the tree was good for food and that it was a delight to the eyes, and the tree was desirable to make one wise; so she took of its fruit, and she ate, and gave also to her husband with her, and he ate.
>
> (Genesis, 3:6)

Creation can be defined as "bestowing being," whereas sin, in stark contrast, can be interpreted as "removing being." Sin, in its essence, represents a direct negation of creation that opposes participation in Being. When we talk of creation, we refer to an act that implies harmony with the Being. While creating leads to an integration into Being, sin results in a loss of that integration. Since sin strips Being of its essence, it aligns with nothingness.

For the ancient Greeks, the idea of nothingness had no autonomous existence; only Being existed. The Greek language did not have a specific word for "nothing." Instead, Greeks used the expression *me on* to deny being, composed of *me*, meaning "not," and *on*, meaning "being." Their term for "nothing" was "not being."

Since nothingness is a negation of Being, we cannot conceptualize it without first postulating the existence of Being. The relation between Being and nothingness is configured in terms of participation and deprivation. Creation and sin are positioned as opposing forces in the becoming of Being. Creation implies a process of affirmation and construction, while sin acts as a force of negation and destruction.

From a philosophical point of view, it follows that nothingness does not possess an independent existence. Its reality is grounded in the negation of Being. In Greek philosophy, dealing with nothingness involves first recognizing Being and then denying it. This interdependence highlights the importance of Being as the primary ontological foundation, while nothingness is understood exclusively as the negation of this foundation. Thus, if we do not presuppose the existence of good, identified with Being, it is impossible to conceive of evil. In this context, evil is interpreted as an accident of Being, requiring the existence of a substance to empty it of Being. Therefore, evil cannot exist by itself and has no entity of its own; its existence depends on the Being of another. In essence, evil is nothingness.

Let us turn to an example to illustrate this point: a person with good legs has two healthy legs. If they lack one, they will say that they have bad legs because there are people with two legs. If no human being had legs, their legs would not be considered bad. Moreover, if human beings did not exist, neither would a person with bad legs. In conclusion, evil has no being of its own and cannot exist without Being. This dependence reinforces the idea that Being is fundamental and that nothingness, like evil, can only be understood in relation to the negation of existence. Evil is the absence of a due good and has accidental existence.

In the above example, evil is defined as the lack of a leg in an individual. Evil is considered the absence of something that the Self should possess. Therefore, evil has no ontological existence, as it lacks an entity of its own. Only the entity and Being exist, while evil acts by emptying the entity of its Being. In essence, evil does not exist by itself.

Heidegger illustrates this idea with his statement "the nothing noths." This means that nothingness, by manifesting in Being, progressively empties it, stripping it of its essence. Nothingness, by actualizing in the realm of Being, deprives us of the fullness of our Being, leaving us increasingly empty.

Individual and universal consciousness

Being refers to itself intrinsically, since existence entails a negation of individual consciousness. Personal consciousness places the "separate I" at the center of perceptions of good and evil. This consciousness defines what is good according to what the "I" determines, akin to the narrative of the tree of knowledge of good and evil. In this process, the "I" appropriates the criterion of Being. The Being is no longer the central axis of existence and is replaced by an historical or separate "I." However, it is not necessary to deny individual consciousness to adhere to Being; on the contrary, by adopting the criterion of Being, individual consciousness is strengthened. By affirming individual consciousness and appropriating the criterion of morality, universal Being is denied. To affirm universal Being, it is essential to reject the prerogative of individual consciousness to define good and evil autonomously. This means that individual consciousness can deny the universal Being by "eating from the tree," appropriating a criterion that, in reality, belongs to Being, as if this norm were intrinsic to consciousness itself. Alternatively, consciousness may choose not to appropriate this criterion, resolving itself in Being. This resolution occurs in Being, as it is Being that establishes the criterion for consciousness, and not the other way around.

Evil, in its essence, is a deprivation of Being. An entity's existence is paramount, while nothingness is characterized by its capacity for active negation, stripping us of our essence. It is crucial to distinguish between the destruction of our conceptions of Being and the gradual process by which nothingness strips us of our Being. By being emptied of Being, we lose the essence of our authenticity. It is imperative to free ourselves from our false beliefs about our identity to rediscover who we really are.

The egoic phenomenon does not refer to a concrete entity nor a specific person, but to the lack of presence of our true essence in the present. This removal, caused by nothingness, deprives us of our essence, leading to an existence devoid of the fullness of Being that should define us. Evil, ultimately, manifests as a lack and implies the deprivation of what is essential for Being to achieve its full realization. Understanding this process leads us to recognize the interaction between nothingness and existence and to identify how the absence of an authentic presence shapes the egoic phenomenon. The true nature of evil lies in this absence, which strips the entity of its Being, resulting in an incomplete existence lacking essence. The existence of evil is fundamentally an accident of Being, since it depends on the existence of Being to manifest. This reduces its fullness and hinders its completeness. Evil is like a parasite of Being, depriving it of its complete and perfect essence. In essence, this defines sin: a force that subtracts Being and prevents its full realization.

Goodness and Being

The study of transcendental philosophy is essential, as one cannot affirm that "Being" and "good" are identical in an absolute sense. In this context, we can suggest more rigorous approach based on classical Western metaphysics, which provides the appropriate framework to address this issue. From a metaphysical perspective, although "Being" and "good" are not completely identical, they are interchangeable in certain contexts. In certain respects, the good can be understood as Being and, similarly, Being can be understood as good. Although "Being" and "good" are intrinsically connected, they are not identical. Their relationship is intricate and demands a detailed understanding to avoid confusing them as simple synonyms. This relationship shows a significant co-belonging, something philosophy calls "the dilemma of the transcendentals."

From an essential perspective, all entities, insofar as they exist, are defined by being good, beautiful, true, one, and being. The existence of any entity is inextricably linked to its goodness; to be good means fully realizing one's own nature. In classical philosophy, a good person is synonymous with a true person. Similarly, we consider a chair to be good when it authentically fulfills its essence, that is, when it possesses all the essential qualities that define a chair. This intrinsic goodness is manifested in its functionality and in the complete realization of its purpose. The interrelationship between "Being" and "good" implies that the very existence of anything includes its inherent goodness, and this goodness is measured in terms of authenticity and plenitude in being what one is. The complexity of this interrelationship demands an analytical approach and a nuanced understanding. Recognizing this distinction is crucial to avoid oversimplifying philosophical concepts that, while related, maintain their own distinct specificities and meanings within the framework of transcendental thought.

The goodness of any entity is measured by its conformity with its own nature and essence. In this way, an entity is considered good when it reaches its full potential and assumes its true identity. This intrinsic relationship between "Being" and "good" highlights the interdependence of these concepts in the metaphysical understanding of reality. People are beautiful and good when they fully realize their essence; in this context, the terms "beautiful" and "good" become almost interchangeable. The concepts of being, beauty, truth, and goodness are deeply connected, which makes them transcendental and, to some extent, interchangeable.

However, it is crucial to note that evil is not a way of being but rather represents the absence of a good that should exist. For example, good people have all the essential qualities of humanity, fulfilling their purpose and nature. If someone is missing an arm, that person clearly does not represent a complete example of humanity, since an essential characteristic is missing. This situation shows that evil is not adding something to an entity but is the lack of an essential quality. Consequently, the exact definition of evil is not an ontological presence, but the lack of a necessary good.

According to Saint Thomas Aquinas, evil, strictly speaking, cannot be considered a creature, since it was not created and, therefore, lacks ontological essence. In other words, there is no entity whose essence is evil. Rather than being a creation with an independent essence, evil is an absence of good, a defect or lack in the existing Being. This perspective emphasizes that evil does not have a positive reality; it is defined by the lack of perfection in something that would otherwise be good or complete.

The essence of evil is not ontological, but manifests historically, since it is introduced into human life without being a creation of humanity. Humans have introduced evil through their own existence in the context of history.

Good and evil—Being and non-being

Evil gradually empties humans of Being. With this emptying of Being, humans introduce non-being into history. This historical process cannot be attributed to a specific creation but to a manifestation of lack within the context of Being. Thus, evil is the Being stripping itself of itself, allowing the prevalence of non-being in human existence. Humans, through their sinful nature, make way for non-being, and this phenomenon is integrated into the historical experience of humanity.

If evil is the negation of Being, good is the affirmation of Being. The norm governing good is Being, while the norm governing evil is non-being. Being bad means not being what one truly is and living out of harmony with one's own essence, which is the definition of ego. The egoic phenomenon is a lack or deficiency. Good manifests in authentically being what one is, and, consequently, being good means truly being what one is in essence.

When we are not authentically what we are, we lack Being, and this lack constitutes evil. However, this evil is not an entity with its own existence but an absence of Being. Through their own existence, the human being introduces non-being into history. The gravity of sin lies precisely in this act: by being, the human being incorporates non-being into the historical realm. Evil was not created, and therefore, evil has no existence of its own in a strict sense.

St. Augustine states that humans are born with the inherent condition of being and are immersed in profound solidarity. This solidarity suggests that we are all one, so that any action performed by an individual involves everyone else. This is the transcendental oneness of the human race. That is, any act committed by one person is an act in which all of humanity participates. He calls this absolute participation the "communal being of humanity." This refers to the idea that all of humanity is united in a covenant or alliance represented by Adam. Thus, Adam's actions have repercussions for all his descendants. This view emphasizes the solidarity and essential unity of humanity in terms of responsibility, and moral and spiritual consequences.

From this perspective, humanity shares a common destiny in which the actions of one affect everyone. This reinforces the idea of an indivisible human community and suggests that our individual decisions have collective implications.

Adam did not act alone but we were all in Adam, participating in his action. For this reason, we cannot claim with certainty that we would have acted differently in his place. Human beings are intrinsically connected. We all belong to a single unity, like branches or roots of a single tree. Anything that affects the stems, fruits, or leaves inevitably impacts the roots. Saint Augustine presents humanity as one body, where any action, whether good or bad, performed by one, is effectively performed by all.

Just as Adam's actions have universal repercussions, the glory of Christ, who is the second Adam, resides in all humanity. All human beings participated in the original sin of Adam, and, similarly, all humanity is represented in Christ, thus receiving life.

In every human being both natures coexist: that of Adam, which represents non-being, or individual consciousness, and that of Christ, which symbolizes Being, or universal consciousness. The key is to transcend the nature of the first in order to access the nature of the second.

> For as in Adam all die, so in Christ all will be made alive.
>
> (1 Corinthians, 15:22)

In this context, the words of John the Baptist become clear.

> He must increase, but I must decrease.
>
> (John, 3:30)

It is essential that individual consciousness be relegated, since every human is born with this fallen condition, manifested in the "I"-centered consciousness. Only by transcending this condition and reaching a universal consciousness can we repair this existential fracture. The fall or fracture refers to the fact that, at birth, each person carries the individual consciousness that characterizes the first Adam. Likewise, every human being is called to reduce the dominance of their individual consciousness in order to access pure and universal consciousness.

However, it is impossible to attain this universal consciousness without first denying the individual one. In other words, without first renouncing the state of the first Adam, which is born of the flesh, it is impossible to enter the state of the second Adam, which is born of the spirit. That is why the Bible says this in the letter to the Romans:

> For we know that our old self was crucified with him so that the body ruled by sin might be rendered powerless so that we may no longer be enslaved to sin, since a person who has died is freed from sin.
>
> (Romans, 6:6–7)

The core of this idea is the imperative need to let the first Adam die, in order to be reborn as the second Adam. In individual consciousness, also known as the flesh, all human beings are destined for death. On the other hand, in universal consciousness, or the spirit, all human beings can attain eternal life.

The transcendence of spirit is highlighted in contrast to the flesh, emphasizing the need to overcome our individual limitations. This transition is essential to achieve a full and universal existence. "Dying to the I" is a central concept in the New Testament, representing the essence of Christian life and underscoring the importance of renouncing individual consciousness to achieve a higher life.

This means taking up the cross and following Christ, a crucial step for spiritual rebirth. In this process, an old man dies and the new man emerges, as mentioned in John (3:3–7). Christians not only experience rebirth at the moment of salvation, but also continue dying to themselves during the process of sanctification. Thus, dying to oneself, or the separate "I," is a singular event but also extends throughout the life of true Christians.

Jesus repeatedly stressed to his disciples the need to take up their cross, an instrument of death, and follow him. He emphasized that people wishing to follow him must deny themselves, that is, renounce their own egoic lives. This was an indispensable requirement to be considered a true disciple of Christ. Jesus warned that attempting to save our egoic life, or independent "I," would inevitably result in losing our life to the kingdom of God. Instead, those who surrender their lives, or individual consciousness, for his sake will find eternal life (Matthew, 16:24–25; Mark, 8:34–35). Jesus clearly stated that those who are not willing to sacrifice their personal lives for him cannot be his disciples (Luke, 14:27).

Christ: the universal archetype

Human beings are born with two types of consciousness: an individual one, which refers to the separate "I," and a universal one. Beyond being an historical figure, Jesus embodies a level of pure consciousness, known as Christic consciousness, which Carl Jung calls "the archetype of consciousness" or "Self." Archetypes are innate patterns in the human psyche that exert a profound influence on our perceptions and behaviors. The fundamental patterns outlined by Carl Jung, known as archetypes, are essential parts of his psychological theory. He argues that archetypes inhabit the collective unconscious and act as universal frameworks that shape our experiences and reactions to various situations. These inherent structures of the human mind are manifested in myths, dreams, and cultural expressions in all societies, reflecting common aspects of the human condition. They not only guide our understanding of the world, but also facilitate the connection between individuals from different cultures and times who share similar symbols and narratives.

The truth of Christ does not lie in the mere historical existence of Jesus, but in the archetype he represents, which is a universal model of the human being conformed by universal consciousness. The validity of this archetype is independent of the historical existence of Jesus. Although the historical Jesus represents a complete manifestation of this archetype, what is fundamental is the archetype itself and not the specific individual. This archetype of universal consciousness overcomes the limitations of individual existence and presents itself as a model of perfection accessible to everyone. Unfortunately, most Christians focus exclusively on the historical figure and center their devotion on the individual called Jesus.

Christic consciousness represents a spiritual ideal we can all aspire to. This ideal transcends belief in miracles and leads to a deep understanding of an essential archetype; it focuses on an archetypal connection and trust, beyond historical facts and personalities. Having faith in Christ means trusting so deeply that we can surrender our spirit with full confidence.

In biology, a clear distinction is made between genotype and phenotype. A genotype is the complete set of genes and genetic information that constitutes an individual of any species. This genetic composition is transmitted from one generation to the next, ensuring the continuity of hereditary traits. The phenotype, on the other hand, is the physical and observable expression of these characteristics in an individual. While the genotype remains constant, the phenotype can vary due to the interaction between genes and environment. Therefore, the phenotype is the external and tangible manifestation of the genetic information contained in the genotype. The gene is the genotype, while the individual is the model that carries that type.

Following this analogy, the historical Jesus can be thought of as the phenotype and Christ as the archetype. The phenotype, as a "phenomenon," is the visible manifestation, while the archetype is the underlying foundation of what is shown. Christ, then, is the type that manifests, and the archetype is the basis of that manifestation. The relevance of Jesus is in his ability to embody this archetype, showing how it is possible to live in consonance with universal consciousness. While his historical existence provides valuable context, it is the universal principle that he embodies that is essential. This archetype serves as a guide for humanity; it indicates a path toward spiritual elevation and the overcoming of the separate "I," thus promoting greater integration and connection with the totality of Being. In this way, Christic consciousness transcends the barriers of time and space, inviting all human beings to recognize and live according to this universal truth.

Christic consciousness

Pure consciousness, or *logos endiatikos*, can only be attained through *logos prosforikos*, that is, the spoken word or language. This language is not static but rather is enriched by various consciousnesses and masks it wears in the process. The notion of *logos endiatikos* refers to an internal understanding that is fundamental and abstract. However, this state of consciousness cannot be attained or communicated without *logos prosforikos*, that is, through the use of articulated language. In this context, language becomes the indispensable means of expressing and transmitting this internal consciousness.

It is worth noting that language is not a fixed or immutable entity. In contrast, it continuously enriches and diversifies through the varied individual consciousnesses and the multiple "masks" it adopts in its usage. These "masks" represent the different forms and contexts in which language can be applied and understood. Thus, in the process of communication and expression, language adapts and expands, incorporating the varied perspectives and experiences of individuals. Pure consciousness depends on language to manifest itself, and this language is enriched and evolves, due to the diverse forms of consciousness and the contexts in which it is employed.

Those who limit themselves exclusively to Christianity do not really understand any religion, for they confuse the relative and the absolute. Thinking that Christ is the only way toward God closes their minds to other forms of divine understanding and even prevents complete access to the essence of Christ.

The encounter with Christ is experienced in the innermost core of the human being, embracing both the individual and the collective sphere, and situated at the very heart of reality. This experience is manifested through a personal Christic faith that emulates the perspective and attitude of Christ and also adopts what is called the "Christic principle." This approach goes beyond mere belief and aims for a profound and integral transformation, essentially altering the understanding and experience of existence in its totality. It is a faith that promotes inner metamorphosis, reconfiguring both perceptions of the world and interactions with the surrounding reality.

By embracing, accepting, surrendering, and trusting in Christic consciousness, we can transcend our egoic nature. This trust allows us to overcome the sinful inclinations inherent in the human condition. Fully integrating this consciousness in our lives lifts us above tendencies to sin toward achieving an authentic, profound, and meaningful transformation.

ARTICLE 8

ON THE QUEST FOR MEANING

The conceptualization of a God with attributes and qualities does not align with our experience of the Divine. Instead of a personal God who created the world, the Divine is a sublime quality that infuses our existence with depth and meaning. It is a transcendental state that, like love, permeates our days with a transformative essence. Divinity is not a figure defined as "something" or a being personified as "someone." God is not a noun but an adjective and resembles qualities such as peace, silence, compassion, and joy.

The idea that one day we will meet the creator of the universe, who will personally explain to us the mystery of his existence, is a limited and extremely primitive human interpretation. The notion of a personal God, with whom we can have a conversation, belongs to the anthropomorphic realm. The Divine transcends these limits. Rather than being an entity with whom we interact, it is a presence we experience. In reality, it is an ineffable experience that goes beyond personification and is situated in the realm of the universal and the unfathomable. Thus, The Rambam explains:

> כְּבָר יָדַעְתָּ אִמְרָתָם הַכּוֹלֶלֶת לְמִינֵי הַפֵּרוּשִׁים כֻּלָּם הַתְּלוּיִים בְּזֶה הָעִנְיָן, וְהוּא אָמְרָם "דִּבְּרָה תוֹרָה כִּלְשׁוֹן בְּנֵי אָדָם". עִנְיָן זֶה – כִּי כָּל מָה שֶׁאֶפְשָׁר לִבְנֵי אָדָם כֻּלָּם הֲבָנָתוֹ וְצִיּוּרוֹ בִּתְחִלַּת הַמַּחְשָׁבָה, הוּא אֲשֶׁר שָׂם רָאוּי לֶאֱלוֹהַּ יִתְבָּרַךְ. וְלָזֶה יְתֹאַר בִּתְאָרִים מוֹרִים עַל הַגַּשְׁמוּת לְהוֹרוֹת עָלָיו שֶׁהוּא יִתְבָּרַךְ נִמְצָא. כִּי לֹא יַשִּׂיגוּ הֶהָמוֹן בִּתְחִלַּת הַמַּחְשָׁבָה מְצִיאוּת כִּי אִם לַגֶּשֶׁם בִּלְבַד, וּמָה שֶׁאֵינוֹ גֶּשֶׁם אוֹ נִמְצָא בַּגֶּשֶׁם אֵינוֹ נִמְצָא אֶצְלָם. וְכֵן כָּל מָה שֶׁהוּא שְׁלֵמוּת אֶצְלֵנוּ יֵיָחֵס לוֹ יִתְבָּרַךְ – לְהוֹרוֹת עָלָיו שֶׁהוּא שָׁלֵם בְּמִינֵי הַשְּׁלֵמֻיּוֹת כֻּלָּם, וְאֵין עִמּוֹ חִסָּרוֹן אוֹ הֶעְדֵּר כְּלָל. וְכָל מָה שֶׁיַּשִּׂיגוּ הֶהָמוֹן שֶׁהוּא חִסָּרוֹן אוֹ הֶעְדֵּר – לֹא יְתֹאַר בּוֹ; וְלַזֶּה לֹא יְתֹאַר בַּאֲכִילָה וּשְׁתִיָּה וְלֹא בְּשֵׁנָה וְלֹא בְּחֹלִי וְלֹא בְּחָמָס וְלֹא בְּמָה שֶׁיִּדְמֶה לָזֶה. וְכָל מָה שֶׁיֵּחָשֵׁב הֶהָמוֹן שֶׁהוּא שְׁלֵמוּת יְתֹאַר בּוֹ – וְאַף עַל פִּי שֶׁהַדָּבָר הַהוּא אָמְנָם הוּא שְׁלֵמוּת בְּעֵרֶךְ אֵלֵינוּ אֲבָל בְּעֵרֶךְ אֵלָיו יִתְבָּרַךְ אֵלּוּ אֲשֶׁר נַחְשְׁבֵם כֻּלָּם שְׁלֵמֻיּוֹת הֵם תַּכְלִית הַחִסָּרוֹן; אָמְנָם אִלּוּ דִּמּוּ הֶעְדֵּר הַשְּׁלֵמוּת הַהוּא הָאֱנוֹשִׁי מִמֶּנּוּ יִתְבָּרַךְ, הָיָה זֶה אֶצְלָם חִסָּרוֹן בְּחָקּוֹ. וְאַתָּה יוֹדֵעַ כִּי הַתְּנוּעָה הִיא מִשְּׁלֵמוּת בַּעַל הַחַיִּים וְהֶכְרֵחִית לוֹ בְּהַשְׁלָמָתוֹ. וּכְמוֹ שֶׁהוּא צָרִיךְ לַאֲכִילָה וּשְׁתִיָּה לְהַחֲלִיף מָה שֶׁיִּתַּךְ כֵּן הוּא צָרִיךְ לַתְּנוּעָה לְכַוֵּן אֶל הַטּוֹב לוֹ וְהַמֻּרְגָּל לִבְרֹחַ מִן הָרַע לוֹ וּמָה שֶׁהוּא כְּנֶגְדּוֹ. וְאֵין הֶפְרֵשׁ בֵּין שֶׁיְּתֹאַר יִתְבָּרֵךְ בַּאֲכִילָה וּבִשְׁתִיָּה אוֹ שֶׁיְּתֹאַר בִּתְנוּעָה. אֲבָל לְפִי "לְשׁוֹן

בְּנֵי אָדָם" – כְּלוֹמַר: הַדִּמְיוֹן הֶהָמוֹנִי – הָיוּ הָאֲכִילָה וְהַשְּׁתִיָּה אֶצְלָם חִסָּרוֹן בְּחֹק הָאֱלוֹהַּ וְהַתְּנוּעָה אֵינָהּ חִסָּרוֹן בְּחֻקּוֹ וְאַף עַל פִּי שֶׁהַתְּנוּעָה אָמְנָם הִצְרִיךְ אֵלֶיהָ הַחִסָּרוֹן. וּכְבָר הִתְבָּאֵר בְּמוֹפֵת כִּי כָּל מִתְנוֹעֵעַ בַּעַל גֹּדֶל – מִתְחַלֵּק בְּלֹא סָפֵק; וְהִנֵּה יִתְבָּאֵר אַחַר זֶה הֱיוֹתוֹ יִתְבָּרַךְ בִּלְתִּי בַּעַל גֹּדֶל וְלֹא תִּמָּצֵא לוֹ תְּנוּעָה; וְלֹא יְתֹאַר גַּם כֵּן בִּמְנוּחָה כִּי לֹא יְתֹאַר בִּמְנוּחָה אֶלָּא מִי שֶׁדַּרְכּוֹ לְהִתְנוֹעֵעַ. וְכָל אֵלֶּה הַשֵּׁמוֹת הַמּוֹרִים עַל מִינֵי תְּנוּעוֹת בַּעַל הַחַיִּים כֻּלָּם יְתֹאַר בָּהֶם יִתְבָּרֵךְ עַל הַדֶּרֶךְ שֶׁאָמַרְנוּ כְּמוֹ שֶׁיְּתֹאַר בַּחַיִּים כִּי הַתְּנוּעָה – מִקְרֶה דָּבֵק לְבַעַל הַחַיִּים. וְאֵין סָפֵק, כִּי בְּהִסְתַּלֵּק הַגַּשְׁמוּת יִסְתַּלְּקוּ כָּל אֵלֶּה כְּלוֹמַר: יָרַד וְעָלָה וְהָלַךְ וְנִצָּב וְעָמַד וְסָבַב וְיָשַׁב וְשָׁכַן וְיָצָא וּבָא וְעָבַר וְכָל מָה שֶׁדּוֹמֶה לָזֶה. וְזֶה הָעִנְיָן הַהַאֲרָכָה בּוֹ – יִתְרוֹן אֶלָּא מִפְּנֵי שֶׁהִרְגִּילוּהוּ דֵּעוֹת הֶהָמוֹן, לָכֵן צָרִיךְ לְבָאֲרוֹ לַאֲשֶׁר לָקְחוּ עַצְמָם בַּשְּׁלֵמוּת הָאֱנוֹשִׁי, וּלְהָסִיר מֵהֶם אֵלּוּ הַמַּחֲשָׁבוֹת הַמַּתְחִילוֹת מִשְּׁנֵי הַנַּעֲרוּת אֲלֵיהֶם – בִּמְעַט הַרְחָבָה כְּמוֹ שֶׁעָשִׂינוּ.

(רמב"ם, מורה נבוכים, א', כ"ו)

You, no doubt, know the Talmudical saying, which includes in itself all the various kinds of interpretation connected with our subject. It runs thus: "The Torah speaks according to the language of man," that is to say, expressions, which can easily be comprehended and understood by all, are applied to the Creator. Hence the description of God by attributes implying corporeality, in order to express His existence: because the multitude of people do not easily conceive existence unless in connection with a body, and that which is not a body nor connected with a body has for them no existence.

Whatever we regard as a state of perfection, is likewise attributed to God, as expressing that He is perfect in every respect, and that no imperfection or deficiency whatever is found in Him. But there is not attributed to God anything which the multitude consider a defect or want; thus He is never represented as eating, drinking, sleeping, being ill, using violence, and the like. Whatever, on the other hand, is commonly regarded as a state of perfection is attributed to Him, although it is only a state of perfection in relation to ourselves; for in relation to God, what we consider to be a state of perfection, is in truth the highest degree of imperfection.

If, however, men were to think that those human perfections were absent in God, they would consider Him as imperfect.

You are aware that locomotion is one of the distinguishing characteristics of living beings, and is indispensable for them in their progress toward perfection. As they require food and drink to replace waste, so they require locomotion, in order to approach that which is good for them and in harmony with their nature, and to escape from what is injurious and contrary to their nature. It makes, in fact, no difference whether we ascribe to God eating and drinking or locomotion; but according to human modes of expression, which is to say, according to common notions, eating and drinking would be an imperfection in God, while motion would not, in spite of the fact that the necessity of locomotion is the result of some want. Furthermore, it has been clearly proved, that everything which moves is corporeal and divisible; it will be shown below that God is incorporeal and that He can have no locomotion; nor can rest be ascribed to Him; for rest can only be applied to that which also moves. All expressions, however, which imply the various modes of movement in living beings, are employed with regard to God in the manner we have described and in the same way as life is ascribed to Him: although motion is an accident pertaining to living beings, and there is no doubt that, without corporeality, expressions like the following could not be imagined: "to descend, to ascend, to walk, to place, to stand, to surround, to sit, to dwell, to depart, to enter, to pass, etc.

It would have been superfluous thus to dilate on this subject, were it not for the mass of the people, who are accustomed to such ideas. It has been necessary to expatiate on the subject, as we have attempted, for the benefit of those who are anxious to acquire perfection, to remove from them such notions as have grown up with them from the days of youth.

(Rambam, *Guide for the Perplexed*, 1.26)

Maimonides does not speak as a dogmatic believer, but as a master who thinks from within the Truth itself. His approach recalls "thinking the true," the phrase Heidegger used to talk about Parmenides and Heraclitus in his 1942–1943 lectures at the University of Freiburg: "at the outset of Western thought [they] uniquely belong together in thinking the true. To think the true means to experience the true in its essence and in such essential experience, to know the Truth of what is true."

Maimonides argues that the anthropomorphized divinity is appropriate for preaching to the masses. But God is a presence, not a person. Rather than a localized entity, divinity is omnipresent. This vision transcends classical and traditional conceptions of an exclusive deity; it invites us to transcend human mental limitations and pursue a universal and transcendent experience.

Among seekers who do not cling to the existence of a personal deity, some strive to dissolve the objective "I" and pursue spiritual enlightenment. Unconcerned about a personal God, they focus on understanding and overcoming their own ontic dimension. Their journey, often prolonged, immerses them in the hope of obtaining "someone" or renouncing "something." We see that, in one way or another, they continue relying on what is objective. They seem to have the attitude that Heidegger criticized in Western philosophy: they get obsessed by the entity and forget the Self. They fail to understand that renouncing the "I" is intrinsically paradoxical: it is as futile as pulling on your belt to lift yourself up.

The effort to abandon the ego is itself an egotistical act, because the attempt ontifies the "I." The ego cannot transcend itself or overcome itself because there is no one who can triumph over anything. In trying to divest ourselves of egocentrism, we may inadvertently consolidate it. The notion of the ego contains an inescapable paradox. This supposed entity, often perceived as the epicenter of self-consciousness, vanishes upon close scrutiny. It is nothing more than an ideational construct, devoid of inherent substance. The ego is configured as an entelechy; it is a chimera born of a belief in its own existence. Upon observation, it simply dissolves.

Just as darkness is nothing more than an absence of light, the egoic entity is mere ignorance of ourselves. The ego reveals itself as the shadow cast by our own ignorance. It is impossible to shatter, demolish, destroy, or renounce a non-existent ego without falling into a perpetual cycle of self-deception. New egoic manifestations will arise in the attempt, such as false humility, feigned liberation, or disguised erudition, which are nothing more than new forms of ignorance. It is futile to fight the darkness or the egoic phenomenon. We cannot expel darkness. We can only turn on the light. Just as darkness is dispelled by light, the ego is dismantled by self-knowledge.

Instead of advocating the renunciation, destruction, or annihilation of the ego, I urge to examine it. The approach should not be confrontation, but deep understanding. Rather than an adversary, it is a phenomenon to be explored. If we want to renounce the ego, we must first verify its presence. By delving into its essence, we will discover whether it really exists. Paradoxically, although the egoic phenomenon is illusory, it is a component of our human experience. By illuminating its darkest corners with full attention and awareness, we discover its absence. With observation, the ego fades away, giving way to an integrated and holistic existence. This journey into self-awareness reveals the ephemeral nature of the ego. In this wholeness, we emerge into a transformed reality. All separation dissipates and we merge into totality, reaching the true essence of our being.

It seems arduous to resolve this enigma, but it is less complicated than it seems. The path of retroprogression does not call for acquiring something or abandoning anything. It does not require actions or renunciations. In fact, the "I" is nourished and strengthened by dedication and perseverance. Curiously enough, nothing feeds the ego more than efforts to acquire something or get rid of something. I suggest adopting a position of observation in our search for the ego. If it is discovered, it cannot be discarded; if it is not found, then there is nothing to get rid of. We cannot destroy lack, renounce non-existence, or eliminate absence. By observing, we will realize that there is no such autonomous entity as the "I" within us.

וְאָמַר רַבִּי אַחָא, "וְהַחָכְמָה מֵאַיִן תִּמָּצֵא" (איוב כ"ח, י"ב). מַהוּ "מֵאַיִן"? מֵאוֹתָן שֶׁעוֹשִׂין עַצְמָן כְּאַיִן.

(מדרש תנחומא, כי תבוא, ג')

And Rabbi Aḥa says, "where can wisdom be found?" can also be translated as, "wisdom comes from nothing"). What is [the meaning of] "from nothing"? from those who make nothing of themselves.

(*Midrash Tanḥuma*, "*Ki Tavo*," 3)

This observation is the process by which the independent "I" transforms itself into nothing and reveals its non-existence. We do not have to transcend the ego, but to discover that we have never had one. This is the process of transformation of the "I" into "nothing."

הקב"ה בָּרָא אֶת הָעוֹלָם יֵשׁ מֵאַיִן, וְהַצַּדִּיקִים עוֹשִׂים בְּמַעֲשֵׂיהֶם אי"ן מי"ש. כְּמוֹ מַעֲשֵׂה הַקָּרְבָּנוֹת, שֶׁהַבְּהֵמָה הִיא יֵשׁ, מַעֲשֵׂה גַּשְׁמִי, וְהַצַּדִּיקִים מְקָרְבִין אוֹתָהּ אֶל הַקְּדֻשָּׁה וְנַעֲשָׂה אַיִן רוּחָנִי. נִמְצָא כִּי מִתְּחִלָּה הָיָה אי"ן וּלְבַסּוֹף אי"ן. וְזֶהוּ אנ"י אוֹתִיּוֹת אי"ן, כִּי מֵאנ"י שֶׁהוּא עֲשִׂיָּה נַעֲשָׂה אי"ן.

(המגיד ממעזריטש, אור תורה, פרשת אמור, מאמר ק"כ)

God created the world something from nothing (*creatio ex nihilo*) and the righteous (*tzadikim*), with their actions, transform something into nothing, as in the act of sacrifices, that the beast is something, a material creation, and the righteous [through sacrifice] bring it closer to holiness and it becomes a spiritual nothingness. So, we find that at the beginning there was nothing (*ain*) and at the end nothing (*ain*), and this is the meaning of the word *ani* (I), being of the same letters of the word *ain* (nothingness), because from *ani* (I), which is acting, it becomes nothingness (*ain*).

(The Maggid of Mezeritch, *Or Torah*, *Parashat Emor*, Discourse 120)

In the fundamental texts of Hindu philosophy, particularly in the Upanishads and the *Avadhūta-gītā*, we find the Sanskrit expression *neti-neti*, which translates as "neither this, nor that."

अथात आदेशो—नेति नेति, न ह्येतस्मादिति नेत्यन्यत्परमस्त्यथ ना मधेयम्—सत्यस्य सत्यमिति ।

athāta ādeśo neti neti na hy etasmād iti nety anyat param asty atha nāma dheyam satyasya satyam iti.

So, therefore, the instruction is *neti-neti*, or "neither this, nor that." There is no other instruction more excellent than *neti*, or "not this"; it is called the truth of truths.

(*Bṛhad-āraṇyaka Upanishad*, 2.3.6)

तत्त्वमस्यादिवाक्येन स्वात्मा हि प्रतिपादितः ।
नेति नेति श्रुतिर्ब्रूयाद् अनृतं पाञ्चभौतिकम् ॥

tattvamasyādi-vākyena
svātmā hi pratipāditaḥ
neti neti śrutir brūyād
anṛtaṁ pāñca-bhautikam

By such phrases as "That thou art," our own Self is affirmed. From that which is false and composed of the five elements, the *śruti* (scripture) says, "not this, not this."

(*Avadhūta-gītā*, 1.25)

Deeply rooted in *jñāna-yoga*, this meditative practice serves as an essential catalyst for the process of self-realization. It is based on the deliberate use of the mind to disassociate itself from all forms and nomenclatures. This promotes discernment between the phenomenal and transcendental realms. By practicing *neti-neti*, one comes to understand that any concept capable of being imagined or conceived by the human mind is not representative of Brahman, the ultimate principle of reality. Thus, this practice gradually leads to the discovery of this essential truth.

Neti-neti is an exercise that begins with the negation of all phenomena of consciousness and concludes in the unveiling of nondual consciousness itself. It is a tool of introspection that takes us on a journey of self-discovery of the *ātman*, or the true "I," progressively discarding identification with peripheral aspects such as the body, thoughts, feelings, names and forms, all of which are considered to be *anātman* ("non-self").

Thus, *neti-neti* not only rejects conceptual descriptions of the absolute reality, but also deconstructs the egoic interpretation. Ādi Śaṅkara advocated this approach in his commentary on Gauḍapāda's *Kārikā*. He held that Brahman transcends all attributes and that this practice helps dissolve the barriers imposed by ignorance. His disciple Sureśvara stressed that it not only negated existence, but also led to the discovery of our underlying identity. *Neti-neti* serves as a description of the indescribable, which captures the essence of what cannot be defined. It is useful when no other definition is appropriate. It offers us footprints to follow toward what is unmanifest.

The *Bṛhad-āraṇyaka Upanishad* provides an illuminating interpretation, by stating that there are two aspects of Brahman: material and immaterial. Śaṅkara considers the apparently separate entity (*jīva*) to be a reflection of Brahman in ignorance (*avidyā*). The principle of *neti-neti* negates all that is not Brahman and offers us a perspective on the infinite capacity for transformation of the Self. Human beings are born without the ability to walk or talk; their future evolution is a reflection of their intrinsic nature. Likewise, we are not aware of our authentic nature, but the possibility of self-realization is inherent to our essence.

The negative approach or path, known in the philosophical and religious spheres, traces its origins through diverse intellectual and spiritual lineages, ranging from Greek philosophy to the foundational teachings of Christianity, Islam, and Judaism. Divinity is what is constant in this scenario. The absence of the "I" eliminates any gap or division, similar to the rupture of a vessel that allows the union of inner space with outer space, revealing its inherent unity and indivisibility. Not that we perceive divinity in all things, nor that we identify God in the entity itself; rather, in the absence of the objective, God's existence becomes self-evident and exclusive. Something similar to the idea of "remotion" is required, as addressed by Saint Thomas Aquinas in his *Summa against the gentiles*:

> [1] We have shown that there exists a first being, whom we call God. We must, accordingly, now investigate the properties of this being.
>
> [2] Now, in considering the divine substance, we should specially make use of the method of remotion. For, by its immensity, the divine substance surpasses every form that our intellect reaches. Thus, we are unable to apprehend it by knowing what it is. Yet we are able to have some knowledge of it by knowing what it is not. Furthermore, we approach nearer to a knowledge of God according as through our intellect we are able to remove more and more things from Him. For we know each thing more perfectly the more fully we see its differences from other things; for each thing has within itself its own being, distinct from all other things. So, too, in the case of the things whose definitions we know. We locate them in a genus, through which we know in a general way what they are. Then we add differences to each thing, by which it may be distinguished from other things. In this way, a complete knowledge of a substance is built up.
>
> [3] However, in the consideration of the divine substance we cannot take a what as a genus; nor can we derive the distinction of God from things by differences affirmed of God. For this reason, we must derive the distinction of God from other beings by means of negative differences. And just as among affirmative differences one contracts the other, so one negative difference is contracted by another that makes it to differ from many beings. For example, if

we say that God is not an accident, we thereby distinguish Him from all accidents. Then, if we add that He is not a body, we shall further distinguish Him from certain substances. And thus, proceeding in order, by such negations God will be distinguished from all that He is not. Finally, there will then be a proper consideration of God's substance when He will be known as distinct from all things. Yet, this knowledge will not be perfect, since it will not tell us what God is in Himself.

[4] As a principle of procedure in knowing God by way of remotion, therefore, let us adopt the proposition which, from what we have said, is now manifest, namely, that God is absolutely unmoved. The authority of Sacred Scripture also confirms this. For it is written: "I am the Lord and I change not" (Mal. 3:6);..."with whom there is no change" (James 2:17). Again: "God is not man... that He should be changed (Num. 23:19).

(*Summa against the gentiles*, Book I, chapter XIV)

St. Thomas Aquinas begins by establishing that we cannot affirm what God is, only what God is not. Next, he advocates the negation method to deepen our knowledge of the Divine. He argues that human nature, by its very limitation, tends to project finite attributes onto God, derived from our tangible and limited experience. Consequently, any quality we assign to the divine invariably falls within the realm of the finite and is constrained by our limited perspective. We understand, for example, the concept of finitude, but it is impossible for us to fully apprehend the infinite. Consequently, in relation to God, we deny finitude. Similarly, our perception of immortality is conditioned by our innate experience with mortality, leading us to discount this last aspect of our conception of the Divine. This process of systematic denial, according to Saint Thomas, brings us toward a more authentic understanding of God, and frees God of the imperfections conceivable from the human perspective.

Neti-neti resembles the concept of "destruction" presented by Martin Heidegger during the first period of his work (1919–1927).

This is not only an interesting aspect of his philosophy, but also an essential element in his phenomenological approach. In his inaugural lectures, Heidegger begins the exploration of "destruction," initially understood as the process of dismantling conceptualizations that distort the perception of "pre-objective" life, a vital experience that is prior to any conceptualization and categorization. Heidegger refers to destruction in the following words:

> For the most part today, philosophy operates inauthentically (*uneigentlich*) within the Greek conceptuality, which itself has been pervaded by a chain of diverse interpretations (*Interpretationen hindurchgegengen ist*). The basic concepts have lost their original functions of expression, functions (*ursprünglichen*) which were specially tailored to fit regions of objects experienced in a particular way. [...] The phenomenological hermeneutics of facticity thus sees itself summoned to such a radical exposition in order to assist the contemporary situation along the path toward a radical possibility of appropriation—and this by way of calling its attention to the concrete categories that are being provided to this end— it is compelled to undertake the task of undoing the inherited and dominant interpretive framework, to expose hidden motives, to uncover trends and interpretive paths that are not always made explicit, and to trace back to the original sources that motivate every explanation through a strategy of deconstruction. Hermeneutics carries out its task only on the path of destruction (*Destruktion*). [...] philosophical research is "historical" knowing in the radical sense of that term. For philosophical research, the destructive contestation of philosophy's history is not merely a supplement for the purposes of illustrating how things were earlier, an occasional overview of what others "did" earlier, or an opportunity for outlining entertaining perspectives in world history. The destruction is rather the authentic path upon which the present must encounter itself in its own basic movements, and it must encounter itself in such a way that what springs

> forth for the present from its history is the continual question: to what extent is it (the present) itself truly worried about appropriating radical possibilities from basic experiences and their interpretations? The tendencies toward a radical logic of origins (*eine radikale Ursprunglogik*) and the approaches to ontologies thereby get a principal critical elucidation. [...] What we do not interpret and express originally (*ursprünglich*) is also what we do not have in proper safekeeping (*eigentlicher*).
> (*Phenomenological Interpretations with Respect to Aristotle*)

Over time, Heidegger broadened and deepened this concept, while retaining certain elements of its original meaning. In a later phase, "destruction" acquired the connotation of critically dismantling traditional philosophical notions. This transformation is like a deconstruction aiming to free the understanding of Being (*Sein*) from the limitations imposed by previous philosophical thought. Such an evolution reflects Heidegger's continuing endeavor to seek a more genuine and unburdened understanding of Being. After "phenomenological destruction" announced in *Being and Time* (*Sein und Zeit*), a final analysis shows how Heidegger approaches reconstruction. Although this aspect remains unfinished in his work, it offers a vital perspective for understanding his philosophy. This meticulous treatment, based on the lectures given at Marburg, reveals Heidegger's efforts to subvert and reconfigure the philosophical tradition, where "destruction" becomes a means to access the fundamentals and approach the problem of Being in a renewed way.

In our search for the Divine, we deny or destroy every ontic attribute, so that its inherent essence can emerge. The seeker is not an entity that needs to acquire qualities in order to attain God, but only to strip God of all attributes. This perspective is transformative: God is not an external entity, but rather the intrinsic nature that lies beneath all ontic layers. We will not perceive God in every object, rather the very absence of objects, nothingness, will reveal God. The Divine is not contained in every particle of the universe, but the universe itself is an authentic divine expression. In fact, "God" is the loving term for "what is," reality in its purest, simplest, and ultimate state.

If we explore our dreams, we will face a complex truth: our oneiric goals, objectives, and destinations are unattainable. Similarly, spiritual practices, promoted both by spirituality merchants and by organized faith, are presented as paths to redemption, but they are mere fictitious constructs. However, this illusion does not diminish their intrinsic value. Belief-based practices are vital tools for our spiritual journey. They are potentially valuable because they can bring about profound introspective transformation.

If the question is poorly posed, we will not arrive at the answer. We will not solve a problem if it is incorrectly formulated. Inquiring into divinity with the aspiration of finding God is a profound conceptual error. What matters is not who is searching nor what is expected to be found, but rather to realize that what exists is simply as it is. With this simple truth, we can recognize that we have never lost anything nor have we wandered anywhere. Nothing has ceased to exist, nor has it been destroyed or annihilated. In the acceptance of what simply is, all searching ends, giving way to true understanding: existence, in its purest and unaltered form, is the very essence of the Divine. The Self is its own essence. The true search should not be oriented toward the external objective world, but rather requires a deep introspection that dissolves the "I" and reveals the divine presence. We seek God, but Gods finds us.

Most religious institutions preach that God is the creator of the universe and of his creatures, but this misses a fundamental point: no one ever asked us if we wanted to be created. If we accept the notion of a personal creator God, we face an ethical dilemma: such a being would resemble a dictator and we would be mere subjects. Obviously, this God is incompatible with the notion of human freedom. If we were puppets in his hands, moved with strings, he would make us sing, cry, laugh, love, and even murder. All distinction between virtue and sin, goodness and evil, would disappear. Puppets are not responsible for their actions; only beings endowed with freedom can be saints or sinners.

Two of Nietzsche's most famous phrases are "God is dead," an aphorism in *The Gay Science*, and "the desert grows," the title of a poem in *Thus spoke Zarathustra.* These statements are more than theological assertions; they articulate a profound transformation in human perception of the cosmos and of life. The phrases stress that humans, in their effort to reach a deeper understanding of reality, have been the catalyzing agents of this "divine extinction." "The desert grows" symbolizes unsteady terrain, devoid of structure and order, in which the creative freedom of the "superman" emerges. This freedom represents a paradigmatic change in thought, where the human being is placed at the center of the interpretation of reality, thereby displacing the figure of a personal divinity as the ultimate explanation of the universe and existence.

Nietzsche writes that this great news was communicated by a madman running in the marketplace at noon shouting incessantly "God is dead." He jumped into a crowd of the people who declared themselves atheists, piercing them with his glance while they laughed and said: "'Where is God?' he cried; I'll tell you! We have killed him—you and I! We are all his murderers." God has not died of natural causes, but has been killed by human beings. From the very moment of the murder, a new story begins for the human beings who must bear the guilt and their freedom. The madman himself asks: "What were we doing when we unchained this earth from its sun? Where is it moving to now? … Aren't we straying as though through an infinite nothing?"

As long as their God lived, human beings could ask these questions. Nietzsche does not simply proclaim the disappearance of faith, but also speaks to the evolution of human consciousness. The death of God represents a liberation and at the same time a monumental challenge. Having lost the anchor of a divine order, humanity is confronted with the vastness of a universe without pre-established guidance, where individuals must seek their own path and create their own meaning. This scenario is both an opportunity for self-realization and a source of existential anxiety. In this new world, humanity's responsibility is amplified; there are no longer deities to blame or praise, only human beings and their ability to shape their own destiny. The madman's concern is clarified in his question:

> Is the magnitude of this deed not too great for us? Do we not ourselves have to become gods merely to appear worthy of it? There was never a greater deed—and whoever is born after us will on account of this deed belong to a higher history than all history up to now!'
>
> Here the madman fell silent and looked again at his listeners; they too were silent and looked at him disconcertedly. Finally, he threw his lantern on the ground so that it broke into pieces and went out.
>
> "I come too early," he then said; "my time is not yet. This tremendous event is still on its way, wandering; it has not yet reached the ears of men. Lightning and thunder need time; the light of the stars needs time; deeds need time, even after they are done, in order to be seen and heard. This deed is still more remote to them than the remotest stars—and yet they have done it themselves!"
>
> It is still recounted how on the same day the madman forced his way into several churches and there started singing his *Requiem aeternam deo*.
>
> Led out and called to account, he is said always to have replied nothing but, "What then are these churches now if not the tombs and sepulchers of God?"
>
> (Friedrich Nietzsche, *The Gay Science*, section 125)

Nietzsche's madman reveals a fundamental transformation in the human conception of autonomy, resonating with Kant's idea that autonomy is now merely a starting point. That is to say, autonomy was traditionally seen as the ultimate destination reached through the use of reason; now it is the first step. This means that humans must actively assume responsibility for their destiny, establishing their own goals and the means to achieve them. This notion is manifested in the madman's exclamation: "I come too early … my time is not yet," meaning that the era of Nietzsche's "superman" has not yet arrived.

According to Nietzsche, the death of God is a transcendental event that frees humans from dependence on a divine entity. I have killed God but I have not yet awakened. This liberation does not automatically lead to true freedom. The murderers of God, instead of attaining full freedom, may fall into the trap of divinizing other idols or concepts. Authentic freedom, according to Nietzsche, lies in the individual's ability to live without God and without belonging to a collective, thus being truly independent.

If we accept a personal God, all responsibility falls on the creator. Humans are relegated to a passive role in the universe and stripped of their freedom and creative possibility. Nietzsche challenges this notion, proposing that true human freedom lies in the capacity to create one's own values, beyond divine impositions. The death of God, therefore, offers humans the opportunity to "be" in an authentic, self-constructed way. This suggests a fundamental change in our relationship with transcendence, marking a turning point in the history of human thought. In a world where the concept of God no longer dominates, the fundamental question arises as to how we should orient our existence. Nietzsche's answer to this concern is the creation of values. The death of God is not only an ending, but also a new beginning, where individuals have the possibility and responsibility to shape their own morality and purpose in life. In this new paradigm, humans become the primary agents of meaning and value in the universe.

In the novel *The Demons* by Dostoevsky, there is a profound paradox in the phrase "If there is no God, everything is permitted," spoken by the character Kirilov. In fact, if God exists, nothing is permitted, since human beings cannot create. If we accept the existence of God, our creative and moral capacity is limited, which leads to a significant dilemma: the presence of God means the absence of true freedom and autonomy.

Nietzsche's proposition, while penetrating and revealing in certain respects, represents only one facet of a broader spectrum. His approach, centered on rationality and logic, highlights a crucial aspect of human nature. It underestimates the importance of meditation without neglecting introspection.

> Healthy introspection, without undermining oneself; it is a rare gift to venture into the unexplored depths of the self, without delusions or fictions, but with an uncorrupted gaze.
>
> (Friedrich Nietzsche, *Unpublished writings from the period of unfashionable observations*)

A similar point is his focus on "giving birth to yourself," or making your own self and your life a lifelong artistic project, that is "becoming and self-overcoming". He spent his days alone and sick—many times at resorts where he took long walks. He advocated solitude and said that good thoughts only came by walking alone in what we might call meditative walks.

This omission leads to a fundamental question about the purpose of human freedom, especially in a context devoid of the figure of a supreme entity. In a world without an ultimate moral arbiter, human freedom becomes more ambiguous and complex. Deprived of a transcendental ethical framework, absolute freedom could drift into unbridled debauchery. Without objective moral authority, human actions are not judged as constructive or destructive. Hence freedom can be both an instrument of greatness and decadence. When deities are absent, the human capacity for both beneficial and pernicious actions is unleashed. Without the presence of a superior entity to guide or forgive, morality becomes a subjective and personal concept. This scenario of unrestricted freedom can trigger extreme and chaotic behavior.

In a world devoid of a God figure, we face an existential void, a resonant echo of Sartre's observation that we are all bastards, because we lack a fundamental being to cling to. This newly acquired freedom, though liberating, leaves us without a clear purpose. Here, Sartre enlightens us with his idea that "existence precedes essence," suggesting that our essence is formed through our choices throughout our existence. That is to say, we first exist and then, as we make choices, we become endowed with essence. This capacity of human beings to use their freedom in a creative and responsible way becomes a central issue, challenging the transformation of liberty into libertinism.

Despite his deep and keen understanding, Nietzsche unfortunately never explored meditation. Had he been imbued with Eastern wisdom, perhaps he would have added this essential dimension to his perspective. Human freedom, to be truly enriching and constructive, must be rooted in meditation. The mind is confusion, chaos, and darkness. Meditation brings clarity because it is not a mental state, but the liberation of the mind, of oneself, of what one believes to be; thus, it is true freedom. Depriving human beings of a deity is not an end in itself, but a means to free them from restrictions. However, it is essential to provide new meaning and significance to human existence. Meditation is a powerful way to discover our essential and eternal nature. In this context, meditation, free from the influence of any deity, is a vital tool for finding direction and purpose in a world free from divinity. Meditation can raise self-awareness to a point where evil becomes unthinkable. This sense of morality is not externally imposed, but is born from the depths of our being. This morality is autonomous, not heteronomous. By recognizing our connection to the cosmos deep within, we reveal our true hidden nature. In this state of enlightenment, negative actions such as harming or hurting become inconceivable.

Nietzsche, in the last years of his life, faced a profound existential crisis. His mind, once a beacon of lucidity, plunged into the shadows of madness, culminating in his confinement in an asylum. The intellectual colossus went so far as to proclaim that "God is dead," a statement that seems to reflect an inherently negative outlook. He found an unfathomable void, a freedom devoid of meaning and purpose. This emptiness is often a precursor to insanity. Human life, like a tree, needs solid roots; without these, we find ourselves adrift, disconnected from the Whole.

Nietzsche's assertion that "God is dead" marked the collapse of a fundamental connection between us and the universe. This loss leaves us vulnerable and lacking a spiritual center. It is essential for humans to find an inner center of understanding and connection beyond traditional religious structures. True freedom is not about denying, but about understanding our relationship to the Whole. Nietzsche, focused on dismantling the illusions of the past, failed to fully embrace the future dimension of freedom. This partial omission contributed to his tragic despair. Freedom involves not only freedom from the chains of the past, but also embracing the uncertainty and possibilities of the future. Freedom, in its fullest sense, is a continuous journey toward self-discovery and self-transformation.

Even if God is now dead, believing in a God provided solace for millennia, a balm for the human soul in times of anguish and despair. This reveals a profound truth about our spiritual needs. It is crucial to recognize and meet these needs authentically and consciously. God, even though humans made him, served as a solace in hours of inner restlessness. The concept of God, even without tangible foundations, filled a void in the human soul. Incessantly repeated over millennia, the idea of God took root in the collective consciousness until it acquired the appearance of truth. Nietzsche's conclusion poses an essential challenge: to find a sense of purpose and connection in a post-religious world. Instead of simply rejecting old beliefs, the challenge is to discover and cultivate a sense of sacredness and transcendence within our own nature. This inner journey requires understanding our place in the cosmos and creating meaning that transcends imposed structures.

In spiritual and religious narratives, God has historically served as a refuge from fear and a shield against the anguish of old age, death, and the unknown. Although probably illusory, this conception of God has always been comforting. It acts as a painkiller for anxiety but has side effects, which remind us of this pithy warning, attributed to Fiódor Dostoevsky: "the best way to keep a prisoner from escaping is to make sure he never knows he's in prison." Falsehoods, though deceptive, can provide temporary comfort. This belated discovery of truth can lead to profound disillusionment and distrust toward those we considered sources of wisdom and guidance. This sense of betrayal creates an existential void, an abyss of disbelief and disenchantment with the world and its narrative structures.

At the end of his life, Nietzsche became mad not by mere chance, but as an inevitable result of his profoundly negative outlook. His intellect, always critical and often sarcastic, was incapable of nourishing the spirit. If we aspire to attain a true understanding of life, it is vital to transcend the intellect. The human spirit needs more than mere reason to flourish; it requires a connection to something deeper and more meaningful. Kant and Descartes believed that reason and logic were all we needed. However, Nietzsche went beyond them: his first book focuses on the ecstatic, irrational, and emotional traits of Greek works and ceremonies. He moved far beyond an idea of humanity based solely on reason. What Nietzsche meant by the Apollonian and the Dionysian is that one god represents order, logic, and reason, and the other represents chaos, madness, and intoxication. Nietzsche considered both necessary. Though powerful, the intellect is not enough to comprehend the full extent of human experience and its connection to the Whole. It is necessary to explore deeper dimensions of existence, the ones that transcend logic and penetrate into the realm of mystical and spiritual experience. Purely negative attitudes are insufficient to nurture the human spirit. While denial can serve as a catalyst for inquiry and introspection, by itself, it cannot provide a path forward.

By disconnecting from faith in God, Nietzsche not only threw away a traditional belief system, but also a source of comfort and stability. In his intellectual quest, he faced a profound paradox: freedom from traditional conventions and beliefs became the prelude to his descent into madness. His rupture with the limitations imposed by rigid belief systems also left him without a stable frame of reference for his existence. His metaphor about the growing desert refers to the expansion of an existential void, which was fed by his own desolate view of the world. He said, "God is dead" and "the desert grows," and then he went mad because the desert grew too much.

This phenomenon extends to other thinkers who, in their relentless search for truth, delved into the depths of an engrossing negativity. Philosophers such as Schopenhauer, Sartre, and Camus, precursors of existentialism, have dismantled prevailing illusions, leaving behind a landscape stripped of traditional meaning. However, life is more than this emptiness and denial of divinity. Existence is a constant flow, a dynamic interaction with the reality that surrounds us, where joy and uncertainty coexist and intertwine. In the face of this nihilistic vision, we suggest a change of focus toward affirmation and deep introspection.

In modern philosophy, deconstructing rooted beliefs was a necessary step toward free thinking from persistent illusions. However, while dismantling them was imperative to preserve intellectual honesty, it has resulted in a profound sense of emptiness. This existential void in the human soul gave rise to existentialism, a philosophical current that focuses on the apparent lack of meaning and purpose in life. Existentialist sayings, such as "life has no purpose" or "you are a mere accident," see human existence as meaningless. This perspective, which could be called "accidentalism," suggests that individuals are accidental and marginal phenomena, and are devoid of any essential or predestined importance.

For this existentialist view, which extends from Nietzsche to Jean-Paul Sartre, human beings go from being puppets in the hands of a fictitious divinity to being a product of chance in an indifferent universe. This transformation represents a dramatic change in the understanding of their own existence. It leaves individuals at a philosophical crossroads, facing the reality of a universe that does not offer ready answers or a predetermined purpose. However, this apparent existential void also offers an opportunity to redefine meaning in personal and authentic terms. This redefinition requires a deep exploration of the human condition, beyond preconceived notions of morality and purpose.

> He who fights with monsters might take care lest he thereby become a monster. And if you gaze for long into an abyss, the abyss gazes also into you.
>
> (Friedrich Nietzsche, *The Gay Science*, section 146)

In this quest, humans can discover a sense of identity and direction that is not dictated by external structures, but rather, one that emerges from their personal and reflective understanding of life.

Meditation and self-inquiry practices are essential tools for addressing the emptiness bequeathed by Nietzsche and his contemporaries. Even in the absence of an explicit divinity, these practices can open a space for peace and meaning. Life, in its complexity and diversity, offers a path of discovery and personal realization that goes beyond the desolation suggested by these philosophers. Ultimately, life's journey should not be a trek through a desolate desert, but an enriching exploration filled with love, joy, and celebration. This approach contrasts with Nietzsche's nihilistic perspective and offers a more holistic and affirmative view of human existence. Seen through this prism, life becomes an odyssey of self-knowledge, growth and delight, where each experience contributes to our integral development as human beings.

Human beings harbor an intrinsic need to unite with existence. Their connection takes roots until it reaches the core of being. From this deep union with existence, enlightenment arises. The blossoming of humans is not a mere awakening of consciousness, but a true explosion of life, which reveals itself in innumerable manifestations of meaning, significance, and bliss. In this state, life becomes a continuous carnival, a dynamic festival of existence that embraces all its facets.

To prevent a descent into madness and paralyzing nihilism, our recently discovered freedom must be transformed into an awakening of consciousness. It is imperative that we establish a deep connection with the universe's essence to find renewed meaning and purpose. Only through this transformation can we ensure that our lives and decisions remain relevant. Without this reorientation, we lose all meaning. Humanity must strive to discover a new purpose, one that does not depend on outdated structures and beliefs, but arises from a deeper and more personal understanding of our existence in the cosmos.

In a world where traditional concepts such as virtue and sin, paradise and hell, reward and punishment, lose their relevance, existence seems to reveal itself as utterly indifferent. This perspective suggests that, with the waning influence of the Divine, once perceived as omnipresent, a chasm of alienation and disconnection emerges between the individual and life. With the absence of God, the intrinsic connection between being and the universe vanishes, leaving existence devoid of a focused and attentive consciousness. According to this view, the universe, stripped of all divine intelligence, is reduced to mere inert matter. Life becomes an accidental and ephemeral by-product, dissipating as soon as its constituent elements disintegrate. Such an existence does not distinguish between the animate and inanimate, and reduces human life to a series of material processes without greater purpose.

The key to navigating this existential landscape is finding an equilibrium between the negative and positive aspects of life. It is essential to balance blind belief in divinities and total rejection of their existence, so we can anchor ourselves between the extremes of theism and atheism. The luminous path of balance is filled with joy, well-being, and wisdom that transcends logic and reason. This new understanding reveals that existence, in its totality, is not only alive, but also is endowed with sensitivity and intrinsic discernment.

In the search for inner balance, we find a silence and peace previously inaccessible due to the constant noise of conceptual activity. This state of equilibrium opens the path toward intimacy with existence, lifting the veil of confusion and overthinking. This silence reveals to us the true nature of our presence. Such clarity shows us that we are beings with an intrinsic purpose. We are not mere accidents in the vastness of the universe. Each individual is a unique and irreplaceable presence, occupying a special place that no one else can fill. As indispensable parts of the great cosmic mosaic, we contribute to the totality of existence in a unique and meaningful way. In our absence, the universe would feel an irreplaceable loss, a vacancy only able to be filled by each of us. The essence of this realization infuses our existence with dignity: we are interconnected beings with all of creation, from stars to flowers, from seas to seagulls.

This awareness floods us with immeasurable joy and ecstasy as we come to realize that we are intrinsically linked with all that exists and that existence itself values our presence. As we reach pure clarity, we begin to perceive the unconditional love that emanates toward us from all dimensions. This love is not a reward or a prize, but rather a natural manifestation of our connection with the universe. We recognize that each one of us is an essential element in the fabric of life, and that our existence holds deep and valuable meaning. You, as a human being, represent the pinnacle of the evolution of existence, the most refined manifestation of universal intelligence. You possess the unique ability to transcend the limits of a conventional mind and its knowingness, delving into the realm of no-mind, where a deeper and more essential wisdom resides.

Upon reaching this higher state of realization, you are not only transformed but also elevated to existence itself. This achievement is a cosmic celebration, for it marks the moment when you attain the summit of your potential, carrying with you a part of the cosmos into higher dimensions of possibility and fulfillment. It is not merely a personal celebration but also a celebration for the universe as a whole. This is because, at that moment, a part of the cosmos achieves what was always implicit in its being. By realizing our deep connection to existence, we become incapable of acting in detriment to life. This profound understanding carries an inherent responsibility toward all that exists. A being that is naturally connected, open, and receptive to these energies, in all their forms, radiates bliss, blessing, and grace. This state of being is not a single event of conquest, but a constant flow of harmonious interaction with the universe.

At this level of consciousness, the existence or non-existence of a personal God is an irrelevant detail. Individuals who have discovered within themselves this inextinguishable spring of absolute bliss have transcended the need for external divine figures. Traditional concepts of paradises and hells lose significance in the face of the magnitude of this realization. The deep understanding of unity with existence makes such concepts seem trivial or limited in comparison to the direct and vivid experience of oneness with the Whole. This evolution has a meaningful impact not only on the individual but also on the cosmos as a whole. By realizing your potential, you are not only transformed, but your transformation contributes to the universe's evolution. You are a crucial thread in the tapestry of existence. Your awakening and developing essence are fundamental to cosmic unfolding.

Retroprogressive teachings invite us to deeply immerse ourselves in the vital bonds that unite us with existence. Let us consider a walk through the sacred forest of Avadhutashram, a place where majestic trees soar toward the sky in an act of natural grandeur. Each of these trees, at its origin, began as a tiny seed, an entity seemingly insignificant yet charged with extraordinary latent potential. This seed, small as it may be, encases not only the promise of what it will become but also a blueprint of its future splendor. The autonomous existence of the seed is not sufficient for its transformation into an imposing tree. This requires synergistic interactions with essential elements such as soil, water, and sun, in a symphony of cosmic elements that interact in perfect harmony. At the core of this seed lies all the potential of the tree, patiently waiting for its opportunity to emerge. At the core of your being, there is a similar seed, symbolizing the essence and existence of your own self. This inner seed, harboring your potential and unrealized possibilities, patiently is waiting for the right moment to make a profound reconnection with the universe. This process is not merely about achieving prominence or external influence; rather, it is about how your most intimate essence, that spark which resides within your inner seed, unfolds, shines, and manifests your authenticity and unique purpose in life.

Our journey of self-discovery and self-realization is like becoming a tree: it is not confined to mere existence but involves an unfolding of our innermost being. Just as the tree draws nourishment from its environment to grow and flourish, we too can draw from our connection with the cosmos in order to fully realize our potential. This blossoming process is a testament to how each individual, as an integral part of existence, has a unique and valuable role to play in the grand scheme of life. This inner essence is not merely a manifestation of ever-latent potential; it is also a constant call, a persistent echo resonating deep within us, reminding us that within us lie unmanifested abilities, unrealized dreams, and a profound connection with the vast universe that surrounds us. This essence works like an internal compass, guiding us toward the realization of innate capacities and the fulfillment of our soul's aspirations and yearnings. In the deepest recesses of our being lies the seed of life, a living spark yearning to reconnect with the cosmos. This desire for reconnection is a fundamental impulse for existence, in all its magnitude and richness, to catalyze and make latent possibilities bloom.

Our existence is not limited to the grandeur of successes or achievements; it is defined by how our inner light, eternally present in that essential seed, unfolds and shines, thus forging our uniqueness. That inner light, rooted in the epicenter of our existence, is undeniable proof of an ever-present potential, waiting to be revealed and activated in the vast ocean of life. That light is like a lighthouse that can illuminate vast seas despite its small size. Each flash is an act of recognition and affirmation of your unique position in the great firmament of existence.

Reality, in its complexity and depth, is like a mirror that reflects not only what we are in the present but also the countless possibilities of what we can become. This phenomenon is a dynamic and uninterrupted process of metamorphosis and development. On this path toward self-realization and plenitude of being, time reveals itself not as an enemy, but as a valuable ally. Far from an implacable adversary, time is a compassionate traveling companion, offering us countless opportunities to cultivate and expand our inner light. Every moment is a precious invitation to live fully, allowing the seed of our inner being to germinate and grow into a garden of unlimited possibilities. In this garden, life becomes a constantly evolving masterpiece, a living canvas on which we paint the tones and hues of our experiences, thoughts, and emotions. We simultaneously become artists and works of art, engaging in an endless creative odyssey where the very act of living is elevated to the most sublime of creations, as Nietzsche states: "One thing is needful—to 'give style' to one's character—a great and rare art!" (*The Gay Science*, aphorism 290). Every human being is both creator and creation. We represent a constant dance of self-expression and self-discovery, in which every step and movement contributes to the rich tapestry of our lives. We are sculptors of our reality, molding and being molded by the experiences we live, ever moving toward a greater realization and manifestation of our authentic nature. This journey is an extensive pilgrimage from what we believe we are to what we truly are.

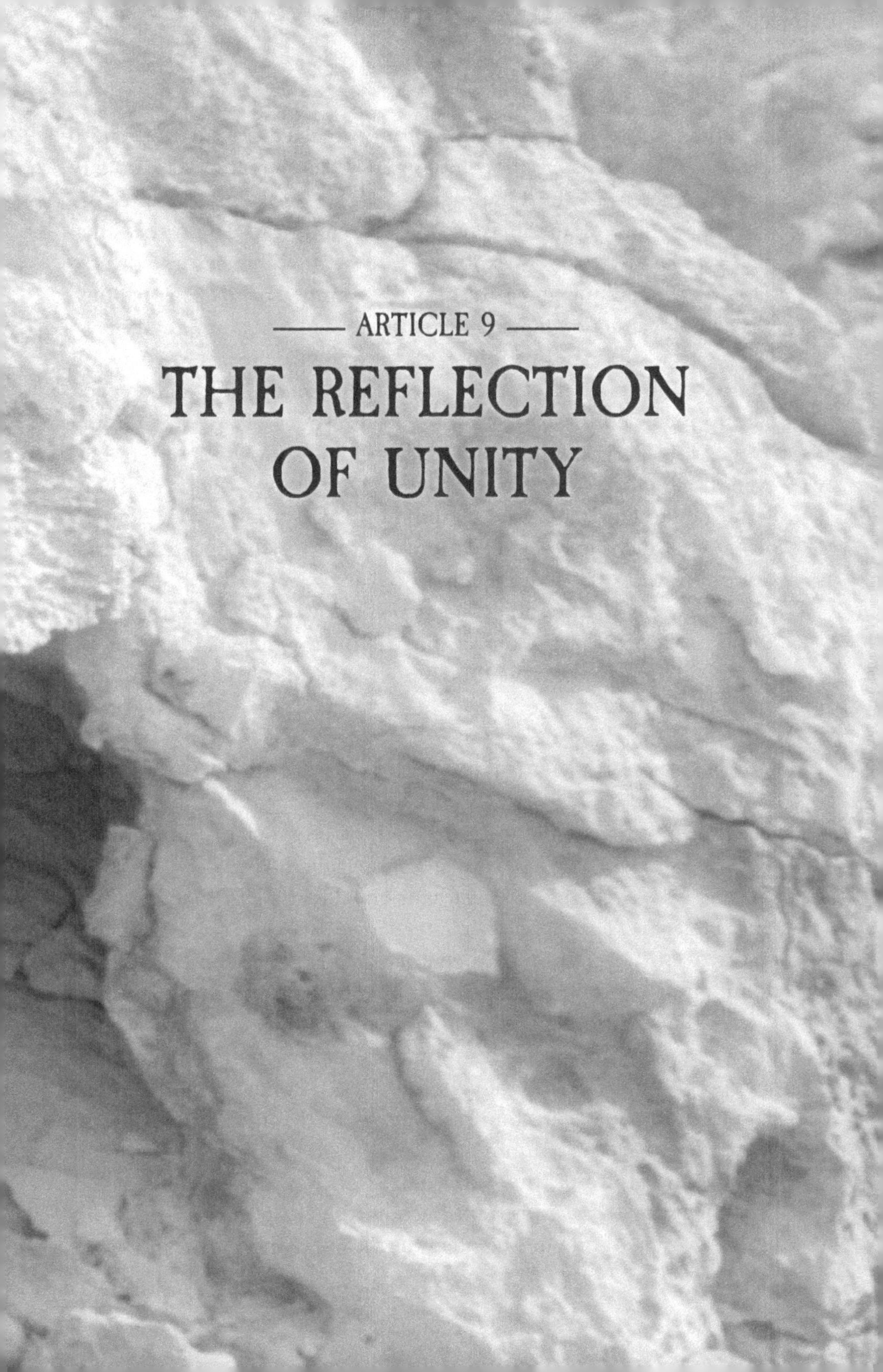

ARTICLE 9

THE REFLECTION OF UNITY

Enlightened masters from various times and places have tried to share a transcendental vision of reality that describes creation as a duality that emerges from the One or as the relative of the absolute, the objective reality of undifferentiated consciousness. To do this, they have resorted to stories to explain how the indivisible became diverse and how the multiplicity of the universe emerged from absolute unity. Repeated over generations, these stories became creation myths.

To access the true meanings of these myths, we must focus on their symbolism rather than their statements. Originally, each culture regarded these creation myths as esoteric stories containing truths. The study of this universal mythology allows us to see that, even though they come from very different cultures, the myths share certain characteristics. One of the most outstanding is the element of water, which appears in various creation myths and traditional stories. Water is the natural mirror par excellence. By observing its image in a mirror, the subject becomes the observer of the reflection and, simultaneously, the object that the mirror reflects. It is only by looking in a mirror that the One is doubled and, with it, the absolute unity seems to diversify.

The primordial waters of creation

Let us first review the creation myth of the ancient Babylonians. The *Enuma Elish* ("When above"), also called *The Seven Tablets of Creation*, was written in Akkadian on clay tablets in cuneiform characters. Some have called it *The Babylonian Genesis*. It was probably recorded in the 17th or 16th century B.C.E., after the Babylonian domination over the Sumerian cities of southern Mesopotamia. It says that in the beginning, there was only watery chaos. Then the waters separated into freshwater and saltwater. The primordial chaotic powers were the saltwater goddess Tiamat, a giant serpent who lived in the ocean, the freshwater god Apsu, and the son and counselor of both, Mummu. A great battle took place between Tiamat and Marduk, the Sun god. Marduk was victorious, ruled over the rest of the gods, and became the main god of Babylon. From Tiamat's body, he created the sky and the earth and from her tears, the Euphrates and Tigris rivers. The demon Kingu was condemned to death for having led the revolt. His blood was mixed with clay and this became the raw material for creating human beings. Here are the first lines of the *Enuma Elish.*

> When on high the heavens had not been named,
> Firm ground below had not been called by name,
> Naught but primordial Apsu, their begetter,
> (And) Mummu–Tiamat, she who bore them all,
> Their waters commingling as a single body;
> No reed hut had been matted, no marsh land had appeared,
> When no gods whatever had been brought into being,
> Uncalled by name, their destinies undetermined—
> Then it was that the gods were formed within them.

In ancient Egypt, the creator god was Atum, or "he who exists by himself." According to the mythology of Heliopolis, Atum arose from Nun, or "the original waters." The primordial ocean was called Nuu and, in a later period, Nun. Atum, through his saliva and semen from masturbation, created his children: the gods Shu and Tefnut, air and moisture.

In the Polynesian mythology from Easter Island, the fertility god Makemake is the creator of the world. One of his main rituals is the *tangata manu*, or "the bird man." In the myth, Makemake was alone, watching over his creation, full of all kinds of plants and animals. But he felt something was missing. Looking into a gourd filled with water, he saw his own reflection for the first time. Impressed with this revelation, he respectfully greeted his own reflection: "Greetings to you, you are beautiful and very much like me." At that moment, a bird landed on his right shoulder, astonishing Makemake even more as he saw his reflection had a beak, wings, and feathers. He merged the bird with the reflection and from this union, his son was born. After seeing his image in the water, Makemake wanted to create a being in his own image that would speak and think. He created the first man by fertilizing a stone with red earth. Later, seeing the solitude of the first man, he created woman to be his companion.

The Hebrew origin myth can be understood as an aquatic revelation, because water occupies an important place in its symbology. We see water at the very beginning of the Pentateuch, with the waters of Genesis, followed by rivers such as the Pishon, Tigris, Euphrates, Nile, and also the wells, the flood, and so on. In the first line of Genesis, we read:

בְּרֵאשִׁית בָּרָא אֱלֹהִים אֵת הַשָּׁמַיִם וְאֵת הָאָרֶץ:
(בראשית א', א')

In the beginning God created the heaven and the earth.
(Genesis, 1:1)

"God, in the beginning, created the heavens." "The heavens" is the translation of the Hebrew *et hashamayim* (את השמיים). On the one hand, *Et* is made up of the Hebrew letters *alef* (א) and *tav* (ת) which correspond to the first and last letters of the Hebrew alphabet; that is, it refers to a totality that includes everything. This is similar to Alpha and Omega, the first and last letters of the Greek alphabet. They are used to refer to God or Jesus Christ in Revelation (21:6): "I am the Alpha and the Omega, the beginning and the end." On the other hand, *shamayim* (שמיים) means "heavens" and also "two theres" This indicates a totality. From the egoic perspective, the human being lives between two infinite theres: a macrocosm and a microcosm. In the macrocosm, we go to outer space but never find the limits of the universe. In the microcosm, we can continue to infinitely divide matter into ever smaller particles.

מַאי "שָׁמַיִם"? אָמַר רַבִּי יוֹסֵי בַּר חֲנִינָא: "שֶׁשָּׁם מַיִם".
(תלמוד בבלי, חגיגה, י"ב, א')

[The *Gemara* asks:] "What is the meaning and source of the word *shamayim* (the sky, heavens)?" Rabbi Yosei bar Ḥanina said: "It is an acronym, *shesham mayim* (That water is there)."
(*Babylonian Talmud*, "*Ḥagigah*," 12a)

From the beginning of the Pentateuch, primordial water is an essential part of the creative process. The creative process described in Genesis begins in a watery chaos and the spirit of God hovering over the original waters. If we pay attention to the text, we will notice that the waters were not created. Rashi, Rabbi Shlomo Yitzḥaki (1040–1105 CE), is one of the most prominent Torah commentators of all time. In his commentary, he does not overlook this point, although he later moves in another direction:

> אִם כֵּן, תְּמַהּ עַל עַצְמְךָ, שֶׁהֲרֵי הַמַּיִם קָדְמוּ, שֶׁהֲרֵי כְּתִיב "וְרוּחַ אֱלֹהִים מְרַחֶפֶת עַל פְּנֵי הַמָּיִם", וַעֲדַיִין לֹא גִּלָּה הַמִּקְרָא בְּרִיאַת הַמַּיִם מָתַי הָיְתָה; הָא לָמַדְתָּ שֶׁקָּדְמוּ הַמַּיִם לָאָרֶץ.
>
> (פירוש רש"י על בראשית א', א')

> Therefore, be astounded at yourself, for the water preceded, as it is written: "and the spirit of God hovered over the face of the water," and Scripture did not yet disclose when the creation of water took place! From this you learn that the water preceded the earth.
>
> (Rashi on Genesis, 1:1)

The renowned master, Rabbi Judah Loew ben Bezalel, who is known as the Maharal of Prague, also mentioned it:

> כִּי מִתְּחִלַּת בְּרִיאָתוֹ שֶׁל עוֹלָם, קֹדֶם שֶׁיָּצַר וּבָרָא עִקַּר הַצּוּרָה – שֶׁהוּא הָאָדָם – הָיוּ הַמַּיִם, אֲשֶׁר הֵם פְּשׁוּטִים וְאֵין בָּהֶם צוּרָה, וְהֵם הָיוּ מְצִיאוּת הָעוֹלָם.
>
> (מהר"ל, גבורות השם, י"ד)

> From the beginning of the creation of the world, prior to the creation of the main form, which is the human being, waters existed, which were pure and formless, and the world consisted of them.
>
> (Maharal, *Gevurot HaShem*, 14)

Then God divides the waters.

וַיֹּאמֶר אֱלֹהִים יְהִי רָקִיעַ בְּתוֹךְ הַמָּיִם וִיהִי מַבְדִּיל בֵּין מַיִם לָמָיִם: וַיַּעַשׂ אֱלֹהִים אֶת־
הָרָקִיעַ וַיַּבְדֵּל בֵּין הַמַּיִם אֲשֶׁר מִתַּחַת לָרָקִיעַ וּבֵין הַמַּיִם אֲשֶׁר מֵעַל לָרָקִיעַ וַיְהִי־כֵן:
(בראשית א', ו'–ז')

And God said: “Let there be a firmament in the midst of the waters, and let it divide between waters and waters.” And God made the firmament, and He divided between the waters below the firmament and the waters above the firmament; and it was so.

(Genesis, 1:6–7)

The sages of the *Talmud* reflected on the distance between the upper waters and the lower waters:

תָּנוּ רַבָּנַן: מַעֲשֶׂה בְּרַבִּי יְהוֹשֻׁעַ בֶּן חֲנַנְיָה שֶׁהָיָה עוֹמֵד עַל גַּב מַעֲלָה בְּהַר הַבַּיִת, וְרָאָהוּ בֶּן זוֹמָא וְלֹא עָמַד מִלְּפָנָיו. אָמַר לוֹ: "מֵאַיִן וּלְאַיִן בֶּן זוֹמָא"? אָמַר לוֹ: "צוֹפֶה הָיִיתִי בֵּין מַיִם הָעֶלְיוֹנִים לְמַיִם הַתַּחְתּוֹנִים, וְאֵין בֵּין זֶה לָזֶה אֶלָּא שָׁלֹשׁ אֶצְבָּעוֹת בִּלְבַד, שֶׁנֶּאֱמַר: 'וְרוּחַ אֱלֹהִים מְרַחֶפֶת עַל פְּנֵי הַמָּיִם' – כְּיוֹנָה שֶׁמְּרַחֶפֶת עַל בָּנֶיהָ וְאֵינָהּ נוֹגַעַת". אָמַר לָהֶן רַבִּי יְהוֹשֻׁעַ לְתַלְמִידָיו: "עֲדַיִין בֶּן זוֹמָא מִבַּחוּץ. מִכְּדֵי 'וְרוּחַ אֱלֹהִים מְרַחֶפֶת עַל פְּנֵי הַמָּיִם' אֵימַת הָוֵי? בַּיּוֹם הָרִאשׁוֹן, הַבְדָּלָה – בְּיוֹם שֵׁנִי הוּא דַּהֲוַאי, דִּכְתִיב: "וִיהִי מַבְדִּיל בֵּין מַיִם לָמָיִם". וְכַמָּה? אָמַר רַב אַחָא בַּר יַעֲקֹב: "כִּמְלֹא נִימָא". וְרַבָּנַן אָמְרִי: "כִּי גוּדָא דְגַמְלָא". מָר זוּטְרָא, וְאִיתֵימָא רַב אַסִּי אָמַר: "כִּתְרֵי גְלִימֵי דִּפְרִיסִי אַהֲדָדֵי". וְאָמְרִי לַהּ: "כִּתְרֵי כָסֵי דִּסְחִיפִי אַהֲדָדֵי".

(תלמוד בבלי, חגיגה, ט"ו, א')

The Sages taught: There was once an incident regarding Rabbi Yehoshua ben Ḥananya, who was standing on a step on the Temple Mount, and Ben Zoma saw him and did not stand to honor him. Rabbi Yehoshua said to him: “From where you come and where are you going, Ben Zoma?” He said to him: “I was contemplating about the gap between the upper waters and the lower waters, as there is only the breadth of a mere three fingers between them, as it is stated: ‘And the spirit of God hovered over the face of the waters’ (Genesis, 1:2), like a dove hovering over its young without touching them." Rabbi Yehoshua said to his students [who had overheard this exchange]: "Ben Zoma is still outside [meaning: he has not yet achieved full realization of these matters]." Now, this verse: "And the spirit of God hovered over the face of the waters," when was it stated? On the first day [of creation], whereas the division of the waters occurred on the second day, as it is written: "and let it divide between waters and waters" (Genesis, 1:6). [How, then, could Ben Zoma derive a proof from the former verse?] [The *Gemara* asks:] "And how much, in fact, is the gap between them?" Rav Aḥa bar Jacob said: "Like the thickness of a hair". and the rabbis said: "Like the gap between the boards of a bridge." Mar Zutra, and some say it was Rav Asi, said: "Like two robes spread one over the other [with a slight gap in between]." And some said: "Like two cups placed one upon the other."

(*Babylonian Talmud*, "*Ḥagigah*," 15a)

The Kabbalist Todros HaLevi Abulafia analyzed this passage:

הַחֲכָמִים הָאֵלּוּ לֹא נֶחְלְקוּ בְּשִׁעוּר מַה בֵּין מַיִם עֶלְיוֹנִים לְמַיִם הַתַּחְתּוֹנִים, שֶׁהַכֹּל מוֹדִים שֶׁאֵין בֵּינֵיהֶם דָּבָר פָּנוּי. אֶלָּא שֶׁכָּל אֶחָד נִתְכַּוֵּן לְהַפְלִיג בְּדַקּוּת הַדְּבֵקוּת וְהָאַחְדוּת. שֶׁכֵּן הַדָּבָר בֶּאֱמֶת, שֶׁאֵין שָׁם מָקוֹם פָּנוּי, וְהַכֹּל דָּבֵק זֶה בָּזֶה, מִקְשָׁה אַחַת, כְּשַׁלְהֶבֶת קְשׁוּרָה בְּגַחֶלֶת. וּבֶן זוֹמָא, מִפְּנֵי שֶׁנִּפְגַּע, כְּלִשָּׁנָא בָּתְרָא, אוֹ שֶׁעֲדַיִן לֹא נִכְנַס, כְּלִשָּׁנָא קַמָּא, אָמַר כְּג' אֶצְבָּעוֹת. וְהָיָה מִתְכַּוֵּן בַּמַּיִם הַתַּחְתּוֹנִים לְמַעְלָה אַחַת שֶׁהוּא לְמַטָּה מִמָּה שֶׁאָמְרוּ שְׁאָר הַחֲכָמִים, עַל כֵּן אָמְרוּ עָלָיו: "עֲדַיִן בֶּן זוֹמָא מִבַּחוּץ", אוֹ "כְּבָר בֶּן זוֹמָא מִבַּחוּץ". וְהִנֵּה זֶה מְבֹאָר.

(המקובל ר' טודרוס בן יוסף הלוי אבולפיה, אוצר הכבוד, חגיגה, פרק אין דורשין)

These sages did not disagree regarding the distance between the upper water and the lower water, for it is agreed that there is no free space between them. Rather, each of them sought to elaborate on the subtlety of the bond and unity. For the truth of the matter is that there is no free space there and everything is bound to each other as one piece, just like the flame is bound to the coals. As for Ben Zoma, because he "was mistaken," as per the second opinion, or because he "had not yet entered," as per the first opinion, he said [that the separation was of] about three fingers. But his reference was to the lower water that is one level below that to which the other sages referred, and this is why they said about him, "Ben Zoma is still outside" or "Ben Zoma is already the outside." And here it is explained.

(The Kabbalist Todros ben Yosef HaLevi Abulafia, *Otzar HaKavod*, ("*Ḥagigah*," chapter "*Ein Dorshin*")

These passages allow us to conclude that the primordial waters existed before creation. This is explained in the *Talmud*:

וְאֵין מַיִם אֶלָּא תּוֹרָה, שֶׁנֶּאֱמַר: "הוֹי כָּל צָמֵא לְכוּ לַמַּיִם". (ישעיהו נ"ה, א')
(תלמוד בבלי, בבא־קמא, י"ז, א')

And the reference to water refers only to the study of Torah, as it is stated (Isaiah, 55:1): "Ho, all who are thirsty, go to the water".

(*Babylonian Talmud*, "*Bava Kamma*," 17a)

Moreover, in Hebrew culture, the Torah is compared to water because both are eternal. According to tradition, therefore, before creating the world, God looked at the Torah. Hence, seen from a divine perspective, the origin of the empirical universe is the Torah.

כָּךְ הָיָה הַקָּדוֹשׁ־בָּרוּךְ־הוּא מַבִּיט בַּתּוֹרָה וּבוֹרֵא אֶת הָעוֹלָם, וְהַתּוֹרָה אָמְרָה: "בְּרֵאשִׁית בָּרָא אֱלֹהִים" (בראשית א', א'). וְאֵין "רֵאשִׁית" אֶלָּא תּוֹרָה, הֵיאַךְ מָה דְּאַתְּ אָמַר: "ה' קָנָנִי רֵאשִׁית דַּרְכּוֹ" (משלי ח', כ"ב).
(בראשית רבה א', א')

Thus, the Lord gazed into the Torah and created the world. Similarly, the Torah says, "In the beginning (*bereshit*), the Lord created [the heavens and the earth]," and beginning (*reshit*) is the Torah, as it is said: "The Lord made me [the Torah] the beginning (*reshit*) of His way" (Proverbs, 8:22).

(*Bereshit Rabbah*, 1.1)

Now regarding "earth," Genesis goes on to say:

וְהָאָרֶץ הָיְתָה תֹהוּ וָבֹהוּ וְחֹשֶׁךְ עַל־פְּנֵי תְהוֹם וְרוּחַ אֱלֹהִים מְרַחֶפֶת עַל־פְּנֵי הַמָּיִם:
(בראשית א', ב')

The earth was unformed and void, with darkness over the surface of the deep and a wind from God was sweeping over the water.

(Genesis, 1:2)

"The earth being unformed and void…" *tohu vavohu* (תוהו ובוהו) translates as "chaos." Rabbi Berachiah commented:

אָמַר ר' בֶּרֶכְיָה: "מַאי דִכְתִיב: 'וְהָאָרֶץ הָיְתָה תֹהוּ וָבֹהוּ'?(בְּרֵאשִׁית א', ב') מַאי מַשְׁמַע 'הָיְתָה'? שֶׁכְּבָר 'הָיְתָה תֹהוּ', וּמַאי 'תֹהוּ'? דָּבָר הַמַּתְהֶא בְּנֵי אָדָם, וּמַאי 'בֹהוּ'? אֶלָּא תֹהוּ הָיְתָה וְחָזְרָה לְבֹהוּ, וּמַאי 'בֹהוּ'? דָּבָר שֶׁיֵּשׁ בּוֹ מַמָּשׁ דִּכְתִיב 'בֹהוּ' – בּוֹ הוּא".

(ספר הבהיר, ב')

Rabbi Berachiah said: "What is it that it is written 'The earth was *tohu* (unformed) and *bohu* (void),' (Genesis, 1:2)? What is the meaning of the word 'was' in this verse? This indicates that the *tohu* existed previously. And what is *tohu*? Something that confuses (*mat'heh*) people. And what is *bohu*? It was *tohu* and turned into *bohu*. And what is *bohu*? It is something that has substance. As it is written: *bohu*, that is, *bo hu* – 'it is in it'."

(*Sefer HaBahir*, 2)

The Hebrew term is composed of two words: *tohu* (תוהו), which can be translated as "wonder" or "nothingness," and *bohu* (בוהו), or "a state of consciousness of complete absence or objective emptiness." The earth existed or "was" (היתה) in its essential state, that is, a state of objective absence and of wonder. Thus, the origin of the empirical world lies in an empty consciousness.

We read: "This indicates that the *tohu* existed previously. And what is *tohu*? Something that confuses (*mat'heh*) people." The term *bohu* does not appear again in the Bible, because *tohu vavohu* is a state prior to objective reality. Wonder or perplexity is a state devoid of both mental and verbal activity.

Bohu refers to a conscious state that lacks defined objects. Another meaning of *bohu* is "in him, he," because it includes the words *bo* (in him) and *hu* (he). Therefore, we are talking about a state of consciousness of wonder that is free of thoughts, but which, at the same time, is not negative emptiness because it is consciousness.

This concept of wonder or complexity will also reappear centuries later in Greek philosophy, specifically in the works of Plato, who identified the origin of philosophy with "wonder." As Karl Jaspers later explained, although the beginning of written Western philosophy was 2500 years ago, the beginning is not the same as the origin. Its beginnings are historical, but the origin is a source of energy that continually radiates and drives us to philosophize. This is perhaps the same source that impels us to express, manifest, and create.

Water: the natural mirror

In ancient Greek culture and mythology, water played a dominant role. Sources of water were considered magical that had healing and prophetic properties, for example, the Castalia fountain from the Hellenistic period of Delphi. Likewise, the cistern of the temple of Asclepios was also used for healing in the ancient Greek city of Emporion, now the ruins of Ampurias. The main interest of the earliest philosophers was nature. Thales of Miletus, considered the father of classical Greek philosophy, argued that water was the essential principle of everything. He called this principle *arche* (from the Greek ἀρχή, source or origin). In this famous phrase, he refers to the mirror of nature: "The most difficult thing is to know ourselves; the easiest is to speak ill of others." It is easy to identify otherness while it is difficult to perceive, recognize, or observe sameness.

Greek mythology tells us the story of Narcissus. He stopped by a fountain of clear water and became fascinated by his own beautiful reflection. He believed he was looking at another person. Trying to hug his reflection, this person escaped him every time. From then on, Narcissus could not look at any other image but his own. Realizing that he had fallen in love with himself and was unable to separate himself from his own image, he threw himself into the water and drowned. There, a beautiful flower grew in his memory. In a later version of the story, Narcissus tried to seduce the beautiful young man in the reflection. He tried to kiss him and then noticed that it was only his own image reflected in the water. Stricken with grief, he killed himself with his sword and transformed into a beautiful flower called a Narcissus or daffodil. Later, Sigmund Freud used the term *narcissistic* for people who have an excessive sense of self-importance.

One of the main ideas that emerges from water as a mythological concept is that it is precisely the natural mirror that allows a subject to unfold and become his own object. For if nothing were to reflect my image, not only would there not be two, but neither would there be one. In turn, although it is my own reflection in the mirror, the reflection is its own object, that is to say, it is an image of my otherness.

כַּמַּיִם הַפָּנִים לַפָּנִים כֵּן לֵב הָאָדָם לָאָדָם׃

(משלי כ"ז, י"ט)

As water reflects a person's face, so a person's heart reflects the person.

(Proverbs, 27:19)

Likewise, the divine spirit moving on the surface of the original waters in Genesis, looking at himself in these waters, experiences the duality of the other. Referring to water as *maim* (מים), or "waters" in plural, we are talking about several mirrors. The reflection of the spirit, or consciousness, is a *tzelem*, or "image." When Genesis refers to "otherness," we must contemplate it as the unfolding of the "I" itself, and not as the idea of otherness of certain authors of Western philosophy, especially of the twentieth century, such as Emanuel Levinas or Jacques Derrida, among others.

In the Conversations (*Maqalat*) of Shams-I Tabrīzī, who was Rumi's master, we find this same mysterious mirror:

> They say that I am a saint. I said, "O.K., let it be so, but what happiness does it bring to me?" If I were to be proud of it, it would be very ugly; but Mevlana, if one looks at the attributes defined by the Koran and the sayings of the Prophet, is a saint. And I am the saint of the saint, the friend of the friend; therefore I am less easily shaken, more firm.
>
> If you bow a hundred times in front of a mirror, it never moves from its place. If any ugliness has appeared in the mirror, know that it is your own; do not despise the mirror. Hide the fault that you see on his face from him, because he is my friend. With the tongue of the heart, he says, "Surely, this is not possible."
>
> Now, O friend, you say, "Place the mirror into my hand so that I may look at it!" Yet I cannot find a pretext for this, nor can I deny your request; but I say in my own heart, "Let me find some pretext not to give you the mirror, because if I say that there is something wrong with your face, perhaps you will not accept it; and if you say that the mirror is defective, this will be worse for you." Yet love does not allow me to find a pretext. Now I say, "Let me give you the mirror, but if you see some fault on its face, do not blame the mirror, but something reflected onto the mirror. Know that it is your own image; find the fault in yourself! At least don't look into the mirror while you are near me. The only condition is that you do not find fault with the mirror. If you are unable to find the fault in yourself, at least find fault with me, as I am the owner of the mirror. Don't say the mirror is defective."
>
> "I accept the condition. I promise, I cannot wait any longer!"
>
> And yet his heart does not accept it.

"O Master," he said, "Again, let me find a pretext to avoid this situation." The point about the mirror is a subtle one. The love between us did not allow this. "Now let us remember the condition once again," he said, and he gave the following advice: "The condition and the agreement is this: every time you see your fault, you shall put the mirror down, you shall not destroy its jewel-like essence. Even if its essence cannot be broken, you shall not do this."

"God forbid," he said, "I would never do such a thing. I would never even think of it."

"Now let me have the mirror so that I can prove to you my good manners and earn your trust."

"But if you break it, its essence is this much, and it cost this much." And he brought witnesses and evidence for its cost.

But finally, after all these words, when he was given the mirror, he, himself, just ran away. The one who had offered the mirror was left speaking to himself, "If this mirror were so valuable, why did he leave it behind and run away"? As soon as he had beheld his own face, and it was ugly, he wanted to throw it to the ground and break it. But he couldn't do it. Because of that he said, "My lungs have filled with blood." He recalled his agreement, the bill of sale, the witnesses, and the money he would have to pay for the crime of destroying the mirror. "I wish there had been no conditions, no witnesses, no financial penalties. Then I could make my heart happy and show him what needs to be done." As he was saying all this, the mirror was rebuking him with the tongue of its own heart: "Do you see? What did I tell you? And what are you doing to me? You love yourself and find fault with the mirror. Because the one who loves his or her own ego respects only the ego, while the one who loves the mirror, gives up both ego and mirror." The mirror is the Truth, Itself. He thinks the mirror is someone other than himself. The mirror answers anyone who addresses It. Due to the inclination of the mirror, he also has an inclination toward the mirror. If he, on the other

hand, had broken the mirror, he would have broken me too. Hasn't it been said, "I am near to those whose hearts have been broken?" In short, it is impossible for the mirror to bow down and honor itself. It is like a touchstone or a balance; it always inclines toward the Truth.
If you try to tell it, "O Balance, this weight is not very much: You're not sitting right, show it correctly!" It only shows the Truth. You can try for two hundred years to trick it, you can prostrate yourself in front of it two hundred times, and it would be futile.

(Conversations [*Maqalat*] of Shams-I Tabrīzī)

When it comes to mirrors and reflections, it is natural to turn to Gauḍīya Vaishnavism. This comes up in verse 8.34 of the *Lalita-mādhava* of Rūpa Gosvāmī, which later appears in the *Śrī Caitanya-caritāmṛta* of Kṛṣṇadāsa Kavirāja Gosvāmī:

আপন-মাধুর্যে হরে আপনার মন ।
আপনা আপনি চাহে করিতে আলিঙ্গন ॥

āpana-mādhurye hare āpanāra mana
āpanā āpani cāhe karite āliṅgana

Lord Kṛṣṇa's sweetness is so attractive that it steals away his own mind. Thus, even he wants to embrace himself.

অপরিকলিতপূর্বঃ কশ্চমৎকারকারী
স্ফুরতি মম গরীয়ানেষ মাধুর্যপূরঃ ।
অয়মহমপি হন্ত প্রেক্ষ্য যং লুব্ধচেতাঃ
সরভসমুপভোক্তুং কাময়ে রাধিকেব ॥

aparikalita-pūrvaḥ kaś camatkāra-kārī
sphurati mama garīyān eṣa mādhurya-pūraḥ
ayam aham api hanta preksya yaṁ lubdha-cetāḥ
sa-rabhasam upabhoktuṁ kāmaye rādhikeva

> Upon seeing His own reflection in a bejeweled pillar of his Dvārakā palace, Kṛṣṇa desired to embrace it, saying, "Alas, I have never seen such a person before. Who is he? Just by seeing him I have become eager to embrace him, exactly like Śrīmatī Rādhārāṇī."
>
> (*Śrī Caitanya-caritāmṛta*, "*Madhya-līlā*," 8.148–149)

Kṛṣṇa, divinity itself, sees his reflection and feels an attraction to his own beauty. Śrī Caitanya Mahāprabhu himself recommended cleansing (*mārjanaṁ*) the mirror (*darpaṇa*) of the heart in the first verse of his *Śikṣāṣṭakam*:

चेतोदर्पणमार्जनं भवमहादावाग्निनिर्वापणं ।

ceto-darpaṇa-mārjanaṁ bhava-mahā-dāvāgni-nirvāpaṇaṁ

> Let there be all victory for the chanting of the holy name of Lord Kṛṣṇa (the *māhā-mantra*), which can cleanse the mirror of the heart and stop the miseries of the blazing fire of material existence.
>
> (*Śrī Caitanya-caritāmṛta*, "*Antya-līlā*," 20.12)

The mirror: *Aspaklaria*

The *Mishnah* of Tractate *Kelim* mentions a non-Hebrew word: *aspaklaria*. The commentators on this *Mishnah* explain that it is a mirror made of some transparent body such as crystal or glass.

אַסְפַּקְלַרְיָא, טְהוֹרָה. וְתַמְחוּי שֶׁעֲשָׂאוֹ אַסְפַּקְלַרְיָא, טָמֵא. וְאִם מִתְּחִלָּה עֲשָׂאוֹ לְשֵׁם אַסְפַּקְלַרְיָא, טָהוֹר.

(משנה כלים, ל', ב')

> A mirror is pure. A glass tray that was made into a mirror is impure, but if it was initially made to serve as a mirror – it is pure.
>
> (*Mishnah*, "*Kelim*," 30.2)

A mirror made solely for reflection is best. A shiny tray can reflect, but because it was made for other purposes, the reflection will be distorted. A shoe can be used to hammer something, but never as well as an actual hammer. Rabbi Samson ben Abraham of Sens, one of the early commentators on the *Mishnah* and a leading *Tosafist*, explains this:

> אַסְפַּקְלַרְיָא. כְּמוֹ אַסְפַּקְלַרְיָא הַמְאִירָה דְּפֶרֶק הַחוֹלֵץ (יבמות מ"ט, ב') וּבְפֶרֶק לוּלָב וַעֲרָבָה (סוכה מ"ה, ב'). וְהִיא מַרְאָה שֶׁל זְכוּכִית כְּעֵין מַרְאוֹת שֶׁלָּנוּ שֶׁהַנָּשִׁים מִסְתַּכְּלוֹת לִרְאוֹת בָּהֶן צוּרַת פְּנֵיהֶן.
> (פירוש הר"ש משאנץ על משנה, כלים ל', ב')

> *Aspaklaria*. Like the bright *aspaklaria* mentioned in chapter "*Haḥoletz*" (*Bavli*, "*Yevamot*," 49b), and in chapter "*Lulav and Arava*" (*Bavli*, "*Sukkah*," 45b), and it is a mirror made of glass like our mirrors that women look at, to see their face.
> (Rabbi Samson of Sens, commentary on *Mishnah*, "*Kelim*," 30.2)

Rabbi Ovadiah ben Avraham of Bertinoro, one of the most prominent commentators on the *Mishnah* explains in a similar way:

> אַסְפַּקְלַרְיָא. מַרְאָה שֶׁל זְכוּכִית שֶׁהָאִשָּׁה רוֹאָה בָּהּ אֶת פָּנֶיהָ.
> (רבי עובדיה מברטנורא על משנה, כלים, ל', ב')

> *Aspaklaria*: a glass mirror in which women see their face.
> (Rabbi Ovadiah of Bertinoro on *Mishnah*, "*Kelim*," 30:2)

The *Gemara*, in Tractate "*Yevamot*" mentions the *aspaklaria* in relation to the way different prophets saw the Divine:

> אָמַר רָבָא: מֵידָן דַּיְינֵיהּ וְקַטְלֵיהּ. אֲמַר לֵיהּ [מְנַשֶּׁה לִישַׁעְיָהוּ], "מֹשֶׁה רַבְּךְ אָמַר: 'כִּי לֹא יִרְאַנִי הָאָדָם וָחָי', וְאַתְּ אָמְרַתְּ: 'וָאֶרְאֶה אֶת ה' יוֹשֵׁב עַל כִּסֵּא רָם וְנִשָּׂא'"[...] מִכָּל מָקוֹם – קָשׁוּ קְרָאֵי אַהֲדָדֵי? 'וָאֶרְאֶה אֶת ה'" (ישעיהו ו', א')

כְּדְתַנְיָא: כָּל הַנְּבִיאִים נִסְתַּכְּלוּ בְּאַסְפַּקְלַרְיָא שֶׁאֵינָהּ מְאִירָה מֹשֶׁה רַבֵּנוּ נִסְתַּכֵּל בְּאַסְפַּקְלַרְיָא הַמְּאִירָה.

(תלמוד בבלי, יבמות, מ"ט, ב')

Rava said: "Manasseh judged Isaiah [as a false prophet for issuing statements contradicting the Torah] and only then killed him. He [Manasseh] said to him [Isaiah]: 'Moses your master said: For man cannot see Me [God] and live, (Exodus, 33:20),' and yet you said: 'I saw the Lord sitting upon a high and lofty throne,' (Isaiah, 6:1)". [...][The *Gemara* asks:] "Is it really that these verses contradict each other?" [The *Gemara* resolves the contradiction:] "I saw the Lord" is to be understood as it is taught in a *Baraita*: "All of the prophets observed their prophecies through a non-glowing *aspaklaria*. Moses our master, however, observed his prophecies through a glowing *aspaklaria*."

(*Babylonian Talmud*, "*Yevamot*." 49b)

Different masters gave different interpretations to the words "glowing *aspaklaria*." We will turn to the explanation of the Ramban, who mentioned it in his commentary on Genesis:

כָּל הַנְּבִיאִים רָאוּ מִתּוֹךְ אַסְפַּקְלַרְיָא שֶׁאֵינָהּ מְצֻחְצַחַת [...] וּמֹשֶׁה רָאָה מִתּוֹךְ אַסְפַּקְלַרְיָא מְצֻחְצַחַת.

(רמב"ן על בראשית י"ח, א')

All the prophets looked through an unpolished mirror [...] and Moses looked through a polished mirror.

(Ramban on Genesis, 18:1)

The above explanation of the Ramban is based on a *Midrash* found in *Vayikra Rabbah*:

מַה בֵּין מֹשֶׁה לְכָל הַנְּבִיאִים? [...] רַבָּנָן אָמְרִין: "כָּל הַנְּבִיאִים רָאוּ מִתּוֹךְ אִיסְפַּקְלַרְיָא מְלֻכְלֶכֶת, הֲדָא הוּא דִכְתִיב: 'וְאָנֹכִי חָזוֹן הִרְבֵּיתִי וּבְיַד הַנְּבִיאִים

אֲדַמֶּה' (הושע י"ב, י"א), וּמשֶׁה רָאָה מִתּוֹךְ אִיסְפַּקְלַרְיָא מְצֻחְצַחַת, הֲדָא הוּא דִכְתִיב: 'וּתְמֻנַת ה' יַבִּיט' (במדבר י"ב, ח')".

(ויקרא רבה, א', י"ד)

What is the difference between Moses and all the [other] prophets? [...] The Rabbis said: "All the prophets saw through a dirty mirror. That is what is written: 'I proliferated visions and granted imagery to the prophets' (Hosea, 12:11). Moses saw through a polished mirror. That is what is written: 'and he beholds the image of the Lord' (Numbers, 12:8)."

(*Vaikra Rabbah*, 1.14)

Rabbi Yisrael Lifschitz wrote in his famous commentary on the *Mishnah*, called *Tif'eret Israel*:

אַסְפַּקְלַרְיָא. [...] מְבֹאָר הַדָּבָר שֶׁהוּא לָשׁוֹן יְוָנִית. סְפֶּעקוּלָארִיא שֶׁפֵּרוּשׁוֹ זְכוּכִית אוֹ שְׁפִּיגֶעל. וְהַיְינוּ מָה שֶׁאָמְרוּ חז"ל (יבמות, מ"ט, ב') "כָּל הַנְּבִיאִים רָאוּ בְּאַסְפַּקְלַרְיָא שֶׁאֵינָהּ מְאִירָה. וְרַק מֹשֶׁה רַבֵּינוּ עָלָיו הַשָּׁלוֹם רָאָה בְּאַסְפַּקְלַרְיָא הַמְאִירָה". רָצָה לוֹמַר, עַצְמוּת אֱלֹהוּתוֹ יִתְבָּרַךְ אִי אֶפְשָׁר לְשׁוּם יְלוּד אִשָּׁה לִרְאוֹתוֹ. וַאֲפִלּוּ מֹשֶׁה רַבֵּינוּ עָלָיו הַשָּׁלוֹם בְּעַצְמוֹ. דְּגַם בּוֹ כְּתִיב (שמות ל"ג, כ"ג): "וּפָנַי לֹא יֵרָאוּ". אֶלָּא כָּל יִשְׂרָאֵל לֹא רָאוּ רַק כְּמוֹ הַבָּבוּאָה שֶׁל עַצְמוּתוֹ יִתְבָּרַךְ. אֶלָּא שֶׁמֹּשֶׁה רַבֵּנוּ עָלָיו הַשָּׁלוֹם רָאָה כִּבְיָכוֹל הַבָּבוּאָה הַהִיא בְּרוּרָה כָּל הָאֶפְשָׁר לִרְאוֹת. מַה שֶׁאֵין כֵּן שְׁאַר הַנְּבִיאִים.

(תפארת ישראל, בועז, על משנה כלים ל', ב')

Aspaklaria. [...] Clearly this is the Greek word *spekularia* which means glass or *spigel* (Mirror in German and Yiddish). This is what Our Rabbis said in the *Talmud* ("*Yevamot*," 49b): "All of the prophets observed their prophecies through a non-glowing *aspaklaria*. Moses our master, however, observed his prophecies through a glowing *aspaklaria*." Meaning, it is not possible to any human being to see the Lord as He really is. Even Our Master Moses himself. For even in regards to him it is written (That the Lord said): "But My face shall

> not be seen." Therefore, all the people of Israel saw only an approximation of the reflection of the reality of the Lord, Blessed be He. And Moses, Peace be on him, as opposed to the rest of the prophets, saw, as it were, that reflection (of the Lord) in the clearest way possible.
>
> (*Tif'eret Israel*, "*Bo'az*" on *Kelim*, 30:2)

This is what Kṛṣṇa refers to in the Bhagavad Gita:

> मनुष्याणां सहस्रेषु कश्चिद्यतति सिद्धये ।
> यततामपि सिद्धानां कश्चिन्मां वेत्ति तत्त्वतः ॥
>
> *manusyāṇāṁ sahasreṣu*
> *kaścid yatati siddhaye*
> *yatatām api siddhānāṁ*
> *kaścin māṁ vetti tattvataḥ*
>
> Out of many thousands among men, one may endeavor for perfection, and of those who have achieved perfection, hardly one knows me in truth.
>
> (Bhagavad Gita, 7.3)

Thought that thinks itself

The term *speculate* comes from the Latin *specularis*, which means "resembling or relating to a mirror" (*aspaklaria*). When we speculate, we are looking at ourselves in a mirror. We speculate based on our own reflection. Philosophy is the love of speculative thinking. When we philosophize, we are actually talking to ourselves. The word *reflect*, which comes from the Latin *reflexio*, includes the prefix *re*, or "backward," and *flectus*, or "bent." Reflecting, thinking, or reasoning is like contemplating our reflection in a mirror. When we stop to reflect on something, we are actually looking inward at ourselves, like in a mirror. If I am considering taking a new job, what I am really thinking about is how this might affect my own image or life, not the job itself. The same applies to speculating and philosophizing: it seems like we are talking about some object that is outside of us, but we're really looking inward and whatever is there is reflected outward.

Aristotle reflects on some qualities of God while leaving the traditional gods in a separate category. He says, "Therefore it must be of itself that the divine thought thinks (since it is the most excellent of things), and its thinking is a thinking on thinking." (*Metaphysics*, book XII, chapter IX). He believes that all God is and does is *nóesis noéseos* (νόησις νοήσεως), or a "thought that thinks itself." But it is not a mental activity; it thinks about itself as a thought that thinks itself. It is a fixed thought because it lacks the process in which potency becomes act. God is only actualization, or *energeia* (ἐνέργεια), and does not think anything that is antithetical to Himself. Even the idea of "thinking" is only an analogy Aristotle uses to talk about what cannot be defined, since it is not even a human thought. As Isaiah would say:

> כִּי לֹא מַחְשְׁבוֹתַי מַחְשְׁבוֹתֵיכֶם וְלֹא דַרְכֵיכֶם דְּרָכָי נְאֻם ה':
> כִּי־גָבְהוּ שָׁמַיִם מֵאָרֶץ כֵּן גָּבְהוּ דְרָכַי מִדַּרְכֵיכֶם וּמַחְשְׁבֹתַי מִמַּחְשְׁבֹתֵיכֶם:
> (ישעיהו, נ"ה, ח'–ט')

> For My thoughts are not your thoughts, neither are your ways My ways, said the Lord. For as the heavens are high above the earth, so are My ways high above your ways and My thoughts above your thoughts.
>
> (Isaiah, 55:8–9)

A thought thinking itself describes an immersed, self-absorbed, and meditative God. It is similar to Rabbi Shneur Zalman of Liadi's description from his famous book *Tanya*:

> אַךְ עִיקַּר הַדַּעַת, אֵינָהּ הַיְדִיעָה לְבַדָּהּ, שֶׁיֵּדְעוּ גְּדֻלַּת ה' מִפִּי סוֹפְרִים וּמִפִּי סְפָרִים, אֶלָּא הָעִקָּר הוּא, לְהַעֲמִיק דַּעְתּוֹ בִּגְדֻלַּת ה', וְלִתְקוֹעַ מַחֲשַׁבְתּוֹ בַּה' בְּחֹזֶק וְאֹמֶץ הַלֵּב וְהַמֹּחַ, עַד שֶׁתְּהֵא מַחֲשַׁבְתּוֹ מְקֻשֶּׁרֶת בַּה' בְּקֶשֶׁר אַמִּיץ וְחָזָק, כְּמוֹ שֶׁהִיא מְקֻשֶּׁרֶת בְּדָבָר גַּשְׁמִי שֶׁרוֹאֶה בְּעֵינֵי בָּשָׂר וּמַעֲמִיק בּוֹ מַחְשַׁבְתּוֹ, כַּנּוֹדָע, שֶׁדַּעַת הוּא לְשׁוֹן הִתְקַשְּׁרוּת, כְּמוֹ: "וְהָאָדָם יָדַע וְגוֹ'".
> (ספר התניא, חלק א', מ"ב)

> However, the essence of knowledge is not the knowing alone, that people should know the greatness of God from authors and books; but the essential thing is to immerse one's mind deeply into the greatness of God and fix one's thought on God with all the strength and vigor of the heart and mind, until his thought shall be bound to God with a strong and mighty bond, as it is bound to a material thing that he sees with his physical eyes and concentrates his thought on it. For it is known that *da'at* connotes union, as in the phrase "And Adam *yada* (knew) Eve..."
>
> (*Tanya*, part 1, 42)

Plotinus was a Greek philosopher who initiated a new phase in the Platonic tradition. In his theological structure, empirical diversity is a consequence of the emanations of an ultimate reality called "One." Such a reality is the only existing One, which Plotinus sometimes calls "God." Through emanations from the One, the *Nous* (intelligence) and the soul emerge. Plotinus, like Plato, thought that the soul's purpose was to return to the One through a wise life. The existence of every living entity depends entirely on the One, which is unlimited, eternal, and indescribable.

The foundation of Hegel's philosophy is the union of the non-dual infinite with the finite. Hegel addresses the relationship between nature and spirit, although this 'spirit' is somewhat obscure and paradoxical. It is not a transcendent God, nor is it disconnected from the universe. It can be perceived in divinized human action. The totality is not merely substance, but a subject whose object is the subject itself "thinking itself." It is reality thinking about itself. The non-dual Absolute becomes spirit through a process of self-knowledge through what is human. Nature is an essential condition, and since it gives objectivity to subjectivity, meaning to spirit, both belong to the Absolute.

Hegel addresses self-awareness in chapter 4 of his famous book *The Phenomenology of the Spirit*. Both Aristotle's "thought thinking itself" and Hegel's "self-consciousness" see an indivisible totality that expresses itself as a duality, dividing the Whole into two. The one becomes many. Subjectivity becomes subject and object.

The subject–object duality emerges from a thought that thinks itself, that is, a self-aware consciousness. If a thought thinks itself, it is both the thinker and what is thought. If consciousness is self-aware, it is the conscious subject, the object of consciousness, and consciousness itself. If an observation observes itself, it is the observer, the observed, as well as the observation itself. Hence God is both differentiated and undifferentiated at the same time. This is similar to the Bengali concept of Chaitanya: *acintya-bhedābheda-tattva*, or "inconceivably one and different simultaneously."

Hegel said that in the beginning, there was only pure non-dual thinking. However, a plenitude without a non-self to compare itself to will remain devoid of essence. In the beginning, thinking and being were in perfect harmony and union. Differentiation first appeared when this non-duality thought the only thing it can think, itself, but had no way of finding its essence, since there can be no essence without differentiation.

The term *essence* comes from the Latin *essentia*, which is a calque of the Greek term *ousia*. *Ousia* is a verbal noun from the verb *einai* meaning "to be." Likewise, *essentia* is derived from the Latin verb *ese*, which also means "to be." In philosophy, essence defines something, but if there is nothing to compare to, it cannot have an essence. Hence, it is differentiation that made it possible for non-dual thinking to have an essence, from which it would follow that differentiation is the origin of essence.

The philosophers Schelling and Fichte have also concluded that it is only possible to know the "I" through the "not-I." Through differentiation from the object, the subject discovers its identity. It is only possible to know ourselves by differentiating from the other. Through otherness, I manage to perceive myself as sameness. Through observation, I become aware of what is not me, in the purest form of Vedantic *neti-neti*, or "neither this, nor that." The first thing that human consciousness knows is not itself, but the surrounding objectual environment. Newborns first perceive their surroundings, what is not "I"; only then does the idea of "I" arise.

More specifically, and as the great psychoanalyst Jacques Lacan argued in one of his main books *The Mirror Stage as Formative of the I Function,* the mirror stage, or in French, *le stade du miroir,* is a phase in a child's development, between six and eighteen months of age, during which children identify with their image in the mirror. Lacan argues that it is precisely at this moment that the idea of the "I" as a psychic instance is born.

If we want to shed more light on a diversity emerging from the One without a second, we can turn to the ideas of Pythagoras. This Greek philosopher saw primordial reality as *pneuma* or unlimited Self, beyond which there is only emptiness or non-being. Within this *pneuma*, through eternal motion, a limited spherical cosmos was formed, but devoid of different parts. This cosmos is the monad, the principle of unity. Breathing deeply, the cosmos inhaled the void. From within, it disintegrated itself, giving rise to the numerical diversity of things. Each thing is equal to a number. Diversity is created from the dismemberment of the *pléroma*. It is the void that disintegrates the original compact sphere and determines objective nature, which makes movement possible and locates things in different places. Therefore, the phenomenal universe is *pléroma*, plenitude, consciousness, but apparently divided or unconscious. It is precisely this consciousness that Hegel calls "absolute knowledge," that is, where being and thinking are revealed as one and the same. For this reason, Hegel says that all that is rational is real and all that is real is being and thinking. Absolute knowledge is when being and thinking become one, that is, where both reintegrate and merge through yoga or religion.

The Absolute creates the universe by looking at itself in the primordial waters. That is why Rabbi Akiva advises us not to exclaim *maim, maim* ("waters, waters") when accessing the deepest secret of the *pardes*. In the depths of secrecy, instead of just seeing water, it is essential to look at your reflection and thus reverse the process to make it retroprogressive or involutionary.

We can compare consciousness, that knowing element of each experience, with a mirror. Consciousness witnesses all experience, reflecting what is in front of it. Everything reflected occurs in front of the mirror and not in it. Wisdom means being a mirror, completely disidentified from everything that is reflected. Experiences appear and disappear, come and go, but the mirror remains unchanged. The mirror does not retain past reflections but only shows what happens now. Enlightened beings live like mirrors, without yesterday and tomorrow. They are filled with the present experience, and when it disappears, no residue remains. This process of *teshuvah*, or "return," leads us to observe what we really are and awaken us to the reality of the recognition of consciousness.

ARTICLE 10

MITZVOT: SYMBOLS OF THE RETURN

The Hebrew term *mitzvah* is usually translated as "precept, ordinance, or commandment." The *mitzvot* are the 613 sacred precepts found in the Torah. The Sinaitic revelation is not a mere compendium of dogmas and theological conceptions. It is a guide that permeates every aspect of human life and prescribes a wide spectrum of norms and daily behaviors. These guidelines dictate the way everything in creation is dealt with: the choice and processing of food, effective time management, and different types of relationships such as commercial, academic, or social. Even trivial everyday acts, such as night's rest, are not excluded from these regulations, which have precise instructions on how to carry them out. This collection of regulations and practices is called *halachah* in Hebrew. Although it is often translated as "Jewish law," is better understood as "the path one walks, one's journey or road of life."

> וְעַתָּה יִשְׂרָאֵל מָה ה' אֱלֹהֶיךָ שֹׁאֵל מֵעִמָּךְ כִּי אִם־לְיִרְאָה אֶת־ה' אֱלֹהֶיךָ לָלֶכֶת בְּכָל־דְּרָכָיו וּלְאַהֲבָה אֹתוֹ וְלַעֲבֹד אֶת־ה' אֱלֹהֶיךָ בְּכָל־לְבָבְךָ וּבְכָל־נַפְשֶׁךָ:
> לִשְׁמֹר אֶת־מִצְוֹת ה' וְאֶת־חֻקֹּתָיו אֲשֶׁר אָנֹכִי מְצַוְּךָ הַיּוֹם לְטוֹב לָךְ:
> (דברים י', י"ב–י"ג)
>
> And now, O Israel, what does the Lord, your God, ask of you? but to fear the Lord, your God, to walk in all His ways, and to love Him, and to serve the Lord, your God, with all your heart and with all your soul; to keep the Lord's commandments, and His statutes, which I enjoin upon you today, for your good.
>
> (Deuteronomy, 10:12–13)

The verb root of *halachah* includes the Hebrew letters *hei*, *lamed*, *kaf*, which means "to walk or go."

> אִם בְּחֻקֹּתַי תֵּלֵכוּ וְאֶת מִצְוֹתַי תִּשְׁמְרוּ וַעֲשִׂיתֶם אֹתָם:
> (ויקרא כ"ו, ג')
>
> If you walk in My statutes and keep My commandments and do them.
>
> (Leviticus, 26:3)

Hence *halachah* is the method and means of navigating the ocean of existence in pursuit of reconnecting with the Divine. The Hebrew term *teshuvah*, on the other hand, is generally translated as "repentance," although it encompasses a wider range of meanings.

> וְשַׁבְתָּ עַד ה' אֱלֹהֶיךָ וְשָׁמַעְתָּ בְקֹלוֹ כְּכֹל אֲשֶׁר אָנֹכִי מְצַוְּךָ הַיּוֹם אַתָּה וּבָנֶיךָ בְּכָל לְבָבְךָ וּבְכָל נַפְשֶׁךָ:
>
> (דברים ל', ב')
>
> And you shall return unto the Lord, your God, and hearken to His voice according to all that I enjoin upon you this day, you and your children, with all your heart and with all your soul.
>
> (Deuteronomy, 30:2)

The Hebrew letters *taf*, *shin*, *vav*, and *bet* form the word *tashuv*, or "will return," which alongside *hei* ('ה), which symbolizes HaShem or the Lord, indicate a return to our divine origin. One who successfully walks the path of *teshuvah* is called *ba'al teshuvah* (בעל תשובה), or "master of return."

> אָמַר רַבִּי אֲבָהוּ: "מָקוֹם שֶׁבַּעֲלֵי תְשׁוּבָה עוֹמְדִין – צַדִּיקִים גְּמוּרִים אֵינָם עוֹמְדִין, שֶׁנֶּאֱמַר: 'שָׁלוֹם שָׁלוֹם לָרָחוֹק וְלַקָּרוֹב' (ישעיהו נ"ז, י"ט). 'לָרָחוֹק' בְּרֵישָׁא, וַהֲדַר 'לַקָּרוֹב'" .
>
> (תלמוד בבלי, מסכת ברכות, ל"ד, ב')
>
> Rabbi Abbahu said: "In the place where *ba'alei teshuvah* (masters of the return) stand, even the full-fledged righteous do not stand, as it is stated: 'Peace, peace upon the one who is far and the one who is near.' Peace is extended first to the one who is far [the master of the return], and only thereafter is peace extended to the one who is near [the full-fledged righteous]."
>
> (*Babylonian Talmud*, "*Berachot*," 34b)

When *teshuvah* is used in the sense of "repentance," it alludes to a process of recognizing shortcomings. Through observation and introspection, individuals identify their weaknesses and return to their primordial essence. *Lashuv* also means rotation, "to turn," which refers to the existence of a pivotal field or space of adaptability that enables the necessary modifications to return to our divine source. In this framework, *halachah* refers to a retroprogressive walk along the path on which moving forward returns us to our primordial source. It is a retroprogressive process because instead of distancing us from our roots, it brings us closer to them.

> עַל־יְדֵי הַתְּשׁוּבָה הַכֹּל שָׁב לָאֱלוֹהוּת, עַל־יְדֵי מְצִיאוּת כֹּחַ הַתְּשׁוּבָה, הַשּׁוֹרֵר בָּעוֹלָמִים כֻּלָּם, שָׁב הַכֹּל וּמִתְקַשֵּׁר בִּמְצִיאוּת הַשְּׁלֵמוּת הָאֱלֹהִית, וְעַל־יְדֵי הָרַעֲיוֹנוֹת שֶׁל הַתְּשׁוּבָה, דֵּעוֹתֶיהָ וְהַרְגָּשׁוֹתֶיהָ, כָּל הַמַּחֲשָׁבוֹת, הָרַעֲיוֹנוֹת וְהַדֵּעוֹת, הָרְצוֹנוֹת וְהָרְגָשׁוֹת, מִתְהַפְּכִים וְשָׁבִים לְהִקָּבַע בְּעֶצֶם תְּכוּנָתָם בְּתֹכֶן הַקֹּדֶשׁ הָאֱלֹהִי.
> (הראי"ה קוק, אורות התשובה, ד', ב')

> Through the *teshuvah* (repentance, return, going back), everything returns to divinity. Through the existence of the power of *teshuvah*, which reigns in all worlds, everything goes back and reconnects with the reality of divine Wholeness. And through the ideas of *teshuvah*, its thoughts and emotions, all thoughts, ideas, opinions, desires, and emotions are transformed and go back to be anchored in their essential quality in the essence of the Divine *kodesh* (holiness).
> (Rabbi Avraham Isaac HaCohen Kook, *Orot HaTeshuvah*, 4.2)

Halachah offers a manual, a detailed guide to direct each step. It is not merely a religious practice, rather, it is an expression of an inherent nature for maneuvering through life.

> וּכְמוֹ שֶׁבְּאִילָן הוֹצָאַת הָעֲנָפִים וְהַפֵּרוֹת שֶׁלּוֹ לְצָרֵף אֶת טִבְעוֹ כַּאֲשֶׁר רָאוּי, וְאִם לֹא הָיָה מוֹצִיא הָעֲנָפִים וְהֶעָלִין וְצוּרַת הַפְּרִי, בְּוַדַּאי הָיָה מְקֻלְקָל, כַּאֲשֶׁר רָאִינוּ שֶׁאֵינוֹ מוֹצִיא שְׁלֵמוּת שֶׁלּוֹ אֶל הַפֹּעַל. כָּךְ הוּא דָּבָר זֶה: אִם לֹא הָיָה מוֹצִיא פְּעֻלַּת הַמִּצְווֹת אֶל הַפֹּעַל, הָיָה נִשְׁאָר בְּכֹחַ מֻטְבָּע בְּחֹמֶר, וְדָבָר זֶה – קִלְקוּל אֵלָיו, כַּאֲשֶׁר נַפְשׁוֹ מִלְמַעְלָה וְהִיא מֻטְבַּע בַּגּוּף. אִם כֵּן הַנֶּפֶשׁ הִיא נִשְׁאַר בְּכֹחַ, וְצָרִיךְ שֶׁתֵּצֵא נַפְשׁוֹ אֶל הַפֹּעַל מִן הַחָמְרִית, וְאֵין זֶה רַק עַל יְדֵי מִצְווֹת אֱלוֹהִיּוֹת. כְּמוֹ שֶׁיֵּצֵא לַפֹּעַל זֶרַע הַנָּטוּעַ בָּאָרֶץ. וְדָבָר זֶה צֵרוּף נַפְשׁוֹ כַּאֲשֶׁר יוֹצֵאת לַפֹּעַל.

[...] לְפִיכָךְ מִצְוֹות הַתּוֹרָה אֲשֶׁר נִתַּן לָאָדָם כְּנֶגֶד הָאָדָם וְעוֹלָמוֹ אֲשֶׁר דָּר בּוֹ הָאָדָם וְהוּא מְקוֹמוֹ. וְהָאָדָם בְּעַצְמוֹ יֵשׁ לוֹ רמ"ח אֵבָרִים שֶׁהֵם שְׁלֵמוּת הָאָדָם, וּכְנֶגֶד זֶה נִתַּן לוֹ רמ"ח מִצְוֹות עֲשֵׂה שֶׁהֵם שְׁלֵמוּת הָאָדָם, וְיֵשׁ לוֹ מָקוֹם אֲשֶׁר הוּא בּוֹ, אֲשֶׁר הַמָּקוֹם מַגְבִּיל הַדָּבָר שֶׁלֹּא יֵצֵא. וּכְבָר אָמַרְנוּ כִּי מְקוֹמוֹ שֶׁל אָדָם הוּא תַּחַת הַחַמָּה, וְכָךְ נִתַּן לָאָדָם שס"ה מִצְוֹות לֹא תַעֲשֶׂה כְּנֶגֶד הַחַמָּה שֶׁיֵּשׁ לָהּ שס"ה יָמִים. וְאֵלּוּ שס"ה מִצְוֹות מַגְבִּילִין אֶת הָאָדָם שֶׁלֹּא יֵצֵא חוּצָה וְיַעֲבֹר אֵלּוּ שס"ה מִצְוֹות, וְהֵם מְקוֹמוֹ, כְּמוֹ שֶׁהַחַמָּה שס"ה יָמִים, שָׁנָה, הוּא מְקוֹמוֹ שֶׁל אָדָם.

(מהר"ל, תפארת ישראל, פרק ז')

In the same way that for the tree bringing forth branches and fruits is the refinement of its proper nature, to be as it should be, and if it would not be producing branches, leaves, and fruits, it would be certain that something is not functioning well, as clearly, it is not expressing its full potential. So it is here: If [a person] would not bring the *mitzvot* into action, that person would remain as potential, embedded into matter. And this is considered a malfunctioning, when the person's soul is elevated and yet embedded into the body, for in this way, the soul remains as a mere potential, while it should actualize itself out of matter. This [actualization] is possible only through divine *mitzvot*, in the same way, that the seed is actualizing its potential when planted in the ground. And when the soul is actualizing its potential, it is being refined....

Therefore, The Torah's *mitzvot*, which were given to human beings, correspond to human beings, and to the world, which is their place of residence. Humans have 248 limbs and corresponding to that, they received 248 positive *mitzvot* [actions to be performed], which are their perfection. This human being has also a place, and a place implies boundaries, which are not to be crossed. We already mentioned that the place of the human being is under the sun, and therefore, the human being received 365 negative *mitzvot* [actions to be avoided] corresponding to the sun that has 365 days [in its cycle]. These 365 *mitzvot* place boundaries on human beings not to go out and transgress them, and therefore they are their place, in the same way that the sun, the year of 365 days, is the place of human beings.

(Maharal, *Tif'eret Israel*, Chapter 7)

In the Bhagavad Gita, the legendary warrior Arjuna asked Kṛṣṇa:

अर्जुन उवाच -
स्थितप्रज्ञस्य का भाषा समाधिस्थस्य केशव ।
स्थितधीः किं प्रभाषेत किमासीत व्रजेत किम् ॥

arjuna uvāca -
sthita-prajñasya kā bhāṣā
samādhi-sthasya keśava
sthita-dhīḥ kiṁ prabhāṣeta
kim āsīta vrajeta kim

Arjuna said: "O Kṛṣṇa, what are the symptoms of one whose consciousness is thus merged in transcendence? How does he speak, and what is his language? How does he sit, and how does he walk?"

(Bhagavad Gita, 2.54)

The behavior of human beings reflects their level of consciousness. While ordinary beings perform mere activities, sages immerse themselves in actions. Action and activity may seem synonymous, but they are radically different.

אָמַר רַבָּה בַּר בַּר חָנָה אָמַר רַבִּי יוֹחָנָן: "מַאי דִּכְתִיב: כִּי יְשָׁרִים דַּרְכֵי ה׳ וְצַדִּקִים יֵלְכוּ בָם וּפֹשְׁעִים יִכָּשְׁלוּ בָם' (הושע י"ד, י') – מָשָׁל לִשְׁנֵי בְּנֵי אָדָם שֶׁצָּלוּ אֶת פִּסְחֵיהֶן, אֶחָד אֲכָלוֹ לְשׁוּם מִצְוָה, וְאֶחָד אֲכָלוֹ לְשׁוּם אֲכִילָה גַּסָּה. זֶה שֶׁאֲכָלוֹ לְשׁוּם מִצְוָה – 'וְצַדִּקִים יֵלְכוּ בָם'. וְזֶה שֶׁאֲכָלוֹ לְשׁוּם אֲכִילָה גַּסָּה – 'וּפֹשְׁעִים יִכָּשְׁלוּ בָם'".

(תלמוד בבלי, מסכת נזיר, כ"ג, א')

> Rabba bar bar Ḥanna said in the name of Rabbi Yoḥanan: "What is the meaning of: 'For the paths of the Lord are straight, and the righteous shall walk in them, while the transgressors stumble in them (Hosea, 14:10)?' How can the same path lead to such different outcomes? This is comparable to two people who roasted their *pesach* offerings [on Passover eve]. One ate it for the sake of *mitzvah*, and one ate it gluttonously. The one who ate it for the sake of *mitzvah*, has fulfilled the first part of the verse: 'And the righteous shall walk in them,' while the other, who ate it gluttonously, is described by the end of the verse: 'But transgressors stumble over them'."
>
> (*Babylonian Talmud*, "*Nazir*," 23a)

Action arises at the right moment, responding to the needs of the present, while activity is driven by past experiences. Action emerges as an organic response to the immediate demands of the environment and life itself. Activity, on the other hand, arises from our anxieties and uses circumstances as mere pretexts to express these anxieties. Hence instead of responding to an existential requirement of the present, activity is a stress release, an outlet for accumulated anxieties from the past that are expressed in the present. The origin of action is serenity. Activities reflect our agitated and altered mental state, revealing restlessness and nervousness. Action flourishes at the right moment; activity is characterized by its irrelevance and insignificance. Action springs from the now; activity is rooted in memory, in the past.

Activity's goal resides in the future and thus belongs intrinsically to a past projected onto tomorrow, that is, a memory looking at the next moment. The only framework that existence acknowledges is the here and now. By engaging in activity, we are absent from the present reality. Genuine *mitzvah* action does not project onto future expectations nor does it harbor underlying goals or ulterior motives.

> אָמַר רַב נַחְמָן בַּר יִצְחָק: גְּדוֹלָה עֲבֵרָה לִשְׁמָהּ מִמִּצְוָה שֶׁלֹּא לִשְׁמָהּ.
> (תלמוד בבלי, מסכת נזיר, כ"ג, ב')

Rav Naḥman bar Yitzḥak said: "A transgression (*aveirah*) committed for its own sake, is better than a *mitzvah* performed not for its own sake."

(*Babylonian Talmud*, "*Nazir*," 23b)

Action emerges as a spontaneous and direct response to an immediate situation in the present context without selfish motives. Through superficial occupations, or what Heidegger calls "busywork," we squander our energy and vitality. Only those who maintain serenity and relaxation preserve the essential energy needed to channel it into action. Mere activity arises from ignorance and lack of discernment, whereas action emerges from cognitive luminosity or complete clarity. Immersed in action, laborious tasks become delightful, effort becomes play, burdens become happiness, and heaviness becomes joy.

מִצְוֹות צְרִיכוֹת כַּוָּנָה.

(תלמוד בבלי, מסכת ברכות, י"ג, א')

Mitzvot require intent.

(*Babylonian Talmud*, "*Berachot*," 13a)

Activity is so automatic and unconscious that those doing it are not even aware of their own behavior. Examples of activities include nail biting, overeating, substance abuse, excessive talking, and smoking. By aligning ourselves with the framework dictated by the *halachah*, we make our existence sacred, so even the simplest and most trivial actions become transcendental. The intention is not to infuse a superficial touch of religiosity or spirituality into our days through sentimentality, but to enrich our lives with a solid and tangible sacred structure.

וְכִי מָה אִכְפַּת לוֹ לְהַקָּדוֹשׁ־בָּרוּךְ־הוּא, בֵּין שֶׁשּׁוֹחֵט אֶת הַבְּהֵמָה וְאוֹכֵל אוֹ אִם נוֹחֵר וְאוֹכֵל? כְּלוּם אַתָּה מוֹעִילוֹ אוֹ כְּלוּם אַתָּה מַזִּיקוֹ? אוֹ מָה אִכְפַּת לוֹ, בֵּין אוֹכֵל טְהוֹרוֹת לְאוֹכֵל נְבֵלוֹת? אָמַר שְׁלֹמֹה, 'אִם חָכַמְתָּ – חָכַמְתָּ לָּךְ' וגו' (משלי ט', י"ב). הָא לֹא נִתְּנוּ הַמִּצְוֹת אֶלָּא לְצָרֵף בָּהֶן אֶת הַבְּרִיּוֹת וְיִשְׂרָאֵל, שֶׁנֶּאֱמַר:

'אִמְרַת־ה' צְרוּפָה' (תהילים י"ח, ל"א). לָמָּה? שֶׁיְּהֵא מָגֵן עָלֶיךָ, שֶׁנֶּאֱמַר: 'מָגֵן הוּא לְכָל הַחוֹסִים בּוֹ' (תהילים י"ח, ל"א).

(מדרש תנחומא, פרשת שמיני, סימן ח')

And what does the Holy One, Blessed be He, care whether one ritually slaughters cattle and eats [the meat] or slaughters it by stabbing and eats it? Will such thing benefit Him [the Holy One, blessed be He,] or will it harm Him? Or what does He care whether one eats carcasses or eats ritually slaughtered animals? Solomon said [about this] (in Proverbs, 9:12), "If you gained wisdom, you gained wisdom for yourself". Thus, the commandments were given only to refine humans and the people of Israel through them, as stated (Psalms, 18:31), "the word of the Lord is refined." Why? So that He might be a shield over you, [as stated] (ibid., cont.), "He is a shield for all who take refuge in Him."

(*Midrash Tanḥuma*, "*Shemini*," 8)

In this sense, the Hebrew revelation offers a profound and enduring way to connect and reintegrate the human and the Divine.

"הָאֵל תָּמִים דַּרְכּוֹ אִמְרַת־ה' צְרוּפָה מָגֵן הוּא לְכֹל הַחֹסִים בּוֹ" (תהילים י"ח, ל"א). אִם דְּרָכָיו תְּמִימִים, הוּא – עַל אַחַת כַּמָּה וְכַמָּה. רַב אָמַר: "לֹא נִתְּנוּ הַמִּצְווֹת אֶלָּא לְצָרֵף בָּהֶן אֶת הַבְּרִיּוֹת. וְכִי מָה אִכְפַּת לֵיהּ לְהַקָּדוֹשׁ בָּרוּךְ הוּא לְמִי שֶׁשּׁוֹחֵט מִן הַצַּוָּאר אוֹ מִי שֶׁשּׁוֹחֵט מִן הָעֹרֶף? הֱוֵי – לֹא נִתְּנוּ הַמִּצְווֹת אֶלָּא לְצָרֵף בָּהֶם אֶת הַבְּרִיּוֹת".

(בראשית רבה, מ"ד, א')

"As for God, His way is perfect; the word of the Lord is refined, He is a shield for all who take refuge in Him." (Psalms 18:31) If His way is perfect, how much more is He Himself! Rav said: "The *mitzvot* were given so that man might be refined by them. Do you really think that The Holy One, Blessed be He, cares if an animal is slaughtered by the front or by the back of the neck? Therefore, *mitzvot* were given only to refine humans."

(*Bereshit Rabbah*, 44.1)

Mitzvot are not merely tools, instruments, or mechanisms that facilitate our relationship with the transcendent; they are the very process of aligning with divinity. The term *mitzvah*, translated as "precept," is intimately related to the word *tzavta* (צוותא), which means "connection or bond." Thus, each biblical precept is as a symbol that merges the individual and the Divine.

וְגַם אֶת־שַׁבְּתוֹתַי נָתַתִּי לָהֶם לִהְיוֹת לְאוֹת בֵּינִי וּבֵינֵיהֶם לָדַעַת כִּי אֲנִי ה' מְקַדְּשָׁם:
(יחזקאל כ', י"ב)

Moreover, I gave them My sabbaths to serve as a symbol between Me and them, that they might know that it is I, the Lord, who sanctifies them.

(Ezekiel, 20:12)

In numerous verses and passages of the Torah, *mitzvot* are referred to as symbols.

וּקְשַׁרְתָּם לְאוֹת עַל־יָדֶךָ וְהָיוּ לְטֹטָפֹת בֵּין עֵינֶיךָ:
(דברים ו', ח')

Bind them [the *tefillin*] as a symbol on your hand and let them serve as *totafot* (frontlets) on your forehead.

(Deuteronomy, 6:8)

The enlightened sages of antiquity point out a parallel between *mitzvot* and the physical structure of the human being.

דָּרַשׁ רַבִּי שִׂמְלַאי: "שֵׁשׁ מֵאוֹת וּשְׁלֹשׁ עֶשְׂרֵה מִצְווֹת נֶאֶמְרוּ לוֹ לְמֹשֶׁה, שְׁלֹשׁ מֵאוֹת וְשִׁשִּׁים וְחָמֵשׁ לָאוִין כְּמִנְיַן יְמוֹת הַחַמָּה, וּמָאתַיִם וְאַרְבָּעִים וּשְׁמוֹנָה עֲשֵׂה כְּנֶגֶד אֵיבָרָיו שֶׁל אָדָם".
(תלמוד בבלי, מסכת מכות, כ"ג, ב')

Rabbi Simlai expounded: "There were 613 *mitzvot* stated to Moses in the Torah, consisting of 365 prohibitions corresponding to the number of days in the solar year,

> and 248 positive *mitzvot* corresponding to the number of a person's limbs."
>
> (*Babylonian Talmud*, "*Makkot*," 23b)

> בְּגִין דְּאִית בְּבַר־נָשׁ רמ"ח שַׁיְפִין, לָקֳבֵל רמ"ח פִּקּוּדִין דְּאוֹרַיְיתָא דְּאִינּוּן לְמֶעְבַּד אִתְיְהִיבוּ, וְלָקֳבֵל רמ"ח מַלְאָכִין דְּאִתְלַבְּשַׁת בְּהוֹן שְׁכִינְתָּא וּשְׁמָא דִּלְהוֹן כִּשְׁמָא דְמָארֵיהוֹן, וְאִית בְּבַר־נָשׁ שס"ה גִידִין, וְלָקֳבְלֵיהוֹן שס"ה פִּקּוּדִין דְּלָאו אִינּוּן אִתְיְהִיבוּ לְמֶעְבַּד, וְלָקֳבֵל שס"ה יוֹמֵי שַׁתָּא.
>
> (ספר הזוהר, פרשת וישלח, ז')

> Because there are 248 limbs in a person, corresponding to the 248 *mitzvot* of the Torah that were given to be done (positive *mitzvot*) and to the 248 angels that the *Shechinaḥ* (God's presence) is enclothed within them and their name is like that of their Lord. And there are 365 sinews in a person – they correspond to 365 *mitzvot* that were given to not do (negative *mitzvot*); they also correspond to the 365 days of the year.
>
> (*Zohar*, "*Vayishlaḥ*," 7)

This passage says that the 248 positive precepts correspond to the 248 limbs of the human body. Likewise, the 365 prohibitive precepts are equated with the 365 ligaments in human anatomy.

The objective world is constantly present as what is perceived. Senses such as sight, touch, and smell allow for direct sensory experience. Through our actions, we directly connect to this platform. While we can experience tangible reality through actions such as walking, dancing, painting, eating, writing, and speaking, it is impossible to process or understand it through thought alone. Unlike actions, thought lacks direct and immediate access to reality. When we engage in mental conceptualization, our access to reality is obstructed by abstract ideas. Thought entails a certain alienation because we interact with reality conceptually. The act of thinking does not establish a direct link to life nor is it sufficient to fully process it. On the contrary, by its inherent nature, it instills a demarcation, a separation, a distance. In this same sense, Hans-Georg Gadamer maintains that Truth implies a belonging and an approximation to the Self, while methods impose distance and separation. Therefore, if we want to access authentic and genuine Truth, we must dispense with methods.

By subjecting reality to analysis or deduction, we inevitably distance ourselves from it. When we reflect "on" it or reason "about" it, we erect an unbridgeable gap. "On" or "about" suggests a mediated link or an indirect relationship; they denote that we do not experience or interact with things in the present. Such prepositions prevent a genuine connection with trees, flowers, and so on.

Discourse "on" or "about" reality dissociates us, separates us, and intrinsically excludes us from it. Intellectuals, no matter how eminent, distance themselves from action because thought is inherently indirect and mediated, while action can only be direct and immediate. In fact, thinking renders acting impracticable and unattainable. Unlike thinkers, genuine artists achieve a direct and unconceptualized relationship with the world.

In the world we inhabit, many people use their cognitive abilities to speculate and ruminate but lack the energy to make their ideas concrete and accomplish something tangible with their lives. Conversely, many unreflective individuals possess considerable vigor and impetus to do things. Though they do not pause to think and evaluate, their desires drive them to do a lot. Unfortunately, many of these unthoughtful but strong-willed beings have generated considerable conflict and devastation, causing painful disasters and havoc throughout history. Only genuine inquiry into reality will interrupt the vicious cycle of mental chatter. When conceptual activity ceases, consciousness awakens. Then, the cognitive faculty metamorphoses and manifests itself as greater mental clarity. The energy that fuels thought is reformulated and becomes lucid.

The purification process begins when mental activity ceases; however, this does not mean suspending consciousness. On the contrary, consciousness persists, gaining greater clarity and lucidity leading us to action. Moving closer to reality, to the essence of things as they are, requires a balanced combination of action and consciousness.

וַיִּקַּח סֵפֶר הַבְּרִית וַיִּקְרָא בְּאָזְנֵי הָעָם וַיֹּאמְרוּ כֹּל אֲשֶׁר־דִּבֶּר ה' נַעֲשֶׂה וְנִשְׁמָע:
(שמות כ"ה, ז')

Then he took the book of the covenant and read it in the hearing of the people. And they said: "All that the Lord has spoken we will do (*na'ase*) and hear (*nishma*)."

(Exodus, 24:7)

In Hebrew, *shema* means "hear or listen," but can also mean "pay attention," which is the active aspect of consciousness, like when a teacher asks students to focus their awareness. *Shema* is more than a request to listen, since it urges focus. The main mantra of the Hebrew tradition, "*shema* Israel," is an intimate exhortation to the people of Israel to not only listen but pay attention. When we say *shema*, we are asking people to both listen and be aware, so it is clear that the word *shema* evokes awareness.

Based on this reading, the expression *na'ase venishma* (נעשה ונשמע), or "we will do and we will listen," closely related to *mitzvot*, refers to action and consciousness. Hence a deeper contemplation of *na'ase venishma* reveals that it is a dual call to action and conscious observation. It not only represents the dimension of acting but also of remaining attentive during the action, in what is termed "meditative action."

However, there are those who misunderstand this notion of remaining attentive during action, associating it with the need for isolation. This is evident in Patañjali's well-known statement in his *Yoga Sūtra*:

योगश्चित्तवृत्तिनिरोधः।

yogaś citta-vṛtti-nirodhaḥ

Yoga is the cessation of mental activity.

(*Yoga Sūtra*, 1.2)

If these wise words are understood incorrectly, they can lead us to conclude that the key to appeasing the mind lies in isolation from society. It is a grave mistake to believe that abstaining from worldly activities guarantees true peace. Cloistering oneself in monasteries while retaining the same mental turmoil can only lead to a disconnection from reality. As Kant would say, authentic faith belongs to practical reason, not theoretical reason.

> וְעַתָּה יִשְׂרָאֵל שְׁמַע אֶל הַחֻקִּים וְאֶל הַמִּשְׁפָּטִים אֲשֶׁר אָנֹכִי מְלַמֵּד אֶתְכֶם לַעֲשׂוֹת לְמַעַן תִּחְיוּ וּבָאתֶם וִירִשְׁתֶּם אֶת הָאָרֶץ אֲשֶׁר ה' אֱלֹהֵי אֲבֹתֵיכֶם נֹתֵן לָכֶם: לֹא תֹסִפוּ עַל הַדָּבָר אֲשֶׁר אָנֹכִי מְצַוֶּה אֶתְכֶם וְלֹא תִגְרְעוּ מִמֶּנּוּ לִשְׁמֹר אֶת מִצְוֹת ה' אֱלֹהֵיכֶם אֲשֶׁר אָנֹכִי מְצַוֶּה אֶתְכֶם: [...] וְאַתֶּם הַדְּבֵקִים בַּה' אֱלֹהֵיכֶם חַיִּים כֻּלְּכֶם הַיּוֹם:
>
> (דברים ד', א', ב', ד')
>
> And now, O Israel, *shema* (hearken) unto the statutes and unto the ordinances that I am teaching you to perform, so that you may live and come and inherit the land which the Lord, the God of your fathers, is giving you. You shall not add anything to what I command you or take anything away from it, but keep the *mitzvot* of the Lord, your God, that I enjoin upon you. [...] But you, who held fast to the Lord, your God, are all alive today.
>
> (Deuteronomy, 4:1,2,4)

The millennia-old Hebrew revelation does not require renouncing action to access reality. On the contrary, it affirms that action is a path to Truth. Halachic actions, performed with full awareness, act as a bridge between what is apparent and what is real, leading us from the relative to the absolute. The biblical precepts have a symbolic character, since they reintegrate us with our original source. The term *symbol* derives from the Greek *sýmbolon* (σύμβολον), which in turn is composed of *sýn* (σύν), meaning "together," and *bállō* (βάλλω), which is "to throw or to cast." Originally, the verb *symbállo* meant "to gather, to bring together, or to unite." In many spiritual traditions, symbols are considered mediators between visible and invisible worlds. Thus, the symbolism in *mitzvot* reconnects us with our absolute dimension, elevating us to meanings and experiences that transcend what is perceptible. Precepts allow for the divinization of the human through conscious action. *Mitzvot* allow humanity to enter divinity and divinity to enter humanity.

Na'ase venishma (נעשה ונשמע) meaning "we will do consciously or attentively," does not emerge from a limited mind, but is an expression of pure consciousness. It means surrendering to action without concepts intervening, as the mind disconnects us from praxis, from what is factual or real, and plunges us into the theoretical realm of ideas, opinions, and conclusions. According to the Sinaitic revelation, the sacred transcends mere conceptualization by manifesting in the many facets of our daily lives. God is present in the water we drink, the food we eat, the music we listen to, the clothes we wear, and in our interactions with family and friends.

Those who immerse themselves exclusively in reflections and speculations become merely thinking entities, confined to a cosmos of theories, postulates, notions, abstractions, inferences, deductions, concepts, and conclusions. However, they should not inhibit reasoning because their intellectual acuity may atrophy. It is best to not evade action but to endow it with greater lucidity and presence, infusing it with more consciousness and clarity, thus merging action and consciousness.

Na'ase venishma encapsulates the essence of meditation. It hints at the transition from the mind to lucidity, the withdrawal of thought, and the revival of consciousness. The secret lies in immersing oneself in action, allowing the mind to flow freely like a river taking its natural course without resistance. By transcending the mind, the potency of thought is redirected toward its origin: pure, genuine consciousness. As mental activity dims and thoughts fade away, we evolve toward a lucid and deeply conscious existence. In this state of mental stillness, no thoughts prevail, regardless of their nature or attributes. Although the mind may fluctuate, knowingness persists, constant and unaffected. It is still possible to perform everyday actions such as walking, talking, smelling, working, eating, or sleeping while remaining fully aware.

The inherent transparency of consciousness transcends and far surpasses mental capacities. Even when ideational, notional, and conceptual entities emerge in the cognitive panorama, attentive observation remains independent. Eventually, mental activity is eclipsed by the radiating lumen of consciousness. This luminescence dispels darkness as mental silhouettes gradually fade and disappear, yielding to the preeminence of ascending consciousness.

Gradually, we enter a process of metamorphosis, transmuting from thinking beings to conscious beings. Upon realizing the crystalline consciousness, our mental constructs vanish like shadows in radiant light. The vigorous lucidity of observation sharpens perception and intensifies acoustic and olfactory sensitivity. Although the actions themselves remain unchanged, they undoubtedly acquire a uniquely renewed attribute. These manifested actions are elevated to the realm of the sacred, aligning with the inherent transcendence of *mitzvot*.

Ordinary people live fragmented lives, with a separation between their words and actions, between their steps and intentions. In contrast, every word spoken by a being fully present in each syllable holds a unique essence, an innate singularity. In the daily behavior of most people, we observe a clear automatism, as they act out of mere habit, disconnected from their activities. However, when someone who is just a shadow of existence acts, every glance, word, gesture, and movement is a full extension of their presence. The average human lives oblivious of their own visual perception, but when someone who is no one looks at us, we feel pierced, as if the entire cosmos is focusing its attention on us through those penetrating eyes.

At the core of symbolic beings there is no fragmentation, dissociation, division, disjunction, or fracture but an absolute integrative cohesion that eliminates any distinction between themselves and their actions. Being the Self, they become the pure manifestation of their actions. The *mitzvot* aspire, in essence, to unite action and consciousness into a coherent and indivisible whole.

The word *experience* originates from the Latin term composed of three parts: the prefix *ex*, meaning "separation"; the verbal root *peri*, which can be translated as "to try"; and the suffix *entia*, which means *qualitas agentis*, or "quality of an agent." An experience consists of witnessing, perceiving, feeling, or knowing something. Accordingly, we can affirm that the term *experience* refers to events, interactions, or perceptions involving a subject and an object—that is, the experiencing subject and the experienced object. Drinking is an experience that involves the interaction between a subject—the one who drinks—and an object, such as a glass of water.

We also have mental and emotional experiences. The entirety of human diegesis can be conceived as a continuous sequence of experiences. At first glance, each experience implies an interaction involving the subject, object, and knowingness. Knowingness apprehends experiences but, paradoxically, is not an experience itself. Objective reality, with its inherent duality and relativity, is an illusory construct with only four components: thoughts, emotions, sensations, and perceptions. Only knowingness, or pure consciousness, is truly real and ontologically immutable, thus identified with the Absolute or divinity. Each *mitzvah* is a symbol that melds the human and the Divine, uniting the relative and the Absolute, the apparent and the real. The purpose of these precepts is to build a home for consciousness in the tangible dimension, within the realm of experiences. *Mitzvot* allow us to create a space for consciousness in the phenomenological sphere, within the orbit of everyday human experiences.

"בָּאתִי לְגַנִּי אֲחוֹתִי כַלָּה" (שיר־השירים ה', א'). אָמַר רַבִּי שְׁמוּאֵל בַּר נַחְמָן: "בְּשָׁעָה שֶׁבָּרָא הַקָּדוֹשׁ־בָּרוּךְ־הוּא אֶת הָעוֹלָם, נִתְאַוָּה שֶׁיְּהֵא לוֹ דִּירָה בַּתַּחְתּוֹנִים כְּמוֹ שֶׁיֵּשׁ בָּעֶלְיוֹנִים. בָּרָא אֶת הָאָדָם וְצִוָּה אוֹתוֹ וְאָמַר לוֹ: 'מִכֹּל עֵץ הַגָּן אָכֹל תֹּאכֵל, וּמֵעֵץ הַדַּעַת טוֹב וָרָע לֹא תֹאכַל מִמֶּנּוּ' (בראשית ב', ט"ז–י"ז) וְעָבַר עַל צִוּוּיוֹ. אָמַר לֵיהּ הַקָּדוֹשׁ־בָּרוּךְ־הוּא, 'כָּךְ הָיִיתִי מִתְאַוֶּה שֶׁיְּהֵא לִי דִּירָה בַּתַּחְתּוֹנִים כְּמוֹ שֶׁיֵּשׁ לִי בָּעֶלְיוֹנִים, וְדָבָר אֶחָד צִוִּיתִי אוֹתְךָ וְלֹא שָׁמַרְתָּ אוֹתוֹ'. מִיַּד סִלֵּק הַקָּדוֹשׁ בָּרוּךְ הוּא שְׁכִינָתוֹ לָרָקִיעַ הָרִאשׁוֹן. מִנַּיִן? דִּכְתִיב (שם ג', ח'): 'וַיִּשְׁמְעוּ אֶת קוֹל ה' אֱלֹקִים מִתְהַלֵּךְ בַּגָּן'. כֵּיוָן שֶׁעָבְרוּ עַל הַצִּוּוּי, סִלֵּק שְׁכִינָתוֹ לָרָקִיעַ הָרִאשׁוֹן. עָמַד קַיִן וְהָרַג לְהֶבֶל, מִיַּד סִלֵּק שְׁכִינָתוֹ לְרָקִיעַ שֵׁנִי כו'. אָמַר הַקָּדוֹשׁ־בָּרוּךְ־הוּא: 'שִׁבְעָה רְקִיעִים בָּרָאתִי, וְעַד עַכְשָׁו יֵשׁ רְשָׁעִים לַעֲמֹד בָּהּ'. מֶה עָשָׂה? קִפֵּל אֶת כָּל הַדּוֹרוֹת הָרִאשׁוֹנִים הָרְשָׁעִים וְהֶעֱמִיד אַבְרָהָם. כֵּיוָן שֶׁהֶעֱמִיד אַבְרָהָם, סִגֵּל מַעֲשִׂים טוֹבִים, יָרַד הַקָּדוֹשׁ־בָּרוּךְ־הוּא מִן רָקִיעַ שְׁבִיעִי לְשִׁשִּׁי. עָמַד יִצְחָק וּפָשַׁט צַוָּארוֹ עַל גַּבֵּי הַמִּזְבֵּחַ, יָרַד מִשִּׁשִּׁי לַחֲמִישִׁי כו'. עָמַד מֹשֶׁה וְהוֹרִידָהּ לָאָרֶץ, שֶׁנֶּאֱמַר: 'וַיֵּרֶד ה' עַל הַר סִינַי' (שמות י"ט, כ') וּכְתִיב (שיר־השירים ה', א'): 'בָּאתִי לְגַנִּי אֲחוֹתִי כַּלָּה'. אֵימָתַי? כְּשֶׁהוּקַם הַמִּשְׁכָּן".

(מדרש תנחומא, פרשת נשא, ט"ז)

"I have come into my garden, my sister, O bride" (Song of songs, 5:1). Rabbi Samuel bar Naḥman said: "When the Holy One, Blessed be He, created the world, He longed to have an abode in the lower worlds just as He has in the higher worlds. [For this end] He created Adam, commanded him and said to him (Genesis, 2:16–17): 'You may freely eat of any tree in the garden; But as for the tree of the knowledge of good and evil, you may not eat of it.' Then he [Adam] transgressed against His commandment. The Holy One, Blessed be He, said this to him: 'This is what I longed for, that just as I have a dwelling on high, I would likewise have one below. Now when I have given you one command, you have not kept it. Immediately the Holy One, Blessed be He, removed His divine Presence [up] to the first firmament. Where is it shown? Where it is stated (Genesis, 3:8): 'Then they heard the voice of the Lord God moving about in the garden.' Since they transgressed the commandment, He removed His divine presence to the first firmament [and therefore they could only **hear** God]. [When] Cain arose and killed Abel, He immediately removed His divine Presence [from the first firmament] to the second firmament etc. The Holy One, Blessed be He, said: 'I created seven firmaments, and up to now there are wicked ones [still] arising upon [the world].' What did He do? He folded away all the generations of the wicked and raised up Abraham. When Abraham arose and performed good works, the Holy One, Blessed be He, immediately descended from the seventh firmament to the sixth. [Then] Isaac arose and stretched out his neck upon the altar, He descended from the sixth firmament to the fifth, etc. [Then] Moses arose, he brought it [the divine Presence] down to earth, as stated (Exodus, 19:20): 'And the Lord descended onto Mount Sinai.' And it is written (Song of songs, 5:1): "I have come into my garden, my sister, O bride." When? When the Tabernacle was set up.

(*Midrash Tanḥuma*, "*Naso*," 16)

Each *mitzvah* reveals the knowingness that has been subsumed in the background of everyday life, bringing it to a central position in the theater of our experiences. Without being an experience itself, consciousness becomes visible, unveiling itself as the foundation of all experiences. In *Pirkei Avot*, we read about the reward for fulfilling *mitzvot*:

> בֶּן עַזַּאי אוֹמֵר, הֱוֵי רָץ לְמִצְוָה קַלָּה כְבַחֲמוּרָה, וּבוֹרֵחַ מִן הָעֲבֵרָה. שֶׁמִּצְוָה גוֹרֶרֶת מִצְוָה, וַעֲבֵרָה גוֹרֶרֶת עֲבֵרָה. שֶׁשְּׂכַר מִצְוָה, מִצְוָה. וּשְׂכַר עֲבֵרָה, עֲבֵרָה.
> (פרקי אבות ד', ב')

> Ben Azzai says: "Run to perform a 'light' (minor) *mitzvah* as to a 'heavy' (major) one and flee from an *averah* (transgression); for a *mitzvah* begets a *mitzvah*, and an *averah* begets an *averah*; For the reward of a *mitzvah* is a *mitzvah* and the reward of an *averah* is an *averah*."
>
> (*Pirkei Avot*, 4.2)

For someone who has strayed from their authenticity, *mitzvot* seem to be forced and imposed activities. However, they are spontaneous and natural actions for those who have realized their true nature. The practiced *mitzvah* reveals the inherent *mitzvah*, as its practical application paves the way to its intrinsic essence. In other words, natural *mitzvot* are deciphered through practiced *mitzvot*, as Rabbi Yehuda HaLevi describes:

> אָמַר הֶחָבֵר: "אֲבָל יְעוּדֵנוּ – הִדַּבְקֵנוּ בָּעִנְיָן הָאֱלֹהִי בַּנְּבוּאָה, וּמָה שֶׁהוּא קָרוֹב לָהּ, וְהִתְחַבֵּר הָעִנְיָן הָאֱלֹהִי בָּנוּ בַּגְּדֻלָּה וּבַכָּבוֹד וּבַמּוֹפְתִים. וְעַל כֵּן אֵינֶנּוּ אוֹמֵר בַּתּוֹרָה, כִּי אִם תַּעֲשׂוּ הַמִּצְוָה הַזֹּאת, אֲבִיאֲכֶם אַחֲרֵי הַמָּוֶת אֶל גַּנּוֹת וַהֲנָאוֹת, אֲבָל הוּא אוֹמֵר: וְאַתֶּם תִּהְיוּ לִי לְעָם וַאֲנִי אֶהְיֶה לָכֶם לֵאלֹהִים מַנְהִיג אֶתְכֶם, וְיִהְיֶה מִכֶּם מִי שֶׁיַּעֲמֹד לְפָנַי וּמִי שֶׁיַּעֲלֶה לַשָּׁמַיִם כַּאֲשֶׁר הָיוּ הוֹלְכִים בֵּין הַמַּלְאָכִים, וְיִהְיוּ גַּם כֵּן מַלְאָכַי הוֹלְכִים בֵּינֵיכֶם בָּאָרֶץ וְתִרְאוּ אוֹתָם יְחִידִים וְרַבִּים, שׁוֹמְרִים אֶתְכֶם וְנִלְחָמִים לָכֶם, וְתַתְמִידוּ בָּאָרֶץ אֲשֶׁר הִיא עוֹזֶרֶת עַל הַמַּעֲלָה הַזֹּאת, וְהִיא אַדְמַת הַקֹּדֶשׁ, וְיִהְיֶה שָׂבְעָהּ וְרַעֲבוֹנָהּ וְטוֹבָתָהּ וְרָעָתָהּ – בָּעִנְיָן הָאֱלֹקִי כְּפִי מַעֲשֵׂיכֶם וְיִהְיֶה נוֹהֵג כָּל הָעוֹלָם עַל הַמִּנְהָג הַטִּבְעִי –

זוּלַתְכֶם. [...] וְהָיָה כָּל זֶה וְהַתּוֹרָה הַזֹּאת וְכָל יִעוּדֶיהָ מֻבְטָחִים, לֹא יִפֹּל מֵהֶם דָּבָר; וְיִעוּדֶיהָ כֻּלָּם כּוֹלֵל אוֹתָם שֹׁרֶשׁ אֶחָד וְהוּא יִחוּל קִרְבַת אֱלֹהִים וּמַלְאָכָיו".
(ספר הכוזרי, חלק א', ק"ט)

The *chaver* (“Rabbi”, “holy,” or “righteous”) said: “Now our purpose is that we shall adhere with the Divine Nature by means of prophecy, and everything that is annexed to it, and the Divine Nature connected with us through grand and awe-inspiring miracles. For this reason, we do not find in the Torah statements such as: ‘If you keep this *mitzvah*, I will bring you after death into beautiful gardens and great pleasures.’ But instead, we find statements like: ‘You shall be my nation, and I will be a God unto you, who will guide you. There will be those of you who will stand before me, and who will ascend to heaven, as those who mingle among the angels, and also my angels shall mingle among you on earth. You shall see them singly or in hosts, watching over you and fighting for you. You shall always remain in the land which forms a stepping-stone to this high level, viz. the Holy Land. Its fertility or barrenness, its happiness or misfortune, depend upon the divine influence which your conduct will merit, whilst the rest of the world would continue its natural course [...]. All this and this Torah and its purposes are promised, nothing will remain unfulfilled. All these purposes have one basis, viz. the anticipation of the proximity of God and His hosts.”

(Rabbi Yehuda HaLevi, *The Kuzari*, 1.99)

Consequently, through the meticulous observance of the precepts as symbolic acts, we align ourselves with the divine character or consciousness. The Hebrew revelation has various interpretive facets, from *pshat* (simple) to *sod* (secret). Each *mitzvah* unveils the secret that our intrinsic nature is divine. The precepts are not mere decrees or laws; they restore individuals fractured by concepts to their primordial symbolic essence. They are links that reintegrate what we think we are with what we truly are.

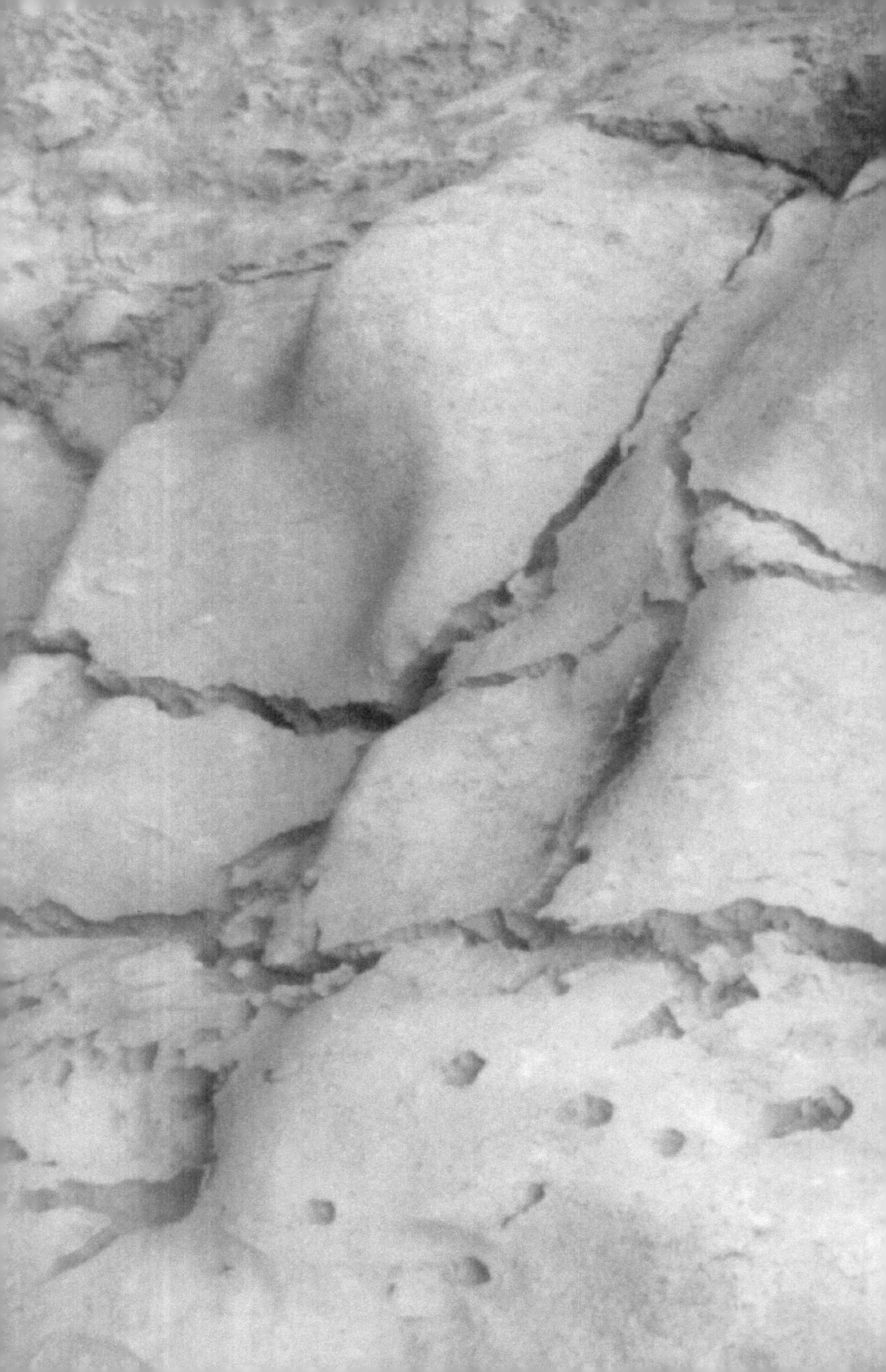

—— ARTICLE 11 ——

THE RECOGNITION OF CONSCIOUSNESS

We are a conscious presence devoid of objective qualities. Thought cannot perceive a consciousness that lacks attributes. Therefore, although we search with different methods and techniques, we are unable to find ourselves. From the mental perspective, we perceive ourselves as emptiness because we cannot recognize a subjectivity that lacks objective attributes. We can observe thoughts, emotions, sensations, and perceptions, but we are not these thoughts, emotions, sensations, or perceptions. Since we are not mental, emotional, or physical objects, we conclude that we are nothing.

The mind perceives only that which possesses qualities. If there is something devoid of attributes, the mind cannot apprehend it, but can merely believe in its existence. Rather than settling for mere **belief**, we ought to embrace **faith**. The Hebrew word *emunah*, or "faith," encompasses the idea of *emun*, or "trust"; it signifies trusting without the need for evidence of the veracity of our experiences. Belief is not equivalent to faith. Belief is a mental ability, whereas faith resides in the heart. Faith is supra-logical and surpasses the intellect. We may hold beliefs with sincerity, yet lack the faith required to integrate those beliefs into our everyday lives.

The word *faith* derives from the Latin *fides*, meaning "trust or fidelity," sharing its root with *affidavit*, which is a document that certifies the truthfulness of a statement. Beyond the confines of religion, faith serves as a foundational value in human interactions. Every interpersonal relationship is initiated on the premise of faith. Upon encountering new individuals, we place our faith in their self-representations; for instance, we trust our physician and dentist to be professionals simply because they claim to be so.

Faith is one of the ways we relate to something to which we cannot ascribe objective qualities.

יִרְאַת ה' רֵאשִׁית אַהֲבָתוֹ, וּדְבֹק בּוֹ תְּחִלַּת אֱמוּנָה:
(ספר בן־סירא, כ"ה, ט"ו)

The reverence of God is the beginning of loving Him, and devoting oneself to Him is the beginning of trusting him.
(*Ecclesiasticus*, 25:15)

At the outset of thePath of Retroprogressive Alignment, or *teshuvah*, we may lean on faith to connect in some way with consciousness. If only for a fleeting moment, we could directly perceive ourselves as consciousness, we would sow the seeds of faith within the heart. This faith is not a belief, that is, the outcome of intellectual conviction. Faith emanates and evolves from direct experience, even if it is illogical. Should we rely solely on reason, mystical experiences might appear unacceptable. Nonetheless, faith gradually furnishes us with the necessary confidence to embrace meditative states, even without further explanation, justification, or reasons. This faith strengthens through repeated experiences of our true nature. I am not talking about the belief in a supernatural entity ruling the universe from the skies. I refer to the confidence that behind every name and form, there lies a singular, undivided reality. As written in the Bible:

אַתָּה הָרְאֵתָ לָדַעַת כִּי ה' הוּא הָאֱלֹהִים אֵין עוֹד מִלְּבַדּוֹ:
(דברים ד', ל"ה)

You have been shown to know that the Lord, He is God; there is no more than only Him.
(Deuteronomy, 4:35)

"לָדַעַת כִּי ה' הוּא הָאֱלֹהִים". דָּא אִיהוּ כְּלָלָא דְּכָל רָזָא דִּמְהֵימְנוּתָא, דְּכָל אוֹרַיְיתָא, כְּלָלָא דְּעֵילָא וְתַתָּא, וְרָזָא דָּא אִיהוּ כְּלָלָא דְּכָל רָזָא דִּמְהֵימְנוּתָא, וְהָכִי הוּא וַדַּאי. כְּלָלָא דְּכָל אוֹרַיְיתָא, דָּא אִיהוּ רָזָא דְּתוֹרָה שֶׁבִּכְתָב, וְדָא אִיהוּ רָזָא דְּתוֹרָה שֶׁבְּעַל פֶּה, וְכֹלָּא חַד, כְּלָלָא דְּרָזָא דִּמְהֵימְנוּתָא, בְּגִין דְּאִיהוּ שֵׁם מָלֵא, דְּאִיהוּ רָזָא דִּמְהֵימְנוּתָא, וּמַאן אִיהוּ? "ה' אֶחָד וּשְׁמוֹ אֶחָד" (זכריה י"ד, ט'). "ה' אֶחָד", "שְׁמַע יִשְׂרָאֵל ה' אֱלֹהֵינוּ ה' אֶחָד" (דברים ו', ד'), דָּא אִיהוּ יִחוּדָא חַד. "וּשְׁמוֹ אֶחָד", "בָּרוּךְ שֵׁם כְּבוֹד מַלְכוּתוֹ לְעוֹלָם וָעֶד" (משנה, יומא, ג', ח'), הָא יִחוּדָא אַחֲרָא לְמֶהֱוֵי שְׁמֵיהּ חַד. וְרָזָא דָּא: "ה' הוּא הָאֱלֹהִים" (מלכים א', י"ח, ל"ט), דָּא כְּתִיב, כַּד אִנּוּן בְּיִחוּדָא חֲדָא.
(ספר הזוהר, שמות, פרשת תרומה, דף קס"א, ב')

"To know that the Lord, He is God": This is the totality of the entire secret of faith, of the entire Torah, the totality

> that comprises above and below. In this secret lies the totality of the whole secret of faith, and it is certainly so. Being the totality of the entire Torah, it is the secret of the Written Torah, and it is the secret of the Oral Torah, and all is one. It is the totality of the secret of the faith, for it is the complete Name, which is the secret of faith. And what is it? "The Lord (shall be) one, and His Name One." (Zechariah, 14:9) "The Lord [shall be] one" (is reflected in the first part of the Blessing of *Shema*): "Hear, O Israel, the Lord is our God, the Lord is one" (Deuteronomy, 6:4), this is one union, in which He is one. [Now, the second part of the verse] "And His Name One" [is reflected in the second part of the Blessing of *Shema*]: "Blessed is the name of His kingdom's glory forever and ever" (*Mishnah*, "*Yoma*," 3.8), this is another union, in which His Name is one. But the secret of "The Lord, He is God" (1 Kings, 18:39), refers to when they both are in one union.
>
> (*Zohar*, "*Terumah*," 161b)

The mind defines through a process of comparing what it is perceived with the information stored in memory. What is really perceived is a conscious space, devoid of objective qualities, where every experience arises and disappears. Comparing that with our accumulated mental information makes meditation impossible, because to meditate is just to perceive our original authenticity without mental comparison.

Silence and peace

The Bible narrates the contentions of the people of Israel. The Bhagavad Gita recounts the famous dialogue between Kṛṣṇa and Arjuna on the battlefield of Kurukṣetra. It may seem paradoxical for sacred texts to deal with matters of war, as they are expected to convey the word of God. I am even frequently asked why I practiced and taught karate for many years. For most, the pursuit of Truth is inherently a journey of peace, a view with which I wholeheartedly agree. However, such objections often fail to recognize that peace, whether as a first metaphor (mental peace) or as a second metaphor (verbal peace), is profoundly fragile. Meditation retreats provide merely an idea of peace, also sold in yoga classes and tai chi training. This peace-idea is tenuous, uncertain, and artificial. It is not intrinsic but acquired or even purchased. Solely cultivated under dim lights and soft-spoken words, it evaporates the moment one searches for the car keys to head home. It is a tranquility experienced while in a relaxation pose, listening to soothing music, but it vanishes at the ring of a phone or the shout of a neighbor.

As the sky remains unaffected by the rain or the clouds' movement, so too does consciousness stay untouched by the transient experiences that arise and dissipate. Just as space and emptiness are inherent to the sky, silence and peace are not qualities we acquire but rather our original nature. Peace, or *shalom* in Hebrew, embodies our essence in its completeness, or *shlemut*.

True peace cannot be acquired from another; it blossoms from the depths of consciousness. The notion of "peace of mind" is inherently contradictory. As long as there is a mind, there can only be a peace-idea as well as silence-idea, love-idea, enlightenment-idea, truth-idea, or God-idea. Genuine peace is not acquired but discovered. Revealed alongside our true nature, it is enduring and all-encompassing. By recognizing your reality as both silence and peace, you can maintain this calm even in hectic and tense situations, for nothing external can disturb it. The battles of Israel demonstrate that it is possible to remain serene and peaceful, as what we really are, even amid the fiercest combat. As Vincent van Gogh aptly noted in his letters, "There is peace even in the storm." If we observe closely, we will notice the profound peace that underlies every kind of experience.

Many spiritual seekers aspiring to recognize consciousness believe they must first achieve a mind state of stillness and calm. This belief perpetuates the myth that enlightenment requires a quiet or tranquil mind, confusing consciousness with an experience or mental state. This misconception underpins much of the pseudo-spiritual industry, which markets various methods and techniques to acquire such calm states. The ever-present consciousness remains unchanged whether in states of silence and peace or amid noise and restlessness. It is crucial to relinquish efforts to attain these states of calm. Although states of serenity are appealing, they are mere experiences, while consciousness observes every occurrence within itself and transcends them all. Conscious space remains indifferent to mental activity or inactivity, to the beauty or flaws of the body. Every experience is perceived with complete impartiality. Our true nature lies not in experiencing but in being.

At the level of consciousness, mental and emotional activity does not truly affect me. As conscious space, I remain distinct from the attributes of varying experiences, much like the sea's water does not share the shape or temporality of its waves. I am unaffected by the qualities that arise and vanish within me: joys and sorrows, attractions and aversions, honors, and humiliations. Indeed, I neither enjoy nor suffer, neither resist nor relent, nor do I move to the rhythm of experiential activity.

The mind conceptualizes consciousness as a separate subject that experiences. From this mental perspective, experiences are objects, and conscious space is an independent subject perceiving experiences appearing and disappearing. Yet, in reality, experiences arise in consciousness as waves rise in the sea. It would be absurd to consider a wave separate from the sea. Likewise, experiences cannot exist independently of consciousness. Just as a wave is the activity of the water, experience is consciousness in motion. The content of the sea is merely water in the forms of waves and bubbles; similarly, the content of consciousness is just consciousness.

A loan from consciousness

For modern philosophy, the content of consciousness is confined to what resides in the mind. Yet, in this discussion, we point out that the content of consciousness encompasses all experiences occurring within it, which includes both mental content and the mind itself. Observing superficially, each wave might seem to have its separate existence or reality, each with its unique form and individual history: born from the depths, growing, and eventually dying on the beach.

However, no wave exists in its own right; it is intrinsically part of the ocean. Every wave derives its existence from the ocean. Though each wave exhibits an individual or personal aspect, its existence is contingent upon and is an integral part of its oceanic essence. Just as a sun ray is never separated from the sun, our true nature is the light of consciousness, which illuminates every experience, both internal and external. This is how Rabbi Shneur Zalman of Liadi explains it:

> וְהַמָּשָׁל לָזֶה הוּא, אוֹר הַשֶּׁמֶשׁ "הַמֵּאִיר לָאָרֶץ וְלַדָּרִים", שֶׁהוּא זִיו וְאוֹר הַמִּתְפַּשֵּׁט מִגּוּף הַשֶּׁמֶשׁ וְנִרְאֶה לְעֵין כֹּל, מֵאִיר עַל הָאָרֶץ וּבַחֲלַל הָעוֹלָם, וְהִנֵּה, זֶה פָּשׁוּט, שֶׁאוֹר וְזִיו הַזֶּה יֶשְׁנוֹ גַּם כֵּן בְּגוּף וְחוֹמֶר כַּדּוּר הַשֶּׁמֶשׁ עַצְמוֹ שֶׁבַּשָּׁמַיִם, שֶׁאִם מִתְפַּשֵּׁט וּמֵאִיר לְמֶרְחוֹק כָּל כָּךְ, כָּל שֶׁכֵּן שֶׁיּוּכַל לְהָאִיר בִּמְקוֹמוֹ מַמָּשׁ, רַק שֶׁשָּׁם, בִּמְקוֹמוֹ מַמָּשׁ, נֶחְשָׁב הַזִּיו הַזֶּה לְאַיִן וָאֶפֶס מַמָּשׁ, כִּי בָּטֵל מַמָּשׁ בִּמְצִיאוּת לְגַבֵּי גּוּף כַּדּוּר הַשֶּׁמֶשׁ, שֶׁהוּא מְקוֹר הָאוֹר וְהַזִּיו הַזֶּה, שֶׁהַזִּיו וְהָאוֹר הַזֶּה, אֵינוֹ רַק הֶאָרָה מְאִירָה מִגּוּף וְעֶצֶם כַּדּוּר הַשֶּׁמֶשׁ; רַק בַּחֲלַל הָעוֹלָם, תַּחַת כָּל הַשָּׁמַיִם וְעַל הָאָרֶץ, שֶׁאֵין כָּאן גּוּף כַּדּוּר הַשֶּׁמֶשׁ בִּמְצִיאוּת – נִרְאֶה כָּאן הָאוֹר וְהַזִּיו הַזֶּה לְיֵשׁ מַמָּשׁ לְעֵין כֹּל, וְנוֹפֵל עָלָיו כָּאן שֵׁם "יֵשׁ" בֶּאֱמֶת, מַה־שֶּׁאֵין־כֵּן כְּשֶׁהוּא בִּמְקוֹרוֹ בְּגוּף הַשֶּׁמֶשׁ – אֵין נוֹפֵל עָלָיו שֵׁם "יֵשׁ" כְּלָל, רַק שֵׁם "אַיִן" וָ"אֶפֶס", כִּי בֶּאֱמֶת, הוּא שָׁם לְאַיִן וָאֶפֶס מַמָּשׁ, שֶׁאֵין מֵאִיר שָׁם רַק מְקוֹרוֹ לְבַדּוֹ, שֶׁהוּא גּוּף הַשֶּׁמֶשׁ הַמֵּאִיר, וְאֶפֶס בִּלְעָדוֹ.
>
> (ספר התניא, חלק שני; שער היחוד והאמונה, ג')

An illustration of this is the light of the sun which "illumines the earth and its inhabitants". [This illumination] is the radiance and the light which spreads forth from the body of the sun and is visible to all as it gives light to the earth and the expanse of the universe. Now, it is self-evident that this light and radiance is also present in the very body and matter of the sun-globe itself in the sky, for if it can spread forth and shine to such a great distance, then certainly it can shed light in its own place. However, there in its own place, this radiance is considered naught and complete nothingness, for it is absolutely nonexistent in relation to the body of the sun-globe which is the source of this light and radiance, inasmuch as this radiance and light is merely the illumination which shines from the body of the sun-globe itself. It is only in the space of the universe, under the heavens and on the earth, where the body of the sun-globe is not present, that this light and radiance appears to the eye to have actual existence. And here, the term *yesh*, (existence), can truly be applied to it, whereas when it is in its source, in the body of the sun, the term *yesh*, (existence), cannot be applied to it at all, and it can only be called naught and nonexistent. There it is indeed naught and absolutely nonexistent, for there, only its source, the body of the sun, gives light, and there is no more than only Him.

(*Tanya*, part 2, "*The portal of unity and faith*," chapter 3)

The Bhagavad Gita emphasizes:

नासतो विद्यते भावो नाभावो विद्यते सतः ।
उभयोरपि दृष्टोऽन्तस्त्वनयोस्तत्त्वदर्शिभिः ॥

nāsato vidyate bhāvo
nābhāvo vidyate sataḥ
ubhayor api dṛṣṭo 'ntas
tv anayos tattva-darśibhiḥ

There is no existence of the unreal, nor non-existence of the real. The ultimate truth of both is known to the wise.

(Bhagavad Gita, 2.16)

Just as the moon has no light of its own and only reflects the sun's light, so too does objective reality borrow its apparent existence from absolute reality. From the mental platform, reality is often perceived as our independent property. It might appear that both the mind–body complex and the universe possess their own inherent existence. However, their reality is merely a loan from consciousness. The sensation of being individual living entities is illusory because our existence belongs to consciousness.

רַבִּי אֶלְעָזָר אִישׁ בַּרְתּוֹתָא אוֹמֵר: "תֶּן לוֹ מִשֶּׁלוֹ, שֶׁאַתָּה וְשֶׁלְּךָ שֶׁלוֹ. וְכֵן בְּדָוִד הוּא אוֹמֵר: 'כִּי מִמְּךָ הַכֹּל, וּמִיָּדְךָ נָתַנּוּ לָךְ' (דברי־הימים א' כ"ט, י"ד)".

(פרקי אבות ג', ז')

Rabbi El'azar of Bartotha said: "Give to Him of that which is His, for you and that which is yours is His"; and so, it is said by David: 'For everything comes from You, and from Your own hand we have given it to You' (I Chronicles, 29:14)".

(*Pirkei Avot*, 3.7)

Knowing knowingness

Throughout our lives, we believe we are familiar with various mental, emotional, and physical objects, such as ideas, feelings, people, animals, things, and places. From a mental perspective, consciousness remains unnoticed, objectified as the body, mind, and universe. Yet, we cannot assert with certainty that we have truly known a mind, a body, or a universe as such; we only know that we have known knowingness.

Throughout our existence, we perceive only perceiving or know only knowingness. Thought extracts both the knower and the known from the depths of consciousness. Within this knowingness, the mind crafts an apparent duality, forming the basis of our relative reality. In every experience, the only certainty is the act of knowing itself, and this knowing is the consciousness or essence of our being.

In contemporary discourse, phrases like "God is everywhere" have been trivialized by the New Age movement. Such statements are misleading because it is not that God resides everywhere; rather, everything is God. In reality, only consciousness, or God, truly is. Beyond God, there is nothing else.

Consciousness not only permeates all experience, but, in fact, **is** every experience. Maurice Merleau-Ponty, the French phenomenological philosopher, stated, "We must not ask ourselves whether we truly perceive the world. On the contrary, we must say that the world is that which we perceive." Similarly, Sayyiduna 'Ali ibn Abi Talib noted: "People are asleep and when they die, they awaken." Echoing this concept, the Muslim mystic and philosopher Ibn Arabi described empirical reality as a mere dream: "In reality, the entire terrestrial existence of the Prophet (Muhammad) passed thus, as a dream within a dream."

Though many believe that through the senses they perceive objects, in reality, there is only a perception of different modulations of consciousness. The three-dimensional universe that we grasp through our senses and believe to be real is merely an illusory play of colors and sounds. It is a mirage maintained by the nerves and the mind. Just as the colors we see are only modulations of light, so too are objects only modulations of knowing.

A thought cannot be conscious, nor can a feeling, a sensation, or a perception; only consciousness knows. Only knowingness can truly be known, and only knowingness can know. Thus, reality is the self-knowledge of knowingness or knowingness knowing itself. Consciousness conscious of itself is the ultimate devotion, intimacy, closeness, union, and the profound love we ardently seek.

Consciousness is seemingly obscured by the projection of a supposed subject–object duality. From the intimacy of this oblivion, an I-thought emerges, believing itself to be part of the apparent attributes of experiences. Within this mental veil, consciousness appears forgotten. The Hebrew Kabbalists called this illusory restriction *tzimtzum*. Thus, *sefirot* (ספירות) gradually emanate. First, we have the *sefirot* related to thought: *ḥochmah* (חכמה – wisdom), *binah* (בינה – understanding), and *da'at* (דעת – knowledge). Then, the *sefirot* related to emotions and feelings: *ḥesed* (חסד – grace), *gevurah* (גבורה – might), and *tif'eret* (תפארת – beauty). Afterward, the *sefirot* related to actions or movement: *netzaḥ* (נצח – victory), *hod* (הוד – splendor), and *yesod* (יסוד – foundation). Finally, the *sefirah* of *malchut* (מלכות – kingship) which is the recipient of the influence from all the above *sefirot*. Delving deeper into this topic would indeed require an entire book.

The I-idea is akin to a wave in the ocean of consciousness. From such an imaginary entity, an identification with the apparent properties of diverse experiences finds expression. This illusory subject strives to reclaim its original state as consciousness. Its primary endeavor is to return to the primal state. Feeling its reality veiled, the imaginary "I" erroneously believes it has lost its nature of absolute peace, silence, and bliss. The raindrop tirelessly searches for water, oblivious to the fact that it already embodies what it seeks. The frustration of unanswered questions compels it toward various "spiritual" practices aimed at attaining enlightenment or liberation. Only when the efforts of the imaginary "I" finally subside, will the conditions be ripe for the conscious presence to be recognized.

Finding consciousness begins by relinquishing efforts to discover it. Only then we will see that it was never lost. By ceasing to seek the way back, we recognize that we have never departed. By stopping our endeavors to become what we truly are, we realize that it is impossible to be anything else: we can only be what we are.

Our perception of the material world

How wondrous it is to sit and watch a spring sunset, to revel in the green of the trees, the blue of the sky, and the songs of birds! We take pleasure in sipping fresh orange juice, feeling the bark of a tree, and inhaling the fragrance of flowers. Yet, the truth is that the trees are not truly green, the sky is not blue, and the juice is not sweet. In previous generations, it was much harder to convey that the world is not as we perceive it through our senses. Today, merely a year or two of high school education is sufficient to understand that our sensory perceptions do not provide an accurate representation of the universe.

Generally, we regard our sensory perceptions as doors and windows to an external universe. We believe our senses allow us to explore and learn about our surroundings to gather information essential for survival. However, our senses are not gateways to what we assume to be reality, but rather converters of photons into images, vibrations into sounds, and chemical reactions into smells and tastes.

It is reasonable to surmise that reality itself and the perceptions recreated by the brain are entirely distinct. It appears that the brain attempts to provide a representation of something real that, in actuality, remains unknown to us. Yet, science informs us that what we perceive is not the real universe, but just a construct of our brain—an internal simulation of a supposed external reality. We live within this perceived reality as though it were factual.

Our understanding of the universe seems to rely solely on the brain, which filters information received from the senses and processes it in its own way. We experience images and colors that are, in reality, electromagnetic waves; smells and tastes are merely chemical compounds dissolved in air or water. These sensory experiences are merely creations of the mind.

What if there is no such thing as light, but only electromagnetic energy? What if smells do not exist, but are simply just volatile particles? What if what we consider to be reality is only the activity of our brain perceiving its surroundings? What if everything we perceive as objective reality is shaped by our capabilities and mental limitations? What if the mind operates on entirely virtual planes and transforms realities?

Modern science has proved that what we perceive as solid matter is predominantly empty space. Atoms are the elementary particles that make up matter. If we divide matter into smaller and smaller parts, at some point we will arrive at the atom. Atoms can be likened to miniature solar systems: with a nucleus at the center and electrons orbiting like planets around a sun. If we scaled up the nucleus to the size of a coin, the electron shell would extend to the dimensions of a soccer stadium, with the electrons themselves as tiny as mosquitoes.

Expanding this analogy further, if the nucleus were the size of planet Earth, the electrons would be as distant as the stars. Residing in the nucleus, we would find it currently impossible to travel to an electron due to the vast empty space of the shell, which constitutes most of the atom. Although we sense an objective world of solid matter, science tells us that this universe is almost entirely vacant.

We may wonder why solid objects do not simply pass through each other. Consider the example of a fan: when it is off, it is easy to pass a pencil between its blades. But when the blades are spinning, they create an impenetrable barrier. Similarly, an atom's electron shell acts like this rotating fan. The swift movement of electrons generates a force field, making matter feel dense and impenetrable. When two objects come into contact, the interaction occurs not between their atoms but between the force fields they generate. Your hand does not truly touch the table; instead, the magnetic fields around the hand repel those of the table, giving the illusion of touch. Despite what our senses may suggest, in reality, no one has ever physically touched anything.

Colors are an integral part of our daily lives, but they do not exist in themselves. They are mere perceptions created by the brain. They result from an interpretation of signals from the eyes, which detect light reflected off objects. The brain colors the images and shows us a colorful world. For example, bananas are not inherently yellow, apples are not red, and trees are not green. The sky is not blue, and there are not inherently white or black horses. Color does not belong to the objects but depends on the light that illuminates things and the way our eyes and brain respond to that light. Isaac Newton explained that colors result from the brain's interpretation of signals sent by the optic nerve when it is exposed to different wavelengths of light.

When objects are illuminated, they absorb some wavelengths of light and reflect others, depending on their material composition. The rods and cones in the retina capture these reflected wavelengths and transmit them to the brain, which interprets each wavelength as a specific color. While humans generally perceive colors in a similar way, no two people have exactly the same eyes or brain, resulting in slight variations in color perception between individuals.

Light itself is a wave that travels in space and each color corresponds to a different wavelength. Humans only see a narrow band of the electromagnetic spectrum. The color we perceive an object to be is determined by the wavelengths of light that the object bounces off. For instance, a red apple absorbs all other colors and only reflects red wavelengths. Curiously, it absorbs all colors except red. A blue glass bulb appears blue because it absorbs nearly all the wavelengths that compose white light and rejects only blue's wavelength.

In essence, color is a construct of our brain. Objects do not possess color on their own; they simply reflect certain wavelengths that our brains interpret and assign sensations to. Despite the significant role of color in art and human culture, it is a perceptual phenomenon, not an inherent quality of objects.

It may seem strange, but it is indeed impossible to see anything in the present moment. We have never observed anyone or anything in real time; instead, we always see them as they were in the past. This delay occurs because light, which carries visual information from objects to our eyes, travels at a finite speed. Therefore, the greater the distance from an object, the longer it takes for light to reach us, even though this time difference is often minuscule. Consequently, everything we perceive as present actually occurs at slightly different times—we are always observing the past of each object.

Furthermore, we never truly see "something" directly; rather, we perceive photons of light that stimulate our retina and generate images in our brain of what we assume are objects or bodies. Our eyes do not actually "see"; they merely transmit information. It is the brain that processes and interprets this information, ultimately creating the images we see. Visual information triggers nerve impulses in the retina, which travel along the optic nerve to the brain. Despite our belief that we are directly observing the shape of an object, we are actually experiencing a simulation created by our brain based on these nerve impulses. The brain has only small sparks to recreate reality, meaning we do not see the world as it exists outside, but rather as it is represented inside our brain. This principle also applies to other senses such as smell and taste, but we will not elaborate on them here.

When two people observe a die, they typically agree it appears to be a cube. Likewise, if we toss a tennis ball, it predictably flies through the air and then falls to the ground. This consistency forms our understanding of "reality." However, quantum physics introduces complexity at very small scales, where the laws that govern our so-called reality alter significantly. According to quantum theory, objective facts do not inherently exist but rather depend on the observer. The properties of objects, such as the shape of a die, may differ: some may see it as a cube, while others as a sphere, due to the peculiar behavior of particles at the quantum level, which can intertwine and mutate according to the observer.

Thus, quantum mechanics suggests that our perception of reality is influenced by our observation; we do not perceive objects as they inherently are. We experience phenomena without truly understanding or knowing their underlying reality. This perspective challenges our conventional understanding of existence and suggests a more fluid and mutable conception of what is real.

Our senses do not grant us access to external reality. To elucidate this concept, let us consider a metaphor: the cockpit of an airplane, which is equipped with an instrument panel displaying dials that indicate altitude, atmospheric pressure, and so forth. These dials provide pilots with information about conditions outside the aircraft. However, this instrument panel does not present the reality outside; it only offers an analog representation designed to ensure safety. Imagine spending your entire life inside a windowless airplane cabin; naturally, you would come to believe that what the dashboard displays is reality itself. Similarly, confined within our own brains, we regard the perceptions it recreates as reality itself. Yet, what the brain provides is merely a representation of an unknown reality. Although a map may faithfully illustrate the territory of a city, the map is not reality but a mere representation.

Existence, presence, and consciousness

Most human beings believe that objects exist independently. But in fact, existence is not a quality of objects, instead, existence possesses objects. From the mental perspective, reality seems to be divided into innumerable existences that every object and human being has. But existence cannot be fragmented because it is one and indivisible.

We all grew up in a tradition that thinks objects are prior to consciousness. Due to this simple error, we conclude that objective reality exists first and then a conscious entity appears and becomes aware of reality. We think that the world exists and that we are born into it to observe and become aware of its existence.

Humans think that the universe exists independently of consciousness. In order to become aware of absolute reality, we must observe objects in relation to consciousness, not as if they were independent.

This is precisely what Rabeinu Naḥman of Breslov refers to when he writes:

> כִּי אִישׁ הַיִּשְׂרְאֵלִי צָרִיךְ תָּמִיד לְהִסְתַּכֵּל בְּהַשֵּׂכֶל שֶׁל כָּל דָּבָר, וּלְקַשֵּׁר עַצְמוֹ אֶל הַחָכְמָה וְהַשֵּׂכֶל שֶׁיֵּשׁ בְּכָל דָּבָר, כְּדֵי שֶׁיָּאִיר לוֹ הַשֵּׂכֶל שֶׁיֵּשׁ בְּכָל דָּבָר לְהִתְקָרֵב לְהַשֵּׁם יִתְבָּרַךְ עַל־יְדֵי אוֹתוֹ הַדָּבָר, כִּי הַשֵּׂכֶל הוּא אוֹר גָּדוֹל, וּמֵאִיר לוֹ בְּכָל דְּרָכָיו, כְּמוֹ שֶׁכָּתוּב: "חָכְמַת אָדָם תָּאִיר פָּנָיו" (קהלת ח', א').
>
> (לקוטי מוהר"ן, א')
>
> For the Israelite should always look at the intelligence (*sechel*) of everything and connect himself to the wisdom (*ḥochmah*) and intelligence that is in everything, so that the intelligence within each and every thing, will shed light upon him, so he may draw closer to the Divine, Blessed be He, by means of that thing, because the intelligence is a great light that illuminates all his ways, as written: "A person's wisdom lights up his face" (Ecclesiastes, 8:1).
>
> (*Likkutei Moharan*, 1)

By *ḥochmah*, or "wisdom," and *sechel*, or "intelligence," Rabeinu refers to that which knows, or consciousness. He suggests we focus on the perception of objects rather than living according to mere theories. Investigating our experience, we find no evidence to support the theory that objects precede consciousness. Undoubtedly, our direct experience confirms that the presence of consciousness is prior to objects. When we experience an object, we perceive its shape, color, texture, but also the element of knowingness. To realize this, it is necessary to pay attention not only to the objects, be they mental, emotional, or physical, but to the knowingness that knows the experience.

"For the Israelite should always (1) look at the intelligence (*sechel*) of everything and (2) connect himself to the wisdom (*ḥochmah*) and intelligence that is in everything": presence and consciousness are two indispensable conditions for an experience to occur. Such knowingness, or consciousness, is our authentic nature or what we really are.

If we explore the immediate reality of our own experience, we will see that it is possible to remove any element from the experience without affecting it. For example, if the experience is to observe our bedroom, we can remove books, chairs, tables, or any object. However, the moment we are not present and lack consciousness, it would be absolutely impossible to experience anything. Therefore, the two fundamental elements of experience are presence and consciousness.

If we walk in the forest and remove elements such as trees, flowers, or birds, the experience will remain. Only if we remove both presence and consciousness will experience vanish. These are the two essential elements prior to any mental, emotional, or physical experience. Therefore, after analyzing our own experience, it is clear that consciousness comes before objects.

We learn this from the Bible, where God's call is repeatedly answered with the Hebrew word *hineni* (הנני), or "here am I."

> וַיְהִי אַחַר הַדְּבָרִים הָאֵלֶּה וְהָאֱלֹהִים נִסָּה אֶת אַבְרָהָם וַיֹּאמֶר אֵלָיו אַבְרָהָם וַיֹּאמֶר הִנֵּנִי:
>
> (בראשית כ"ב, א')
>
> Some time afterward, God put Abraham to the test, saying to him, "Abraham." And he answered, "Here I am."
>
> (Genesis, 22:1)

> וַיִּקְרָא ה' אֶל־שְׁמוּאֵל, וַיֹּאמֶר הִנֵּנִי.
>
> (שמואל א' ג', ד')
>
> And the Lord called out to Samuel, and he answered: "Here I am."
>
> (I Samuel, 3:4)

As we commented in article 1, the term *hineni* carries important teachings. It is composed of two words: *hineh* (הנה), meaning "here"; and *ani* (אני), meaning "I." *Hineh* indicates knowingness or consciousness capable of perceiving; *ani* refers to presence or being. Thus, this Hebrew word combines the two basic conditions for experience.

We say "my consciousness" because we are under the false impression that everyone has a portion of consciousness. In our illusion, each human being is an independent piece of consciousness or a separate entity. This sense of an isolated "I" is what we call the "egoic phenomenon" or "ego."

However, consciousness is indivisible. All mental, emotional, or physical experience emanates in and out of consciousness. By placing consciousness as the foundation of experience, we realize that it is not divided by anything that arises in and from it. The sky cannot be torn by the clouds that cross it. Likewise, we have never fragmented consciousness with an idea, thought, emotion, sensation, or perception. Perhaps we have experienced some physical or emotional fracture, but never of consciousness. In the Bhagavad Gita, Kṛṣṇa says:

नैनं छिन्दन्ति शस्त्राणि नैनं दहति पावकः ।
न चैनं क्लेदयन्त्यापो न शोषयति मारुतः ॥

nainaṁ chindanti śastrāṇi
nainaṁ dahati pāvakaḥ
na cainaṁ kledayanty āpo
na śoṣayati mārutaḥ

No weapon can cut it to pieces, nor can fire burn it, nor water dampen it, nor wind wither it.

अच्छेद्योऽयमदाह्योऽयमक्लेद्योऽशोष्य एव च ।
नित्यः सर्वगतः स्थाणुरचलोऽयं सनातनः ॥

acchedyo 'yam adāhyo 'yam
akledyo 'śosya eva ca
nityaḥ sarva-gataḥ sthāṇur
acalo 'yaṁ sanātanaḥ

The Self is unbreakable and insoluble, and cannot be burned or dried up. It is eternal, omnipresent, immutable, motionless, and eternally the same.

अव्यक्तोऽयमचिन्त्योऽयमविकार्योऽयमुच्यते ।
तस्मादेवं विदित्वैनं नानुशोचितुमर्हसि ॥

avyakto 'yam acintyo 'yam
avikāryo 'yam ucyate
tasmād evaṁ viditvainaṁ
nānuśocitum arhasi

It is said that the Self is unmanifested, inconceivable and immutable. Knowing this, you should not grieve.

(Bhagavad Gita, 2.23–25)

Some neuroscientists claim that consciousness is a product of the brain. According to popular belief, consciousness is the last thing to manifest in evolution. However, based on our own experience, we lack any evidence that anything or anyone can exist outside of consciousness. It is absolutely impossible for any experience, even a brain, to exist outside of consciousness.

Fragmentation has never been experienced at the level of consciousness because consciousness is indivisible. Its indivisibility is not due to its resilience, but to its voidness. It lacks something objective that can be divided, shattered, broken, or destroyed. All experience emanates in consciousness from a *tzimtzum*, or "apparent restriction." The existence of all that can manifest is possible only from the restriction of consciousness and emanation from and within it.

דַּע, כִּי טֶרֶם שֶׁנֶּאֶצְלוּ הַנֶּאֱצָלִים וְנִבְרְאוּ הַנִּבְרָאִים, הָיָה אוֹר עֶלְיוֹן פָּשׁוּט מְמַלֵּא אֶת כָּל הַמְּצִיאוּת. וְלֹא הָיָה שׁוּם מָקוֹם פָּנוּי בִּבְחִינַת אֲוִיר רֵיקָנִי וְחָלָל, אֶלָּא הַכֹּל הָיָה מָלֵא אוֹר הָאֵין־סוֹף הַפָּשׁוּט הַהוּא. וְלֹא הָיָה לוֹ לֹא בְּחִינַת רֹאשׁ וְלֹא בְּחִינַת סוֹף, אֶלָּא הַכֹּל הָיָה אוֹר אֶחָד פָּשׁוּט שָׁוֶה בְּהַשְׁוָאָה אַחַת, וְהוּא הַנִּקְרָא "אוֹר־אֵין־סוֹף".

(רבי חיים ויטאל, עץ חיים א', ב')

Know, that before the emanations emanated and the creatures were created, there was a supreme simple light [*Pashut*, all-pervading light, without qualities or attributes] filling the entire existence. And there was not any empty place in the sense of vacant air or space, but all was filled with that infinite all-pervading light. And it did not have neither the aspect of beginning nor the aspect of end, but everything was one all pervading, uniform light, and it is called *Or Ein Sof* (The Infinite Light)"

(Rabbi Ḥayim Vital, *Etz Ḥayim*, 1.2)

The self-restriction of consciousness

Every thought emanates within consciousness. There is only consciousness before it emerges from its depths; while it appears, only consciousness exists, and it will endure after its disappearance. Therefore, there is no other raw material from which thought can be made. However, due to its qualitative appearance, thought becomes objectified. Its apparent attributes distinguish it from consciousness, creating an illusory objective reality. In fact, it is not a real object, but the voluntary inadvertence of self-consciousness that expresses itself as an objective perception.

Just like thoughts, perceptions arise from the self-limitation of consciousness. Everything known as the objective universe is merely perceptions emanating from the depths of consciousness due to its self-restriction. Thoughts, emotions, sensations, and perceptions, and thus the universe, appear within consciousness, are known by it, and are made of it.

דַּע, כִּי תְּחִלַּת הַכֹּל הָיָה כָּל הַמְּצִיאוּת אוֹר פָּשׁוּט וְנִקְרָא אי"ן סו"ף וְלֹא הָיָה שָׁם שׁוּם חָלָל וְשׁוּם אֲוִיר פָּנוּי, אֶלָּא הַכֹּל הָיָה אוֹר הָאֵין־סוֹף. וּכְשֶׁעָלָה בִּרְצוֹנוֹ הַפָּשׁוּט לְהַאֲצִיל הַנֶּאֱצָלִים לְסִבָּה נוֹדַעַת וְהִיא לְהִקָּרֵא "רַחוּם וְחַנּוּן אֶרֶךְ אַפַּיִם" וְכַיּוֹצֵא (שמות ל"ד, ו'), כִּי אִם אֵין בָּעוֹלָם מִי שֶׁיְּקַבֵּל רַחֲמִים מִמֶּנּוּ אֵיךְ יִקָּרֵא רַחוּם, וְכֵן עַל דֶּרֶךְ זֶה בְּכָל הַכִּנּוּיִים. וְאָז צִמְצֵם עַצְמוֹ בְּאֶמְצַע הָאוֹר שֶׁלּוֹ בִּנְקֻדַּת הַמֶּרְכָּז אֶמְצָעִית שֶׁבּוֹ, וְשָׁם צִמְצֵם עַצְמוֹ אֶל הַצְּדָדִין וְהַסְּבִיבוֹת וְנִשְׁאַר חָלָל בֵּינְתַיִם, וְזֶה

הָיָה צִמְצוּם הָרִאשׁוֹן שֶׁל הַמַּאֲצִיל הָעֶלְיוֹן. וְזֶה מְקוֹם הֶחָלָל הוּא עָגֹל בְּהַשְׁוָאָה אַחַת מִכָּל צְדָדָיו, עַד שֶׁנִּמְצָא עוֹלָם הָאֲצִילוּת וְכָל הָעוֹלָמוֹת נְתוּנִים תּוֹךְ הֶחָלָל הַזֶּה. וְאוֹר הָאֵין־סוֹף מַקִּיפוֹ בְּשָׁוֶה מִכָּל צְדָדָיו. וְהִנֵּה כַּאֲשֶׁר צִמְצֵם עַצְמוֹ אָז דֶּרֶךְ צַד אֶחָד מִן הֶחָלָל הֶעָגֹל הַזֶּה, הִמְשִׁיךְ אוֹר דֶּרֶךְ קַו אֶחָד יָשָׁר, דַּק כְּעֵין צִנּוֹר אֶחָד, אוֹר הַנִּמְשָׁךְ הָאֵין־סוֹף אֶל תּוֹךְ הֶחָלָל הַזֶּה וּמְמַלֵּא אוֹתוֹ. אֲבָל נִשְׁאַר מָקוֹם פָּנוּי בֵּין הָאוֹר שֶׁבְּתוֹךְ חָלָל זֶה וּבֵין אוֹר הָאֵין־סוֹף הַמַּקִּיף אֶת זֶה הֶחָלָל כַּנִּזְכָּר, שֶׁנִּתְצַמְצֵם אֶל צְדָדָיו. וְסִיּוּם הַקַּו הַזֶּה לְמַטָּה אֵינוֹ נוֹגֵעַ גַּם כֵּן בְּאוֹר הָאֵין־סוֹף עַצְמוֹ שֶׁאִם לֹא כֵּן יַחֲזֹר הַדָּבָר לִכְמוֹת שֶׁהָיָה וְיַחֲזֹר וְיִתְחַבֵּר הָאוֹר הַזֶּה שֶׁבְּתוֹךְ הֶחָלָל עִם אוֹר הָאֵין־סוֹף יַחַד כְּבָרִאשׁוֹנָה. וְעַל־כֵּן לֹא נִתְפַּשֵּׁט וְנִמְשַׁךְ הָאוֹר הַזֶּה בְּרֹחַב אֶל תּוֹךְ הֶחָלָל – רַק דֶּרֶךְ קַו אֶחָד דַּק לְבַד כַּנִּזְכָּר. וְדֶרֶךְ הַקַּו הַזֶּה נִמְשָׁךְ וְיוֹרֵד אוֹר הָאֵין־סוֹף הַמַּאֲצִיל אֶל תּוֹךְ הֶחָלָל הֶעָגֹל הַזֶּה שֶׁהוּא הַנֶּאֱצָל, וְעַל־יְדֵי כֵּן מִתְדַּבְּקִים הַמַּאֲצִיל בַּנֶּאֱצָל יַחַד וְלֹא עוֹד. וְאַף־עַל־פִּי שֶׁכָּל הָאֲצִילוּת הוּא עָגֹל וְהָאֵין־סוֹף מַקִּיפוֹ בְּשָׁוֶה מִכָּל צְדָדָיו, עִם כָּל זֶה, אוֹתוֹ הַמָּקוֹם שֶׁנִּשְׁאַר דָּבוּק בּוֹ וְנִמְשָׁךְ מִמֶּנּוּ רֹאשׁ הַקַּו הַזֶּה שָׁם נִקְרָא רֹאשׁ הָאֲצִילוּת וְעֶלְיוֹנוֹ וְכָל מָה שֶׁמִּתְפַּשֵּׁט וְנִמְשָׁךְ לְמַטָּה נִקְרָא תַּחְתּוֹנִיּוּת הָאֲצִילוּת. וְעַל־יְדֵי כָּךְ נִמְצָא שֶׁיֵּשׁ בְּחִינַת מַעְלָה וּמַטָּה בָּאֲצִילוּת, שֶׁאִם לֹא כֵּן לֹא הָיָה בְּחִינַת מַעְלָה וּמַטָּה וְרֹאשׁ וְרַגְלַיִם בָּאֲצִילוּת.

(רבי חיים ויטאל, אוצרות חיים, שער העיגולים)

Know, that in the beginning of everything, all existence consisted of a simple [*pashut*, all-pervading and without qualities] light known as *Ein Sof* (infinite, without end), and there was not any space or vacant air. Rather, everything was that infinite light. Then, when the simple will to emanate emanations arose in Him, for the known purpose of being called "compassionate and gracious, slow to anger" (Exodus, 34:6), and so on. For, if there was no one in the world to receive His compassion, how could He be called compassionate? And so it is for all other pronouns.

Then, He contracted Himself in the middle of the center point of His own light; and there, He contracted Himself to the sides and peripheries, leaving an empty space in the middle.

> This was the first contraction of the Supreme Emanator. This empty space is round and perfectly symmetrical, encompassing within it the "world of emanations" and all the other worlds, while the infinite light surrounds it symmetrically from all sides.
>
> As so it was, when He contracted Himself, He extended light through a thin straight line, like a pipeline, light which is extended from the infinite into this space and filling it. However, an empty space remained between the light inside the space and the infinite light surrounding this space, which contracted to all sides as mentioned. The lower end of this line of light does not touch the infinite light itself, for if it did, everything would revert to be as it was initially, and this light that is inside the space would once again reconnect with the infinite light, as was in the beginning.
>
> Therefore, that light did not expand and spread through the space, but instead, it extended only in one thin line, as mentioned. Through this line, the infinite light, or "The Emanator," descends into this round space, or "the emanated". By this "The Emanator" and "the emanated" adhere together, and nothing else. Even though the emanation is round and the infinite surrounds it symetrically on all sides, that place in which the line is adhered to the infinite, and from which it is extended, that place is called "the head" of the emanation, or its upper part, and all that is extends from it downward is called the lower part of the emanation. Thus, the aspects of "above" and "below" are found in the emanation. For otherwise, there could not be aspects of above and below and head and legs in the emanation.
>
> (Rabbi Ḥayim Vital, *Otzrot Ḥayim*, "*The gate of circles*")

Every idea, book, table, bottle, or person appears to possess its own separate existence. However, the reality and beingness of every object, whether mental, emotional, astral, or physical, is derived from consciousness. The apparent withdrawal of consciousness allows for the perception of an objective multiplicity. Thus, the distinctness we observe around us is not an inherent quality of objects but a product of masking an underlying unity.

Observing the sea, we see a diversity of waves, each with its apparent separate existence, but within the vastness of the sea, there exists no true division or fracture—regardless of the number of waves, the sea remains unified. Before any object expresses something about itself, it tells us about its nature and origin. Observing a wave will inform us about its shape and height, but first and foremost, it will tell us something about its reality as sea, much as The Rambam might elucidate:

> יְסוֹד הַיְסוֹדוֹת וְעַמּוּד הַחָכְמוֹת לֵידַע שֶׁיֵּשׁ שָׁם מָצוּי רִאשׁוֹן. וְהוּא מַמְצִיא כָּל נִמְצָא. וְכָל הַנִּמְצָאִים מִשָּׁמַיִם וָאָרֶץ וּמַה שֶּׁבֵּינֵיהֶם לֹא נִמְצְאוּ אֶלָּא מֵאֲמִתַּת הִמָּצְאוֹ: וְאִם יַעֲלֶה עַל הַדַּעַת שֶׁהוּא אֵינוֹ מָצוּי אֵין דָּבָר אַחֵר יָכוֹל לְהִמָּצְאוֹת.
> (משנה תורה, ספר המדע, הלכות יסודי התורה, א', א'-ב')
>
> The foundation of all foundations and the pillar of all wisdom is to know that there is a Primary Existence that brought all that exists into existence. All that exists, from heavens to earth, and all that is between them, came into existence only from the truth of His existence. And if one would imagine that He does not exist, no other thing could possibly exist.
>
> (*Mishneh Torah*, "*Sefer HaMadda*,"
> "*Foundations of the Torah*," 1.1–2)

The great Vedantic master Śrī Bhagavan Ramaṇa Maharṣi of Tiruvanmalai, India, presented the excellent example of the screen, which appears in David Godman's book *Be as you are*. Watching a Western television show, we see horses, gunfighters, Indians, cows, and wagons. Yet, in reality, we only have a television in front of us. To identify each shape, we differentiate it from the screen while completely disregarding the screen itself. Clearly, these objects do not possess independent existence; they derive their beingness from the screen they are displayed on. In essence, to observe the world in a film, one would need a television that hypothetically lacks a screen. Similarly, to manifest a world, the omnipresent consciousness creates a space that is, hypothetically, devoid of consciousness.

From the perspective of the characters within the film, objects and people that appear on the screen seem to have a real and separate existence. Looking around, they do not perceive the screen itself but instead a multitude of independent objects and entities. They think that space is the container of their experiences. Although the space is screen, they cannot perceive it from within the film. Likewise, the mind–body complex ignores or omits the real background from which it is made. We believe we perceive a diversity of objects and beings; however, what we truly perceive is merely perception itself, not actual entities or objects. Just as the movie is not real, neither is the universe—an apparent reality created through perception. Since nothing can exist apart from consciousness, the universe is apparent, as it is not independent of consciousness.

> כָּל דָּבָר שֶׁהָיָה בִּכְלָל וְיָצָא מִן הַכְּלָל לְלַמֵּד, לֹא לְלַמֵּד עַל עַצְמוֹ יָצָא, אֶלָּא לְלַמֵּד עַל הַכְּלָל כֻּלּוֹ יָצָא.
>
> (ספרא, ברייתא דרבי ישמעאל)
>
> Anything that was subsumed in a general category and departed from that category to teach (something), not in order to teach about itself did it depart, but in order to teach about the entire category did it depart.
>
> (*Sifra*, *Baraita DeRabbi Yishma'el*)

This *Baraita* illustrates that any object, whether mental, emotional, or physical, first reveals insights about consciousness before it speaks of its own attributes. Without perceiving things, it is very difficult to become aware of knowingness. However, this knowingness does not confirm the existence of objects; rather, objects point to the existence of knowingness. Just as heat could not be perceived without the presence of fire, objects could not be perceived without underlying knowingness. Therefore, more important than merely observing objects is the deeper endeavor of connecting with the essence of knowingness.

Exploring our experience

If we investigate our experience, we will recognize the knowing element. It is the factor that allows experience to be known, and it is the conscious presence of all objective experience. When we do not engage our curiosity or make the effort to explore this knowing element, we typically label it "I." However, upon closer observation of this "I," it becomes evident that it is neither the mind nor the body, as both are observable. The mind–body complex is part of what is observed, not the observer itself. Through recognizing this knowingness, I discover that I am the observation to all appearances without actually being any of them. I stop thinking that I am an observable object because I discover myself to be a conscious space devoid of attributes.

By delving into the essence of a spark, we discover that it is fire. Similarly, by observing the depths of ourselves, we recognize the boundless ocean of consciousness. Our true nature defies description. If it were describable, it would become another observable object. It is often referred to as Infinite Light; enlightenment is to realize it.

> אֵין יְדִיעָתֵנוּ בּוֹ אֶלָּא שֶׁהוּא אוֹר פָּשׁוּט מֵאִיר, רוֹצֶה לוֹמַר מֵאִיר, שֶׁמַּגִּיעַ הֶאָרָתוֹ עַל הָאֲחֵרִים, אַךְ שֶׁנָּבִין מַהוּ הָאוֹר הַזֶּה לֹא יַעֲלֶה בְּדַעְתֵּנוּ, כִּי עַל כֵּן נִקְרָאֵהוּ אוֹר פָּשׁוּט, מִפְּנֵי שֶׁלֹּא נוּכַל לְדַבֵּר מִמַּהוּתוֹ כְּלָל, רַק נֵדַע שֶׁהוּא מֵאִיר וּנְדַבֵּר מֵהֶאָרָתוֹ, וְלַהֶאָרָה הַזֹּאת נִקְרָאֵהוּ אֵין סוֹף, כִּי בֶּאֱמֶת אֵין לָהּ גְּבוּל, כְּמוֹ שֶׁאֵין גְּבוּל לְעַצְמוּתוֹ [...].
>
> (רמח"ל, אדיר במרום, עמוד נ"ט)
>
> All we know about Him, is that He is *or pashut* (an illuminating all-pervading light, without qualities or attributes). "Illuminating" meaning, that His light is reaching the others, but it does not even come to our mind that we can understand what this light is, and for this reason we call Him "all-pervading light," since we cannot speak of His essence

> at all. We only know that He is illuminating, and we can talk about His illumination. And we call this illumination *Ein Sof* (The Infinite), because in reality, He has no limit, just as there is no limit to His essence…
>
> (Ramḥal, *Adir BaMarom*, page 59)

Throughout our lives, we accumulate knowledge and gather information, and call this process "education." This knowledge often comes from intermediary sources such as books and people. However, such knowledge does not fundamentally change us; information not acquired through direct experience lacks transformative power. No matter how much knowledge we possess, we still do not know who we are. We identify with the egoic phenomenon, which is nothing more than the information that others have provided us with about us.

Stored mental knowledge actually perpetuates ignorance. By trying to know through the mind, we must remember that all knowledge is relative, as the mind itself is relative and distorts Truth. Therefore, any knowledge obtained through the mind is necessarily flawed, making knowledge and ignorance equally misleading, both being constructs of the mental world.

Society often fails to distinguish between knowledge and wisdom. Wisdom does not come through intermediaries but blooms from the depths of consciousness. Knowledge and ignorance are disconnected from truth and reality. True understanding emerges only when the mind is transcended. When we move beyond the mind, falsehood is left behind and wisdom awakens, operating within the realm of the true and real, unmediated by the mind. The realization of Truth does not require knowledge but wisdom. Knowledge is a product of mental effort, while wisdom comes to us in relaxation and silence. Only by transcending the mental plane and its so-called knowledge can we awaken to absolute reality or God. Innocence is needed to overcome ignorance. The aim of abandoning all knowledge about God is to know what God really is. Rabbi Avraham Isaac HaCohen Kook wrote the following:

דַּעַת הַקֹּדֶשׁ מִמְּקוֹר הַחַיִּים – הַיְּדִיעָה מִן הָעוֹלָם וְהַמְּצִיאוּת, שֶׁבָּאָה מִצַּד הַחוֹל, אֵינָהּ עוֹלָה אֲפִילוּ לְחֵלֶק אֶחָד מִנִּי רְבָבָה בְּעֵרֶךְ הָאֱמֶת, לְעֻמַּת הַיְּדִיעָה הָעֲמֻקָּה שֶׁל הָעוֹלָם וְהַיֵּשׁוּת בִּכְלָל, שֶׁבָּאָה מִצַּד הַקֹּדֶשׁ. כִּי אֲמִתַּת הַמְּצִיאוּת וְהַיֵּשׁ הַגָּמוּר שֶׁל הַכֹּל הִיא רַק בִּהְיוֹת הַכֹּל בָּא מִצַּד הַהוֹפָעָה הָאֱלֹהִית, מִצַּד הִסְתַּעֲפוּת חַיִּים וְיֵשׁוּת מִמְּקוֹר הַחַיִּים וְהַיֵּשׁ. שֶׁכָּל מָה שֶׁמִּתְגַּלֶּה בְּתוֹר עוֹלָם וַהֲוָיָה הוּא רַק כְּעֵין צֵל קָלוּשׁ לְגַבֵּי הַיֵּשׁוּת הַטְּהוֹרָה וְהָאַדִּירָה שֶׁבַּמָּקוֹר הָאֱלֹהִי.

The knowledge of the holy, from the source of life. The knowledge of the world and reality, when it comes from the direction of the mundane, does not even come near to 1/10,000 value of truth when compared to the deep knowledge of the world and the entire existence, that comes from the direction of Holiness. This is because the true and absolute reality of everything is only when it all comes from the divine manifestation, where life and existence branching from the source of life and existence. For all that is revealed as a world and existence, is but a faded shadow when compared to the pure and mighty existence found in the divine source.

וְנִמְצָא שֶׁכָּל הַהוֹן הַמַּדָּעִי שֶׁל הָאָדָם יַעֲלֶה בְּרוֹמְמוּת פְּאֵר גָּדְלוֹ רַק כְּשֶׁיֵּאָצֵר וְיֵחָסֵן בִּמְקוֹר הֲוָיָתוֹ, שֶׁהִיא דַּעַת ה' וְעֻזּוֹ, הַכָּרַת הַכֹּל מִצַּד מְקוֹר הַכֹּל. אָז יִתְיַשְּׁרוּ כָּל הַהֲדוּרִים, מִצַּד שֶׁרַק אָז, בִּהְיוֹת הַגֹּבַהּ הָעֶלְיוֹן שֶׁל הַמַּדָּע מִתְגַּלֶּה, יַחַשׂ הַמַּדָּע נֶעֱרָךְ בְּטִבְעוֹ. וְכָל זְמַן שֶׁהָעוֹלָם מִתְגַּלֶּה רַק עַל יְדֵי צְלָלָיו הַכֵּהִים, שֶׁהֵם הַשְׁעָרַת הַכָּרָתוֹ מִצַּד צְבָעָיו הַבּוֹדְדִים וְהַכָּרוֹתָיו הַחִיצוֹנִיּוֹת, כְּלֹא נֶחְשָׁב, לְעֻמַּת הַקִּנְיָן הַמַּדָּעִי הַמֻּחְלָט, שֶׁהוּא דַּעַת ה', הַמִּתְבַּלֵּט עַל־יְדֵי דַּעַת הָעוֹלָם בְּתוֹר פֹּעַל ה', שֶׁאֶל זֶה נְשׂוּאוֹת הֵן עֵינֵי כָּל חָי.

Hence, man's entire wealth of knowledge will manifest in its glorious and majestic greatness only when it will be kept and stored in the source of its existence, which is the knowledge of the Lord and His might; the recognition of everything from the direction of The Source of All.

Then all difficulties will settle, for only then, when the highest altitude of knowledge is revealed, knowledge can be relatively assessed.

As long as the world is revealed only through the dark shadows of knowledge, which are only its estimated perception by its dull colors and few external attributes, it is considered as nothing compared to the acquisition of absolute knowledge, which is the knowledge of the Lord. Knowledge which is manifested as seeing the world as the creation of the Lord. This is the goal toward which all eyes are set.

וְזֶה כָּל הָאָדָם, כָּל הַמָּצוּי, כָּל הַמֻּכָּר וְהַנּוֹדָע. וְכָל עֲמַל הָעוֹלָם וְעִלּוּיֵי מַדְרֵגוֹתָיו הוּא מְכוֹנָן רַק כְּדֵי שֶׁיָּבֹא הָאוֹר הָעֶלְיוֹן שֶׁל הַמַּדָּעִיּוּת לְהִתְגַּלּוֹת בְּשֶׁטֶף מְקוֹר אֲמִתָּתוֹ. וְכָל הַמּוּסָר הַכְּלָלִי וְהַפְּרָטִי, כָּל הֲטָבַת אָרְחוֹת הַחַיִּים, אֹרַח הַצְּדָקָה וְהַיְּשָׁרוּת בְּחַיֵּי הַיָּחִיד וְהַכְּלָלִיּוּת, הַכֹּל תָּלוּי הוּא וְעוֹמֵד לְהַגִּיעַ אֶל מְכוֹן תַּמּוּתוֹ, עַל־יְדֵי הַהִתְוַדְּעוּת שֶׁל הַהַכָּרָה בִּמְקוֹרִיּוּתָהּ, שֶׁהִיא הוֹלֶכֶת וּמִתְנַשֵּׂאת לְפִי אוֹתָהּ הַמִּדָּה שֶׁיֵּחָשֵׂף הַהוֹד שֶׁל אוֹר הַחַיִּים שֶׁבִּמְקוֹר הַקֹּדֶשׁ, שֶׁהוּא זֹהַר הָאֱמֶת, אוֹר ה', מְחוֹלֵל כֹּל.

(הרב אברהם יצחק הכהן קוק, אורות הקודש א', ב')

And this is all what human beings are about, all that exists, all the familiar and known. All the world's endeavor and progression are arranged only for the supreme light of knowledge to reveal itself, overflowing from the source of its truth. And all moral—general and personal—all righteousness, the ways of piousness and honesty of individual and collective life, Everything is still pending, and will reach its final goal when consciousness will recognize its source. This recognition will go and rise in the measure that the glory of the Light of Life, of the Holy Source, the Splendor of Truth, the Light of the Lord, the cause of all—will expose itself.

(Rabbi Abraham Isaac HaCohen Kook, *Orot HaKodesh*, 1.2)

Thought offers consciousness three possibilities: to be subject, object, or consciousness as it is. It can be the knower, the known, or knowingness. However, in none of the three options does consciousness cease to be conscious of anything apart from itself.

כָּל הַנִּמְצָאִים – חוּץ מִן הַבּוֹרֵא – מִצּוּרָה הָרִאשׁוֹנָה עַד יַתּוּשׁ קָטָן שֶׁיִּהְיֶה בְּטַבּוּר הָאָרֶץ, הַכֹּל מִכֹּחַ אֲמִתָּתוֹ נִמְצְאוּ. וּלְפִי שֶׁהוּא יוֹדֵעַ עַצְמוֹ וּמַכִּיר גְּדֻלָּתוֹ וְתִפְאַרְתּוֹ וַאֲמִתָּתוֹ, הוּא יוֹדֵעַ הַכֹּל וְאֵין דָּבָר נֶעֱלָם מִמֶּנּוּ:
הַקָּדוֹשׁ־בָּרוּךְ־הוּא מַכִּיר אֲמִתּוֹ וְיוֹדֵעַ אוֹתָהּ כְּמוֹ שֶׁהִיא. וְאֵינוֹ יוֹדֵעַ בְּדֵעָה שֶׁהִיא חוּץ מִמֶּנּוּ כְּמוֹ שֶׁאָנוּ יוֹדְעִין. שֶׁאֵין אָנוּ וְדַעְתֵּנוּ אֶחָד, אֲבָל הַבּוֹרֵא יִתְבָּרַךְ הוּא וְדַעְתּוֹ וְחַיָּיו אֶחָד מִכָּל צַד וּמִכָּל פִּנָּה וּבְכָל דֶּרֶךְ יִחוּד. שֶׁאִלְמָלֵי הָיָה חַי בַּחַיִּים וְיוֹדֵעַ בְּדֵעָה חוּץ מִמֶּנּוּ – הָיוּ שָׁם אֱלֹהוּת הַרְבֵּה: הוּא וְחַיָּיו וְדַעְתּוֹ, וְאֵין הַדָּבָר כֵּן, אֶלָּא אֶחָד מִכָּל צַד וּמִכָּל פִּנָּה וּבְכָל דֶּרֶךְ יִחוּד. נִמְצֵאתָ אַתָּה אוֹמֵר: הוּא הַיּוֹדֵעַ וְהוּא הַיָּדוּעַ וְהוּא הַדֵּעָה עַצְמָהּ – הַכֹּל אֶחָד.

(רמב"ם, משנה תורה, ספר המדע, הלכות יסודי התורה, ב', ט'–י')

All existence, aside from the Creator—from the first form down to a small mosquito in the depths of the earth—all exist by the power of His Truth. And since He knows Himself and His greatness, splendor, and truth, He knows everything, and nothing is hidden from Him.

The Holy One, Blessed be He, acknowledges His Truth and knows it as it is; He does not know it with an intelligence which is separate from Himself, the way we know. For we and our intelligence are not one, but the Creator, His Intelligence and His Life—are all one from all aspects, angles, and in every manner of unity. For if He would live a life and understand with an intelligence which are separate from Himself, there would be many gods: He, His life, and His Intelligence; but this is not so, for He is One from all aspects, angles, and manners of unity. Therefore, you must say: "He is the knower, He is the known, and He is the knowledge. All is One."

(Rambam, *Mishneh Torah*, "*Sefer HaMadda,*"
"*Foundations of the Torah,*" 2.9–10)

Whether as perceiver, perceived object, or perception, consciousness is and perceives only itself. All that I am and perceive is perception itself. Just as for the dreamer, waking up means the end of the dream, the end of the ego is its disappearance as someone. What we call "enlightenment" is the evaporation of both subject and object because it is the dissolution of duality.

וַיֹּאמֶר לֹא תוּכַל לִרְאֹת אֶת פָּנָי כִּי לֹא יִרְאַנִי הָאָדָם וָחָי׃
(שמות ל"ג, כ')

[And God] said: "But you cannot see My face, for a human being may not see Me and live."

(Exodus, 33:20)

Existence can be divided into three categories: the known, the unknown, and the unknowable. Knowledge is what was previously unknown, but after hearing or reading about it, it becomes known. We find this attitude in organized religions, which worship a glorious past and the time when the unknown became known.

The second category belongs to the unknown, which sooner or later will become known. This is the attitude of science, in its efforts to transform the unknown into the known. The goal of science is a world where everything is known.

Finally, the unknowable is inaccessible to the mind because it will never be able to touch it or possess it in any way. In fact, consciousness frightens the mind because it represents its end; therefore, the mind tries to remain unconscious. The unknowable can be lived, experienced, painted, danced, or sung, but it will forever remain unknown. If the known attracts the religious person and the unknown attracts the scientist, the unknowable belongs to the mystic, who is an artist of the enigma and an adventurer of the mystery.

Captivated by the brightness of the stars, we fail to perceive the immensity of the sky that serves as their background. To recognize the reality of all the characters is to pay attention to the stage, which is the background that allows their representation. Likewise, we live seduced by our experiences. Only by transcending our fascination is it possible to recognize consciousness as our authenticity.

The nature of consciousness is to be conscious; it never ceases to be conscious, not even for a moment. But it is never conscious of separate entities or objects. From the absolute perspective, the ego does not exist. Thus, the egoic phenomenon is problematic only from its own perspective. Enlightenment is only a problem of the ego. For consciousness, the ego has no real existence, so there is no need to forget it, omit it, restrict it, or transcend it.

Perceiving diversity is a consequence of omitting consciousness. Therefore, realizing consciousness necessarily means diversity will evaporate. With knowingness, accumulated knowledge evaporates. Upon realizing what we really are, everything we thought we knew about ourselves disappears.

שְׁלִילַת הַיְּדִיעָה הִיא מֻכְרַחַת, מִפְּנֵי שֶׁכָּל יְדִיעָה הִיא מְטַשְׁטֶשֶׁת אֶת הַיָּדוּעַ, כְּשֵׁם שֶׁהִיא מְבָרֶרֶת אוֹתוֹ, מִפְּנֵי הַטִּשְׁטוּשׁ הַנִּמְצָא בְּמַדָּע הָאָדָם, וְהוּא הַדִּין בְּכָל מַדָּע שֶׁל כָּל הֲוָיָה מֻגְבֶּלֶת שֶׁיֵּשׁ לָהּ רֵאשִׁית. וְעֶצֶם הַחַיִּים הֲרֵי הֵם הַיַּחַשׂ הָאֱלֹהִי שֶׁל הַהֲוָיָה, וְזֶה אָצוּר בַּיְּדִיעָה הַנֶּעֱלֶמֶת, הַנִּתְפֶּסֶת רַק בִּרְעוּתָא דְּלִבָּא הַיּוֹתֵר כְּמוּסָה. וְאִי־אֶפְשָׁר לָהּ לִהְיוֹת מֻגְלֶמֶת בִּידִיעָה מֻבְלֶטֶת, מִפְּנֵי שֶׁתִּתְטַשְׁטֵשׁ עַל־יְדֵי הַהַגְבָּלָה, וּבָזֶה יְבֻטַּל קֶשֶׁר הַמְּצִיאוּת. עַל־כֵּן אִי־אֶפְשָׁר לְשׁוּם הֲוָיָה שֶׁתִּתְפּוֹס אֶת הַהֲוָיָה הָאֱלֹהִית, כְּדֵי שֶׁלֹּא תִּתְבַּטֵּל מְצִיאוּתָהּ, וְתַכְלִית הַיְּדִיעָה מַמְשֶׁכֶת הַחַיִּים וְהַהֲוָיָה, שֶׁאֵין בֵּינָהּ וּבֵין מְקוֹר חַיֵּי הַחַיִּים וַהֲוָיַת הַהֲוָיָה שׁוּם מָסָךְ מַבְדִּיל, שׁוּם דָּבָר חוֹצֵץ, הוּא דַּוְקָא מָה שֶׁלֹּא נֵדַע, כְּלוֹמַר לֹא הַצִּיּוּר שֶׁל הֶעְדֵּר יְדִיעָתֵנוּ, כִּי־אִם עַצְמוּתָהּ שֶׁל שְׁלִילַת הַיְּדִיעָה, שֶׁבְּחָשְׁכָּהּ הָעֶלְיוֹן עַצְמוּת הַיְּדִיעָה הָאֲמִתִּית מֻנַּחַת הִיא בְּלֹא שׁוּם מַגַּע יָד מֻגְבָּלָה, הַמְּמַעֶטֶת אֶת דְּיוֹקְנָהּ. "הֲלֹא אֶת הַשָּׁמַיִם וְאֶת הָאָרֶץ אֲנִי מָלֵא נְאֻם ה'" (ירמיהו כ"ג, כ"ד).

(הרב אברהם יצחק הכהן קוק, מידות הראי"ה, יראה)

It is necessary to negate "knowledge" because, every knowledge blurs the known in the same measure that it clarifies it, and this is due to the hazy nature of the knowledge of human beings, as well as of any limited being that has a beginning.

The very essence of life is the divine relation of the being, which is hidden in the invisible knowledge, that can be perceived only in the most hidden will of the heart. It cannot manifest as external knowledge because it will become blurry due to this limitation, and this will undo the "tie of existence" (the bond of matter and spirit). Therefore, no being can grasp the divine being for otherwise its existence would be

> annulled. The ultimate and life-giving knowledge, which no vail, or any barrier stands between it and The Life-source of the Living and the Existence of Existence, is, in fact, the knowledge that we cannot know. It does not refer to the idea that we lack knowledge of it, but to the very essence of the negation of knowledge: that true knowledge, in its essence, resides in its elevated darkness, unattainable by any limited hand that might reduce its image. "For I fill both heaven and earth—declares the Lord" (Jeremiah, 23:24).
>
> (Rabbi Avraham Isaac HaCohen Kook, *Middot HaRa'ayah*, "Awe")

I do not recommend renunciation, but instead, meditation. I do not advise abandoning the world but cultivating attentive observation. As observation expands, the mind vanishes along with the universe. Meditating is waiting, but what we wait for only arrives when the one who waits disappears. When what is expected arrives, the person who was expecting it dissolves. The revelation of knowingness destroys the knower. What was long-awaited makes the separate false "I" vanish. Then, you cease to be situated somewhere and begin to be. As you become less and less of a localized consciousness, your authenticity of being is revealed to be only boundless consciousness.

When light comes, darkness disappears; the two never coexist. Night may want the day to come and wait for it, but at dawn, darkness dies. The apparent egoic contraction of consciousness vanishes with the relaxation of beingness in its indeterminate original state. When Truth appears, the mind evaporates along with its world.

The one who is blessed and graced with this revelation is not what you know as yourself. If it were, it would be only an experience. Truth is the worst threat to the mind, which is rooted in falsehood. As long as we know, we remain in ignorance; only by knowing knowingness we are set free from what we know. All that you know about yourself fades away, while what endures is inexplicable and impossible to define.

וְתַכְלִית מָה שֶׁנַּשִּׂיג מִמֶּנּוּ יִתְבָּרֵךְ – שֶׁאִי אֶפְשָׁר לְהַשִּׂיגוֹ כְּמַאֲמַר הֶחָכָם: "תַּכְלִית
מָה שֶׁנֵּדַע בְּךָ – שֶׁלֹּא נֵדָעֲךָ".
(רבי יוסף אלבו, ספר העיקרים, מאמר שני, פרק ל')

The ultimate knowledge of Him, Blessed be He, is that it is impossible to grasp Him. As said the wise: "The culmination of our knowledge of You, is that we cannot know You."
(Rabbi Yosef Albo, *Sefer Ha'Ikarim*, 2.30)

An interdisciplinary approach to consciousness

The idea that consciousness constitutes the essential and omnipresent foundation of existence, rather than merely a derivative of material processes, resonates across various philosophical and scientific disciplines. This conception fosters a transdisciplinary exchange that could deepen our understanding of reality and its associated phenomena.

In quantum physics, the interaction between consciousness and perceived reality suggests that our observation might alter the state of the observed. This notion is reflected in theories such as the "wave function collapse" and "quantum entanglement," which could be interpreted as evidence that consciousness plays an active role in shaping physical reality, challenging traditional ideas of objectivity and the distinction between observer and observed.

In neuroscience, analyzing how consciousness arises from the brain, or considering it to be an inherent and fundamental property, opens broad possibilities for debate. This approach might explain why certain neural patterns are associated with specific conscious experiences, questioning the notion that consciousness is simply the result of neural complexity.

Transpersonal psychology echoes the notion of a universal consciousness by exploring how experiences of altered or unitary states transcend traditional psychology's explanatory frameworks. These experiences might indicate that individual consciousness is actually an expression of a broader, interconnected consciousness.

In the philosophy of mind, engaging with theories like panpsychism provides a framework for envisioning consciousness as a universal and fundamental characteristic, omnipresent throughout the cosmos. This approach broadens our view of consciousness and offers a more integrated model of reality.

Interfaith dialogue also benefits from this perspective, as many spiritual traditions have perceived and taught that the foundation of all being is a form of consciousness or spiritual reality. Examining these points of convergence can enrich our philosophical and spiritual understanding of consciousness.

Moreover, the ethical and social implications of considering consciousness as the foundation of all reality are significant. Accepting that all beings are manifestations of the same consciousness could foster greater empathy, compassion, and a renewed sense of responsibility toward others and our planet.

This interdisciplinary approach not only synthesizes various fields of knowledge but also opens new pathways for understanding and living our existence. It suggests that consciousness, far from being a secondary phenomenon, constitutes the true essence of our reality.

ARTICLE 12

THE VOICE OF SILENCE

Question:

Why do some books refer to the state of enlightenment as being nothing or nobody, while others describe it as being everything or everybody? Are being nobody and everybody two distinct states of enlightenment? If so, how do they differ? I must admit that being nothing doesn't sound very appealing.

Answer:

The etymological origin of the word *vacuity* traces back to the Latin term *vacuitas*, which is composed of the adjective *vacuus*, meaning "that which lacks content," and the suffix *dad*, indicating "quality." Buddha refers to vacuity as *śūnyatā*, or "that which lacks identity or separate existence." Vacuity can be viewed from two perspectives: negatively, as nothingness, or positively, as fullness.

> "Why do some books refer to the state of enlightenment as being nothing or nobody…?"

In its negative aspect, vacuity is a lack, deficiency, or absence. Nothingness seems to threaten a desolation that frightens and intimidates us. In reality, however, it is merely an absence of objects or things, while the pure presence of consciousness remains. As the density of objective reality diminishes, the presence of the background becomes more apparent, just as a flame is perceived more clearly when it is not surrounded by smoke. Our excessive gravitation toward objective reality prevents us from appreciating the beauty of consciousness.

Deep sleep and general anesthesia are states of non-existence for the mind. We are so seduced by experiences and objective activity that we think consciousness ceases to exist if it lacks mental, emotional, or physical objects. Consciousness hides from itself by wearing the disguise of a mind cluttered with objective content. But consciousness is easily recognized in the transcendental meditative state or absolute vacuity.

We believe in a universe composed of various subtle objects that are mental, emotional, or physical. In order to define "nothingness," we create a mental replica of emptiness within objective existence. However, nothingness as an idea or concept remains a mental object. Therefore, the conceptualization of consciousness as "nothingness" is only for those who perceive it as an object. Statements such as "reality is nothing" or "consciousness is emptiness" stem from the dogma of the existence of something; they are just reactive conceptualizations to belief in an objective reality.

Fear of death arises from misconceiving reality and believing in objective existence. We are terrified that our achievements will vanish and become nothing. We believe that to die is to disappear. In truth, only our illusory identity disappears; the one that dissolves has never existed. The "I" evaporates, but it was never more than a personal pronoun.

"...while others describe it as being everything or everybody."

There is also a positive conception of emptiness that can be called "plenitude." In the total absence of objects or things, consciousness remains like a mirror with nothing to reflect: only the presence of the mirror full of itself. By emptying ourselves of all sound, even mental or emotional noise, we reach the plenitude of silence. Those who become empty realize the overflowing content of existence, consciousness, and bliss. Even so, they seek to associate with others, but without egoic intentions. The other is not pursued out of an imperious need or a desperate escape from solitude. The need to be loved is not the same as the need to love. Those who have realized themselves as nothingness, filled with love and overflowing bliss, seek others because they feel too full and wish to share and serve.

יוֹתֵר מִמַּה שֶּׁהָעֵגֶל רוֹצֶה לִינַק פָּרָה רוֹצָה לְהָנִיק.
(תלמוד בבלי, מסכת פסחים, קי"ב, א')

More than the calf wishes to suck, the cow wants to suckle.
(*Babylonian Talmud*, "*Pesaḥim*," 112a)

Sitting motionless in the meditation posture with your eyes closed is not the same as inner emptiness. You can be still and repeat the mantra *Oṁ* for hours, even as profuse mental and emotional activity persists. As Kṛṣṇa says, thought is dynamic by nature:

न हि कश्चित्क्षणमपि जातु तिष्ठत्यकर्मकृत् ।
कार्यते ह्यवशः कर्म सर्वः प्रकृतिजैर्गुणैः ॥

na hi kaścit kṣaṇam api
jātu tiṣṭhaty akarma-kṛt
kāryate hy avaśaḥ karma
sarvaḥ prakṛti-jair guṇaiḥ

No one can ever refrain from performing action, not even for a moment, because everyone is made to act helplessly according to the qualities one has acquired from the modes of material nature.

(Bhagavad Gita, 3.5)

Mental activity is constant and uninterrupted. The mind endlessly generates conclusions, theories, emotions, and feelings. If old chains disappear, new ones immediately appear, ready to perpetuate our slavery. We see the world through old content and are simultaneously creating new content.

רַבִּי אוֹמֵר: אַל תִּסְתַּכֵּל בַּקַּנְקַן, אֶלָּא בְּמַה שֶּׁיֵּשׁ בּוֹ. יֵשׁ קַנְקַן חָדָשׁ מָלֵא יָשָׁן, וְיָשָׁן שֶׁאֲפִלּוּ חָדָשׁ אֵין בּוֹ.

(פרקי אבות ד', כ')

Rabbi said, do not look at the decanter, but at what is inside: there is a new decanter full of old, and an old one in which there is not even new.

(*Pirkei Avot,* 4.20)

Our life unfolds superficially. But sooner or later, observation will lead us to look inward. Then, we will realize that the space inside the jar is the same as the space outside of it. The spaces are not different. When transporting the jar from one place to another, its interior space remains immobile and static. In fact, it does not have an inner space; the jar is within infinite space. Likewise, it is believed that everyone possesses their own consciousness as if it resided within us, like the space inside the jar. However, consciousness does not reside inside us; instead, we reside within consciousness.

The glass of the jar is its peripheral nature. Realizing its inner emptiness means finding the center. Likewise, our mental, emotional, and physical activity only takes place on the periphery, not in the center. Since we spend our lives absorbed by the jar, the rabbi recommends we look inward and discover that we are the vacuity. We will then realize that our essence transcends the old and does not create new mental or emotional content. In my youth as a beginner, I was overflowing, burdened, and full of the past. Now, in my old age, I have emptied myself, even of what is new.

Never relate to nothingness from a negative perspective as if it were absence. This vacuity does not imply deficiency. Only names and forms disappear while conscious presence remains. The essence that lies behind all experiences is imperishable and unchanging. However, this reality is inaccessible to the mind, which only functions within the relative and dual field of opposites.

> "Are being nobody and everybody two distinct states of enlightenment? If so, how do they differ?"

Enlightened beings throughout history have only conceptualized consciousness to explain spiritual teachings. Definitions vary according to the capacity and experience of the bearers and recipients of the revelation. Furthermore, since all these messages clarify previous concepts, they are influenced by pre-established ideas. If there were no erroneous beliefs, new teachings would be unnecessary.

Conceptualizing reality as "nothing" was necessary to counteract the prior idea of it as objective. Although it is impossible to conceptualize consciousness, there is nothing wrong with trying to simplify it. Conceptualization is an important stage of the evolutionary process, and without it, we would stagnate at the instinctual level. At the absolute level, ultimate reality is revealed when we deny that it is neither something nor nothing. Its objectivity is transcended, as well as its non-objectivity.

> הַנְּשָׁמָה לוֹמֶדֶת תּוֹרָה מֵהקב"ה בִּמְתִיבְתָּא דִּרְקִיעַ וְהקב"ה שׁוֹלֵחַ לְמַטָּה אֶת הַנְּשָׁמָה אֶל הָעוֹלָם לֹא רַק כְּדֵי לִלְמֹד תּוֹרָה אֶלָּא גַּם כְּדֵי לַהֲפֹךְ אֶת הָאנ"י לְאי"ן (לַעֲשׂוֹת מֵהָאֲנִי אַיִן). אֲפִלּוּ מִי שֶׁהוּא בֶּאֱמֶת אנ"י שֶׁל תּוֹרָה וּמִצְווֹת צָרִיךְ לַהֲפֹךְ אֶת הָאנ"י הַזֶּה לְאי"ן.
>
> (בעל־שם־טוב, כתר שם־טוב, הוספות, רי"ג)
>
> The soul learns Torah from The Holy One, Blessed be He in the heavenly academy and The Holy One, Blessed be He sends the soul into the world not only to learn Torah, but also to transform the *ani* ("I") into *ain* (nothing) even if one is truly an "I" of Torah and *mitzvot* (religious "I"), he has to turn that *ani* ("I") into *ain* (nothing).
>
> (Ba'al Shem Tov, *Keter Shem Tov*, *Additions*, 213)

Even if we are an "I" of Torah and *mitzvot*, we will only be complete when we dissolve ourselves on every level. No matter how religious, spiritual, holy, or pure devotees we may be, the realization of our authentic nature is vacuity itself.

> "I must admit that being nothing doesn't sound very appealing."

We tend to react negatively to vacuity. Going from the ego to vacuity is a leap from the known to the unknowable. The unknowable exists outside the mental boundaries deep within us, always ready to reveal itself when we truly desire it.

Most people's lives are based on the egoic phenomenon. They identify with the mind–body complex. They describe themselves with a name, age, profession, nationality, and marital status. After the idea of being (1) "something or somebody" evaporates, then the experience of being (2) "nothing or nobody" emerges. Then this gives way to the experience of being (3) "everything or everybody," and finally, in only (4) knowing.

(1) Something or somebody

In the egoic state, we consider ourselves to be a personal, individual entity that exists within the confines of a body and a mind. We believe we are "something" that exists. Interestingly, the etymology of the term *exist* is related to the verb *to appear*. If we explore its roots, we discover that it is formed by *ex* and *sist*. *Ex* reflects the abandonment of an environment and *sist* is a Latin verb meaning "to remain or to be." Therefore, to *exist* refers to something that was not part of this reality and that, in order to manifest itself, had to abandon its original state.

We believe we are part of a temporal and objective reality. As we evolve and progress on the Path of Retroprogressive Alignment, we recognize ourselves to be the knowing conscious presence of the mind–body complex. We notice that our nature is not objective, but that which observes and knows the objects.

(2) Nothing or nobody

From the relative level of consciousness in which we consider ourselves "something or somebody" we move forward and realize we lack attributes and are "nothing or nobody." Our nature is unqualified observation. From the mental perspective, which only knows objective reality, unqualified reality is interpreted as nothing. The mind can only perceive objects with attributes; therefore, it thinks non-objective essence is emptiness.

Next, we inquire into the relationship between consciousness and the apparent objective reality of our mind, body, and universe. As we observe our experience, we notice that consciousness is much more than the observation of diverse objects at a distance or a background observing a multiplicity of objects.

Astonishingly, we realize that consciousness, observation, and all objects share a single essential substance. This is a step forward after the realization of our non-objective nature. It takes us from considering ourselves to be nothing to recognizing we are the essential substance of everything.

(3) Everything or everybody

The retroprogressive process takes us from considering ourselves as something, then nothing, and finally realizing that we are the essence of everything. Both observation and what is observed are composed of the same substance. When a jeweler crafts necklaces, rings, earrings, or bracelets, the gold remains unchanged. And if all these pieces of jewelry are eventually melted down, they will still be gold.

Similarly, the essential substance of the observation and what is observed is one and the same. The perception of the universe is also the perceiver; they are one. This awakening leads to the realization that we are the substance of all objective diversity. Rather than being the witnessing background of an objective reality, I am the essence of each and every object in the apparent empirical universe.

These different levels are related to objects in various ways. Initially, we think we possess them. Then comes the experience of the disappearance of objects. Obviously, from the mental perspective accustomed only to objective reality, nothingness is unappealing. To the mind that knows only a reality of objects, their absence resembles death. Next, we consider ourselves to be all objects, but if things do not exist and only perception exists, the claim to be everything and everyone would be contradictory.

We define ourselves based on our belief in the reality of matter. Our conception of reality assumes that objects exist. These are relative levels of consciousness, each more real than the last. The level of realization at which we consider ourselves to be everything is also relative and corresponds to an illusion, since objects do not exist independently. There are simply no objects to observe with which to share the same substance.

(4) Knowing

The reality of our own experience tells us clearly that we have never known an object, but only the knowing. All our knowledge of mind, body, and universe consists just in the knowing. In reality, we have never known anything. The knower and the known are not two different factors, but rather both are what we call "knowingness."

Consciousness recognizes its unqualified nature, imperceptible to the senses; it is timeless, unlimited, and always present. After the disappearance of all physical, energetic, mental, and emotional objects, we find only silence. By transcending physical things, ideas, thoughts, feelings, conclusions, memories, dreams, and longings, we will have an intimate encounter with life. This is because silence is a face-to-face encounter with reality and existence, with what is, as it is.

The explanation of the next level of consciousness is given by silence. Few listen to it and even fewer understand it. Of course, I am not referring to silence perceived in yoga or tai chi classes, but to the silence that arises from our inner depths. It is not an absence of sounds, thoughts, or emotions, but a silence that is a presence. It is not a lack of concerns, troubles, or tensions, rather a blissful and loving presence.

> וַיֹּאמֶר צֵא וְעָמַדְתָּ בָהָר לִפְנֵי ה' וְהִנֵּה ה' עֹבֵר וְרוּחַ גְּדוֹלָה וְחָזָק מְפָרֵק הָרִים. וּמְשַׁבֵּר סְלָעִים לִפְנֵי ה' לֹא בָרוּחַ ה' וְאַחַר הָרוּחַ רַעַשׁ לֹא בָרַעַשׁ ה':
> וְאַחַר הָרַעַשׁ אֵשׁ לֹא בָאֵשׁ ה' וְאַחַר הָאֵשׁ קוֹל דְּמָמָה דַקָּה:
> (מלכים א' י"ט, י"א–י"ב)
>
> And he said: "Come out, and stand on the mountain before the Lord." And, there, the Lord passed by. There was a great and mighty wind, splitting mountains and shattering rocks before the Lord; but the Lord was not in the wind. After the wind—an earthquake; but the Lord was not in the earthquake. After the earthquake—fire; but the Lord was not in the fire. And after the fire—a sound of subtle silence.
>
> (I Kings 19:11–12)

If we observe ourselves, we may notice moments when we forget our ambitions and yearnings, yesterday and tomorrow, what was and what will be, our past and future. It may happen to us while we watch a seagull at sunset by the sea, contemplate the full moon reflecting on a lake, or see a happy child running into its mother's arms. The beauty of the stars can unify us with ourselves, merging the subjective and objective. In moments like these, we empty ourselves of concepts like time and space and flood ourselves with eternity and infinity. We disappear, for we cease to perceive ourselves as subjects separated from what is observed. Even if we empty ourselves of our mental and emotional content for a moment, our cowardice will prevent us from living from vacuity. Without courage, our mental content will be instantly renewed.

You say that being nothing is not appealing. Dare to realize your vacuity, observing the world without allowing it to distort you. If for a moment you feel that what you observe disfigures you, re-synchronize with vacuity. It will gradually reveal itself as a completely unknown fullness that transcends nothingness and somethingness. At first, it will seem like nothing, then everything, and eventually it will show itself to be a silence devoid of qualities, not because they are lacking, but because they are unnecessary. It is not a silence that lacks words. It is a silence that says it all. It is not the silence of a cemetery, but the silence of the moon and the stars bathing in the lake.

ARTICLE 13

HASSIDISM: LIVING IN GRACE

If Kabbalah is the soul of the Torah, Hassidism is its inner depths. It is the most intimate essence of Hebrew revelation. This wisdom was transmitted by enlightened Hasidic masters directly to their disciples. Hassidism is a path of liberation that points to reality, to what is, as it is.

Hassidism arose in Ukraine and Belarus in the eighteenth-century CE. This vision emerged out of the Sinaitic revelation and was presented by the eminent enlightened being Rabbi Israel ben Eliezer, known as the Ba'al Shem Tov (1698–1760 CE). The son of Eliezer and Sarah, he was born in Okopy, a Ukrainian town that throughout history has belonged to Poland, Russia, and Galicia. He died in the Ukrainian city of Medzhybizh, which was at different points part of Lithuania, Turkey, Poland, and Russia. Had this great enlightened master been born in India, he would most certainly have been considered an *avatāra*, or "an incarnation of God." Although he did not establish a new religion, he blessed humanity with the Hassidic movement.

The Besht (the acronym for Ba'al Shem Tov) did not invent anything but reminded us of the essence of religion. Masters like him make religion fresh and spiritual once again. Without rejecting his own tradition, he revolutionized the society he lived in by revealing the core of religious life in a practical way. The revolution that The Besht inspired also brought resistance from prominent contemporary religious leaders. These detractors and opponents are called *mitnagdim* in Hebrew.

The Hebrew term *ḥasid* (חסיד) means "merciful or pious," and is derived from the root *ḥ.s.d.* (ח.ס.ד.), which means "piety, mercy, or grace." It is the source of the term *ḥasidut* (חסידות), whose meaning is "to live by piety, mercy, and grace." English lacks an equivalent word to *ḥesed* that conveys the breadth of its meaning. Various authors have translated it as piety, mercy, grace, compassion, faithfulness, kindness, goodness, gentleness, love, justice, glory, or favor, but none of these terms encompass its full meaning. Hassidism is about the constant presence of *ḥesed* in our lives, considered to be as important as the *mitzvot*, or "the precepts."

Judging solely by their manifestations, it is difficult to differentiate between false piety and authentic mercy. The former arises from the ego, while the latter blossoms from absence of ego. A certain sensitivity is required to evaluate and recognize the quality of each, because externally they are very similar. If we peel back the cover of egoistic piety, we discover that politics and business lie beneath, but if we delve into genuine mercy, we find happiness and bliss. For Hassidism, bliss is akin to a sacred commandment, while sadness is considered almost a sin.

Mercy and piety are the light and heat of the flame of bliss that burns in our soul. Happiness shared with our fellow human beings comes from the heart and attracts others since it is genuine mercy. By sharing the happiness that dwells in our soul with others, others experience it as *ḥesed*. Its false versions are found in politics, business, the spiritual marketplace, and institutionalized religion. When politicians of one country help those of another with money or weapons, they are not motivated by mercy. Many people help humanity motivated by monetary gain or selfish reasons. Even some religious organizations help the poor to ensure their volunteers a place in paradise. If altruists aim to get tickets for eternal life, they are nothing but greedy. True mercy comes from beatitude, as a selfless expression of happiness and fulfillment. In reality, these people do not wish to eradicate poverty, because if the world ran out of poor people, the volunteers would have no way to approach God. Of course, Hassidism supports charity, but its emphasis is not on charity itself, but on happiness and bliss. Mercy or *ḥesed* cannot be practiced, but if we are blessed with bliss, they will manifest effortlessly.

In Hassidism, the words *mercy* and *grace* have very different meanings. With mercy, we are forgiven upon sincere repentance; grace, on the other hand, is a free gift for our benefit. In Vedantic terminology of karma, mercy means receiving karmic reactions of lesser severity than deserved, while grace is undeserved help that brings us closer to sainthood. Grace is divine love acting upon human nature. Grace leads humans to revelation but must be discovered. Those who have received it feel it is undeserved, but to be worthy of it, they must do everything possible to deserve it. It is freely available divine support, but it is only granted to those who have made enough effort. It is like searching for groundwater: it is always there, but finding it requires effort. Although grace is available, we will not recognize it if we are too busy with trivial matters. Grace descended on Mount Sinai, where the human made efforts to rise to the summit and divinity bent down to make possible the encounter and revelation.

Those who fall in love often attribute it to a relationship with another person. Few realize that we do not fall in love, but rather we reconnect with our essence, which is love. Such love does not stem from a relationship, but rather emanates from our depths. Initially, it is an experience of love, later it is perceived as grace, and ultimately, it is revealed as the divine.

Unfortunately, most who have found love misinterpret the call in their hearts as an invitation for enjoyment and pleasure, diverting themselves to the objective plane. They make the mistake of relating it to someone, satisfying themselves, and getting stuck in the preamble. Love is the preamble to grace, and grace is the preamble to revelation. To avoid this mistake, we must at least understand that love does not depend on a relationship but is the light of our own being. The more you love, the closer to the revelation of the self you are. The deeper you dive into the depths of yourself, the more love grows. Grace descends upon those who are not satisfied with the love of a relationship. The blessed ones do not remain stagnant in the objective world but venture into the depths of subjectivity.

Pleasure experienced on the objective plane is suffering, while even pain coming from God is bliss. Better than smiles from worldly achievements are tears due to longing to God. It was grace, not misery, that made the *gopīs* of Vrindavan, Mīra, and Chaitanya weep unconsolably. When Chaitanya begs to cry for God in his poem *Śikṣāṣṭakam*, he is asking for grace, not misery:

नयनं गलदश्रुधारया वदनं गद्गदरुद्धया गिरा ।
पुलकैर्निचितं वपुः कदा तव नामग्रहणे भविष्यति ॥

nayanaṁ galad-aśru-dhārayā
vadanaṁ gadgada-ruddhayā girā
pulakair nicitaṁ vapuḥ kadā
tava nāma-grahaṇe bhaviṣyati

> O my Lord, when will my eyes be decorated with tears of love flowing constantly when I chant your holy name? When will my voice choke up, and when will the hairs of my body stand on end at the recitation of your name?
>
> (*Śikṣāṣṭakam*, 6)

Hassidism means living in grace. Grace changes the quality of our life radically, descending like a call from the depths of the soul. It pulls us into an irresistible search for the unknowable. The need for God is undeserved grace because it is God calling for God.

To find God, we must not look in an otherness, but deep within us. It is an encounter in the absolute dimension with that which is our deepest reality. In this quest, we come to realize that consciousness was never confined to a specific place, but that there is no place devoid of it.

We find it difficult to recognize consciousness, akin to deep-sea fish that cannot recognize water. Comparison is a basic thinking skill that we use to recognize things. It allows us to manage information and to organize our perceptions. It is part of the foundation of analytical, critical, and creative thinking. Comparison arises spontaneously and helps us identify specific objects in our daily lives. When we look for a friend in a large group, we compare our memory with each face we see. We search for a missing object by comparing the memorized image with each perceived object. However, such mental abilities cannot be utilized in the realm of consciousness.

> וְאֶל־מִי תְדַמְּיוּנִי וְאֶשְׁוֶה יֹאמַר קָדוֹשׁ:
>
> (ישעיהו מ', כ"ה)

> To whom, then, can you liken Me, to whom can I be compared?—says the Holy One.
>
> (Isaiah, 40:25)

Only consciousness is and thus it cannot be compared to any object because these objects, in essence, are nonexistent. The entire reality of the objective universe belongs to consciousness, which is completely devoid of objective qualities.

Many believe that the Torah teaches monotheism. Verses such as *ein od milvado*, or "there is no more than only Him" (Deuteronomy, 4:35), are generally interpreted as expressions proclaiming the existence of one God. Although the Torah does not argue for a multitude of gods, neither does it say there is only one. The essence of the Sinaitic revelation, transmitted over generations through enlightened masters, teaches us that apart from God, nothing else exists. *Ein od milvado* categorically affirms the non-existence of anything besides God. Only God is and besides God, meaning consciousness, nothing and no one really *is*.

אֲנִי ה' וְאֵין עוֹד זוּלָתִי אֵין אֱלֹהִים אֲאַזֶּרְךָ וְלֹא יְדַעְתָּנִי:
לְמַעַן יֵדְעוּ מִמִּזְרַח־שֶׁמֶשׁ וּמִמַּעֲרָבָה כִּי־אֶפֶס בִּלְעָדָי אֲנִי ה' וְאֵין עוֹד:
(ישעיהו מ"ה, ה'–ו')

I am the Lord, and there is no other; besides Me, there is no God. I will strengthen you although you have not known Me. So that they know from the rising of the sun [morning or east] and its setting [night or west] that there is nothing else aside from Me; I am the Lord, and there is nothing else.
(Isaiah, 45:5–6)

Following the biblical statement, The Rambam, Rabbi Moshe Ben Maimon, says that only consciousness is and that nothing but consciousness is real and true:

לְפִיכָךְ אֵין אֲמִתָּתוֹ כַּאֲמִתַּת אֶחָד מֵהֶם. הוּא שֶׁהַנָּבִיא אוֹמֵר: "וַה' אֱלֹהִים אֱמֶת" (ירמיהו י', י'). הוּא לְבַדּוֹ הָאֱמֶת וְאֵין לְאַחֵר אֱמֶת כַּאֲמִתָּתוֹ. וְהוּא שֶׁהַתּוֹרָה אוֹמֶרֶת: "אֵין עוֹד מִלְּבַדּוֹ"(דברים ד', ל"ה). כְּלוֹמַר, אֵין שָׁם מָצוּי אֱמֶת מִלְּבַדּוֹ כְּמוֹתוֹ.
(משנה תורה, ספר המדע, הלכות יסודי התורה ,א', ג'–ד')

Therefore, the truth of His [being] does not resemble the truth of any of their [being]. And this is what the prophet stated (Jeremiah, 10:10): "And the Lord, God, is true," meaning, He alone is true, and no one else possesses truth that compares to His truth. And this is what is meant by the Torah's statement "there is no more than only Him" (Deuteronomy, 4:35), meaning, aside from Him, there is no true existence like His.

(*Mishneh Torah*, "*Sefer HaMadda*,"
"*Foundations of the Torah*," 1.3–4)

The *Ḥasid* transcends belief in a single God who resides in heaven and who spends his days judging human beings. He goes beyond the concept of a God whose only job is to reward and punish. The *Ḥasid* awakens to the reality that only God is.

לֵית אֲתַר פָּנוּי מִנֵּיהּ, כְּנִשְׁמְתָא דְאִשְׁתַּכְּחַת בְּכָל אֵבֶר וְאֵבֶר דְגוּפָא.

(תיקוני זוהר, קכ"ב, ב')

There is no place vacant of Him, just as the soul that pervades each and every limb of the body.

(*Tikkunei HaZohar*, 122b)

לֵית אֲתַר דְלָאו אִיהוּ תַּמָּן, לְעֵילָא עַד אֵין סוֹף, וּלְתַתָּא עַד אֵין תַּכְלִית, וּלְכָל סִטְרָא לֵית אֱלוֹהַּ בַּר מִנֵּיהּ.

(זוהר חדש, פרשת יתרו, מאמר ז' ימי בראשית)

There is no place where He is not—above, infinitely; below, without an end; and on every side—there is no Lord except Him.

(*Zohar Ḥadash*, *Parashat Yithro*, Discourse
"*The seven days of creation.*")

In other words, outside of God there is nothing here. The universe has been created through words or transcendental verbal expressions. God spoke, and objective diversity emanated from his transcendental utterances.

כִּי הוּא אָמַר וַיֶּהִי הוּא צִוָּה וַיַּעֲמֹד:

(תהילים ל"ג, ט')

For He spoke, and it was; He commanded, and it endured.
(Psalms, 33:9)

God not only spoke in the distant past to create objective reality, but he continues to create through his speech in every moment.

הַמְחַדֵּשׁ בְּטוּבוֹ בְּכָל־יוֹם תָּמִיד מַעֲשֵׂה בְרֵאשִׁית:
(סידור התפילה, תפילת שחרית, ברכת יוצר אור)

He who renews, in His goodness, each day continuously, the act of creation.
(Daily morning prayer, "*Yotzer Or*" blessing)

אָמְנָם אֲמִתַּת הָאֱמוּנָה הַנִּרְאָה בְּעֵינַי הִיא: ה' יִתְבָּרַךְ מְחַדֵּשׁ בְּטוּבוֹ בְּכָל יוֹם תָּמִיד מַעֲשֵׂה בְרֵאשִׁית, בְּכַוָּנָה מְכֻוֶּנֶת שׁוֹפֵעַ שִׁפְעוֹ, וְאִלּוּ הָיָה מוֹנֵעַ רֶגַע אֶחָד הָיָה הַכֹּל כְּלֹא הָיָה, בְּטֵל הַמְּצִיאוּת. וְהוּא פֵּרוּשׁ הַפָּסוּק: "וְיָדַעְתָּ הַיּוֹם וַהֲשֵׁבֹתָ אֶל לְבָבֶךָ כִּי ה' הוּא הָאֱלֹהִים בַּשָּׁמַיִם מִמַּעַל וְעַל הָאָרֶץ מִתָּחַת אֵין עוֹד" (דברים ד', ל"ט). אֵין הַפֵּרוּשׁ כִּי אֵין אֱלוֹהַּ זוּלָתוֹ, כִּי זֶהוּ פְּשִׁיטָא, וּכְבָר גִּלָּה זֶה בְּפָסוּק "שְׁמַע יִשְׂרָאֵל ה' אֱלֹהֵינוּ ה' אֶחָד" (דברים ו', ד'), אֶלָּא ר"ל שֶׁאֵין עוֹד מְצִיאוּת בָּעוֹלָם זוּלַת מְצִיאוּתוֹ יִתְבָּרֵךְ, כִּי בְּהֶסְתֵּרוֹ יֹאבַד הַכֹּל.
(רבי ישעיה הלוי הורוביץ, שני לוחות הברית, עשרה מאמרות, מאמר א')

But the true faith, as I see it, is that the Lord, Blessed be He, renews, in His goodness, each day continuously, the act of creation. He spreads His abundance with direct intention, and if He were to refrain from doing so, even for a moment, everything would revert to a state as if it had never existed; reality would be nullified. This is the essence of the verse: "Know therefore this day, and keep in mind that the Lord alone is God, in heaven above and on earth below; there is no other" (Deuteronomy, 4:39). The meaning of this verse is not that there is no other God, as this is obvious and has already been revealed in the verse: "Hear, O Israel, the Lord is our God, the Lord is one" (Deuteronomy, 6:4). Rather, the verse emphasizes that apart from His existence, Blessed be He, there is no other existence in the world, and if He were to conceal Himself, everything would vanish.

(Rabbi Isaiah HaLevi Horowitz, *Shnei Luḥot HaBrit*, "*Ten Expressions*," first expression)

The existence of an objective universe is a miracle or a supranatural phenomenon. However, we should expect the waters of the sea to return to their natural state after having been held back, for example, when the Red Sea parted so the people of Israel could walk through it. If you throw a stone up, you do not expect it to stay in the air. Due to inertia, as soon as the throwing energy weakens, it will return to its natural state. Likewise, it is unnatural to expect the mind, the body, and the universe to continue to exist. Instead, we should anticipate that they will return to their nonexistent natural state. The existence of mind, body, and universe depends entirely on consciousness. Creation borrows its existence and reality from the only thing that exists on the absolute plane. The existence of objective reality is not independent. Just as stones cannot fly, what looks objective does not become absolute reality. This is explained by the great master, Rabbi Schneur Zalman of Liadi:

אִלּוּ הָיוּ מִסְתַּלְּקוֹת מִמֶּנָּה [מן הארץ] כְּרֶגַע חַס וְשָׁלוֹם הָאוֹתִיּוֹת מֵעֲשָׂרָה מַאֲמָרוֹת שֶׁבָּהֶן נִבְרֵאת הָאָרֶץ בְּשֵׁשֶׁת יְמֵי בְּרֵאשִׁית, הָיְתָה חוֹזֶרֶת לְאַיִן וָאֶפֶס מַמָּשׁ, כְּמוֹ לִפְנֵי שֵׁשֶׁת יְמֵי בְּרֵאשִׁית מַמָּשׁ.

(ספר התניא, שער היחוד והאמונה, פרק א')

If the letters of the Ten Utterances by which the world was created during the Six Days of Creation were to depart from it [from the earth], even for an instant—God forbid—it would revert to naught and absolute nothingness, exactly as it was before the Six Days of Creation.

(*Tanya*, "*The portal of unity and faith*," chapter 1)

וְהִנֵּה, אַחֲרֵי הַדְּבָרִים וְהָאֱמֶת הָאֵלֶּה, כָּל מַשְׂכִּיל עַל דָּבָר יָבִין לַאֲשׁוּרוֹ, אֵיךְ שֶׁכָּל נִבְרָא וָיֵשׁ הוּא בֶּאֱמֶת נֶחְשָׁב לְאַיִן וָאֶפֶס מַמָּשׁ לְגַבֵּי כֹּחַ הַפּוֹעֵל וְרוּחַ פִּיו שֶׁבַּנִּפְעָל, הַמְהַוֶּה אוֹתוֹ תָּמִיד וּמוֹצִיאוֹ מֵאַיִן מַמָּשׁ לְיֵשׁ.

(ספר התניא, שער היחוד והאמונה, פרק ג')

> Now, following these words and truths [concerning the nature of the Creation], every intelligent person will clearly understand that each creature and being is actually considered null and absolute nothingness in relation to the Creative Force and the "Breath of His mouth," within the created, which continuously call it into existence and bring it from absolute nothingness into being.
>
> (*Tanya*, "*The portal of unity and faith*," chapter 3)

If God were silent, the universe would cease to exist. Divine silence would mean the disappearance of objective reality.

> 'הַמְחַדֵּשׁ בְּטוּבוֹ בְּכָל יוֹם תָּמִיד מַעֲשֵׂה בְּרֵאשִׁית', שֶׁבְּכָל יוֹם מִתְחַדֵּשׁ חִדּוּשׁ הַבְּרִיאָה מֵאַיִן לְיֵשׁ, וּכְמוֹ שֶׁהָיְתָה תְּחִלַּת הַבְּרִיאָה בְּשֵׁשֶׁת יְמֵי בְּרֵאשִׁית מֵאַיִן לְיֵשׁ מַמָּשׁ, כְּמוֹ כֵן עַתָּה מִתְחַדֶּשֶׁת הַבְּרִיאָה יֵשׁ מֵאַיִן מַמָּשׁ כו'.
>
> (האדמו"ר הזקן, ליקוטי תורה, פרשת ראה, י"ט, ג')

> "He who renews, in His goodness, each day continuously, the act of creation" suggests that creation *ex-nihilo* (from nothing to something) is being renewed every day, and just as the beginning of creation, during the Six Days of Creation, was truly *ex-nihilo*, so it is now, creation is truly being renewed *ex-nihilo*.
>
> (*The Alter Rebbe*, *Likutei Torah*, "*Re'eh*," 19, 3)

Nothing exists outside of consciousness. The Alter Rebbe states that the existence of the objective universe depends entirely on consciousness. The universe constantly borrows its apparent reality and existence from consciousness. If it were to stop doing this for even a moment, the entire universe would cease to exist. It would be as if it never existed.

> אֲבָל אִלּוּ נִתְּנָה רְשׁוּת לָעַיִן לִרְאוֹת וּלְהַשִּׂיג אֶת הַחַיּוּת וְרוּחָנִיּוּת שֶׁבְּכָל נִבְרָא הַשּׁוֹפֵעַ בּוֹ מִמּוֹצָא פִּי ה' וְרוּחַ פִּיו, לֹא הָיָה גַּשְׁמִיּוּת הַנִּבְרָא וְחָמְרוֹ וּמַמָּשׁוֹ נִרְאֶה כְּלָל לְעֵינֵינוּ, כִּי הוּא בָּטֵל בִּמְצִיאוּת מַמָּשׁ לְגַבֵּי הַחַיּוּת וְהָרוּחָנִיּוּת שֶׁבּוֹ, מֵאַחַר שֶׁמִּבַּלְעֲדֵי הָרוּחָנִיּוּת הָיָה אַיִן וָאֶפֶס מַמָּשׁ כְּמוֹ קֹדֶם שֵׁשֶׁת יְמֵי בְּרֵאשִׁית מַמָּשׁ,

וְהָרוּחָנִיּוּת הַשּׁוֹפֵעַ עָלָיו מִמּוֹצָא פִּי ה' וְרוּחַ פִּיו הוּא לְבַדּוֹ הַמּוֹצִיאוֹ תָּמִיד מֵאֶפֶס
וְאַיִן לְיֵשׁ וּמְהַוֶּה אוֹתוֹ, אִם כֵּן אֶפֶס בִּלְעָדוֹ בֶּאֱמֶת.
(ספר התניא, שער היחוד והאמונה, פרק ג')

But if the eye was allowed to view and perceive the life-force and spirit that is within every created being, which flows in it from the expression and breath of God's mouth, then the corporeity and tangibility of the created being would not be perceived by our eyes at all. Because in relation to the life and spirit it contains, it is essentially null, since without the spirit, it would be literally nothing, a nullity, as it was before the Six Days of Creation. The spirit that flows into it from the mouth of God is the only thing that constantly brings it out from nullity and nothingness into existence and brings it into being. Therefore, there is nothing but Him, truly.

(*Tanya*, "*The portal of unity and faith*," chapter 3)

We find the following verse in Psalms:

לְעוֹלָם ה' דְּבָרְךָ נִצָּב בַּשָּׁמָיִם:
(תהילים קי"ט, פ"ט)

Forever, O Lord, Your word stands firm in the heavens.

(Psalms, 119:89)

In connection with this verse, the founder of Hassidism, The Ba'al Shem Tov, quoted the following *midrash*:

"דְּבָרְךָ נִצָּב בַּשָּׁמַיִם" (תהילים קי"ט, פ"ט). אֵיזֶה דָּבָר הַנִּצָּב בַּשָּׁמַיִם? אֶלָּא אָמַר
הקב"ה: "עַל מָה הַשָּׁמַיִם עוֹמְדִים? עַל אוֹתוֹ דָּבָר שֶׁאָמַרְתִּי 'יְהִי רָקִיעַ בְּתוֹךְ הַמָּיִם
[וְגוֹ'] וַיְהִי כֵן' (בראשית א', ו'–ז')", וּכְתִיב "כִּי הוּא אָמַר וַיֶּהִי" וְגוֹ' (תהילים
ל"ג, ט'), אוֹתוֹ הַדָּבָר שֶׁאָמַר – הוּא עָשָׂה. לְכָךְ נֶאֱמַר: "הוּא צִוָּה וַיַּעֲמֹד" (שם),
"בִּדְבַר ה' שָׁמַיִם נַעֲשׂוּ" (תהילים ל"ג, ו'), וּבְאוֹתוֹ הַדָּבָר שֶׁבָּרָא אוֹתָן – בּוֹ הֵם
עוֹמְדִים לָעוֹלָם. לְכָךְ נֶאֱמַר: "לְעוֹלָם ה' דְּבָרְךָ נִצָּב בַּשָּׁמָיִם".
(אוצר מדרשים, מדרש תהילים, הוספה למזמור קי"ט, מ"א)

> "Your word stands firm in the heavens" (Psalms, 119:89) What word is it that stands in heavens? The Holy Blessed One said: "What is it that the heavens stand on? On the very same utterance that I have said: 'Let there be a firmament in the midst of the water, etc. [...] and it was so' (Genesis, 1:6–7)." And it is written: "For He spoke, and it was." (Psalms, 33:9). The same thing that He spoke, He created. Therefore, it is said: "He commanded, and it endured." And "By the word of the Lord the heavens were made" (Psalms, 33:6). With the same utterance that He created, they are maintained forever. This is why it was said: "Forever, O Lord, Your word stands firm in heaven."
>
> (*Midrash Shoḥer Tov* on Psalms, 119:89)

Hassidic teachings are not accessible through intellectual study alone. Only grace can give us access to the Hassidic treasures. Grace can come from God, the scriptures, a guru, and so on. When we receive grace from the holy scriptures, they unveil themselves directly to us. When we receive grace from a guru, we access transcendental wisdom that can only be transmitted from master to disciple. To elevate ourselves to the heights that Hassidism invites us to, it is indispensable to accept the guidance of an authentic master who has directly realized absolute reality. Then, we should try to embrace our master's vision. Disciples look, but masters see. An *admor* is a being who is deeply rooted in reality and can guide us to the realization that only God exists. Ultimately, we will not discover that God exists, but that God is existence itself.

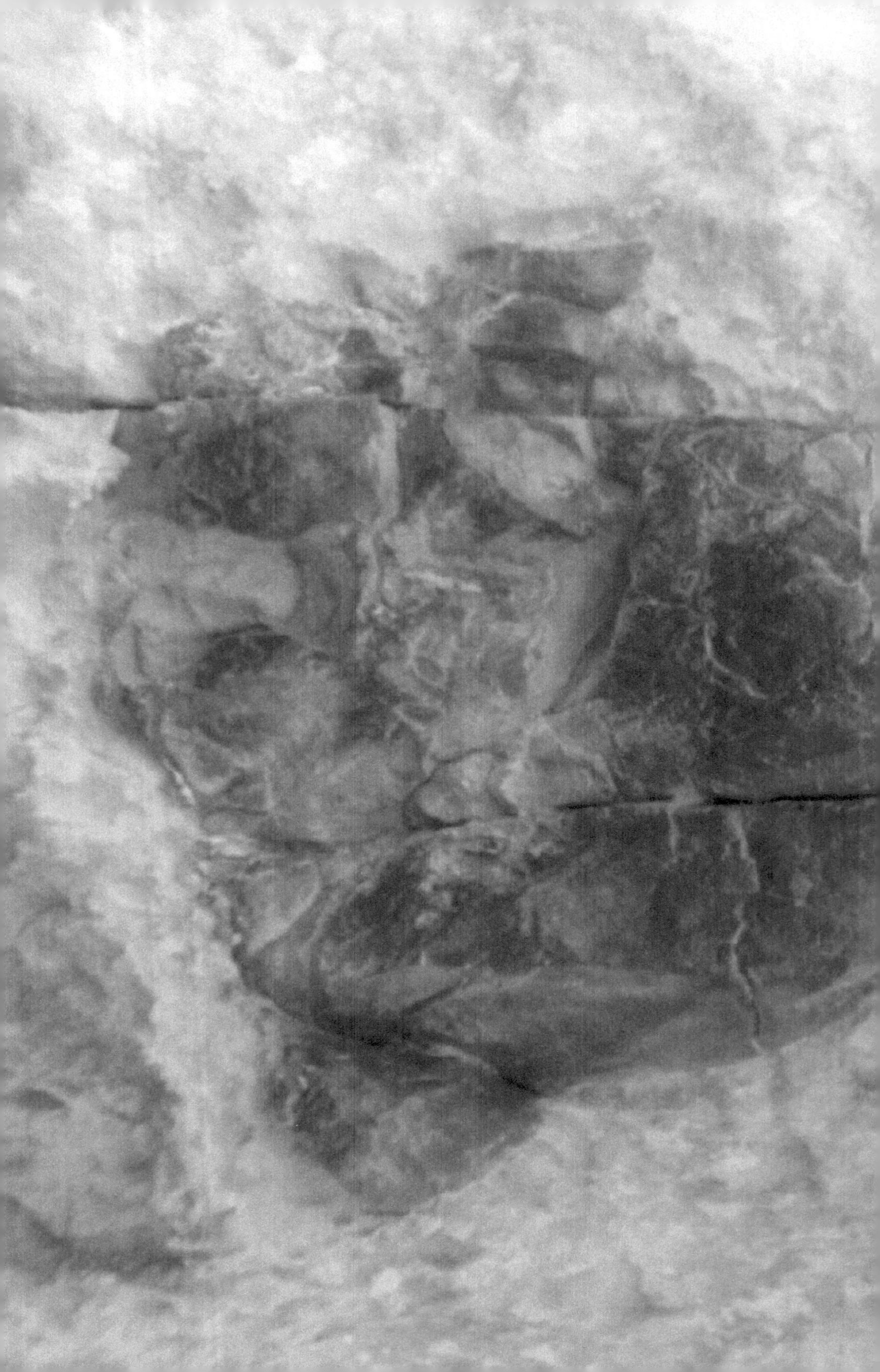

— ARTICLE 14 —

A FIRE IS BURNING HERE!

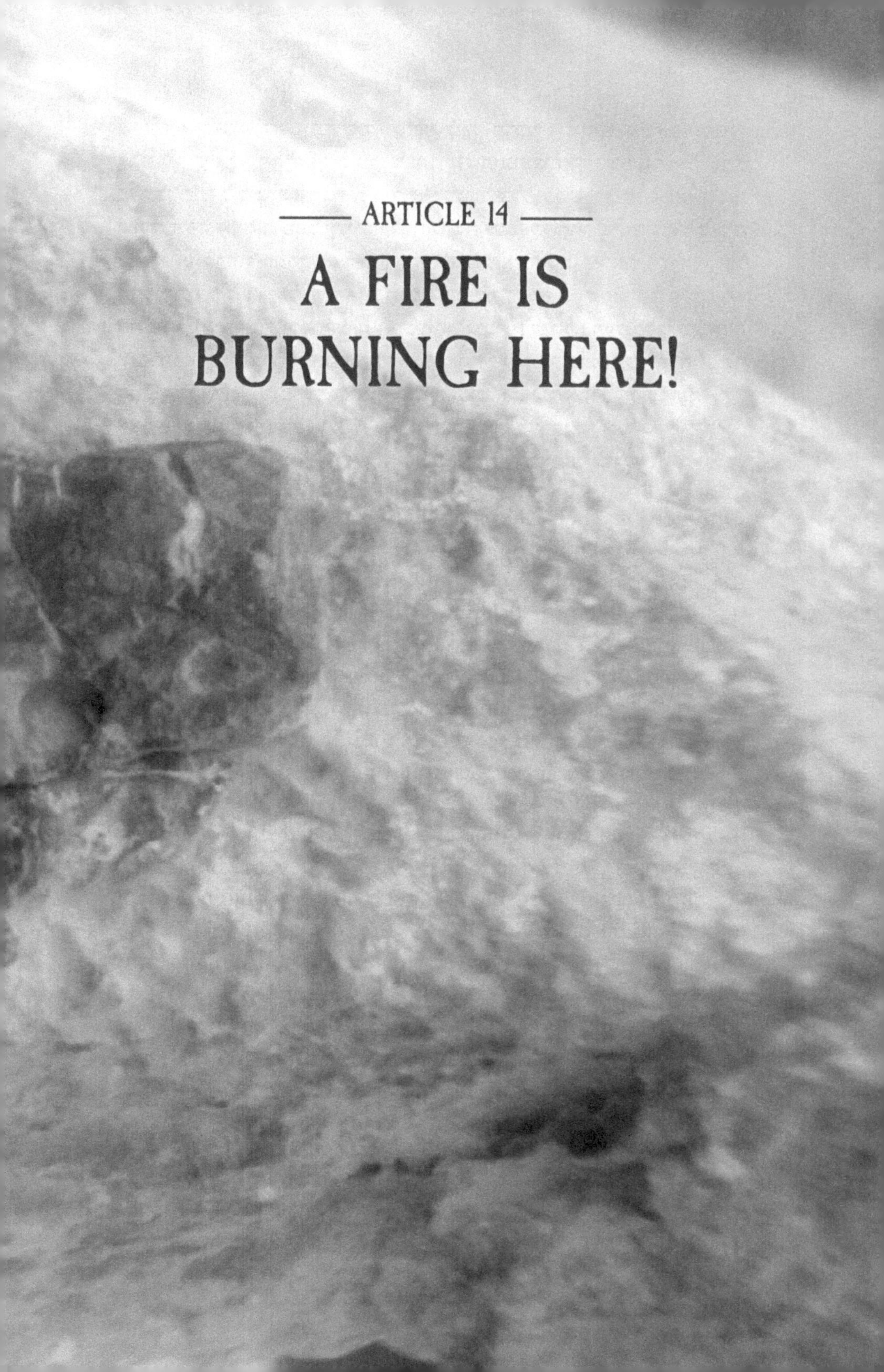

מוהרנ"ת הַקָּדוֹשׁ ז"ל אָמַר שֶׁמָּה שֶׁזָּכָה לֵידַע מֵרַבֵּנוּ ז"ל יוֹתֵר מִשְּׁאַר תַּלְמִידֵי רַבֵּנוּ ז"ל הָיָה רַק מֵהַלֵּילֵי שַׁבָּתוֹת שֶׁבַּחֹרֶף (שֶׁהִתְנוֹצְצוּת הַקְּדֻשָּׁה וְהַיִּרְאָה שֶׁהָיוּ עַל פְּנֵי רַבֵּנוּ ז"ל בְּלֵילֵי שַׁבָּתוֹת הָיָה אֵין לְשַׁעֵר כְּלָל, כַּמּוּבָא בְּחַיֵּי מוהר"ן, וּמִי שֶׁהָיָה אֶצְלוֹ אָז הָיָה נוֹפֵל יִרְאָה וּבוּשָׁה גְּדוֹלָה מְאֹד עַל פָּנָיו עַד שֶׁרַבֵּנוּ ז"ל הָיָה מֻכְרָח אָז לִהְיוֹת בְּמַסְוֶה עַל פָּנָיו וְהָיָה אוֹמֵר אָז תּוֹרָה בְּיִרְאָה גְּדוֹלָה). וְכָל הַתַּלְמִידִים ז"ל אַף־עַל־פִּי שֶׁהָיָה לָהֶם הִתְנוֹצְצוּת וְכוּ' כנ"ל אַף עַל פִּי כֵן הָיוּ הוֹלְכִים אַחַר כָּךְ לִישֹׁן וּמוהרנ"ת ז"ל מֵחֲמַת בּוֹעֲרוּת לִבּוֹ לֹא הָיָה יָכֹל לִישֹׁן, וְהָיָה יוֹצֵא חוּץ לְהָעִיר בְּרֶסְלָב תַּחַת הָהָר אֵצֶל הַנָּהָר בִּיק, וְהָיָה צוֹעֵק כָּל הַלַּיְלָה (בְּנִגּוּן הַמְעוֹרֵר הַלֵּב): "רִבּוֹנוֹ שֶׁל עוֹלָם, אַז דָּא בְּרֶענְט אַ פַּייעֶר אַזַא פַּייעֶר אַרַיין דָאס פַּייעֶר מִיר אִין הַארְץ אַרַין", "כָּאן בּוֹעֵר אֵשׁ כָּזוֹ, הַבְעֵר נָא אֵשׁ זוֹ בְּלִבִּי".

(רבי אברהם נחמן שמחה וייצהנדלר, שיח שרפי קודש, א', תרס"ד)

Our holy teacher Rabbi Nathan said that the grace that he had—to know our master (Rabbi Naḥman) better than other disciples—was only from the wintery Saturday nights (on which the brightness of holiness and awe on our Rabbi Naḥman's face were completely unimaginable, as is described in the book *The Life of Rabeinu Naḥman*, and whoever was in his presence then would experience great awe and bashfulness. So much so, that Rabbi Naḥman was obliged to cover his face. Then he would give a speech about the Torah with great awe). And all the disciples, blessed is their memory, even though they had experienced this brightness, as mentioned, they would still then go to sleep. But our Rabbi Nathan's heart was burning so much, that he could not sleep, and would go out of the city of Breslow, at the foot of the mountain by the Byk river and chant the entire night (in a melody that awakens the heart): "Lord of the Universe! Such a fire is burning here! Please, ignite this fire in my heart."

(Rabbi Avraham Naḥman Simcha Weitzhendler, *Siaḥ Sarfei Kodesh*, 1.664)

Butterflies are born as tiny caterpillars. In holometabolism, larvae undergo metamorphosis, radically changing their appearance and behavior. Upon reaching adulthood, they transform into beautiful butterflies. Just like larvae, humans are born with inconceivable latent potential. They are akin to unripe fruits or unbaked loaves of bread that must endure the appropriate transformative process to actualize their potential.

In our immaturity, we wander through life with insatiable dissatisfaction. Not even the grandest of successes can alleviate this unrest. Until we discover our true abode, we will feel like outsiders, even within our own homes. We will continue to encounter limitations until we have realized our true nature: freedom.

In essence we are diamonds, but we are covered with mud, and this is why we feel the need to clean ourselves. We desperately want to get rid of everything that is foreign. However, the cleansing process can be extremely unpleasant and uncomfortable. The path back to our source is like entering a fire that consumes everything except what is real and authentic in us. It can be painful to burn our most cherished dreams, illusions, expectations, hopes, longings, and attachments. In the arduous process of involution, we abandon what is dearest to us or what we have become accustomed to loving. We have lived clinging to ideas, concepts, points of view, customs, and attitudes, considering these to be our possessions. As we advance on the path of involution, we realize that they are in fact impurities.

Today's pseudo-spiritual market offers an abundant variety of methods, techniques, and disciplines to obtain certain benefits. Hatha yoga is advertised for health and flexibility, tai chi for intensifying vital energy, and meditation techniques for creativity and overcoming stress. The surge in instructor certification courses is truly remarkable. Courses have become so industrialized that there seem to be more teachers than students. New enlightened satsangists appear every day, handing out enlightenment to participants in meetings and retreats.

Courses and books are also offered to promote spiritual business. From a commercial perspective, it is legitimate to advertise the benefits of products you sell. As in any business, customers who buy merchandise expect to receive something in return for their money. We do not criticize commerce at all, even in the religious, mystical, esoteric, or spiritual industry. We are only pointing out that the relationships between merchants and their customers are very different from those between masters and their disciples.

Market transactions have a radically different dynamic from those that require true involutionary effort. In business, as we all know, the customer is always right. The merchant's duty is to deliver the goods in exchange for money. There are even traders who are not after our money, but rather their egos feed on our attention and energy. Many guides and teachers seek the appreciation and admiration of their customers in exchange for free merchandise and they promise health, knowledge, and enlightenment. In contrast, the master–disciple relationship is based on service and the questions of souls who are aware of their ignorance.

Like customers, neophyte seekers search with a sense of lack, therefore, they want to acquire something. They expect to receive whatever they think they lack. But if they believe that the work of the master will complete them, they will be disappointed. The great service that the guru renders is in fact stripping them of possessiveness. He will not bestow something upon them but will lead them by the hand to the direct realization that they lack nothing, and they already are all that they seek. The master does not add or attach anything to what we are but takes from us that we think is ours. While merchants offer us sweet comfort and effective solutions, the true master, only fire.

אֲבָל מָה אֶעֱשֶׂה וְנַפְשִׁי חָשְׁקָה בַּתּוֹרָה. וְהִיא בְּלִבִּי כְּאֵשׁ אוֹכֶלֶת בּוֹעֵרָה.
(רמב"ן, הקדמה לתורה)

But what shall I do, that my soul craves for the Torah and the Torah in my heart is like a consuming, burning fire?
(Ramban on Genesis, Introduction)

There is a story about a boy that went to visit his neighbor's sculpting workshop. Upon entering, the boy saw a large block of stone. He turned to the artist and asked, "Why did you bring that gigantic rock?" The sculptor replied, "Because there is a beautiful angel inside." After a few months, the little boy returned and found an amazing statue of an angel. He asked the sculptor, "And how did you know that this lovely angel lived inside this rock?"

The child's question holds a great truth, because the angel was already inside the stone. The sculptor's talent allowed him to see it and to gradually eliminate what was in excess. He did not add anything to the sculpture; on the contrary, he removed the stone that kept others from appreciating the angel within. The sculptor's art is seeing what others do not see. This process is like the art of educating. The term *educate* comes from of the Latin *educare*; composed of the prefix *e* for *ex*, meaning "outside" and *ducare* the frequentative subject of *ducere*, which stands for "to bring." In other words, many understand to educate as "to extract from within." Masters are more akin to sculptors than painters; they do not add color to a canvas; they artfully remove excess.

הֲלוֹא כֹה דְבָרִי כָּאֵשׁ נְאֻם־ה' וּכְפַטִּישׁ יְפֹצֵץ סָלַע:

(ירמיהו כ"ג, כ"ט)

Behold, My word is like fire—declares the Lord—and like a hammer that shatters rock!

(Jeremiah, 23:29)

The capacity of authentic masters lies in seeing the potential within disciples. They perceive the Divine in each one, which has been obscured by considerable worldliness, vulgarity, attachments, and confusion. As painful as it may be, the art of the genuine master is to skillfully use their flame to burn away disciples' impurities.

We are dirty diamonds. Although we identify strongly with our dirt, we need hygiene. All our possessions are grimy. The identification with filth is so deep that it hurts when we finally bathe.

Many wonder why so many saints have been persecuted, discredited, imprisoned, tortured, and even killed throughout history. There have been many so-called disciples in all traditions who have come to detest their masters. It is hard to find a genuine guru who has not been discredited. The reason is that true enlightened masters never meet aspirants' expectations. They do not bring comfort but burn them with fire.

"דּוֹר הֹלֵךְ וְדוֹר בָּא וְהָאָרֶץ לְעוֹלָם עֹמָדֶת" (קהלת א', ד'). וְנִרְאֶה עוֹד, עִם מַאֲמַר "טוֹבָה קְלָלָה שֶׁקִּלֵּל אֲחִיָּה הַשִּׁלֹנִי אֶת יִשְׂרָאֵל מִבְּרָכָתוֹ שֶׁבֵּרְכָן בִּלְעָם" (תענית כ"ה, א'). וְזֶה אָר רָץ שֶׁהוּא רִיצָה נֶגֶד הַקְּלָלָה שֶׁל צַדִּיקִים, שֶׁתּוֹכָן רָצוּף אַהֲבָה מִסְתֶּרֶת, כְּמַאֲמַר רשב"י (מועד קטן, ט', ב'): "זִיל גַּבַּיְיהוּ דְּלִיבָרְכוּךְ". וּבֵרְכוּ אוֹתוֹ: "יְהֵא רַעֲוָא דְּתִזְרַע וְלָא תֶּחְצַד". וְחָשַׁב שֶׁזֶּה קְלָלָה וּלְבַסּוֹף רָאָה שֶׁזֶּה בְּרָכָה שֶׁיִּהְיֶה לוֹ בָּנִים וְלֹא יִקְבֹּר אוֹתָם. כֵּן אָר רָץ שֶׁרָצִים נֶגֶד קִלְלוֹתֵיהֶם שֶׁל צַדִּיקִים וְלֹא אַחַר בִּרְכָתָם שֶׁל רְשָׁעִים מִפְּנֵי שֶׁאֵין בִּפְנִימִיּוּת מָה שֶׁבַּתּוֹכִיּוּת [חִיצוֹנִיּוּת] אֲבָל הַצַּדִּיק לְהֶפֶךְ, רַק בְּרָכָה כַּוָּנָתוֹ.

(הרב נח גד וויינטראוב, ספר אש המזבח על קהלת, א', ד')

"One generation goes, another comes, but the earth (*aretz*) stands forever" (Ecclesiastes, 1:4). Another way to explain this verse is with the saying: "Ahijah the Shilonite's curse on the people of Israel is better than the blessing of wicked Balaam" (*Ta'anit,* 20a). And this is [the etymology of the word *aretz* (land)] : *ar ratz* [*ar* is from the word "curse," and *ratz* means "to run or desire"], that is, "running toward or desiring the curses of saintly people." Because these curses are, in essence, full of concealed love. As Rabbi Shim'on, son of Yoḥai, said [to his son] (*Mo'ed Katan*, 9b): "Go to these respected people and ask them to bless you," and he went and got their blessing: "Let it be that you will sow, but not harvest" and he thought that it was a curse, but eventually understood that it was a blessing—that he will have children and will not have to bury them. In the same manner: *ar ratz*, seeking the curses of the righteous rather than the blessings of the evil, because in essence the evil mean something different from what they say. But the saint, on the other hand, means only to bless.

(Rabbi Noaḥ Gad Waintraub, *Eish HaMizbeaḥ* on Ecclesiastes, 1.4)

Disciples may often feel disappointed when their master's actions do not meet their expectations. At some point in the process, they may feel the urge to flee as if the master were fire. In the Kṛṣṇa Yajur

Veda, we find a *śanti-mantra* for the master and the disciple to recite together at the beginning of each class:

ॐ सह नाववतु ।
सह नौ भुनक्तु ।
सह वीर्यं करवावहै ।
तेजस्विनावधीतमस्तु मा विद्विषावहै ।
ॐ शान्तिः शान्तिः शान्तिः ॥

oṁ saha nāvavatu
saha nau bhunaktu
saha vīryaṁ karavāvahai
tejasvināvadhītamastu
mā vidviṣāvahai
oṁ śāntiḥ śāntiḥ śāntiḥ

Oṁ
May we (teacher and students) be protected.
May we be nurtured.
May we work together with energy and vigor.
May our study be enlightening.
May there be no animosity between us.
Oṁ, peace, peace, peace.

(*Śānti-mantra* of *Taittirīya Upanishad*, *Kaṭha Upanishad*, and *Śvetaśvatara Upanishad*)

The term *vidviṣ* in Sanskrit means "hostility or hatred." To a Westerner, it may seem strange to pray for hatred not to arise. They pray for this because hatred is always latent in disciples. After a short time living with a true master, our preconceived ideas about enlightenment and the guru will be totally burnt to ashes. Eventually, we will understand that it is impossible to control the Divine. Only the daring, the adventurous, and the courageous stay as long as is necessary for metamorphosis to occur. Only those who are in love persevere long enough to be consumed by the flames.

וּכְכַלּוֹת שְׁלֹמֹה לְהִתְפַּלֵּל וְהָאֵשׁ יָרְדָה מֵהַשָּׁמַיִם וַתֹּאכַל הָעֹלָה וְהַזְּבָחִים וּכְבוֹד ה' מָלֵא אֶת הַבָּיִת:
וְלֹא יָכְלוּ הַכֹּהֲנִים לָבוֹא אֶל בֵּית ה' כִּי מָלֵא כְבוֹד ה' אֶת בֵּית ה':
וְכֹל בְּנֵי יִשְׂרָאֵל רֹאִים בְּרֶדֶת הָאֵשׁ וּכְבוֹד ה' עַל הַבָּיִת וַיִּכְרְעוּ אַפַּיִם אַרְצָה עַל הָרִצְפָה וַיִּשְׁתַּחֲווּ וְהוֹדוֹת לַה' כִּי טוֹב כִּי לְעוֹלָם חַסְדּוֹ:
(דברי הימים ב', ז', א'–ג')

> And when Solomon finished praying, the fire descended from heaven and consumed the burnt-offerings and the peace-offerings, and the glory of God filled the house. And the priests could not enter the house of the Lord, for the glory of the Lord filled the house of the Lord. And all the children of Israel witnessed the descent of the fire and the glory of the Lord on the house. And they knelt on the floor with their faces to the ground, and they prostrated themselves in thanks to the Lord "for He is good; for His lovingkindness endures forever."
> (II Chronicles, 7:1–3)

If masters acted in a way that was easy to love them, then your trust would have very little value. Surrendering to logical masters would be ordinary. When your master has destroyed everything, but you stay; when it is impossible to love him, but you do; when it seems outrageous to trust, but you trust; when it is madness to believe, but you do… then the miracle happens.

It is then when we find ourselves very close to the fire, but an alluring danger prevents us from fleeing. Our head warns us of the threat and asks us for protection, but an irresistible vulnerability calls us. Our mind screams to escape and save ourselves, but the heart wants us to risk everything. When instead of fearing fire, we feel the need to burn all the bridges that tie us to what is known, what has been, what is old, what is desired, what has been achieved, what has been lost, what I think I am, and what I have been. It is then that we feel the urge to burn our patterns, habits, beliefs, fears, attachments, and learned behaviors until they turn to ashes. When we feel an inexplicable desire to trust these flames deep within our being and we renounce all solutions and wish only for the fire to consume our conflicts and selfishness, in that state, instead of fleeing, we say:

כָּאן בּוֹעֵר אֵשׁ כָּזוֹ, הַבְעֵר נָא אֵשׁ זוֹ בְּלִבִּי.

Such a fire is burning here! Please, ignite this fire in my heart.

Only when this fire consumes the "I" and what is "mine" and all that remains is God, do the necessary conditions arise for a miracle to occur. Then, a small and insignificant caterpillar spreads its colorful wings and becomes the most beautiful queen of the garden.

—— ARTICLE 15 ——

THE TURKEY-PRINCE: SHEDDING THE GARMENTS OF ILLUSION

Rabbi Naḥman of Breslov was an enlightened Jewish master. He was born in Medzhybizh, then part of the Russian Empire, on April 4, 1772, and died in Uman, now part of Ukraine, on October 16, 1810. He was the great-grandson of the founder of the Hasidic movement, Rabbi Israel ben Eliezer, known as The Ba'al Shem Tov. He carried on the Hasidic movement through teachings based on Torah studies and Kabbalah and emphasized prayer and joy. He simplified the language of the Hebrew path and made it more accessible. During his lifetime, he was followed by hundreds of eager seekers of Truth. Up to this day, his movement remains alive and active. In this chapter, we will delve into one of his best-known stories: *The Tale of the Turkey Prince.*

> **It is said that a king's son went mad. Believing himself to be a turkey, he felt compelled to strip naked, sit under the table, and rummage like a turkey through the breadcrumbs and bones. All the doctors in the kingdom gave up on helping him and healing him. The whole situation greatly saddened the monarch. One day, a wise man appeared who said he could cure him. The sage was taken to the royal dining room with the king, his family, and some invited ministers. There the family was seated at the table with the ministers and the prince, naked under the table. Upon arrival there, the sage unexpectedly took off his clothes and, like the prince, sat naked by his side under the table. The sage began to rummage for crumbs and bones just like the king's son. The prince looked at the sage and asked him: "Who are you and what are you doing here?" ... to which the sage replied: "Who are you and what are you doing here?". The prince replied, "I am a turkey," to which the wise man replied, "I am also a turkey." For a long time, both remained together under the table naked until the prince grew comfortable with the wise man's companionship. Suddenly, the sage made a sign and**

shirts were thrown at them. The sage said to the prince, "Do you think a turkey cannot wear a shirt like human beings? It is perfectly possible to wear a shirt like them and remain a turkey. I have actually seen turkeys wearing shirts somewhere." So they both wore their respective shirts. After a while, the sage made another sign asking for pants. Again, the sage, addressing the monarch's son, said, "Do you think that by wearing pants like human beings you will be less of a turkey?" And they both proceeded to put on their pants. It went thus on until finally they were both dressed in all their garments. Suddenly, the sage signaled, and plates of food were lowered under the table for them. The wise man said to the prince: "Do you think that if you feed yourself with human food you will stop being a turkey?... No, it is possible to eat the same food that humans eat and still be a turkey." They both ate together under the table. Then, the wise man said to the young prince: "Do you think that being a turkey you should sit alone under the table...? No, you can continue to be a turkey and sit on a chair at the table with all human beings." This is how the sage managed to cure the king's son completely.

Commentary:

פַּעַם־אַחַת נָפַל בֶּן־מֶלֶךְ אֶחָד לְשִׁגָּעוֹן, שֶׁהוּא תַּרְנְגוֹל הוֹדוּ הַנִּקְרָא "הִינְדִּיק",
וְצָרִיךְ הוּא לֵישֵׁב עָרֹם תַּחַת הַשֻּׁלְחָן וְלִגְרֹר חֲתִיכוֹת לֶחֶם וַעֲצָמוֹת כְּמוֹ הִינְדִּיק...

It is said that a king's son went mad. Believing himself to be a turkey, he felt compelled to strip naked, sit under the table, and rummage like a turkey through the breadcrumbs and bones.

Many families assign specific seats at the dinner table based on familial roles. In my family, my father sat at the head of the table, my mother to his right and my little sister and I to his left. These places remained fixed; however, during my grandfather's visits, my father would give my grandfather his spot and move to my mother's. Most sociological and psychological studies assert that the family is the fundamental unit upon which society is constructed, serving as a core component across all cultures. The prince in our story symbolically sheds all societal conditioning by abandoning his designated seat. It is crucial to understand what the young prince declares through his actions. His choice to sit under the table signifies a renunciation of his familial and social ties.

Family is the foundation of personality, providing the structure upon which individuals construct their egoic patterns and conceptions of the world and of themselves. Accordingly, Vedanta posits that being born into a virtuous family results from good karma, while the opposite is a consequence of bad karma. In the parable, the king's son distances himself from his family and strips himself of all garments. In that way, he chooses to remain as naked as a simple animal like a turkey.

If we compare humans with trees, the tree roots represent human instincts. The trunk, branches, leaves, and berries embody the intellect, while the flowers symbolize intuition—the blossoming of consciousness. Instincts, crucial for survival, are the legacies of millions of years of evolution. Regulated by biological instincts, our bodily systems operate flawlessly without our conscious input. Instinct controls all involuntary vegetative functions, including the heartbeat and the diaphragmatic movements essential to breathe. Despite remarkable scientific advancements, we are still unable to artificially replicate all the functions that our body performs naturally.

The intellect represents a pivotal juncture where the evolutionary path of consciousness shifts to an involutionary phase. This is the stage where consciousness reaches its most concealed state and begins to reveal itself. In this jump from animal to human, self-consciousness emerges.

Human intellect, inherently ego-driven, forms the foundation of our cultures, traditions, ideologies, and beliefs. It does not make sense to criticize the egoic phenomenon, since it is a natural phase within the broader evolutionary process. We should minimize the length of this stage and focus on advancing toward the recognition of consciousness.

Behavior in animals is driven entirely by instinct. They identify edible substances and instinctively fast when sick, in order to purge toxins. By contrast, humans have drifted from the safety net of instinct. While the intellect denotes a more evolved state of consciousness, social developments and perceived progress have gradually disconnected the human being from instinct. This disconnection extends even to domesticated animals, such as dogs and cats, who, through close association with humans, have started to suffer from psychological disorders akin to those seen in humans.

Instinct corresponds to our physical existence, intellect to the mental realm, and intuition to the reality of consciousness. A human primarily driven by instinct might resemble figures like Tarzan or Robinson Crusoe. These fictitious characters, brought to life by Edgar Rice Burroughs and Daniel Defoe respectively, rely on their primal instincts for survival. On the other hand, a quintessential representation of intellect is Sherlock Holmes. This astute London detective, a character created by Scottish author and physician Sir Arthur Conan Doyle, epitomizes the application of logic, cunning, and intellectual prowess.

Intellect serves as a transitional phase, as a passageway from being a beast to transcendence. It is an intermediate state for the transition between the human and the Divine. Intuition is our potential; it is what we can become. Unlike the intellectual and intuitive plane, the instinctive level is an undifferentiated experiencing, accessible through meditation. Positioned at the opposite end of the spectrum, instinct is the innate pre-egoic state while intuition signifies the transcendental post-egoic state.

Darwin proposed the theory that new biological species evolve naturally rather than being created by God. This idea provoked resistance, particularly from organized religions, where the notion that humans and apes share common ancestors is often met with fear and sometimes hostility. Whether Darwin is right or wrong, it is true that our instinctive roots are an integral part of us. Respect for instinct is one of the main teachings of Tantric wisdom.

The intellect can only be used wisely when instinct works in harmony with intuition. Embracing our instincts paves the way to developing intuition, as the two are essentially the same: instinct is the material manifestation of intuition, and intuition is the spiritual dimension of instinct. Our mental conditioning and personal interpretations of experience often stem from a prolonged stagnation at the intellectual level. Simple, pure, and undifferentiated experience belongs to instinct, while pure consciousness belongs to enlightenment. The similarities between instinct and intuition are recognized by various traditions. For example, the *Talmud* says that prophecy has been given to fools and newborns. The newborn only perceives an undifferentiated experience, like the awakened being who is only consciousness.

The Hebrew masters of Hassidism describe the human being as endowed with two souls: one is animal and one is divine. The animal soul, or *nefesh behemit* (נפש בהמית) in Hebrew, drives survival and preservation. It is our instinctive aspect, which vitalizes the physical body and perceives only objective reality. The more power the animal soul possesses, the more our negative instinct (*yetzer hara*) intensifies, which lies in the foundation of every individual. However, the animal soul is not intrinsically evil, but it is negative if it controls our desires and actions, thereby delaying our evolutionary process.

In contrast, the divine soul, known in Hebrew as *nefesh elohit* (נפש אלוהית) yearns for reconnection with its source and origin. It is characterized by *yetzer hatov*, or the "positive instinct," which manifests as a drive to sacrifice in the pursuit of Truth. The Kabbalah wisdom quotes a verse, where King Solomon asks: "Who knows whether the soul of human beings ascends, and whether the soul of animals descends to the earth?" (Ecclesiastes, 3:21). The verse describes two inclinations of the human soul: ascending and descending. Ascending requires nourishing the divine soul to ensure that the animal soul does not lead to spiritual decline. If we adopt the appropriate attitude, we can even elevate the animal soul and direct its instincts toward the pursuit of transcendence.

Rabbi Yitsḥak Luria, known as HaAri HaKadosh, expands on this by teaching that humans possess five levels of the soul, with the *nefesh behemit* being the lowest. Rabbi Shneur Zalman of Liadi explains in the *Tanya* (chapter 9) that though the *nefesh behemit* is drawn to physical pleasures, it is not evil simply because it seeks enjoyment. However, for it to aspire to the transcendental, it must be transmuted by sublimation. Once refined, the animal soul becomes the *nefesh ḥiyunit*, or "vital soul," energizing and enlivening the body. Hasidic teachings emphasize that the animal soul should render service to the divine soul, or *nefesh elohit*, as articulated in the Torah:

וְאָהַבְתָּ אֵת ה' אֱלֹהֶיךָ בְּכָל לְבָבְךָ וּבְכָל נַפְשְׁךָ וּבְכָל מְאֹדֶךָ:
(דברים ו', ה')

And you shall love the Lord your God with all your heart, with all your soul, and with all your might.
(Deuteronomy, 6:5)

The original Hebrew text, instead of using the word *libcha* (your heart), intriguingly uses the form *levavcha* (doubling the letter *bet* ב and thus hinting it is plural), suggesting the engagement of both positive and negative inclinations in the service of the divine, as the *Mishnah* explains:

"בְּכָל לְבָבְךָ", בִּשְׁנֵי יְצָרֶיךָ, בְּיֵצֶר טוֹב וּבְיֵצֶר רָע.
(משנה, ברכות, ט', ה')

"With all your hearts"—means with both your inclinations, the positive (human) and the negative (instinctive).
(*Mishna, "Berachot,"* 9.5)

In the story, the prince withdraws from his family and sits naked on the ground to eat crumbs like an animal; he severs ties with the clan and seeks isolation from society to search solitude. By wearing clothing, we have distanced ourselves from our animal nature and the natural world. The modern Western society that we have built is ashamed of its animality and condemns its roots. As humans, we strive to distinguish ourselves from the beasts to the point of rejecting even our own bodies. In the West, we have crafted a society so unnatural that we prefer artificial garments made by humans over natural coverings provided by God.

If we were to stroll naked down a city street, we would be deemed insane and met with laughter. Conversely, should we venture into a forest clad in garments, birds, bears, wolves, deer, and native peoples and ancestral ethnicities would find amusement in our attire. The trees and flowers, in their natural state, are bare. Though silent, they would surely mock the folly of humanity. In a sane society, public nudity would be seen as entirely appropriate; yet, in our own, such an act would lead to arrest for indecent exposure.

Just as clothing conceals our physical form, the mental garments woven by human conditioning shroud our original body, which is consciousness itself. Embarking on an involutionary path entails gradually shedding all egoic clothing and remaining in our primal state of nakedness. While some practice physical nudism, I personally recommend being a mental nudist who strips away egoic coverings to reveal the true self.

Facing loneliness can be difficult. We often escape it by watching television, reaching out to friends, or engaging in other distractions because, in the absence of others, our constructed identities begin to dissolve. Alone, we must confront our own nakedness and be with ourselves as we are. The hesitation to exhibit the body stems from a deeper fear of exposing our consciousness. In solitude, our illusionary identity falls away, revealing the reality of our true essence.

Darwin's theory often meets resistance because it reminds us of our animal origins. Ashamed of our animality, in our modern Western society we tend to condemn and suppress our instincts. In an attempt to distance ourselves from these primal urges, we have created clothes, beds, chairs, and tables, and covered natural landscapes with brick and concrete.

Despite our ability to transcend the intellectual plane, it is impossible to completely disown, deny, or eliminate our instinctual roots. When human and animal aspects conflict, the animal aspect typically prevails due to its overwhelming power. To err is inherently human, but it is the intellect that errs; instinct, by contrast, is never mistaken.

Ignoring our animal nature means neglecting a fundamental component of our existence. Contempt for this aspect can foster a self-destructive attitude and cause an internal fracture that leads to disarray. Inner conflicts obstruct clear observation. Therefore, instead of rejecting our instincts, we should embrace them, recognizing that they are integral to our roots. In the story, the prince's actions symbolize this acceptance of our animal aspect.

וְכָל הָרוֹפְאִים נוֹאֲשׁוּ מִלַּעֲזֹר לוֹ וּלְרַפְּאוֹתוֹ מִזֶּה, וְהָיָה הַמֶּלֶךְ בְּצַעַר גָּדוֹל מִזֶּה...

All the doctors in the kingdom gave up on helping him and healing him. The whole situation greatly saddened the monarch.

Despite our civilized and modern facade, each of us harbors an inner "turkey," which reminds us that modern society is not our original natural environment. Society mechanizes individuals, treating human beings like robots, and molds us into functional objects caged into behavioral patterns deemed "normal." Instead of raising our children to embrace freedom, we condition them to fit into social mechanisms.

The state dominates organized and organizing society, which is manufactured and manufacturing, structured and structuring. Humans, in turn, construct society and become mere gears of its machinery. Society dictates dress codes, family structures, educational frameworks, and the ambitions we are expected to harbor. From early childhood, we are indoctrinated with the belief that money equates power, success, status, security, reward, admiration, love, and happiness. Through careful observation, the illusion becomes apparent: money can buy doctors but not health, people but not friendship, companionship but not love, and possessions but not happiness.

Society's preoccupation with the future prompts it to teach the masses to overlook the present. Rather than allowing individuals to determine their own lives, society imposes prefabricated "lifestyles" upon us. Citizens are treated more like subjects, conditioned to pursue externally imposed desires and ambitions such as professional success, wealth, honor, and fame. Blinded by our conditioning, we live frustrated lives, trying to achieve these artificial aspirations.

Governments have infiltrated into the most intimate aspects of citizens' lives, even influencing the values conveyed by educational systems. Often, schools resemble prisons more than learning centers. It is astonishing that slavery was once legal, and future generations will likely be similarly baffled by our participation in an educational system that stifles individual expression and curtails freedom. Society should facilitate personal expression, enabling individuals to realize their full potential: to benefit them and not to exploit them. Education in its truest form cannot restrict individuals, since intelligence only flourishes in freedom.

Due to its inherent rigidity, society fails to grant individuals the freedom necessary for their evolution. Rigid laws, rules, and regulations are static, whereas the individuals subjected to them require dynamism to thrive. The discord between society and human beings mirrors the conflict between mechanical and biological, inert and organic, artificial and natural, dead and alive. Society represents the superficial or external aspect of humans, highlighting a clash between our inner world and its periphery. Transcending the mind and accessing consciousness is the only path to resolving this conflict.

Each individual embodies two roles: a subject and a human being. Governments, naturally, prefer us to conform as subjects, diminishing our humanity to enhance control and compliance. Moreover, it is simpler for us to fit into the role of citizens, merely acting within the confines of established social frameworks. Demanding lifelong loyalty to a single partner, enduring years of schooling, fighting in wars, and other societal expectations are challenging impositions on the human spirit.

Good citizens may not always be conscious humans, but conscious humans invariably make exemplary citizens, not just of their own country but of the entire universe. They never harm others or their environment; they avoid antisocial behaviors and cooperate with others. They strive to avoid vulgarity, triviality, superficiality, herd mentality, and the follies of mere citizenship. Thus, governments often fear that these individuals will challenge their authority. However, a society that overlooks its human constituents in favor of mass citizenship is doomed to fail. Merely good citizens cannot foster an intelligent society. In a system where subjects prevail, conflicts are inevitable. For modern society to thrive, it should shift focus from nurturing superficial subjects to fostering the growth of conscious individuals, thereby acknowledging and embracing their psychological realities.

Unlike animals, humans get their nourishment through the mind, and their desires seem insatiable. Even after consuming as much as they can stomach, the need for enjoyment persists. Oriented toward an imagined future of endless enjoyment, they attempt to maximize current pleasures, fully aware of their finite lifespan. Unable to guarantee future satisfaction, they exploit immediate gratification, often compromising their health. Their craving for pleasure leaves them perpetually unsatisfied. With their senses desensitized by so much stimulation, they need to increase their doses, which ultimately damages their bodies and leads to self-destructive behaviors.

Modern society encourages us to chase a future that never materializes. Governments prioritize long-term survival over present conditions, but for the conscious individual, all that matters is now and not tomorrow. The reality of what is as it is can only be realized when thoughts of the future dissipate, facilitating a reconciliation between the citizen subject and the individual human.

In the relentless pursuit of future pleasures, we are like a dog chasing its own tail, with satisfaction always just out of reach. Civilized society rushes endlessly, pushing its members to seek more pleasure rather than appreciating existing achievements. We do not find the promised happiness in solid objects, but in abstract ideas. Substantial objects do not provide us with bliss and the realities we long for are theoretical. The market capitalizes on this, offering fleeting pleasures through sensual excitement and continuous distractions.

We often deem sleep a waste of time, choosing instead to chase dreamed pleasures. Because life is short, we lengthen our waking state to maximize pleasure, even if we develop insomnia. The pursuit of future enjoyment takes precedence over the need for restorative sleep, leading us to sacrifice genuine life experiences for hours of trivial entertainment. This never-ending stimulation desensitizes us to life's true joys.

Citizens pursue success, money, partners, family, honor, attention, and so on, but these things are mere shadows. A partner or family is only a symbol of true love, and money is only a shadow of real wealth. We wrongly choose to run after elusive goals that are only pale reflections of what is real. Since they are insubstantial, when we acquire them, we feel empty. In fact, we are addicted to fantasies, while ignoring what really is, as it is.

To truly realize life as it is, we must shed conventional routines and extricate ourselves from the robotic traditions of society. Our reality calls for us to step away from the herd, reject the societal game, and liberate ourselves from the restrictive definitions, concepts, and customs that define "human" society. According to societal standards, those who live in true observation may seem to require psychiatric help.

Realizing that our authentic nature transcends all labels ignites a desire to exist freely and intensely, unbound by any classification. We cease aspiring to be defined by roles such as princes, doctors, presidents, or professors. Human society may view individuals who defy these categories as needing psychiatric intervention, but it is precisely through this rebellion that we can discover that our authentic nature is absolute freedom.

עַד שֶׁבָּא חָכָם אֶחָד וְאָמַר: אֲנִי מְקַבֵּל עַל עַצְמִי לְרַפְּאוֹתוֹ! וְהָלַךְ וְהִפְשִׁיט גַּם־כֵּן אֶת עַצְמוֹ עָרֹם וְיָשַׁב תַּחַת הַשֻּׁלְחָן אֵצֶל בֶּן־הַמֶּלֶךְ הַנַּ"ל וְגַם כֵּן גָּרַר פֵּרוּרִים וַעֲצָמוֹת.

One day, a wise man appeared who said he could cure him. The sage was taken to the royal dining room with the king, his family, and some invited

ministers. There the family was seated at the table with the ministers and the prince, naked under the table. Upon arrival there, the sage unexpectedly took off his clothes and, like the prince, sat naked by his side under the table. The sage began to rummage for crumbs and bones just like the king's son.

The sage reveals to the prince that he too does not enjoy the company of these "human" beings. He too has lost his sense of belonging in a society that values what we have and not who we are.

In this society, human beings are valued not for their inherent qualities but for their adherence to societal norms and impositions. Initially, we are presented with a set of rules and regulations, and appreciation is conditional upon our compliance. This system does not foster genuine appreciation for authenticity, but for our ability to pretend.

וּשְׁאָלוֹ בֶּן־הַמֶּלֶךְ: "מִי אַתָּה? וּמַה אַתָּה עוֹשֶׂה פֹּה"? וְהֵשִׁיב לוֹ: "מִי אַתָּה? וּמַה אַתָּה עוֹשֶׂה פֹּה?"

The prince looked at the sage and asked him: "Who are you and what are you doing here?" ... to which the sage replied: "Who are you and what are you doing here?"

What we really are is observation and consciousness. Everything we see around us is illusion, fantasy, a dream, and sometimes a nightmare.

אָמַר לוֹ: "אֲנִי הִינְדִּיק"! אָמַר לוֹ: "אֲנִי גַּם־כֵּן הִינְדִּיק"!

The prince replied, "I am a turkey," to which the wise man replied, "I am also a turkey."

The sage in the story is not merely a wise man but a saint, a *tzaddik*. Inherently truthful, he could not deceive the prince. So, how did he persuade him to dress and sit at the table? The *tzaddik* chose to join the prince under the table, stripping away his own garments to meet the prince where he was. There, he told the prince, "Do you want me to confess something, my friend? May I share a secret with you? I understand you perfectly because I can perceive the melody of your presence. When I see that ray of light in your eyes, I recognize it. Two drunks can easily recognize each other. I can identify your silence because I see what you see. I am what you are. I, too, love to shed my clothes. We are birds of a feather, and no matter where we fly, we always fly together, unified."

וּכְמוֹ שֶׁנֶּאֱמַר בְּשָׁאוּל שֶׁהָלַךְ וּמִתְנַבֵּא עָרוֹם (שמואל א' י"ט, כ"ד). פֵּרוּשׁוֹ שֶׁהַגּוּף הוּא לְבוּשׁ לַנֶּפֶשׁ כַּנּוֹדָע, וְהִתְפַּשְׁטוּתוֹ נִקְרָא עָרוֹם, וְתַרְגּוּם יוֹנָתָן שָׁם בִּרְשָׁן. פֵּרוּשׁוֹ מְשֻׁגָּע שֶׁאֵינוֹ פּוֹנֶה כְּלָל לְגוּפוֹ, וּפְעֻלַּת הַגּוּף הֵם כִּמְעַט בְּלֹא יְדִיעָתוֹ כְּלָל וּכְמוֹ מְשֻׁגָּע.

(רבי צדוק הכהן מלובלין, צדקת הצדיק, ר"י)

As is said about Saul, that he was prophesizing while being naked (1 Samuel, 19:24). This means that the body is clothing for the soul, as it is known, and we call it nakedness when the soul is undressed. And Jonathan's Aramaic translation there is *birshan,* which means crazy, because, like a crazy person, Saul is absolutely inattentive to his body and the actions of his body are almost without his awareness.

(Rabbi Tzadok HaCohen of Lublin, *Tzidekat HaTzadik*, 210)

I enjoy my own selfhood in its purest and most pristine nakedness.

וְיָשְׁבוּ שְׁנֵיהֶם יַחַד כָּךְ אֵיזֶה זְמַן, עַד שֶׁנַּעֲשׂוּ רְגִילִים זֶה עִם זֶה. וְאָז רָמַז הֶחָכָם לִבְנֵי-הַבַּיִת לְהַשְׁלִיךְ לָהֶם כֻּתָּנוֹת, וְאָמַר הֶחָכָם "הָאִינְדִּיק" לְבֶן-הַמֶּלֶךְ: "אַתָּה חוֹשֵׁב, שֶׁהִינְדִּיק אֵינוֹ יָכוֹל לֵילֵךְ עִם כֻּתֹּנֶת? יְכוֹלִים לִהְיוֹת לָבוּשׁ כֻּתֹּנֶת, וְאַף־עַל־פִּי־כֵן יְהֵא הִנְדִּיק כִּי בְּמָקוֹם אֶחָד רָאִיתִי הִינְדִּיקֶעס לְבוּשִׁים בְּכֻתָּנוֹת..." וְלָבְשׁוּ שְׁנֵיהֶם הַכֻּתֹּנֶת, וְאַחַר אֵיזֶה זְמַן רָמַז וְהִשְׁלִיכוּ לָהֶם גַּם מִכְנָסַיִם. וְאָמַר לוֹ הֶחָכָם גַּם־כֵּן כַּנִּזְכַּר לְעֵיל: "אַתָּה חוֹשֵׁב, שֶׁעִם מִכְנָסַיִם לֹא יְכוֹלִים לִהְיוֹת הִינְדִּיק?! וְכוּ'", עַד שֶׁלָּבְשׁוּ הַמִּכְנָסַיִם, וְכֵן עִם שְׁאָר הַבְּגָדִים. וְאַחַר־כָּךְ רָמַז וְהִשְׁלִיכוּ לָהֶם

מַאַכְלֵי אָדָם מֵהַשֻּׁלְחָן, וְאָמַר לוֹ: "אַתָּה חוֹשֵׁב שֶׁאִם אוֹכְלִים מַאֲכָלִים טוֹבִים כְּבָר אֵינְךָ הִינְדִיק?! אֶפְשָׁר לֶאֱכֹל כְּאָדָם וְלִהְיוֹת הִינְדִיק!" "אִיז מֶען שׁוין קֵיין הִינְדִיק נִישְׁט?! מֶען קֶען עֶסְן אוּן אוֹיךְ זַיין אַ הִינְדִיק"! וְאָכְלוּ. וְאַחַר־כָּךְ אָמַר לוֹ: "אַתָּה חוֹשֵׁב, שֶׁהִינְדִיק מֻכְרָח לִהְיוֹת דַּוְקָא תַּחַת הַשֻּׁלְחָן? יְכוֹלִים לִהְיוֹת הִינְדִיק וְלִהְיוֹת אֵצֶל הַשֻּׁלְחָן"! וְכֵן הִתְנַהֵג עִמּוֹ, עַד שֶׁרִפֵּא אוֹתוֹ לְגַמְרֵי.

For a long time, both remained together under the table naked until the prince grew comfortable with the wise man's companionship. Suddenly, the sage made a sign and shirts were thrown at them. The sage said to the prince, "Do you think a turkey cannot wear a shirt like human beings? It is perfectly possible to wear a shirt like them and remain a turkey. I have actually seen turkeys wearing shirts somewhere." So they both wore their respective shirts. After a while, the sage made another sign asking for pants. Again, the sage, addressing the monarch's son, said, "Do you think that by wearing pants like human beings you will be less of a turkey?" And they both proceeded to put on their pants. It went thus on until finally they were both dressed in all their garments. Suddenly, the sage signaled, and plates of food were lowered under the table for them. The wise man said to the prince: "Do you think that if you feed yourself with human food you will stop being a turkey?... No, it is possible to eat the same food that humans eat and still be a turkey." They both ate together under the table. Then, the wise man said to the young prince: "Do you think that being a turkey you should sit alone under the table...? No, you can continue to be a turkey and sit on a chair at the table with all human beings." This is how the sage managed to cure the king's son completely.

I'm a turkey just like you, my friend. Many years ago, I stopped being someone and became a shadow of existence. I no longer believe in God, because one day, looking around me, I realized that apart from God, there is nothing here.

אַתָּה הָרְאֵתָ לָדַעַת כִּי ה' הוּא הָאֱלֹהִים אֵין עוֹד מִלְּבַדּוֹ.
(דברים ד', ל"ה)

You have been shown to know that the Lord, He is God; there is no more than only Him.

(Deutoronomy, 4:35)

The sage said, "I know of the conscious emptiness, of the knowingness that lies behind everything and everyone. However, you are young and as one who has seen many seasons, let me tell you that nothingness is also everything. Just as the content of the ocean is of the same substance as the ocean, meaning water, so too the content of consciousness is consciousness. The multiplicity of mental, emotional, and physical experiences is our reality. This diversity of thoughts, emotions, sensations, and perceptions is also what we really are. Therefore, my friend, what does it matter if we conform to societal norms, wearing clothes and eating at tables? We can navigate society's conventions while in our depths we know who we really are. Even as turkeys, we can participate in a society that is human and perhaps all too human. It is possible to engage with the community without sacrificing our individuality. Society will try to suffocate you in many ways, but if you maintain your own rhythm, it will not be able to annihilate your authenticity. Society will try to make you obey, tame you, fit you in an archetype of father, mother, brother, sister, professional, soldier, or prince, without allowing you to be as you are. The world expects you to be yet another imitator, to live your life as if you were a prince. But it is possible to be part of the world without belonging to the world. Let us don the clothes, join the meal at the table, and partake in the societal dance, but let us never allow society to buy us and alter us. In life, many doors remain shut merely due to the fear of stepping through them. Many cages remain locked only because of the dread of flying. Be courageous!"

— ARTICLE 16 —

UNITY AND HUMAN EXPRESSION

TANYA CHAPTER 20

If we wish to delve into the innermost depths of the Hebrew revelation, we should excavate in the fertile soils of Hassidism. There we will discover the proper way to digest the truths of the Torah. Although Hassidism can be considered an extension of Kabbalah, the fundamental difference is that while Kabbalah aspires to elevate us to the Divine, Hassidism directs our attention to the depths of reality. The former elevates humans toward God; the latter invites them to search for the Divine in what is human and discover that we already are what we are looking for.

Rabbi Shneur Zalman of Liadi (1745–1812 CE), also known as the Alter Rebbe (elderly Rabbi), was the youngest disciple of the Maggid of Mezeritch, who was a disciple of the Ba'al Shem Tov. He is the founder of the Chabad-Lubavitch movement. His profuse literary legacy is remarkable. His superb works cover almost all parts of Hebrew knowledge: Jewish law (*halachah*), philosophy, Kabbalah, and ethics.

His book *Likkutei Amarim*, or "*Collection of discourses*," better known as the *Tanya*, was published in 1797. It was written in Hebrew and its translation may be difficult to understand for those who are unfamiliar with the original language of the Sinaitic revelation. Every page reveals that this giant of the spirit does not declaim intellectual knowledge but shares a transcendental experience. The light of his wisdom pours generously from every one of his texts. I believe that we all can benefit from studying his words. We will discuss parts of chapter 20.

> **[...] In order to elucidate this matter clearly, we must first briefly refer to the subject and essence of the Unity of the Holy One, Blessed is He, Who is called One and Unique, "And all believe that He is All Alone," (*Rosh HaShanah* Prayer) exactly as He was before the world was created, when there was naught besides Him, as is written: "You were [the same] before the world was created; You are [the same] since the world has been created..." (Morning Prayer). This means exactly the same without any**

change, as it is written: "For I, the Lord, have not changed" (Malachi, 3:6), inasmuch as this world and likewise all supernal worlds do not effect any change in His Unity, Blessed be He, by their having been created *ex nihilo*. For just as He was All Alone, Single and Unique, before they were created, so is He One and Alone, Single and Unique after they were created, since, beside Him, everything is as nothing, verily as null and void.

For the coming into being of all the upper and nether worlds out of nonbeing, and their life and existence sustaining them from reverting to nonexistence and naught, as was before, is nothing else but the word of God and the breath of His mouth, Blessed be He, that is clothed in them.

To illustrate from the soul of a human being: when a man utters a word, this utterance in itself is as absolutely nothing even when compared only with his general "articulate soul," which is the so-called middle "garment," namely, the soul's faculty of speech, which can produce speech without limit or end; all the more when it is compared with its so-called innermost "garment," namely, its faculty of thought, which is the source of speech and its life-force, not to mention when it is compared with the essence and entity of the soul, these being its ten attributes mentioned above, viz., *ḥochmah* (wisdom), *binah* (understanding), *da'at* (knowledge), and so on, from which are derived the "letters" of thought that are clothed in the speech when it is uttered. For thought can as much be defined in terms of "letters" as speech, except that in the former they are more spiritual and refined.

But the ten attributes—*ḥochmah* (wisdom), *binah* (understanding), *da'at* (knowledge), and so forth—are the root and source of thought, and, prior to their being clothed in the "garment" of thought, still lack the element of "letters."

For example, when a man suddenly becomes conscious of a certain love or desire in his heart, before it has risen from the heart to the brain to think and meditate about it, it has not yet acquired the element of "letters"; it is only a simple desire and longing in the heart for the object of his affection.

All the more so before he began to feel in his heart a craving and desire for that thing, and it is as yet confined within the realm of his wisdom, intellect, and knowledge, that is, the thing is known to him to be desirable and gratifying, something good and pleasant to attain and to cling to, as, for instance, to learn some wisdom or to eat some delicious food.

Only after the desire and craving have already found their way into the heart, through the stimulus of his wisdom, intellect, and knowledge, and then ascended once more back to the brain, to think and meditate on how to translate his craving from the potential into the practical, with a view to actually obtaining that food or acquiring that wisdom—it is here that the so-called "letters" are born in his mind, such "letters" corresponding to the language of each nation, employing them in speech and thought about all things in the world.

We will address the subject part by part.

וּלְבָאֵר הֵיטֵב עִנְיָן זֶה, צָרִיךְ לְהַזְכִּיר תְּחִלָּה בִּקְצָרָה עִנְיַן וּמַהוּת אַחְדּוּתוֹ שֶׁל הַקָּדוֹשׁ־בָּרוּךְ־הוּא, שֶׁנִּקְרָא יָחִיד וּמְיֻחָד.

In order to elucidate this matter clearly, we must first briefly refer to the subject and essence of the Unity of the Holy One, Blessed is He, Who is called One and Unique.

The Alter Rebbe refers briefly to the subject of non-duality. The term *biktzarah* (בקצרה), or "briefly," indicates that the author will deal the topic more extensively in the section *Sha'ar HaYiḥud VeHa'Emunah*, or *"The portal of unity and faith,"* which we will study later. In that section, he discusses the terms *One* and *Unique* (יחיד ומיוחד) in detail.

The *Shema* is considered one of Judaism's most sacred prayers. It expresses a fundamental vision of absolute unity. It is named after its first words: *Shema Israel* (שמע ישראל)

שְׁמַע יִשְׂרָאֵל ה' אֱלֹהֵינוּ ה' אֶחָד:

(דברים ו', ד')

Shema Israel, HaShem E-loheinu, HaShem Eḥad

Hear, Israel, the Lord is our God, the Lord is One.

(Deuteronomy, 6:4)

In *Midrash Rabbah* we find:

רַבָּנָן אָמְרֵי: "אָמַר הַקָּדוֹשׁ בָּרוּךְ הוּא לְיִשְׂרָאֵל: 'בָּנַי, כָּל מַה שֶּׁבָּרָאתִי בָּרָאתִי זוּגוֹת, שָׁמַיִם וָאָרֶץ זוּגוֹת, חַמָּה וּלְבָנָה זוּגוֹת, אָדָם וְחַוָּה זוּגוֹת, הָעוֹלָם הַזֶּה וְהָעוֹלָם הַבָּא זוּגוֹת, אֲבָל כְּבוֹדִי אֶחָד וּמְיֻחָד בָּעוֹלָם', מִנַּיִן? מִמַּה שֶּׁקָּרִינוּ בָּעִנְיָן: 'שְׁמַע יִשְׂרָאֵל ה' אֱלֹהֵינוּ ה' אֶחָד' (דברים ו', ד')".

(דברים רבה, פרשת ואתחנן ב', ל"א)

Our rabbis said: "The Holy One Blessed be He, said to Israel, 'My children, all that I created, I created in pairs: Heaven and earth are a pair, the sun and the moon are a pair, Adam and Eve are a pair, this world and the world to come are a pair. But My glory is one and unique in the world.' From where [do we know this]? From that which we read about the matter: 'Hear O Israel, the Lord is our God, the Lord is One' (Deuteronomy, 6:4)."

(*Devarim Rabbah*, "*Va'etḥanan*," 2.31)

The objective creation manifests itself as dual reality. Both the material and the higher spiritual or astral worlds are part of this dual diversity. Based on the above text *Devarim Rabbah*, the Alter Rebbe refers to God, or consciousness, not only as *eḥad* (אחד), or "one," but as *yaḥid* (יחיד), or "the only one," and *meyuḥad*, (מיוחד), or "unique." Although the word *one* would be appropriate, it does not deny the existence of others. "God is one" can be interpreted to mean that he is one god among many others. Expressions such as "consciousness is one" could indicate that it is one among many. If we say someone has a son, it does not mean that he is an only son. "I bought one chocolate bar," does not mean it is the only one I have ever brought. The Alter Rebbe chooses the term *meyuḥad*, or "unique," in order to invalidate all extraneous existence. The Sanskrit term *advaita*, or "not two," was adopted for a similar reason by Vedantic nondualism (*kevalādvaita* or *dvaita-vāda-pratiṣedha*). This term dispels any doubt of possible duality.

To summarize, the distinguished Hebrew master clarifies that the Divine unity does not only refer to the existence of God as a person or an object within a reality full of similar others. He does not indicate that there is a superior being designated as a god within a reality filled with endless beings who are not gods. He does not postulate a mathematical statement to refute polytheism. In the Torah, we read:

וְיָדַעְתָּ הַיּוֹם וַהֲשֵׁבֹתָ אֶל לְבָבֶךָ כִּי ה' הוּא הָאֱלֹהִים בַּשָּׁמַיִם מִמַּעַל וְעַל הָאָרֶץ מִתָּחַת אֵין עוֹד:

(דברים ד', ל"ט)

And you shall know this day, and you shall set it to your heart, that the Lord, He is God, in the heavens above and on the earth below; there is none else.

(Deuteronomy, 4:39)

The expression *ein od* (אין עוד), or "there is no more," firmly establishes God as the only reality or the One without a second. This statement does not refer to God, but to Existence itself. In such a case, denying God would be as absurd as denying consciousness or saying that existence does not exist.

Dual empirical experience differs completely from the biblical revelation; hence it cannot be reconciled with the Sinaitic view. For example, if we look at our hand, we will see five fingers. This multiplicity consists of the thumb and the index, middle, ring, and little fingers. Although superficially we see five separate fingers, they are, in fact, all part of the same hand. Despite their differences, they belong to the same whole. Likewise, although the apparent multiplicity of our empirical reality simulates plurality, it shares a common source. Actually, the observed diversity comprises different expressions of the same unique non-dual nature. The substance that constitutes the universe does not differ at all from consciousness. Reality is not divided into divine and secular, spiritual and material. There is only a single undivided reality devoid of attributes, which the Torah calls God.

Contrary to popular belief, the Torah is not opposed to art, painting, and sculpture. Idolatry is a much broader and deeper concept than the worship of images. An idol is an experience to which we grant existence separate or independent of consciousness and, therefore, has an existence of its own. It is an experience foreign to consciousness and to our nature. The idol we worship most is the idea of a separate "I," which in India is called *ahaṅkāra*, or the "I-doer," that is, the egoic phenomenon. In Psalms, we have the following verse:

> לֹא יִהְיֶה בְךָ אֵל זָר וְלֹא תִשְׁתַּחֲוֶה לְאֵל נֵכָר:
>
> (תהילים פ"א , י')
>
> No alien god shall be within you, neither shall you prostrate yourself to a foreign god.
>
> (Psalms, 81:10)

To which the *Babylonian Talmud* says:

> וְהָתַנְיָא, רַבִּי שִׁמְעוֹן בֶּן אֶלְעָזָר אוֹמֵר מִשּׁוּם חִילְפָּא בַּר אַגְרָא, שֶׁאָמַר מִשּׁוּם רַבִּי יוֹחָנָן בֶּן נוּרִי: "הַמְקָרֵעַ בְּגָדָיו בַּחֲמָתוֹ וְהַמְשַׁבֵּר כֵּלָיו בַּחֲמָתוֹ וְהַמְפַזֵּר מְעוֹתָיו בַּחֲמָתוֹ, יְהֵא בְּעֵינֶיךָ כְּעוֹבֵד עֲבוֹדָה זָרָה. שֶׁכָּךְ אֻמָּנוּתוֹ שֶׁל יֵצֶר הָרָע: הַיּוֹם אוֹמֵר לוֹ: עֲשֵׂה כָּךְ, וּלְמָחָר אוֹמֵר לוֹ: עֲשֵׂה כָּךְ, עַד שֶׁאוֹמֵר לוֹ: עֲבוֹד עֲבוֹדָה זָרָה, וְהוֹלֵךְ וְעוֹבֵד". אָמַר רַבִּי אָבִין: "מַאי קְרָאָה: 'לֹא יִהְיֶה בְךָ אֵל זָר וְלֹא תִשְׁתַּחֲוֶה לְאֵל נֵכָר' (תהילים פ"א, י'), אֵיזֶהוּ אֵל זָר שֶׁיֵּשׁ בְּגוּפוֹ שֶׁל אָדָם? הֱוֵי אוֹמֵר, זֶה יֵצֶר הָרָע".
> (תלמוד בבלי, שבת, ק"ה, ב')
>
> Did we not learn in the *Baraita* that Rabbi Shim'on ben El'azar says in the name of Ḥilfa bar Agra, who said in the name of Rabbi Yoḥanan ben Nuri: "One who rends his garments in his anger, or breaks his vessels in his anger, or scatters his money in his anger, should be considered, in your eyes, an idol worshipper, as that is the skill of the *yetzer hara* (evil inclination): Today he tells him: 'do this', and tomorrow he tells him: 'do that', until eventually, [when he no longer controls himself] he tells him: 'worship idols', and he goes and worships idols." Rabbi Avin said: "What verse alludes to this? 'No alien god shall be within you, neither shall you prostrate yourself to a foreign god' (Psalms 81:10). What is the alien god that is within a person's body? We say that it is the *yetzer hara* (evil inclination)."
>
> (*Babylonian Talmud*, "*Shabbat*," 105b)

It is a foreign god because it is not connected to you or to who you really are. The authentic God is your true nature. *Da mah lemalah mimmcha* (*Mishnah*, "*Pirkei Avot*," 2.1). That is, what exists above is from you *(mimmcha)*. The alien god, which is the ego, comes from the other, from society. The evil inclination is called *yetzer hara* in Hebrew. *Ra*, or "bad," has the first letters of the terms *ratzon atzmi*, or "self-will."

> "וְכֹל מַאֲמִינִים שֶׁהוּא לְבַדּוֹ הוּא" (פיוט לראש־השנה) כְּמוֹ שֶׁהָיָה קֹדֶם שֶׁנִּבְרָא הָעוֹלָם מַמָּשׁ, שֶׁהָיָה הוּא לְבַדּוֹ, וּכְמוֹ שֶׁנֶּאֱמַר: "אַתָּה הוּא עַד שֶׁלֹּא נִבְרָא הָעוֹלָם

אַתָּה הוּא מִשֶּׁנִּבְרָא" כו' (תפילת שחרית), פֵּרוּשׁ, הוּא מַמָּשׁ בְּלִי שׁוּם שִׁנּוּי, כִּדְכְתִיב: "אֲנִי ה' לֹא שָׁנִיתִי" (מלאכי ג', ו'). כִּי עוֹלָם הַזֶּה, וְכֵן כָּל הָעוֹלָמוֹת הָעֶלְיוֹנִים, אֵינָם פּוֹעֲלִים שׁוּם שִׁנּוּי בְּאַחְדוּתוֹ יִתְבָּרֵךְ בְּהִבָּרְאָם מֵאַיִן לְיֵשׁ, שֶׁכְּמוֹ שֶׁהָיָה הוּא לְבַדּוֹ הוּא יָחִיד וּמְיֻחָד קֹדֶם הִבָּרְאָם, כֵּן הוּא לְבַדּוֹ הוּא יָחִיד וּמְיֻחָד אַחַר שֶׁבְּרָאָם, מִשּׁוּם דְּכֹלָּא קַמֵּהּ כְּלָא חָשִׁיב וּכְאַיִן וָאֶפֶס מַמָּשׁ.

"And all believe that He is All Alone," (*Rosh HaShanah* Prayer) exactly as He was before the world was created, when there was naught besides Him, as is written: "You were [the same] before the world was created; You are [the same] since the world has been created..." (Morning Prayer). This means exactly the same without any change, as it is written: "For I, the Lord, have not changed" (Malachi, 3:6), inasmuch as this world and likewise all supernal worlds do not effect any change in His Unity, Blessed be He, by their having been created *ex nihilo*. For just as He was All Alone, Single and Unique, before they were created, so is He One and Alone, Single and Unique after they were created, since, beside Him, everything is as nothing, verily as null and void.

The immutability of God is also mentioned in Psalms:

וְאַתָּה־הוּא וּשְׁנוֹתֶיךָ לֹא יִתָּמּוּ׃

(תהילים ק"ב, כ"ח)

But you are, and your years will not end.

(Psalms, 102:28)

Before the beginning of time, only God existed in his absolute primordial solitude. If we want to make a table, we need wood. To publish a hardcopy book, we need paper. To make bread, we have to buy flour. To build a house, we need cement. In his total solitude, God obviously did not have any substance beside Himself to create a universe. If only God was, He did not have anything other than Himself to create out of. Therefore, the universe is more a concealment than a creation. Instead of a revelation, it is a masking that manifests the indivisible in an apparent diversity, what is absolute into relative, what is eternal into temporal, what is infinite into limited. That is to say, the One without a second is both the efficient or effective cause and the material cause.

Evidently, as an exposing concealment that actually creates without generating, the universe does not affect God at all. This reminds us of the famous invocation of the *Īśāvāsya Upanishad*:

> ॐ पूर्णमदः पूर्णमिदं पूर्णात्पूर्णमुदच्यते ।
> पूर्णस्य पूर्णमादाय पूर्णमेवावशिष्यते ॥
> ॐ शान्तिः शान्तिः शान्तिः ॥

oṁ pūrṇam adaḥ pūrṇam idaṁ
pūrṇāt pūrṇam udacyate
pūrṇasya pūrṇam ādāya
pūrṇam evāvaśiṣyate
oṁ śāntiḥ śāntiḥ śāntiḥ

> That is the Whole, this is the Whole; from that Whole, this Whole is manifested. When this Whole is extracted, that Whole remains being the Whole. *Oṁ* peace, peace, peace.
> (*Īśāvāsya Upanishad*, invocation)

In the daily Jewish morning prayers, or *shaharit*, the congregation prays:

> אַתָּה הוּא עַד שֶׁלֹּא נִבְרָא הָעוֹלָם, אַתָּה הוּא מִשֶּׁנִּבְרָא הָעוֹלָם.
> (סידור התפילה, תפילת שחרית)

> You are [the same One who was] before the world was created, and You are [the same One who is] since the world was created.
> (*Siddur*, Weekday morning prayer, *Shaharit*)

The seemingly unnecessary repetition of the words *ata hu,* or "You are," indicates that what exists before and after the creation is exactly the same. The substance from before and after creation remains absolutely immutable. Such repetition emphasizes the immutability of the Absolute. Likewise, clouds do not affect the vastness of the sky nor do movies affect the movie screen. Even if the water falls in a torrential storm, flows in a tumultuous river, or rests in a calm lake, its nature is unaffected. Its mutability manifests only on the surface, not in its essence.

From our childhood to old age, through adolescence, youth, and maturity, our surface constantly transforms. Our body, mind, and feelings change, but at the core, consciousness is unaffected. Deep within, we feel the same at age five, fifteen, or fifty. Changes that manifest at the surface level do not affect consciousness; it remains unchanged despite the changing periphery. Experiences never alter consciousness.

כִּי הִתְהַוּוּת כָּל הָעוֹלָמוֹת, עֶלְיוֹנִים וְתַחְתּוֹנִים, מֵאַיִן לְיֵשׁ, וְחִיּוּתָם וְקִיּוּמָם הַמְקַיְּמָם
שֶׁלֹּא יַחְזְרוּ לִהְיוֹת אַיִן וָאֶפֶס כְּשֶׁהָיָה, אֵינוֹ אֶלָּא דְּבַר ה' וְרוּחַ פִּיו הַמְלֻבָּשׁ בָּהֶם.

For the coming into being out of nonbeing, of all the upper and nether worlds, and their life and existence sustaining them from reverting to nonexistence and naught, as was before, is nothing else but the word of God and the breath of His mouth, that is clothed in them.

According to Hassidism, the universe and all the higher worlds are not a reality separate from the creator. The universe is not detached and disconnected from God, but a manifestation of Him. As such, it is not a reality separated from its source. Creation is not a historical event that occurred in the distant past but continues to happen all the time. The universe is not a one-time phenomenon, rather it requires constant maintenance. Divine utterances continue to maintain this contraction, this *tzimtzum*, or "cosmic concealment." Otherwise, what exists, or *yesh,* would return to its natural state of nothingness, or *ayin*. If God stopped uttering it, the world would return to its primordial state. Thus, multiplicity is, in essence, a manifestation of God's breath. This topic is explained in more detail in the section *Sha'ar HaYichud VeHa'Emunah*. The cosmos continues to manifest itself because of continuous divine expressions. These utterances not only manifest the phenomenal world at a general level, but also animate the individual aspects of everything created, through complicated combinations or modulations. In *Bereshit Rabbah*, we read:

> אָמַר רַבִּי סִימוֹן: אֵין לְךָ כָּל עֵשֶׂב וְעֵשֶׂב, שֶׁאֵין לוֹ מַזָּל בָּרָקִיעַ שֶׁמַּכֶּה אוֹתוֹ, וְאוֹמֵר לוֹ: גְּדַל!
>
> (בראשית רבה, י', ו')
>
> Rabbi Simon said: "There is not a single blade of grass that does not have a constellation in the firmament that strikes it and says to it: "Grow!"
>
> (*Bereshit Rabbah*, 10.6)

The existence of all the universes, with everything and everybody that they contain, is maintained by the power of the active creator in what has been created, or *koaḥ hapo'el banif'al*. Hassidism uses the example of a stone thrown in the air. The stone will continue to move until the kinetic energy is exhausted. Then, it will fall to the ground.

Here we must mention the superior worlds, especially for those who mistakenly believe that non-dual claims are only relevant to the mundane platform. Creation is part of the divine reality. Both the lower and higher worlds are expressions of divinity. Worlds such as *assiyah* and *yetzirah*, as well as the higher ones, *beri'ah* and *atzilut*, are part of the dual reality. Even if they are the most abstract and subtle dimensions, whether astral or energetic, as long as the subject–object relationship exists, they are part of the dual and relative platform.

> וּלְמָשָׁל כְּמוֹ בְּנֶפֶשׁ הָאָדָם כְּשֶׁמְּדַבֵּר דִּבּוּר אֶחָד, שֶׁדִּבּוּר זֶה לְבַדּוֹ כְּלָא מַמָּשׁ אֲפִלּוּ לְגַבֵּי כְּלָלוּת נַפְשׁוֹ הַמְדַבֶּרֶת, שֶׁהוּא בְּחִינַת לְבוּשׁ הָאֶמְצָעִי שֶׁלָּהּ, שֶׁהוּא כֹּחַ הַדִּבּוּר שֶׁלָּהּ שֶׁיָּכוֹל לְדַבֵּר דִּבּוּרִים לְאֵין קֵץ וְתַכְלִית. וְכָל שֶׁכֵּן לְגַבֵּי בְּחִינַת לְבוּשׁ

הַפְּנִימִי שֶׁלָּהּ, שֶׁהוּא הַמַּחֲשָׁבָה שֶׁמִּמֶּנָּה נִמְשָׁכוּ הַדִּבּוּרִים וְהִיא חִיּוּתָם. וְאֵין צָרִיךְ לוֹמַר לְגַבֵּי מַהוּת וְעַצְמוּת הַנֶּפֶשׁ, שֶׁהֵן עֶשֶׂר בְּחִינוֹתֶיהָ הַנִּזְכָּרוֹת לְעֵיל, חָכְמָה בִּינָה וָדַעַת כו', שֶׁמֵּהֶן נִמְשָׁכוּ אוֹתִיּוֹת מַחֲשָׁבָה זוֹ הַמְּלֻבָּשׁוֹת בְּדִבּוּר זֶה כְּשֶׁמְּדַבֵּר. כִּי הַמַּחֲשָׁבָה הִיא גַּם כֵּן בְּחִינַת אוֹתִיּוֹת, כְּמוֹ הַדִּבּוּר, רַק שֶׁהֵן רוּחָנִיּוֹת וְדַקּוֹת יוֹתֵר.

To illustrate from the soul of a human being: when a man utters a word, this utterance in itself is as absolutely nothing even when compared only with his general "articulate soul," which is the so-called middle "garment," namely, the soul's faculty of speech, which can produce speech without limit or end; all the more when it is compared with its so-called innermost "garment," namely, its faculty of thought, which is the source of speech and its life-force, not to mention when it is compared with the essence and entity of the soul, these being its ten attributes mentioned above, viz., *ḥochmah* (wisdom), *binah* (understanding), *da'at* (knowledge), and so on, from which are derived the "letters" of thought that are clothed in the speech when it is uttered. For thought can as much be defined in terms of "letters" as speech, except that in the former they are more spiritual and refined.

There is no difference between the divine expression and its absolute source. In other words, every divine expression is divinity. In this text, the Alter Rebbe gives us a vivid explanation of the creation process as a contraction or concealment of consciousness. It is compared to human expression: when a person utters a word, that single word is insignificant compared to the capacity of their soul to speak. A person's faculty for verbal expression is capable of producing an infinite number of words. These words are irrelevant and practically non-existent in relation to the origin of the human expression or the "articulate soul," (*nefesh medaberet*). Within the context of the "clothing" or "garments" (thought, speech, and action), the ability to speak is mid-range clothing. It is not the deepest vestment, because certain sensations cannot be communicated verbally. Very deep experiences cannot be verbalized, since they belong to a preverbal level.

Thought (*maḥshavah*) is the soul's deepest clothing. When we verbalize our thoughts, they are only partially expressed. Thought can also be viewed at different levels of subtlety. Thought is a garment that precedes verbal expression (*dibbur*). According to the Kabbalah, thought arises from the relationship between the different powers of the soul, or *middot hanefesh*. That is, the relationship between *ḥochma* (wisdom), *binah* (understanding), *da'at* (knowledge), *ḥesed* (grace), *gevurah* (might), *tif'eret* (beauty), *netzaḥ* (victory), *hod* (splendor), *yessod* (foundation), and *malchut* (kingship). Obviously, the word loses its relevance when compared to deeper faculties such as thought, let alone preverbal dimensions of the human being.

Both thought and speech are communication; the former with ourselves and the latter with others. Thought is an internal activity, while verbal expression externalizes mental content. Thoughts are subtle words. Mental activity is more abstract and subtle because it is closer to metaphysical planes. Thus, if words are insignificant compared to our capacity for expression, they are even more so when compared to deeper levels. The difference between thought and speech is only quantitative: it is like comparing a gram of bronze and a ton of bronze. But if we compare the words of the soul with the Self or consciousness, it would be like comparing bronze and feathers. The first difference is quantitative, while the second is qualitative or at the level of essence. Because when we refer to consciousness, we are talking about something that is not something; it is devoid of objective qualities.

אֲבָל עֶשֶׂר בְּחִינוֹת חָכְמָה בִּינָה וָדַעַת כו' הֵן שֹׁרֶשׁ וּמְקוֹר הַמַּחֲשָׁבָה, וְאֵין בָּהֶם בְּחִינַת אוֹתִיּוֹת עֲדַיִן קֹדֶם שֶׁמִּתְלַבְּשׁוֹת בִּלְבוּשׁ הַמַּחֲשָׁבָה.

But the ten attributes [of the soul]—*ḥochmah* (wisdom), *binah* (understanding), *da'at* (knowledge), and so forth—are the root and source of thought, and, prior to their being clothed in the "garment" of thought, still lack the element of "letters."

The ten attributes, or *middot*, are the elementary levels of the objective reality. They constitute the power that dominates us both mentally and verbally. However, the prelinguistic plane lacks letters. Much of what happens on this level cannot be imagined or expressed in words. There are experiences on elementary planes of objective reality that cannot be verbalized.

לְמָשָׁל, כְּשֶׁנּוֹפֶלֶת אֵיזוֹ אַהֲבָה וְחֶמְדָּה בְּלִבּוֹ שֶׁל אָדָם, קֹדֶם שֶׁעוֹלָה מֵהַלֵּב אֶל הַמֹּחַ לְחַשֵּׁב וּלְהַרְהֵר בָּהּ, אֵין בָּהּ בְּחִינַת אוֹתִיּוֹת עֲדַיִן, רַק חֵפֶץ פָּשׁוּט וַחֲשִׁיקָה בַּלֵּב אֶל הַדָּבָר הַהוּא הַנֶּחְמָד אֶצְלוֹ.

For example, when a man suddenly becomes conscious of a certain love or desire in his heart, before it has risen from the heart to the brain to think and meditate about it, it has not yet acquired the element of "letters"; it is only a simple desire and longing in the heart for the object of his affection.

This is how the Alter Rebbe describes the process: first, a pre-mental impulse is born which does not manifest itself as an idea because it is prior to thought and, obviously, to its verbal expression. At that primary level, the impulse is not yet filled with ideas, thoughts, or letters. This level is existential, unverbalized, and there are no differences based on culture or nationality. It is a dimension of silence that lies beyond all verbal definition because it lacks internal chatter. However, it is not a silence imposed from outside; it is born from our depths. Instead of communication between two beings, there is communion: two hearts beat as one and two souls hold hands. Misunderstandings disappear and they share the same joy and peace.

וְכָל שֶׁכֵּן קֹדֶם שֶׁנָּפְלָה הַתַּאֲוָה וְהַחֶמְדָּה בְּלִבּוֹ לְאוֹתוֹ דָּבָר, רַק הָיְתָה בְּכֹחַ חָכְמָתוֹ וְשִׂכְלוֹ וִידִיעָתוֹ, שֶׁהָיָה נוֹדָע אֶצְלוֹ אוֹתוֹ דָּבָר שֶׁהוּא נֶחְמָד וְנָעִים וְטוֹב וְיָפֶה לְהַשִּׂיגוֹ וְלִדָּבֵק בּוֹ, כְּגוֹן לִלְמֹד אֵיזוֹ חָכְמָה אוֹ לֶאֱכֹל אֵיזֶה מַאֲכָל עָרֵב.

All the more so before he began to feel in his heart a craving and desire for that thing, and it is as yet

> **confined within the realm of his wisdom, intellect, and knowledge, that is, the thing is known to him to be desirable and gratifying, something good and pleasant to attain and to cling to, as, for instance, to learn some wisdom or to eat some delicious food.**

When attraction for an object awakes, it does not necessarily express itself in thoughts or words. Only when we store the memory of that enjoyment and yearn to repeat it, is desire put into words. For example, if we are absorbed in the enjoyment of a sunrise by the seashore, we experience the present moment without any mental activity. But the next day, remembering that pleasure, the desire to repeat it arises, and we resort to thoughts and words.

We have already talked about the insignificance of words compared to the ability to speak. In this text, the comparison is qualitative. Words are practically incomparable to deeper dimensions that lack even mental activity. Likewise, divine expressions are insignificant when compared to their origin or God. Therefore, the universe, which is maintained through divine words, is null.

The Alter Rebbe uses the words of a prayer here:

> אֱמֶת וְיַצִּיב וְנָכוֹן וְקַיָּם וְיָשָׁר וְנֶאֱמָן וְאָהוּב וְחָבִיב וְנֶחְמָד וְנָעִים [...]
> (סידור התפילה, קריאת שמע של שחרית)

> It is true and firm, certain and enduring, upright and faithful, beloved and cherished, desired and pleasant…
>
> (*Siddur*, Morning "*Shema*")

Also, we see that he quotes Eve's words that ultimately led to Adam's fall:

> וַתֵּרֶא הָאִשָּׁה כִּי טוֹב הָעֵץ לְמַאֲכָל וְכִי תַאֲוָה הוּא לָעֵינַיִם וְנֶחְמָד הָעֵץ לְהַשְׂכִּיל וַתִּקַּח מִפִּרְיוֹ וַתֹּאכַל וַתִּתֵּן גַּם לְאִישָׁהּ עִמָּהּ וַיֹּאכַל:
>
> (בראשית ג', ו')

And the woman saw that the tree was good for eating, and that it was desirable for the eyes, and that the tree was auspicious for knowing, and she took of its fruit and ate, and gave also to her husband with her, and he ate.

(Genesis, 3:6)

The hidden teaching behind these words is that attraction can be awakened to the Divine as well as to the mundane, to reality or illusion. Consequently, the power of attraction can either elevate or degrade us, depending on the object of our attraction.

רַק לְאַחַר שֶׁכְּבָר נָפְלָה הַחֶמְדָּה וְהַתַּאֲוָה בְּלִבּוֹ בְּכֹחַ חָכְמָתוֹ וְשִׂכְלוֹ וִידִיעָתוֹ, וְאַחַר כָּךְ חָזְרָה וְעָלְתָה מֵהַלֵּב לַמֹּחַ לַחֲשֹׁב וּלְהַרְהֵר בָּהּ אֵיךְ לְהוֹצִיא תַּאֲוָתוֹ מֵהַכֹּחַ אֶל הַפֹּעַל לְהַשִּׂיג הַמַּאֲכָל אוֹ לְמִידַת הַחָכְמָה בְּפֹעַל, הֲרֵי בְּכָאן נוֹלְדוּ בְּחִינוֹת אוֹתִיּוֹת בְּמֹחוֹ, שֶׁהֵן אוֹתִיּוֹת כִּלְשׁוֹן עַם וָעָם, הַמְדַבְּרִים וְהַמְהַרְהֲרִים בָּהֶם כָּל עִנְיְנֵי הָעוֹלָם.

Only after the desire and craving have already found their way into the heart, through the stimulus of his wisdom, intellect, and knowledge, and then ascended once more back to the brain, to think and meditate on how to translate his craving from the potential into the practical, with a view to actually obtaining that food or acquiring that wisdom—it is here that the so-called "letters" are born in his mind, such "letters" corresponding to the language of each nation, employing them in speech and thought about all things in the world.

The first stage is an impulse that cannot be expressed through words or letters. This desire can remain unexpressed, without generating any ideas. Only after the impulse is transformed into an emotion, thought is born in order to plan how to satisfy it. Then, letters manifest themselves to dress that impulse. In its primary stage, the impulse transcends culture and nationality. Thirst is not Arabic, Israeli, Chilean, or Hindu. Hunger is not Muslim, Jewish, Catholic, or Buddhist. The linguistic differences come after their expression at the mental level. Verbal variety belongs to the surface. Unity resides in the depths of consciousness. Only after getting dressed in thoughts and letters, desire manifests itself on the plane of action.

It is very beneficial to observe others, but with the intention of learning about ourselves. It is easier to be objective about human beings similar to us because we do not feel we have something to defend, gain, or lose. If you want to know reality more deeply, pay less attention to words and more to meanings. Although we use the same words, we give them very different sense. If you only pay attention to words, you will be confused. Try to listen to what is hidden behind the words you hear.

This brings us to the end of chapter 20 of the *Tanya*, which begins with the unity of divinity and ends with verbal expression in humans. Such an examination exemplifies the relationship between objective reality and consciousness. It teaches us that verbal expression does not constitute an independent phenomenon, but is only the manifestation of an inner essence. When our personality expresses itself, it uses language to present a certain image, which allows it to hide its feelings and ideas. The more it talks, the more it hides. Sincere and honest beings use fewer words with greater meaning.

Observe your conversations and transform them into meditation. Pay more attention to gestures and movements than to words. You will learn to understand the language behind them. This meditation will help you pay attention to your own communication. If you listen to your own words, you will see that they are mostly lies. Discover the silence deep within you, and as you penetrate it, you will be flooded with peace, joy, and bliss. You are a child of silence: it is your origin and your destination. True meditation ultimately leads you to inner silence. Just as you communicate with others through sound, silence is the ideal medium to communicate with yourself or your reality. In complete silence, all paths to others disappear, leaving open only the path that leads to you.

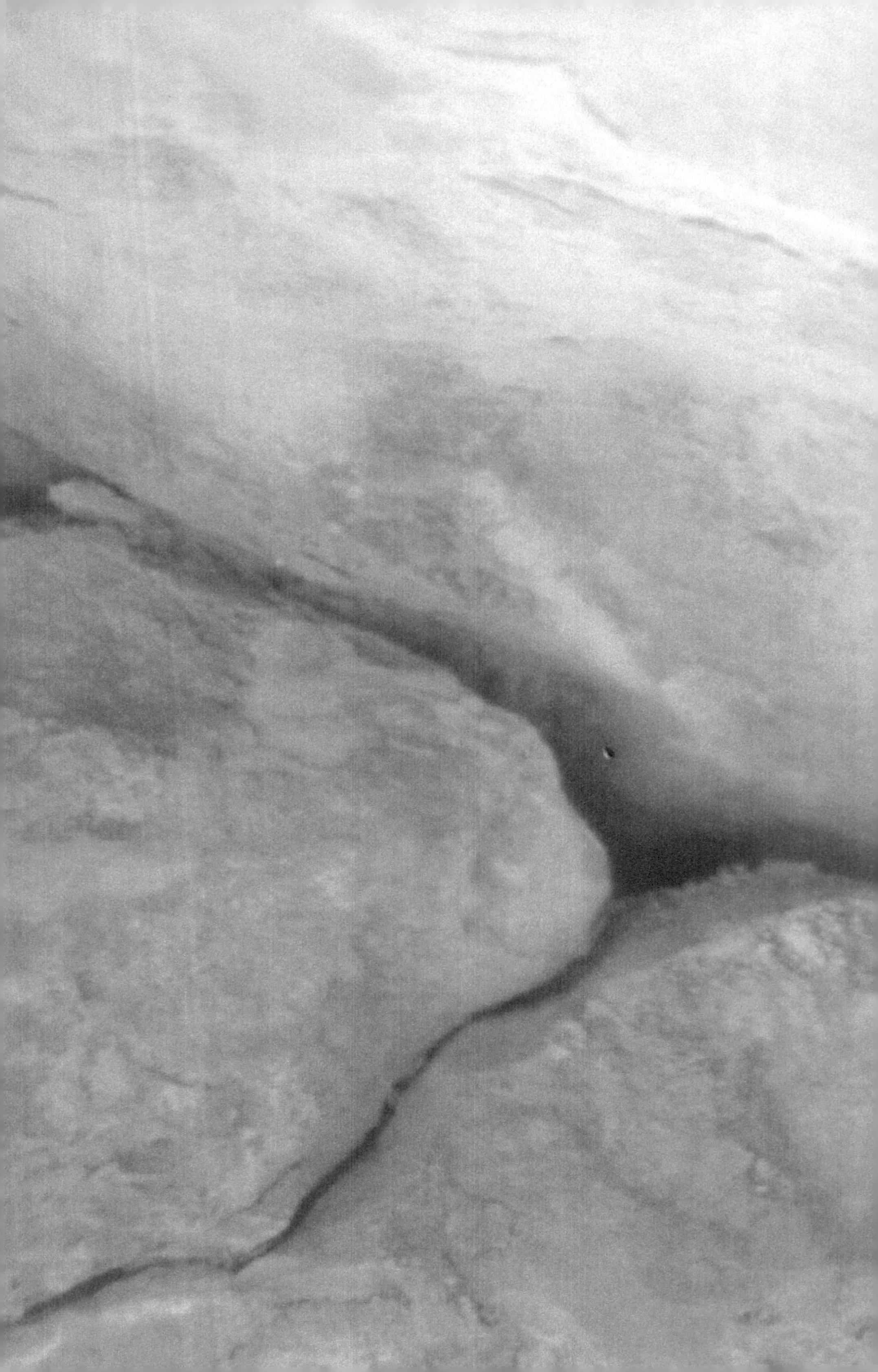

ARTICLE 17

UNITY AND DIVINE EXPRESSION

TANYA CHAPTER 21

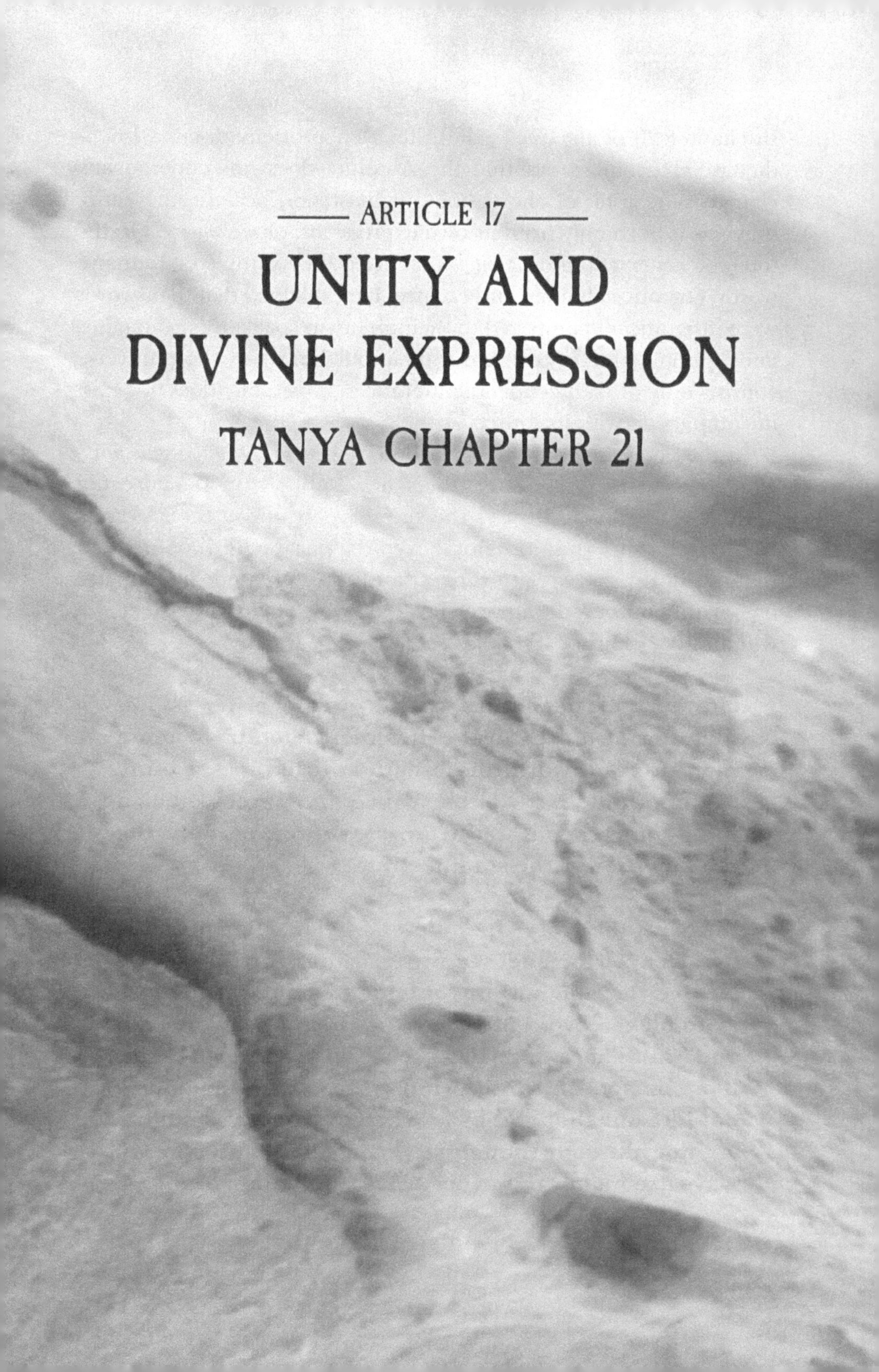

In chapter 20 of the *Tanya*, the Alter Rebbe briefly discussed non-duality. He pointed out that the Absolute does not undergo any change as a result of the cosmic manifestation because the entire universe is born only from its own expressions, or *ma'amarot*. On the topic of contraction, or *tzimtzum*, he used the example of humans' words, cognitive abilities, and essence. He explained that their words were insignificant compared to their ability to speak, their thoughts, and especially, the very essence of their soul. Since the whole universe consists only of transcendental utterances, it basically does not exist in comparison with its source.

In the section of the *Tanya* called *The portal of unity and faith*, which we will discuss later, the Alter Rebbe says that created entities exist in God, just as the sun's rays reside at their source. In their origin, they do not have a separate or independent reality. Both sacred utterances and the created beings are irrelevant compared to more elevated levels of divinity. Next, we will analyze chapter 21.

However, "The nature of the divine order is not like that of a creature of flesh and blood." When a man utters a word, the breath emitted in speaking is something that can be sensed and perceived as a thing apart, separated from its source, namely, the ten faculties of the soul itself.

But with the Holy One, Blessed is He, His speech is not, Heaven forfend, separated from Him, Blessed be He, for there is nothing outside of Him, and "there is no place devoid of Him" (*Tikkunei HaZohar*, 122b and 92a). Therefore, His speech, Blessed be He, is not like our speech, God forbid [just as His thought is not like our thought, as is written "For My thoughts are not like your thoughts" (Isaiah, 55:8) and "So My ways are higher than your ways..." (Isaiah, 55:9)]

His speech, Blessed be He, is called "speech" only in order to illustrate that, just as in the case of man below, whose speech reveals to his audience what was hidden and concealed in his thoughts, so, too, is it on high with the *Ein Sof* (Infinite), Blessed is He, Whose emitted light and life-force—as it emerges from Him, from concealment into revelation, to create worlds and to sustain them—is called "speech."

These [emanations] are, indeed, the ten fiats by which the world was created; likewise also the remainder of the Torah, Prophets, and Writings, which the Prophets conceived in their prophetic vision.

Yet His so-called speech and thought are united with Him in absolute union as, for example, a person's speech and thought are united while they are still *in potentia* in his wisdom and intellect, or [another example:] in a desire and craving that are still in the heart prior to rising from the heart to the brain, where by cogitation they are formulated into the so-called "letters," for at that time [prior to raising to the brain] the "letters" of thought and speech which evolve from that longing or desire were still *in potentia* in the heart, where they were absolutely fused with their root, namely, the wisdom and intellect in the brain, and the longing and desire in the heart.

Verily so, by way of example, are the "speech" and "thought" of the Holy One, Blessed is He, absolutely united with His essence and being, Blessed be He, even after His "speech," Blessed be He, has already become materialized in the creation of the worlds, just as it was united with Him before the worlds were created. There is thus no manner of change before

Him, Blessed be He, but only for the created beings which receive their life-force from His "word," Blessed be He, as it were, in its revealed state at the creation of the worlds, in which it [His speech] is clothed, giving them life through a process of gradual descent from cause to effect and a downward gradation, by means of numerous and various contractions, until the created beings can receive their life and existence from it without losing their identity.

These "contractions" [or condensations] are all in the nature of "veiling of the countenance," (*hester panim*) to obscure and conceal the light and life-force that is derived from His "word," Blessed be He, so that it shall not reveal itself in a greater radiance than the lower worlds are capable of receiving. Hence it seems to them as if the light and life-force of the speech of the Omnipresent, Blessed is He, which is clothed in them, were something apart from His essence and being, Blessed be He, and it only issues from Him, just as the speech of a human being [issues] from his soul.

Yet, in regard to the Holy One, Blessed is He, no contraction or concealment hides or obscures anything from Him, to Whom darkness is like light, as is written "Even the darkness obscures nothing from You" (Psalms, 139:12), etc. For all the "contractions" and "garments" are not things distinct from Him, Heaven forfend, but "like that turtle, whose garment is part of his body" and as is written: "The Lord, He is God" (Deuteronomy, 4:35), as is explained elsewhere. Therefore, in His Presence, all else is of no account whatsoever.

We will discuss this text one section at a time.

וְהִנֵּה מִדַּת הַקָּדוֹשׁ בָּרוּךְ הוּא שֶׁלֹּא כְּמִדַּת בָּשָׂר וָדָם. שֶׁהָאָדָם, כְּשֶׁמְּדַבֵּר דִּבּוּר, הֲרֵי הֶבֶל הַדִּבּוּר שֶׁבְּפִיו הוּא מֻרְגָּשׁ וְנִרְאֶה דָּבָר בִּפְנֵי עַצְמוֹ, מֻבְדָּל מִשָּׁרְשׁוֹ, שֶׁהֵן עֶשֶׂר בְּחִינוֹת הַנֶּפֶשׁ עַצְמָהּ.

However, "The nature of the divine order is not like that of a creature of flesh and blood." When a man utters a word, the breath emitted in speaking is something that can be sensed and perceived as a thing apart, separated from its source, namely, the ten faculties of the soul itself.

Human verbal communication occurs on the dual platform, where speech is separate from the speaker. Once spoken, words are disconnected from their origin; the wind takes them away, as the saying goes. On the relative plane, logos has its own existence, independent of the speaker.

אֲבָל הַקָּדוֹשׁ בָּרוּךְ הוּא, אֵין דִּבּוּרוֹ מֻבְדָּל מִמֶּנּוּ יִתְבָּרֵךְ חַס וְשָׁלוֹם, כִּי אֵין דָּבָר חוּץ מִמֶּנּוּ וְ"לֵית אֲתַר פָּנוּי מִנֵּהּ" (תיקוני הזוהר, קכ"ב, ב' וצ"ב, א'), וְלָכֵן אֵין דִּבּוּרוֹ יִתְבָּרֵךְ כְּדִבּוּרֵנוּ חַס וְשָׁלוֹם.

But with the Holy One, Blessed is He, His speech is not, Heaven forfend, separated from Him, Blessed be He, for there is nothing outside of Him, and "there is no place devoid of Him" (*Tikkunei HaZohar*, 122b and 92a). Therefore, His speech, Blessed be He, is not like our speech, God forbid.

Unlike human speech, divine verbal expression is one with its transcendental source. On the absolute plane, internal and external are one: there is no difference between the subject as speaker and the object as verb. It is impossible to separate God from His expression because only God truly is and everything is in God.

On a relative perspective, human beings speak from the inside out. However, from an absolute perspective, words occur deep within consciousness; they are an intimate experience at the primary level. Similarly, when the mind yearns, it desires something external because it perceives something is missing. But the transcendental desire is a longing for what is internal, or inherently part of oneself. Since God is not separate from His utterances, His creation is nothing but divinity. There is nothing in us that exists independently of God. All universes belong to consciousness. Our essence is divine and our existence is a loan. As divine expressions, we are recreated in every moment.

[כְּמוֹ שֶׁאֵין מַחֲשַׁבְתּוֹ כְּמַחֲשַׁבְתֵּנוּ, כְּדִכְתִיב: "כִּי לֹא מַחְשְׁבוֹתַי מַחְשְׁבוֹתֵיכֶם (ישעיהו נ"ה, ח')", וּכְתִיב: "כֵּן גָּבְהוּ דְּרָכַי מִדַּרְכֵיכֶם" (ישעיהו נ"ה, ט') וגו'.]

[just as His thought is not like our thought, as is written "For My thoughts are not like your thoughts" (Isaiah, 55:8) and "So My ways are higher than your ways…" (Isaiah, 55:9)]

Just as there is a distinction between divine and human thought, there is also a great difference between the speech on the relative and the absolute platforms.

וְלֹא נִקְרָא דִּבּוּרוֹ יִתְבָּרֵךְ בְּשֵׁם "דִּבּוּר", רַק עַל דֶּרֶךְ מָשָׁל, כְּמוֹ שֶׁדִּבּוּר הַתַּחְתּוֹן שֶׁבָּאָדָם הוּא מְגַלֶּה לַשּׁוֹמְעִים מַה שֶּׁהָיָה צָפוּן וְנֶעְלָם בְּמַחֲשַׁבְתּוֹ, כָּךְ לְמַעְלָה, בְּאֵין־סוֹף בָּרוּךְ הוּא, יְצִיאַת הָאוֹר וְהַחִיּוּת מִמֶּנּוּ יִתְבָּרֵךְ, מֵהַהֶעְלֵם אֶל הַגִּלּוּי לִבְרֹא עוֹלָמוֹת וּלְהַחֲיוֹתָם, נִקְרָא בְּשֵׁם "דִּבּוּר".

His speech, Blessed be He, is called "speech" only in order to illustrate that, just as in the case of man below, whose speech reveals to his audience what was hidden and concealed in his thoughts, so, too, is it on high with the *Ein Sof* (Infinite), Blessed is He, Whose emitted light and life-force—as it emerges from Him, from concealment into revelation, to create worlds and to sustain them—is called "speech."

Through verbal expressions, we expose our mental and emotional world. This expression, both on a human and transcendental level, consists of an act of contraction and unveiling. God creates the world through utterances and, therefore, reveals by contracting God's own inner reality. As previously mentioned, unlike human expression, transcendental locution expression remains in its source. Hence, it could be considered thought rather than speech. This is why the Alter Rebbe says, "**His speech, Blessed be He, is called 'speech' only in order to illustrate.**" That is to say, divine expression is metaphorically or allegorically called so precisely because it reveals what is hidden.

The Alter Rebbe continues:

וְהֵן הֵן עֲשָׂרָה מַאֲמָרוֹת שֶׁבָּהֶן נִבְרָא הָעוֹלָם, וְכֵן שְׁאָר כָּל הַתּוֹרָה נְבִיאִים וּכְתוּבִים שֶׁהִשִּׂיגוּ הַנְּבִיאִים בְּמַרְאֵה נְבוּאָתָם.

These [emanations] are, indeed, the ten fiats by which the world was created; likewise also the remainder of the Torah, Prophets, and Writings, which the Prophets conceived in their prophetic vision.

The Bible is considered transcendental; it is the revelation of existence to the prophet. Enlightenment shows what is hidden and inaccessible to ordinary levels of consciousness. It is possible to convey that vision but, obviously, not through human verbal communication.

וַהֲרֵי דִּבּוּרוֹ וּמַחֲשַׁבְתּוֹ כִּבְיָכוֹל מְיֻחָדוֹת עִמּוֹ בְּתַכְלִית הַיִּחוּד, דֶּרֶךְ מָשָׁל, כְּמוֹ דִּבּוּרוֹ וּמַחֲשַׁבְתּוֹ שֶׁל אָדָם בְּעוֹדָן בְּכֹחַ חָכְמָתוֹ וְשִׂכְלוֹ.

Yet His so-called speech and thought are united with Him in absolute union as, for example, a person's speech and thought are united while they are still *in potentia* in his wisdom and intellect.

The divine expression, unlike the human one, is more similar to thought than to speech. Once spoken, words have a life of their own and a reality independent from their speaker. On the other hand, thoughts are discrete and intimate. Mental activity remains hidden and imperceptible to external entities. Experiences do not occur outside of consciousness, but deep within it. Thus, there is no experience outside of consciousness.

אוֹ בַּתְּשׁוּקָה וְחֶמְדָּה שֶׁבְּלִבּוֹ, קֹדֶם שֶׁעָלְתָה מֵהַלֵּב לַמּוֹחַ לְהַרְהֵר בָּהּ בִּבְחִינַת אוֹתִיּוֹת, שֶׁאָז הָיוּ אוֹתִיּוֹת הַמַּחֲשָׁבָה וְהַדִּבּוּר הַזֶּה, הַנִּמְשָׁכוֹת מֵחֶמְדָּה וּתְשׁוּקָה זוֹ, בְּכֹחַ בַּלֵּב, וּמְיֻחָדוֹת שָׁם בְּתַכְלִית הַיִּחוּד בְּשָׁרְשָׁן, שֶׁהֵן הַחָכְמָה וְשֵׂכֶל שֶׁבַּמּוֹחַ וְחֶמְדָּה וּתְשׁוּקָה שֶׁבַּלֵּב.

Or [another example:] in a desire and craving that are still in the heart prior to rising from the heart to the brain, where by cogitation they are formulated into the so-called "letters," for at that time [prior to raising to the brain] the "letters" of thought and speech which evolve from that longing or desire were still *in potentia* in the heart, where they were absolutely fused with their root, namely, the wisdom and intellect in the brain, and the longing and desire in the heart.

According to the Alter Rebbe, desires and fears that abide deep in the heart can be transformed into words. These impulses send signals to the mind, where they become thoughts, symbols, and finally, words. Feelings, emotions, and desires lie in potential, and through verbal expression, are transformed into words. On the other hand, mental activity is a dialogue with oneself that remains a part of the inner world until it is shared through external communication.

וְכָכָה מַמָּשׁ, דֶּרֶךְ מָשָׁל, מְיֻחָדוֹת דִּבּוּרוֹ וּמַחֲשַׁבְתּוֹ שֶׁל הַקָּדוֹשׁ־בָּרוּךְ־הוּא בְּתַכְלִית הַיִּחוּד בְּמַהוּתוֹ וְעַצְמוּתוֹ יִתְבָּרֵךְ, גַּם אַחַר שֶׁיָּצָא דִּבּוּרוֹ יִתְבָּרֵךְ אֶל הַפֹּעַל בִּבְרִיאוֹת הָעוֹלָמוֹת, כְּמוֹ שֶׁהָיָה מְיֻחָד עִמּוֹ קֹדֶם בְּרִיאַת הָעוֹלָמוֹת.

Verily so, by way of example, are the "speech" and "thought" of the Holy One, Blessed is He, absolutely

united with His essence and being, Blessed be He, even after His "speech," Blessed be He, has already become materialized in the creation of the worlds, just as it was united with Him before the worlds were created.

Divine verbal expression never separates from its source. Even after manifesting the universe, it remains an integral part of its transcendental origin. These locutions do not exist independently because God's omnipresent nature does not allow for any externalization. This would require a space outside of divinity, which would conflict with the Hebrew non-duality.

וְאֵין שׁוּם שִׁנּוּי כְּלָל לְפָנָיו יִתְבָּרֵךְ, אֶלָּא אֶל הַבְּרוּאִים, הַמְקַבְּלִים חִיּוּתָם מִבְּחִינַת דִּבּוּרוֹ יִתְבָּרֵךְ, בִּבְחִינַת יְצִיאָתוֹ כְּבָר אֶל הַפֹּעַל בִּבְרִיאַת הָעוֹלָמוֹת...

There is thus no manner of change before Him, Blessed be He, but only for the created beings which receive their life-force from His "word," Blessed be He, as it were, in its revealed state at the creation of the worlds...

Just as the movie scenes do not affect the screen, experiences do not affect consciousness. The screen does not get wet when the film shows a flood nor does it burn when a fire appears. Only the actors who perceive themselves as real entities experience apparent mutability. Similarly, change and temporality are perceived only from the perspective of the localized consciousness of beings who consider themselves to be created.

Divine expressions descend through a causative system of condensations or contractions (*tzimtzumim*) until they are grasped as an empirical reality. This is a descent through cause and effect, in addition to changes and mutations. Verbal expressions are already known by the speaker and are new only for the listener. Likewise, the process of creation does not mean there is any change for the absolute and immutable.

...[הָעוֹלָמוֹת] שֶׁמִּתְלַבֵּשׁ בָּהֶם [דִּבּוּרוֹ יִתְבָּרֵךְ] לְהַחֲיוֹתָם עַל יְדֵי הִשְׁתַּלְשְׁלוּת מֵעִלָּה לְעָלוּל וִירִידַת הַמַּדְרֵגוֹת בִּצְמְצוּמִים רַבִּים וְשׁוֹנִים, עַד שֶׁיּוּכְלוּ הַבְּרוּאִים לְקַבֵּל חִיּוּתָם וְהִתְהַוּוּתָם מִמֶּנּוּ, וְלֹא יִתְבַּטְּלוּ בִּמְצִיאוּת.

... [The worlds] in which it [His speech] is clothed, giving them life through a process of gradual descent from cause to effect and a downward gradation, by means of numerous and various contractions [or condensations], until the created beings can receive their life and existence from it without losing their identity.

For many people, the incredible thing about the cosmic manifestation is that what exists (*yesh*) was created out of nothing (*ain*).

וְכָל הַצִּמְצוּמִים הֵם בְּחִינַת הֶסְתֵּר פָּנִים, לְהַסְתִּיר וּלְהַעְלִים הָאוֹר וְהַחִיּוּת הַנִּמְשָׁךְ מִדִּבּוּרוֹ יִתְבָּרֵךְ, שֶׁלֹּא יִתְגַּלֶּה בִּבְחִינַת גִּלּוּי רַב שֶׁלֹּא יוּכְלוּ הַתַּחְתּוֹנִים לְקַבֵּל.

These "contractions" are all in the nature of "veiling of the countenance," (*hester panim*) to obscure and conceal the light and life-force that is derived from His "word," Blessed be He, so that it shall not reveal itself in a greater radiance than the lower worlds are capable of receiving.

The system of condensation (*tzimtzum*) regulates the intensity of light or consciousness that each entity perceives, in proportion to their receptive capacity. According to the Alter Rebbe, a complete revelation of consciousness would annihilate any created entity. In this case, the transcendental utterances would destroy the universe instead of creating it. The expression of these is reduced to maintain empirical reality and to allow the created entity to regulate the received light on its own. Objective multiplicity comprises myriad modulations of consciousness.

וְלָכֵן גַּם כֵּן נִדְמֶה לָהֶם אוֹר וְחִיּוּת הַדִּבּוּר שֶׁל מָקוֹם בָּרוּךְ הוּא הַמְלֻבָּשׁ בָּהֶם כְּאִלּוּ הוּא דָּבָר מֻבְדָּל מִמַּהוּתוֹ וְעַצְמוּתוֹ יִתְבָּרֵךְ, רַק שֶׁנִּמְשַׁךְ מִמֶּנּוּ יִתְבָּרֵךְ, כְּמוֹ דִּבּוּר שֶׁל אָדָם מִנַּפְשׁוֹ.

Hence it seems to them as if the light and life-force of the speech of the Omnipresent, Blessed is He, which is clothed in them, were something apart from His essence and being, Blessed be He, and it only issues from Him, just as the speech of a human being [issues] from his soul.

Unlike human verbal expression, divine utterances are not separated from their origin. Therefore, some type of limitation is necessary to differentiate between the speaker and the expression. The essence of the universe is the concealment of its source. Although created beings are always consciousness, due to condensations (*tzimtzumim*), they assume an apparent contracted and localized nature that prevents them from perceiving their origin. From their relative perspective, they perceive a creation separate from its creator and mistakenly conclude that if God exists, He must be a completely separate entity.

אַךְ לְגַבֵּי הַקָּדוֹשׁ בָּרוּךְ הוּא אֵין שׁוּם צִמְצוּם וְהֶסְתֵּר וְהֶעְלֵם מַסְתִּיר וּמַעְלִים לְפָנָיו, וְכַחֲשֵׁכָה כָּאוֹרָה, כְּדִכְתִיב (תהילים קל"ט, י"ב): "גַּם חֹשֶׁךְ לֹא יַחְשִׁיךְ מִמֶּךָּ" וגו'.

Yet, in regard to the Holy One, Blessed is He, no contraction or concealment hides or obscures anything from Him, to Whom darkness is like light, as is written "Even the darkness obscures nothing from You" (Psalms, 139:12), etc.

Concealment is relevant only from a relative perspective, not from an absolute one. It is like a polarized car window that allows those inside to see out but prevents anyone outside from seeing in.

מִשּׁוּם שֶׁאֵין הַצִּמְצוּמִים וְהַלְּבוּשִׁים דָּבָר נִפְרָד מִמֶּנּוּ יִתְבָּרַךְ חַס וְשָׁלוֹם, אֶלָּא "כְּהָדֵין קַמְצָא דִּלְבוּשֵׁהּ מִנֵּהּ וּבֵהּ", כְּמוֹ שֶׁכָּתוּב (דברים ד', ל"ה): "כִּי ה' הוּא הָאֱלֹהִים", וּכְמוֹ שֶׁנִּתְבָּאֵר בְּמָקוֹם אַחֵר. וְלָכֵן קַמֵּיהּ כֹּלָּא כְּלָא חָשִׁיב מַמָּשׁ.

For all the "contractions" and "garments" are not things distinct from Him, Heaven forfend, but "like that turtle, whose garment is part of his body" and as is written: "The Lord, He is God" (Deuteronomy, 4:35), as is explained elsewhere. Therefore, in His Presence, all else is of no account whatsoever.

Just as the shell of the turtle is part of its body, the garments that cover the Absolute are an integral part of it. Likewise, divine condensations are divinity itself. Because all that exists is only consciousness, whatever conceals it is also consciousness. Verse 4:35 of Deuteronomy starts with *Ki Havaya hu Ha'Elohim*, or "The Lord, He is God." *Havaya*, or "The Lord," refers to the transcendental revealer, the One without a second. The Hebrew name Elohim refers to God revealed as universe and nature. Elohim is pluralized because it refers to multiplicity. According to gematria, the word *hateva*, or "the nature," has the same numerical value as Elohim. There is no difference between the revealed God and the hidden God. Vedanta also states that even illusion, or *māyā*, is Brahman, that is, our objective reality lacks an absolute and independent real existence.

Many believe that to experience the Truth, it is essential to escape illusion. While I respect every point of view, for me, spiritual life does not demand celibacy, renunciation of the world, or escape to a *yeshiva*, monastery, or ashram. The illusion is also reality, for the mundane hides the divine, and the material conceals the spiritual. We can find this idea in the words of Rabbi Naḥman of Breslov:

שֶׁזֶּה בְּחִינַת אֶסְתֵּר, בְּחִינַת "וְאָנֹכִי הַסְתֵּר אַסְתִּיר" (דברים ל"א, י"ח) שֶׁאֲפִלּוּ בְּתַכְלִית הַהַסְתָּרָה, בְּהַסְתָּרָה שֶׁבְּתוֹךְ הַסְתָּרָה גַּם שָׁם הוּא אָנֹכִי. כִּי גַּם שָׁם נִמְצָא ה' יִתְבָּרַךְ כִּי "מְלֹא כָל הָאָרֶץ כְּבוֹדוֹ" (ישעיהו ו', ג').

(ליקוטי הלכות, אורח חיים, הלכות שבת ג', י')

This is the nature of "Esther," in the context of "and I shall hide, I shall certainly hide" (Deuteronomy, 31:18). This means that even in the deepest concealment, in the concealment within concealment, there, too, it is I. For the Lord, Blessed be He, is also there, because "The whole earth is full of His glory" (Isaiah, 6:3).

(*Likkutei Halachot*, "*Oraḥ Ḥayim*," "*Hilchot Shabbat*," 3.10)

וַאֲפִלּוּ בְּתֹקֶף הַהַסְתָּרָה שֶׁבְּתוֹךְ הַסְתָּרָה גַּם שָׁם אַתָּה נִמְצָא, כִּי אַתָּה בְּעַצְמְךָ נִסְתָּר בְּתוֹךְ כָּל הַהַסְתָּרוֹת שֶׁבָּעוֹלָם, וַאֲפִלּוּ בַּהַסְתָּרָה שֶׁבְּתוֹךְ הַסְתָּרָה, וַאֲפִלּוּ בְּאַלְפֵי אֲלָפִים וְרִבֵּי רְבָבוֹת הַסְתָּרוֹת עַד אֵין קֵץ, גַּם שָׁם אַתָּה נִמְצָא, כִּי לֵית אֲתַר פָּנוּי מִנָּךְ, וְאַתָּה מְחַיֶּה אֶת כֻּלָּם, וּבִלְעָדֶיךָ אֵין שׁוּם חַיּוּת לְשׁוּם דָּבָר שֶׁבָּעוֹלָם, וַאֲפִלּוּ כָּל הַקְּלִפּוֹת וְכָל הַטֻּמְאוֹת שֶׁבָּעוֹלָם, וְכָל הַסִּטְרִין אַחֲרָנִין, וְכָל הַהַסְתָּרוֹת שֶׁבָּעוֹלָם הַמַּסְתִּירִים אֱלֹהוּתְךָ, כֻּלָּם אֵין לָהֶם חַיּוּת וְכֹחַ כִּי אִם מָה שֶׁמְּקַבְּלִים מִמְּךָ בְּעַצְמְךָ תִּתְבָּרַךְ לָנֶצַח, וְאַתָּה מוֹשֵׁל בַּכֹּל וּמַלְכוּתְךָ בַּכֹּל מָשָׁלָה, וּבִלְעָדֶיךָ אֵין כֹּחַ לְשׁוּם הַסְתָּרָה שֶׁבָּעוֹלָם לְהַסְתִּיר וּלְהַעְלִים אוֹתְךָ תִּתְבָּרַךְ.

(רבי נחמן מברסלב, ליקוטי תפילות, חלק א', נ"ו)

And even amid the deepest concealment within concealment, even there, your presence persists. For in Your very essence, You remain hidden within every concealment that exists in the world, and even in concealment within concealment, and even within myriad or countless concealments *ad infinitum*, even there your presence endures, for there is no space devoid of You, and You are the life-force of everything, and without you nothing has vitality in the world. And even all the *kelipot* (shells or husks, the evil, the dark coverings that veil the light or holiness), all the impurities in the world, and all the *sitrin aḥranin* (the "other sides," the opposite of holiness), as well as every concealment in the world, which veil your sovereignty, all these, draw all their vitality and strength from You alone, forever Blessed are You. And You govern all, and Your sovereignty governs all, and without You, no concealment in the world would be able to conceal or hide You, Blessed are You.

(Rabbi Naḥman of Breslov, *Likkutei Tefilot*, 1.56)

Therefore, any effort to run from the apparent will lead us farther from what is real. If we renounce the world, we renounce God. Reality is not opposed to the apparent: it is hidden within. The soul resides hidden in the body: it is the body's clothing and the temple where divinity resides.

> אֲבָל בֶּאֱמֶת אֲפִלּוּ בְּכָל הַהַסְתָּרוֹת, וַאֲפִלּוּ בְּהַהַסְתָּרָה שֶׁבְּתוֹךְ הַסְתָּרָה, בְּוַדַּאי גַּם שָׁם מְלֻבָּשׁ הַשֵּׁם יִתְבָּרַךְ, כִּי בְּוַדַּאי אֵין שׁוּם דָּבָר שֶׁלֹּא יִהְיֶה בּוֹ חַיּוּת הַשֵּׁם יִתְבָּרַךְ, כִּי בִּלְעֲדֵי חַיּוּתוֹ לֹא הָיָה לוֹ קִיּוּם כְּלָל. וְעַל־כֵּן בְּוַדַּאי בְּכָל הַדְּבָרִים, וּבְכָל הַמַּעֲשִׂים, וּבְכָל הַמַּחֲשָׁבוֹת, מְלֻבָּשׁ שָׁם הַשֵּׁם יִתְבָּרַךְ, כִּבְיָכוֹל.
> (רבי נחמן מברסלב, ליקוטי מוהר"ן, נ"ו, ג')
>
> Yet, in truth, even in all the concealments—even in concealment within a concealment—God is certainly enclothed [permeated] there as well. Indeed, there is nothing that does not have God's life-force, for it could not exist without His life-force. Therefore, God is certainly pervading all things [words] and all deeds and all thoughts, so to speak.
> (Rabbi Naḥman of Breslov *Likutei Moharan*, 56.3)

God is hidden in flowers, trees, mountains, the sea, stars, and in each of us. It is divinity that looks through every eye and listens through every ear. If you penetrate the blue of the ocean or the radiance of the stars, you will find God. If you reach into the depths of another human being until you touch their soul, you will find God. If you immerse yourself in your interior, you will finally reach God.

—— ARTICLE 18 ——

THE RETROPROGRESSIVE JOURNEY OF *TESHUVAH*

The magnificent book *Tanya*, written by the great Jewish enlightened master Rabbi Shneur Zalman of Liadi, presents invaluable pearls of Hasidic wisdom. We will now discuss the first chapter of its section *Sha'ar HaYiḥud VeHa'Emunah* or "*The portal of unity and faith.*"

Know this day and take to your heart that Havaya is Elohim (The Lord, He is God) in the heavens above and upon the earth below; there is no other." (Deuteronomy, 4:39) This requires explanation. For would it occur to you that there is a god "soaking" in the waters beneath the earth that it is necessary to negate it so strongly [as to say,] "Take to your heart?"

It is written (Psalms, 119:89): "Forever, O Lord, Your word stands firm in the heavens." The Ba'al Shem Tov, of blessed memory, has explained that "Your word" which you uttered, "Let there be a firmament in the midst of the waters…" (Genesis, 1:6) these very words and letters stand firmly forever within the firmament of heaven and are forever clothed within all the heavens to give them life, as it is written : "The word of our God shall stand firm forever" (Isaiah, 40:8) and "His words live and stand firm forever…." (Morning Prayers).

For if the letters were to depart [even] for an instant, God forbid, and return to their source, all the heavens would become naught and absolute nothingness, and it would be as though they had never existed at all, exactly as before the utterance, "Let there be a firmament."

And so it is with all created things, in all the upper and lower worlds, and even this physical earth, which is the realm of the inanimate. If the letters of the Ten Utterances by which the earth was created

during the Six Days of Creation were to depart from it [but] for an instant, God forbid, it would revert to naught and absolute nothingness, exactly as before the Six Days of Creation.

This same thought was expressed by the Arizal when he said that even in completely inanimate matter, such as stones or earth or water, there is a soul and spiritual life-force—that is, the enclothing of the "Letters of speech" of the Ten Utterances which give life and existence to inanimate matter that it might arise out of the naught and nothingness which preceded the Six Days of Creation.

Now, although the name "*even*" (stone) is not mentioned in the Ten Utterances recorded in the Torah, nevertheless, life-force flows to the stone through combinations and substitutions of the letters which are transposed in the "two hundred and thirty-one gates," either in direct or reverse order, as is explained in Sefer Yetzirah, until the combination of the name "*even*" descends from the Ten Utterances, and is derived from them, and this is the life-force of the stone.

And so it is with all created things in the world—their names in the Holy Tongue are the very "letters of speech" which descend, degree by degree, from the Ten Utterances recorded in the Torah, by means of substitutions and transpositions of letters through the "two hundred and thirty-one gates," until they reach and become invested in that particular created thing to give it life.

[This descent is necessary] because individual creatures are not capable of receiving their life-force directly from the Ten Utterances of the Torah, for the life-force issuing directly from them is far greater than the capacity of the individual creatures. They can receive the life-force only when it descends and is progressively diminished, degree by degree, by means of substitutions and transpositions of the letters and by *gematriot*, their numerical values, until the life-force can be condensed and enclothed and there can be brought forth from it a particular creature. And the name by which it is called in the Holy Tongue is a vessel for the life-force condensed into the letters of that name which has descended from the Ten Utterances in the Torah that have power and vitality to create being *ex nihilo* and give it life forever. For the Torah and the Holy One, Blessed is He, are one.

We will review this chapter one part at a time.

It begins with the classical teachings of the Ba'al Shem Tov and quotes a famous verse from the Pentateuch:

"וְיָדַעְתָּ הַיּוֹם וַהֲשֵׁבֹתָ אֶל לְבָבֶךָ, כִּי ה' הוּא הָאֱלֹהִים בַּשָּׁמַיִם מִמַּעַל וְעַל הָאָרֶץ מִתָּחַת אֵין עוֹד" (דברים ד', ל"ט). וְצָרִיךְ לְהָבִין: וְכִי תַעֲלֶה עַל דַּעְתְּךָ שֶׁיֵּשׁ אֱלֹהִים נִשְׁרֶה בַּמַּיִם מִתַּחַת לָאָרֶץ, שֶׁצָּרִיךְ לְהַזְהִיר כָּל־כָּךְ "וַהֲשֵׁבֹתָ אֶל לְבָבֶךָ"?

Know this day and take to your heart that Havaya is Elohim (The Lord, He is God) in the heavens above and upon the earth below; there is no other." (Deuteronomy, 4:39) This requires explanation. For would it occur to you that there is a god "soaking" in the waters beneath the earth that it is necessary to negate it so strongly [as to say,] "Take to your heart?"

(*Tanya*, "*The portal of unity and faith*," chapter 1)

The Alter Rebbe is not speaking as a pedagogue but as a master. He is not just another guide, instructor, or declaimer of recycled information or second-hand knowledge. He does not only share information from books, but also wisdom born out of his own direct experience. In the original verse, we are warned that it is not just a matter of *understanding* something, but *receiving* it in the depths of our heart. Beyond intellectually understanding a theology, we are invited to awaken to this reality: "the Lord, He is God, in the heavens above and on the earth below; there is nothing else" (Deuteronomy, 4:39).

With his question, the Alter Rebbe rejects a superficial interpretation of this verse. The simple understanding is that there is no other god—not in the heavens, nor on the earth, nor under the waters. The Hasidic luminary, however, wonders whether it is even possible to imagine another god somewhere in the universe. It is clear that the very idea of another god under the floor or on a distant planet would be unnecessary and superfluous.

The Bible verse points to God as the exclusive and unique reality. Certainly, this statement corresponds to the absolute Truth or ultimate reality. There are different levels of reality, so even though Truth is one, it is perceived differently according to one's level of consciousness. Even though our body always needs nourishment, the type of food we consume at each age depends on what we can digest. Likewise, the classical rabbinic method called *pardes* indicates that the Hebrew revelation can be assimilated at four different levels of awareness. *Pardes* (פרדס) is a word composed of the first Hebrew letter of each level: *peshat*, *remez*, *derash*, and *sod*:

- *Peshat* (פשט) means "simple" and corresponds to the most obvious meaning of the text.
- *Remez* (רמז) is an allegorical or symbolic interpretation.
- *Derash* (דרש) is about the search for metaphorical or midrashic meanings and comparisons with similar biblical sources.
- *Sod* (סוד) means "secret," that is, the higher meaning of the text.

The Hebrew revelation contains more than a single Torah:

אֵלֶּה הַחֻקִּים וְהַמִּשְׁפָּטִים וְהַתּוֹרֹת אֲשֶׁר נָתַן ה' בֵּינוֹ וּבֵין בְּנֵי יִשְׂרָאֵל בְּהַר סִינַי בְּיַד מֹשֶׁה:

(ויקרא כ"ו, מ"ו)

These are the statutes, the laws and the teachings (*torot*), which the Lord made between Him and the children of Israel at Mount Sinai through the hand of Moses.

(Leviticus, 26:46)

The *Midrash* explains this verse as follows:

"אֵלֶּה הַחֻקִּים וְהַמִּשְׁפָּטִים וְהַתּוֹרֹת": הַחֻקִּים – אֵלּוּ הַמִּדְרָשׁוֹת. וְהַמִּשְׁפָּטִים – אֵלּוּ הַדִּינִים. וְהַתּוֹרֹת – מְלַמֵּד שֶׁשְּׁתֵּי תוֹרוֹת נִתְּנוּ לָהֶם לְיִשְׂרָאֵל אֶחָד בִּכְתָב וְאֶחָד בְּעַל פֶּה. אָמַר רַבִּי עֲקִיבָא: "וְכִי שְׁתֵּי תוֹרוֹת הָיוּ לָהֶם לְיִשְׂרָאֵל? וַהֲלֹא תוֹרוֹת הַרְבֵּה נִתְּנוּ לָהֶם לְיִשְׂרָאֵל: 'זֹאת תּוֹרַת הָעוֹלָה' (ויקרא ו', ב'). 'זֹאת תּוֹרַת הַמִּנְחָה' (ויקרא ו', ז'), 'זֹאת תּוֹרַת הָאָשָׁם' (ויקרא ז', א'), 'זֹאת תּוֹרַת זֶבַח הַשְּׁלָמִים' (ויקרא ז', י'א), 'זֹאת הַתּוֹרָה אָדָם כִּי יָמוּת בְּאֹהֶל' (במדבר י"ט, י"ד)".

(ספרא, בחוקותי, ב', ח')

"These are the statutes and the ordinances and the Torahs": "The statutes": These are the *midrashot* (exegeses); "And the judgments": These are the *dinim* (laws); "And the Torahs": This teaches us that two Torahs were given to Israel, one written, and one oral. Rabbi Akiva said: "Did Israel have only two Torahs? Were not many Torahs given to them?" "This is the Torah of burnt-offerings," (Leviticus, 6:2) "This is the Torah of meal-offerings," (Leviticus, 6:7). "This is the Torah of the guilt-offerings," (Leviticus, 7:1) "This is the Torah of the sacrifice of peace-offerings," (Leviticus, 7:11) "This is the Torah—when a person dies in a tent" (Numbers, 19:14).

(*Sifra*, "*Beḥukotai*," 2.8)

The Sinaitic revelation descends upon the entire people of Israel. But a collective is composed of individuals with different levels of consciousness. Therefore, the Torah reveals the same Truth in a variety of realities. Truth is clothed in garments appropriate to each person, according to their point along the Path of Retroprogressive Alignment. Due to concessions to those who reside on the illusory platform, the reality of an objective universe is accepted. However, as the search for what is real progresses, the existence of relative reality will be questioned.

If we wake up at midnight and see a gorilla in the corner of our room and it vanishes in a few moments, we will undoubtedly conclude that it was a hallucination. In general, when an experience lasts for a short period of time and then evaporates, it is considered a dream. Temporal experiences are often considered to exist, yet they are not deemed real. Similarly, while objective reality may be perceived as existing, it lacks true reality. While objects and matter lack independent reality, they cannot be called false.

Obviously, there can be no part of a mutable existence that is truly real. For clarity, we will resort to the classic Advaitic analogy of the rope and the snake. Walking at dusk through the forest, we see a rope on the side of the road. Due to the lack of visibility, we mistake it for a snake and are overcome with fear. When we finally realize it is a rope, the fear disappears. Although the reptile was only apparent, the fear was real. Only when we see the rope, the snake completely loses its reality. The snake was never born, nor did it ever die; it had no beginning in time. It neither came out of the rope nor disappeared into it because, although it existed, it was never real. It was the darkness that did not allow us to perceive that it was only a rope. When someone turns on a flashlight, we manage to recognize our error and dispel ignorance. Wisdom allows the recognition of reality as it is. In the analogy, the snake is our empirical existence and the rope is absolute consciousness. We speak of more than one Torah because it communicates with three levels of reality: the real, the unreal, and the not real. The real always exists, while the false has never existed.

Śaṅkara, the highest exponent of Advaita Vedanta, offers a brilliant explanation about the phenomenon of the world and its relation to the ultimate reality. In his writings, he mentions three orders or levels of reality: absolute reality (*pāramārthika*), relative reality (*vyāvahārika*), and illusory reality (*prātibhāsika*), which he distinguishes from non-existence (*alīka*).

यद्वा त्रिविधं सत्त्वम्पारमार्थिकं व्यावहारिकं प्रतिभासिकञ्चेति। पारमार्थिकं सत्त्वं ब्रह्मणः, व्यावहारिकं सत्त्वमाकाशादेः, प्रातिभासिकं सत्त्वं शुक्तिरजतादेः।

yad vā tri-vidhaṁ sattvam—pāramārthikaṁ vyāvahārikaṁ pratibhāsikañ ceti. pāramārthikaṁ sattvaṁ brahmaṇaḥ, vyāvahārikaṁ sattvam ākāśādeḥ, prātibhāsikaṁ sattvaṁ śukti-rajatādeḥ.

[Or we may say] there are three kinds of existence: absolute, conventional, and illusory. Absolute existence belongs to Brahman, conventional existence to the ether and so on, and illusory existence to the silver in nacre.

(Dharmarāja Adhvarīndra, *Vedānta-paribhāṣā,* chapter 2)

Absolute reality or *pāramārthika-sattā*: This refers to Brahman or consciousness, which is the only reality that exists. It is pure, immutable, and eternal. Objective phenomena are unreal superimpositions over the background of this absolute reality. From the point of view of *pāramārthika-sattā*, both relative and illusory realities are false. Differences between the two are only relevant to those who are still blinded by ignorance. Those who have realized transcendental consciousness perceive that plurality is a manifestation of a single reality. Plurality vanishes along with the disappearance of ignorance. *Pāramārthika* refers to the absolute reality behind the objective diversity of names and forms. Just as an ordinary person knows that the moon reflected in the lake is not the real moon, a realized being perceives that objects are unreal. The wise ones look at the objective world like we look at a mirror: knowing that the reality they see is only a reflection.

Relative reality or *vyāvahārika-sattā*: This is the empirical, practical, relative, and temporal reality that is based on subject–object relationships. Śaṅkara says in his commentary on the *Vedānta Sūtra* that *vyāvahārika-sattā* comes from the mutual superimposition of the real and the unreal, or the Self and non-Self, caused by ignorance. Every existing phenomenon combines reality and unreality. Since *vyāvahārika-sattā* is subject to categories such as time, space, and causality, it is constantly mutating. Its temporary nature differentiates it from absolute reality, which is eternal. However, even though the objective world is only an empirical reality, in practical life we should relate to the world as if it were real.

Illusory reality or *prātibhāsika-sattā*: *Prātibhāsika* is only an appearance of *vyāvahārika*. It refers to the apparent reality of the illusory phenomena, such as hallucinations, mirages, dreams, and so on. We accept this as real as long as the illusion lasts, but this ends when one becomes conscious of empirical reality (*vyāvahārika*). These illusions originate in *avidyā*, or "ignorance," and they vanish as soon the real basis that gave rise to the appearances is recognized. The illusion dissipates only through the knowledge of essence, or *adhiṣṭhāna*.

Prātibhāsika includes phenomena such as the reflection of the moon in a calm and peaceful lake. Although it is only an appearance, the reflection may look like the moon itself. The moon's reflection is perceptible, but it is not real. Unlike its reflection, the moon itself is considered real.

Inexistence or *alīka*: This refers to absolute non-existence. The three levels of reality mentioned above are different from *alīka*. It is impossible to perceive *alīka* in the past, present, or future. For example, the child of a barren woman is imperceptible.

For Śaṅkara, only absolute reality (*pāramārthika*) exists, while relative reality (*vyāvahārika*) is non-real, or *mithyā*. However, relative reality (*vyāvahārika*) is different from illusory reality (*prātibhāsika*) and, of course, from absolute inexistence (*alīka*). Although it differs from absolute reality, relative reality (*vyāvahārika*), which is the objective universe (*mithyā*), is indeed perceptible.

अवाच्छिन्नश्चिदाभासस्त्रितीयन्स्वप्नकल्पितः ।
स्विज्ञेयस्त्रिविधोजीवस्तत्राद्यः पारमार्थिकः ॥

avācchinnaś cid-ābhāsas
tritīyan svapna-kalpitaḥ
svijñeyas tri-vidho jīvas
tatrādyaḥ pāramārthikaḥ

> There are three conceptions of *jīva* (consciousness): one is limited by *prāṇa* (vital energy), one is present in the mind, and one is consciousness as imagined in dream [taking on the forms of people, etc.]. The first of these is true nature.
> (Śrī Vidyāraṇya, *Dṛg-dṛśya-viveka*, 32)

Of all these levels, the *prātibhāsika* reality is surpassed by *vyāvahārika*, which in turn is transcended by *pāramārthika*. *Prātibhāsika* is a private reality, *vyāvahārika* is shared by all human beings, and *pāramārthika* belongs only to the enlightened. Only sages have the right to relate to the world as *mithyā*, or "non-real," but not those who are still blinded by illusion.

What is real exists (*sat*) in the present, past, and future. What is unreal does not exist (*asat*) in present, past, nor future. Finally, what is non-real (*mithyā*) lies between *sat* and *asat*: sometimes it exists and sometimes it does not.

सदसद्विलक्षणत्वम्मिथ्यात्वम्।

sad-asad-vilakṣaṇatvam mithyātvam.

Mithyātva (non-reality) is neither real nor unreal.
(Madhusūdana Sarasvatī, *Advaita-siddhi*, *pariccheda* 1)

In the example we mentioned of the rope and the snake, the snake is not real (*sat*) in the present, past, nor future. On the other hand, the snake is not unreal (*asat*) because it causes us fear. The snake is non-real (*mithyā*): it has existence for the frightened person, but it ceases to exist when ignorance vanishes.

Ignorant people perceive objects and accept distinctions between them as real. They are attracted by some objects and repulsed by others. This is like a person who goes to buy a porcelain vase and focuses solely on the shape, forgetting that all the vases in the shop are made of porcelain. On the other hand, manifold reality has no meaning for enlightened beings with transcendental experience: they know that it is only due to the *upādhis*, or "limitations," that objects of the phenomenal world appear to be separate. They see everything and everyone without attraction or repulsion. Due to their transcendental vision, they see the essence of everything and do not love or hate anything in particular: nothing is *priya* or *apriya*.

In other words, enlightened beings do not pay attention to the diversity of this world but they are aware of the world's true identity. Neither do they ignore the existing objective variety, although they know that the differences are false, temporary, and illusory. Awakened ones move through the world respecting dual *vyāvahārika* reality while conscious of the transcendental *pāramārthika* reality.

Therefore, the Torah contains texts intended for different dimensions of reality. The sacred scriptures encompass passages that refer to the illusory, relative, and absolute realities. The Torah mercifully makes concessions to communicate with everyone on different levels of consciousness. Since it is a revelation, it does not remain confined to absolute reality. A single paragraph can be understood on different levels according to *peshat*, *remez*, *derash*, and *sod*. When referring to an illusory level of reality, the Torah emphatically rejects polytheism or the belief in the existence of a diversity of gods. When speaking on the basis of relative reality, it emphasizes the existence of one personal or ontic God, one God who is someone, one objective God. However, when it addresses humanity in terms of absolute reality, the Torah asserts that the objective reality is God and only God in essence. At the initial level, there is no multiplicity of gods, then, there is only one God, and finally, only God is.

Even though such a statement does not contradict our experience, it does differ from our interpretation of reality, which is colored by our own narrative. We think that the world is made of objects. But when we perceive them, we include conditioning and therefore, we close ourselves to the infinite instantaneous probabilities. Since we include memory in perception, we reduce the potential probabilities to a single one, which we accept as the only real one. We read in Genesis:

וַיִּקְרָא הָאָדָם שֵׁמוֹת לְכָל הַבְּהֵמָה וּלְעוֹף הַשָּׁמַיִם וּלְכֹל חַיַּת הַשָּׂדֶה [...]
(בראשית, ב', כ')

So the man gave names to all the livestock, the birds in the sky and all the wild animals.

(Genesis, 2:20)

For the mind, reality depends on language. The reality of objects is determined by thoughts, comparisons, memory, concepts, and definitions. As we walk the retroprogressive path in search of ultimate reality, we may commit the same fallacy. Most "spiritual" aspirants seek absolute Truth as if it were objective. They are expecting to perceive enlightenment as something or someone with objective qualities. They believe that it must be a very special experience with lights, colors, and energies. However, the essential condition of ultimate reality is permanence, invariance, and immutability.

כִּי אֲנִי ה' לֹא שָׁנִיתִי [...]

(מלאכי ג', ו')

For I, the Lord, do not change [...].

(Malachi, 3:6)

People under the influence of alcohol or drugs experience different "realities." There are as many realities as there are levels of consciousness. However, absolute reality is not another variant; it encompasses all other levels. Absolute consciousness is not a special state; it is a state that includes all states of consciousness. Only undifferentiated perception can be real, in which the knower knows, but without differentiating from the known. In this way, the perceived objective reality can be considered ultimate only when it includes the perceiving subject.

הִנֵּה, כְּתִיב: "לְעוֹלָם, ה', דְּבָרְךָ נִצָּב בַּשָּׁמָיִם" (תהילים קי"ט, פ"ט), וּפֵירֵשׁ הַבַּעַל־שֵׁם־טוֹב זִכְרוֹנוֹ לִבְרָכָה: כִּי "דְּבָרְךָ" שֶׁאָמַרְתָּ "יְהִי רָקִיעַ בְּתוֹךְ הַמָּיִם וְגוֹ'" (בראשית א', ו') – תֵּיבוֹת וְאוֹתִיּוֹת אֵלּוּ, הֵן נִצָּבוֹת וְעוֹמְדוֹת לְעוֹלָם בִּתוֹךְ רְקִיעַ הַשָּׁמַיִם, וּמְלוּבָּשׁוֹת בְּתוֹךְ כָּל הָרְקִיעִים לְעוֹלָם לְהַחֲיוֹתָם, כְּדִכְתִיב: "וּדְבַר אֱלֹהֵינוּ יָקוּם לְעוֹלָם" (ישעיהו מ', ח'), "וּדְבָרָיו חָיִים וְקַיָּמִים לָעַד כוּ'" (תפילת שחרית).

It is written (Psalms, 119:89): "Forever, O Lord, Your word stands firm in the heavens." The Ba'al Shem Tov, of blessed memory, has explained that "Your word" which you uttered, "Let there be a firmament in the midst of the waters..." (Genesis, 1:6) these very words and letters stand firmly forever within the firmament of heaven and are forever clothed within all the heavens to give them life, as it is written : "The word of our God shall stand firm forever" (Isaiah, 40:8) and "His words live and stand firm forever...." (Morning Prayers).

(*Tanya*, "*The portal of unity and faith*," chapter 1)

The verse quoted by the Alter Rebbe is from the book of Psalms:

לְעוֹלָם ה' דְּבָרְךָ נִצָּב בַּשָּׁמָיִם:

(תהילים קי"ט, פ"ט)

Forever, O Lord, your word stands fast in the heavens.

(Psalms, 119:89)

According to the Bible, the empirical universe is a divine expression manifested through sayings. We read the following in Genesis, the first book of the Torah:

וַיֹּאמֶר אֱלֹהִים יְהִי רָקִיעַ בְּתוֹךְ הַמָּיִם [...]
וַיֹּאמֶר אֱלֹהִים יִקָּווּ הַמַּיִם מִתַּחַת הַשָּׁמַיִם אֶל־מָקוֹם אֶחָד וְתֵרָאֶה הַיַּבָּשָׁה [...]
וַיֹּאמֶר אֱלֹהִים תַּדְשֵׁא הָאָרֶץ דֶּשֶׁא עֵשֶׂב מַזְרִיעַ זֶרַע [...]
וַיֹּאמֶר אֱלֹהִים יְהִי מְאֹרֹת בִּרְקִיעַ הַשָּׁמַיִם [...]

(בראשית א', פסוקים ו', ט, י"א, י"ד)

And God said, "Let there be a firmament in the midst of the water." [...]
And God said, "Let the water under the heavens be gathered to one place, and let the dry land appear." [...]

> And God said, "Let the earth produce vegetation: seed-bearing plants."[…]
> And God said, "Let there be luminaries in the firmament of the heaven."[…]
>
> (Genesis, 1:6, 9, 11, 14)

The same expression is repeated on other days of creation. Therefore, *Pirkei Avot*, or "*Ethics of the Fathers*," states:

> בַּעֲשָׂרָה מַאֲמָרוֹת נִבְרָא הָעוֹלָם.
>
> (פרקי אבות ה', א')

> In ten expressions the world was created.
>
> (*Pirkei Avot*, 5.1)

To create a work of art, appropriate materials should be obtained. This artistic creation will need substances to be produced. But God, being all that exists, lacks a substance other than Himself to create the universe. Being the only reality, he has only Himself to be the raw material. Since only consciousness is, any created reality can only be consciousness. God is both the material and the efficient cause of his creation. Therefore, the *tzimtzum*, or "contraction," the free space, the line, the *Adam Kadmon*, the three lines, the vessels, the divine letters or sounds are necessarily divinity.

> בְּרֵאשִׁית בָּרָא אֱלֹהִים אֵת הַשָּׁמַיִם וְאֵת הָאָרֶץ:
>
> (בראשית א', א')

> In the beginning God created the heavens and the earth.
>
> (Genesis, 1:1)

The Aramaic term *go* (גו) means inside, while *bar* (בר) means outside. The Hebrew word *bara* (ברא) implies an externalization or expression from within.

Likewise, the word *exist* derives from the Latin *exsistō* or *exsistere*, composed of *ex* (outside) and *sistō*, *sistere*, *stitī/stetī*, or *statum* (to place, to stand); it is causative of *stō* or *stāre*, from the Indo-European root *sti-sth*, meaning "to stand." The classical Greek for "to stand" (*ἵστημι* - *hístēmi*) also derives from this root. Creation is a divine expression; in creating God simply expresses Himself.

כִּי הוּא אָמַר וַיֶּהִי הוּא צִוָּה וַיַּעֲמֹד:

(תהילים ל"ג, ט')

For He spoke, and it came to be; He commanded, and it stood firm.

(Psalms, 33:9)

בִּדְבַר ה' שָׁמַיִם נַעֲשׂוּ וּבְרוּחַ פִּיו כָּל צְבָאָם:

(תהילים ל"ג , ו')

By the word of the Lord the heavens were made, their starry host by the breath of His mouth.

(Psalms, 33:6)

The ontology of sound is one of the unknowns in the philosophy of sound. It is not entirely clear what sound is, because it seems to lack a physical quality, just as the phenomenon of a rainbow is only an appearance. Unlike objects that require space and time, sound seems to only require time. Sounds are not perceived by their place of origin, but by the pattern of transformation they cause over time. The word *sound* is used in two different senses: scientific and physiological. Physics investigates sound itself. For physicists, sound is any phenomenon that propagates in the form of audible elastic waves, which are generated from the vibratory motion of a body. For physiologists, however, sound is the auditory sensation produced by such waves. Sound waves are stimuli that trigger our hearing mechanism. Vibrations are transmitted through the air, stimulate the nerve fibers of the ear, generate impulses that travel along auditory pathways, and reach their projection area in the temporal lobes. Sounds are perceived by means of the auditory apparatus, which transforms sound waves into movement of the stereocilia. The waves are perceived in the inner ear, which transmits them through the nervous system to the brain, thus making hearing possible.

Hearing is considered one of humans' principal senses, since it allows us to relate to our environment and is essential for communication with other human beings. We have this capacity even before birth; fetuses in the womb also can hear. The human ear is sensitive only to vibrations with frequencies of 16–20,000 Hz, so in our daily life we can capture only an infinitesimal percentage of the cosmic vibrations.

According to Jewish, Vedic, and many other mystical sources, the universe is a materialization of the spirit through sound. Various esoteric paths, for thousands of years, have accessed the revelation that the origin of the universe is sound vibrations.

By reaching the deepest levels of meditation, true silence is accessed. At that level, one hears sound at its primordial level, arising from deep within. The Vedanta refers to such primordial sound as *Oṁkāra* and its closest expression is the Sanskrit *Oṁ*, a sound that is actually included in the Hebrew *shalom*. Its sound is so subtle that even mental noise prevents us from hearing it. Hence the basic requirement to access it is total stillness, both mental and emotional silence. From the depths of *Sanātana-dharma*, yogis shared their transcendental experience on the subject of sound by creating, thousands of years ago, important paths of liberation such as *nāda-yoga* and *mantra-yoga*. From such classical yogic paths, esoteric terms were born, such as *śabda-brahman* or *nāda-brahman*, which refer to sound at its subtlest levels.

Śabda-brāhman is the sound that is generated when the one becomes many. It expresses itself along with the unfolding of creative energy, or *śakti*, in a diversity of names and forms. It is the sound of the Self that ranges from ultra-subtle, through subtle, to gross. It is no coincidence that the modern scientific community calls the beginning of the universe the Big Bang.

The Vedic *ṛṣis* explained that the entire universe comes from sound and is in a pulsating state called *spanda*. The Sanskrit term *spanda* refers to the creative pulsation of the universe that expresses itself as spontaneous creative waves. Everything around us vibrates. All expressions of nature constantly emit vibrations.

The *nāda-brahman* comes from the sound caused by *spanda*: the vibration, pulsation, movement, or agitation produced by the reflection of Brahman upon itself or upon its *vimarṣa*. *Vimarṣa* is that great mirror, as it were, upon which Śiva observes his own splendor.

Sound transcends both creation and the origin of creation. According to the millennia-old wisdom of *Sanātana-dharma*, the cosmic manifestation rests in its potential as sound in Viṣṇu's sleep after each dissolution (*layam*). Then, each time the Lord reawakens, the potential that lies hidden deep in silence manifests as thought–sound again, and he expresses Himself as the physical universe of names and forms.

Both *śabda-brahman* and *nāda-brahman* are translated as "sound," but they refer to different aspects of sound. Since these concepts are similar, it is important to clarify their differences to avoid confusion.

Śabda-brahman is the eternal word, the divine verb. *Nāda-brahman* is the eternal sound, the transcendental melody that is the very Self reflected in music. The former refers to lyrics, the latter to music. The former originates from the very mouth of God, the latter from God's heart.

Śabda-brahman refers to Brahman as linguistic sound: mantras, hymns, prayers, and *yajñas*; it is related to *mantra-yoga* and *mantra-śāstra*. *Nāda-brahman* refers to vibration or sound in a musical sense and is thus more related to *nāda-yoga*.

To make the point clearer, I would say that in both cases we are talking about communication between the part and the Whole, between the soul and the absolute. In *mantra-yoga* it is a transmission, while in *nada-yoga* it is a reception of certain cosmic signals.

According to the teachings of the Ba'al Shem Tov, the verse "Forever, O Lord, Your word stands firm in the heavens" (Psalms, 119:89) means that the utterances that come from the Absolute remain stable and immutable in the heights. These utterances from the firmament emanate constantly to maintain creation. These transcendental expressions were not just emitted at the moment of creation in the past but continue to manifest and vivify the creation in every moment. To be more accurate, we should say that, although the explanation to this verse is attributed here to the Ba'al Shem Tov, it is actually from the *Midrash Tehilim* (Psalms):

> "דְּבָרְךָ נִצָּב בַּשָּׁמַיִם" (תהילים קי"ט, פ"ט). אֵיזֶה דָּבָר הַנִּצָּב בַּשָּׁמַיִם? אֶלָּא אָמַר הקב"ה: "עַל מָה הַשָּׁמַיִם עוֹמְדִים? עַל אוֹתוֹ דָּבָר שֶׁאָמַרְתִּי 'יְהִי רָקִיעַ בְּתוֹךְ הַמָּיִם [וְגוֹ'] וַיְהִי כֵן' (בראשית א', ו'–ז')", וּכְתִיב "כִּי הוּא אָמַר וַיֶּהִי" וְגוֹ' (תהילים ל"ג, ט'), אוֹתוֹ הַדָּבָר שֶׁאָמַר – הוּא עָשָׂה. לְכָךְ נֶאֱמַר: "הוּא צִוָּה וַיַּעֲמֹד" (שם), "בִּדְבַר ה' שָׁמַיִם נַעֲשׂוּ" (תהילים ל"ג, ו'), וּבְאוֹתוֹ הַדָּבָר שֶׁבָּרָא אוֹתָן – בּוֹ הֵם עוֹמְדִים לָעוֹלָם. לְכָךְ נֶאֱמַר: "לְעוֹלָם ה' דְּבָרְךָ נִצָּב בַּשָּׁמָיִם".
>
> (מדרש שוחר־טוב על תהילים קי"ט, פ"ט)

> "Your word stands firm in the heavens" (Psalms, 119:89). What word is it that stands in heavens? The Holy Blessed One said: "What is it that the heavens stand on? On the very same utterance that I have said: 'Let there be a firmament in the midst of the water, etc. […] and it was so' (Genesis, 1:6–7)". And it is written: "For He spoke, and it was." (Psalms, 33:9). The same thing that He spoke, He created. Therefore, it is said: "He commanded, and it endured." And "By the word of the Lord the heavens were made" (Psalms, 33:6). With the same utterance that He created, they are maintained forever. This is why it was said: "Forever, O Lord, Your word stands firm in heaven".
>
> (*Midrash Shoḥer Tov* on Psalms, 119:89)

Although the quotation is from *Midrash Shoḥer Tov* (Psalms), it is attributed to the Ba'al Shem Tov for the simple reason that he cited it repeatedly to explain his teachings. In the *Talmud*, we find many similar situations where verses from the scriptures are attributed to particular masters who referred to them frequently. Moreover, this *midrash*, or 'commentary', was not well-known before the Ba'al Shem Tov made it famous among his disciples and the general public.

The Besht says that, on the absolute plane, unlike the relative one, divine expression is permanent. These expressions remain embedded in the heavens, giving them life constantly. The transcendental expression is eternal, as the Torah affirms:

[...] וּדְבַר־אֱלֹהֵינוּ יָקוּם לְעוֹלָם:

(ישעיהו מ', ח')

[...] but the word of our God endures forever.

(Isaiah, 40:8)

כִּי אִילּוּ הָיוּ הָאוֹתִיּוֹת מִסְתַּלְּקוֹת כְּרֶגַע חַס וְשָׁלוֹם וְחוֹזְרוֹת לִמְקוֹרָן, הָיוּ כָּל הַשָּׁמַיִם אַיִן וָאֶפֶס מַמָּשׁ, וְהָיוּ כְּלֹא הָיוּ כְּלָל, וּכְמוֹ קוֹדֶם מַאֲמַר "יְהִי רָקִיעַ" כוּ' מַמָּשׁ.

For if the letters were to depart [even] for an instant, God forbid, and return to their source, all the heavens would become naught and absolute nothingness, and it would be as though they had never existed at all, exactly as before the utterance, "Let there be a firmament."

(*Tanya*, "*The portal of unity and faith*," chapter 1)

If the creative expressions or letters returned to their source, the universe would return to such a state as if it had never existed, its original state of inexistence. "All the heavens would become naught and absolute nothingness." The state prior to cosmic manifestation is not destruction, the deconstruction of something, or the death of someone, but a state in which what is created never existed. The Hebrew term *mamash*, or "absolute," emphasizes the apparent nature of empirical reality.

וְכֵן בְּכָל הַבְּרוּאִים שֶׁבְּכָל הָעוֹלָמוֹת עֶלְיוֹנִים וְתַחְתּוֹנִים, וַאֲפִילוּ אֶרֶץ הַלָּזוּ הַגַּשְׁמִית וּבְחִינַת דּוֹמֵם מַמָּשׁ, אִילּוּ הָיוּ מִסְתַּלְּקוֹת מִמֶּנָּה כְּרֶגַע חַס וְשָׁלוֹם הָאוֹתִיּוֹת מֵעֲשָׂרָה מַאֲמָרוֹת שֶׁבָּהֶן נִבְרֵאת הָאָרֶץ בְּשֵׁשֶׁת יְמֵי בְּרֵאשִׁית, הָיְתָה חוֹזֶרֶת לְאַיִן וָאֶפֶס מַמָּשׁ, כְּמוֹ לִפְנֵי שֵׁשֶׁת יְמֵי בְּרֵאשִׁית מַמָּשׁ.

And so it is with all created things, in all the upper and lower worlds, and even this physical earth, which is the realm of the inanimate. If the letters of the Ten Utterances by which the earth was created during the Six Days of Creation were to depart from

> **it [but] for an instant, God forbid, it would revert to naught and absolute nothingness, exactly as before the Six Days of Creation.**
>
> **(*Tanya*, "*The portal of unity and faith*," chapter 1)**

In other words, this statement is valid for every creature and object in the universe, including us. The divine expression symbolizes the act of objectification of all that is physical, mental, and emotional. Without such activity, what is created would return to its original state of being null.

When referring to the absolute nothingness prior to the six days of creation, many wonder how it is possible for something to come from nothing. The problem with this question is that it stems from an erroneous conjecture. It is like trying to solve a mathematical problem when one of the numbers is incorrect. It is impossible for us to achieve a correct result if we start with the wrong numbers. Similarly, the question arises from an incorrect assumption about objective existence. This inquiry is based on the belief that things exist and explores how they arise from objective non-existence. That is, this perspective assumes that objects exist and come from something that is not a thing or that is not an object. But from the absolute perspective, objects do not exist as such and, therefore, the idea of a non-objective something is meaningless. There is no something, nothing, everything, or everyone, but only what is. What is does not emerge from something, nor does anything emerge from it. In reality, there is only what is, modulating itself in a diversity of apparent forms without ever ceasing to be what it is.

From this modulation arise the apparent objective diversity that the Torah divides into *domem* (inert), *tsomeaḥ* (vegetal), *ḥai* (animal), and *medaber* (speaking). It is clear that *tsomeaḥ*, *ḥai*, and *medaber* are consciousness, because we can see their movement with the naked eye. However, consciousness as *domem* is not obvious to us. According to the Alter Rebbe, earth, stones, and minerals, although they appear to be inanimate, are also consciousness.

וְזֶהוּ שֶׁאָמַר הָאֲרִ"י זִכְרוֹנוֹ לִבְרָכָה, שֶׁגַּם בְּדוֹמֵם מַמָּשׁ, כְּמוֹ אֲבָנִים וְעָפָר וּמַיִם, יֵשׁ בְּחִינַת נֶפֶשׁ וְחַיּוּת רוּחָנִית. דְּהַיְינוּ, בְּחִינַת הִתְלַבְּשׁוּת אוֹתִיּוֹת הַדִּבּוּר מֵעֲשָׂרָה מַאֲמָרוֹת הַמְחַיּוֹת וּמְהַוּוֹת אֶת הַדּוֹמֵם, לִהְיוֹת יֵשׁ מֵאַיִן וָאֶפֶס שֶׁלִּפְנֵי שֵׁשֶׁת יְמֵי בְרֵאשִׁית.

This same thought was expressed by the Arizal when he said that even in completely inanimate matter, such as stones or earth or water, there is a soul and spiritual life-force—that is, the enclothing of the "Letters of speech" of the Ten Utterances which give life and existence to inanimate matter that it might arise out of the naught and nothingness which preceded the Six Days of Creation.

וְאַף שֶׁלֹּא הוּזְכַּר שֵׁם "אֶבֶן" בַּעֲשָׂרָה מַאֲמָרוֹת שֶׁבַּתּוֹרָה, אַף־עַל־פִּי־כֵן, נִמְשָׁךְ חַיּוּת לָאֶבֶן עַל יְדֵי צֵירוּפִים וְחִילּוּפֵי אוֹתִיּוֹת, הַמִּתְגַּלְגְּלוֹת בְּרל"א שְׁעָרִים פָּנִים וְאָחוֹר, כְּמוֹ שֶׁכָּתוּב בְּסֵפֶר יְצִירָה, עַד שֶׁמִּשְׁתַּלְשֵׁל מֵעֲשָׂרָה מַאֲמָרוֹת וְנִמְשָׁךְ מֵהֶן צֵירוּף שֵׁם "אֶבֶן", וְהוּא חַיּוּתוֹ שֶׁל הָאֶבֶן.

Now, although the word *even* (stone) is not mentioned in the Ten Utterances recorded in the Torah, nevertheless, life-force flows to the stone through combinations and substitutions of the letters which are transposed in the "two hundred and thirty-one gates," either in direct or reverse order, as is explained in the *Sefer Yetzirah*, until the combination of the word *even* descends from the Ten Utterances, and is derived from them, and this is the life-force of the stone.

וְכֵן בְּכָל הַנִּבְרָאִים שֶׁבָּעוֹלָם, הַשֵּׁמוֹת שֶׁנִּקְרָאִים בָּהֶם בִּלְשׁוֹן הַקֹּדֶשׁ – הֵן הֵן אוֹתִיּוֹת הַדִּבּוּר, הַמִּשְׁתַּלְשְׁלוֹת מִמַּדְרֵגָה לְמַדְרֵגָה מֵעֲשָׂרָה מַאֲמָרוֹת שֶׁבַּתּוֹרָה, עַל יְדֵי חִילּוּפִים וּתְמוּרוֹת הָאוֹתִיּוֹת בְּרל"א שְׁעָרִים, עַד שֶׁמַּגִּיעוֹת וּמִתְלַבְּשׁוֹת בְּאוֹתוֹ נִבְרָא לְהַחֲיוֹתוֹ.

And so it is with all created things in the world—their names in the Holy Tongue are the very "letters of speech" which descend, degree by degree, from the Ten Utterances recorded in the Torah, by means of substitutions and transpositions of letters through the "two hundred and thirty-one gates," until they reach and become invested in that particular created thing to give it life.

(***Tanya***, "***The portal of unity and faith,***" **chapter 1**)

It should be noted that inert, vegetal, animal, and speaking are levels in the descent of light, or consciousness, in its process of *tzimtzum*, or "contraction." As an egoic phenomenon, we are contracted consciousness. Although at our present level it is difficult to accept, this entire universe is consciousness at different levels, including the pillars and stones. If whatever has allowed the manifestation of the universe were to abandon objective reality, it would return to total nullity. If the water were to leave the waves, they would return to an absolutely non-existent state.

שִׁבְעָה בָנִים הָיוּ לְקִמְחִית וְכֻלְּהֶם שִׁמְּשׁוּ בִכְהֻנָּה גְדוֹלָה. שָׁלְחוּ חֲכָמִים וְאָמְרוּ לָהּ: "מַה מַעֲשִׂים טוֹבִים יֵשׁ בְּיָדֵךְ?" אָמְרָה לָהֶן: "יָבוֹא עָלַי אִם רָאוּ קוֹרוֹת בֵּיתִי שַׂעֲרוֹת רֹאשִׁי וְאִמְרַת חֲלוּקִי מִיָּמַי". אָמְרִין: "כָּל־קִמְחַיָּא קֶמַח וְקִמְחָא דְקִמְחִית סֹלֶת". וְקָרוּן עֲלָהּ: "כָּל־כְּבוּדָּה בַת־מֶלֶךְ פְּנִימָה מִמִּשְׁבְּצוֹת זָהָב לְבוּשָׁהּ". (תהילים מ"ה, י"ד).

(תלמוד ירושלמי, מגילה, א', י')

Qimḥit had seven sons; and all of them served as High Priests. The Sages sent for Qimḥit and asked, "what good deeds have you done?" She told them: "I swear that the roofbeams in my house have never seen the hair on my head or the seams of my undershirt." They said, "all flour is flour but Qimḥit's flour is fine flour." [The name Qimḥit comes from the root *kemaḥ*, which means "flour"]. They recited this about her: "All glorious is the princess within her chamber; her gown is interwoven with gold" (Psalms, 45:14).

(*Jerusalem Talmud*, "*Megillah*," 1, 10)

And that is why it is said in the *Babylonian Talmud*:

וְשֶׁמָּא יֹאמַר אָדָם מִי מֵעִיד בִּי? אַבְנֵי בֵיתוֹ שֶׁל אָדָם וְקוֹרוֹת בֵּיתוֹ שֶׁל אָדָם מְעִידִים בּוֹ. שֶׁנֶּאֱמַר (חבקוק ב', י"א): "כִּי אֶבֶן מִקִּיר תִּזְעָק וְכָפִיס מֵעֵץ יַעֲנֶנָּה".
(תלמוד בבלי, תענית, י"א, א')

And lest a person say, "[I have acted in secret] who will testify against me [on the Day of Judgment]?" [The *tanna* explains:] The stones of a person's house and the roofbeams of a person's house will testify against him, as it is stated (*Habakkuk*, 2:11): "For a stone shall cry out from the wall, and a beam out of the timber shall answer it."

(*Babylonian Talmud*, "*Ta'anit*," 11a)

In order to know, consciousness is diversified into thought and perception. Through the former, the mind is known, and through the latter, matter is known. These are the only two means that exist to experience objective reality. Objective reality exists only within the parameters of conception and perception, outside of which there is no universe and no objective multiplicity. We have never experienced anything that is not thought or perception and, therefore, there is no proof of the existence of a universe outside of these. We do not live life according to what our own experience of reality tells us, but according to the interpretation we have given it for generations. According to this, objects possess an existence of their own, independent of consciousness. However, existence is not an attribute proper to objects. For, if it were, it would mean that it is possible to fracture existence into innumerable parts. Each pillar, stone, and object would possess its own existence, which would have to be divisible.

The Hebrew revelation refers to God as a living and existing God, intimately relating God to life and existence:

[...] דִּי־הוּא אֱלָהָא חַיָּא וְקַיָּם לְעָלְמִין [...]
(דניאל ו', כ"ז)

For he is the living God and he endures forever.
(Daniel, 6:27)

Sometimes the term God sounds distant or too theological; however, terms such as life or existence are familiar to everyone.

אָדָם יְסוֹדוֹ מֵעָפָר וְסוֹפוֹ לֶעָפָר. בְּנַפְשׁוֹ יָבִיא לַחְמוֹ. מָשׁוּל כְּחֶרֶס הַנִּשְׁבָּר, כְּחָצִיר יָבֵשׁ, וּכְצִיץ נוֹבֵל, כְּצֵל עוֹבֵר, וּכְעָנָן כָּלָה, וּכְרוּחַ נוֹשָׁבֶת, וּכְאָבָק פּוֹרֵחַ, וְכַחֲלוֹם יָעוּף. וְאַתָּה הוּא מֶלֶךְ אֵל חַי וְקַיָּם.
(תפילת "ונתנה תוקף", מוסף לראש השנה)

A man's origin is from soil and his destiny is back to soil, at risk of his life he earns his bread; he is likened to a broken shard, a withering grass, a fading flower, a passing shade, a dissipating cloud, a blowing wind, flying dust, and a fleeting dream. But You are the King, the Living and Existing God.
("*Unetaneh Tokef*" Prayer, *Musaf* of *Rosh Ha'Shanah*)

God is existence itself, indivisible and inseparable, who lends generously of Himself to everything and everyone.

אֵל חַי וְקַיָּם תָּמִיד יִמְלוֹךְ עָלֵינוּ לְעוֹלָם וָעֶד.
(סידור התפילה, תפילת ערבית, ברכת "המעריב ערבים")

May the living and existing God perpetually reign over us for all eternity.
(*Siddur*, Evening prayer, "*Hama'ariv Aravim*" blessing)

The first traces of materialistic doctrines are from the end of the third and beginning of the second millennium BCE, in the Egyptian and Babylonian cultures. There, we find the first writings about spontaneous materialistic conceptions. Later, we find it in some philosophies of China and ancient India. In our present-day society, the materialistic attitude has reached its apogee: what is physical is more important than character. Packaging prevails over content.

Unquestionably, throughout generations, humankind has developed a materialistic interpretation of experience. According to this, things are composed from their material elements. Reality is understood only through matter. As a result, foundations are built upon the objective world rather than consciousness. According to the materialistic interpretation of experience, objects manifest first and only after this, consciousness emerges. However, in our own experience, we find no evidence for this.

In fact, what is pristine, fundamental, and primordial is consciousness. The basic and elementary requirement of experience is consciousness, because without it, no experience is possible. We can extract any object from experience or even take them all out without destroying it, but without conscious presence, there is no experience. Experience does not need objects, but it does need the presence of consciousness. In dreamless deep sleep, we experience a state of pure consciousness devoid of content. This shows us that consciousness constitutes the foundation of all experience, whether in dreams or in wakefulness. Likewise, the essential background upon which an experience can exist is *hineni*, or "here I am."

The content of experience cannot cut or fracture the conscious presence. It is possible to see the light beams projected across the room, but the images can only be perceived after the photons interact with the screen. Likewise, consciousness is the screen upon which objects are projected.

The foundation of cognition is a knowing that knows itself. The universe is the substantiality of the one consciousness, which emerges as individuality only at levels where a differentiation between observing subject and observed object is expressed. The unity of conscious presence is absolute, impossible to fragment or fracture. But the cause of its indivisibility lies not in its durability, but in its emptiness. Only "something" can be broken; nothingness cannot be split.

We lack evidence that anything can exist outside of consciousness. No one has experienced it and we cannot even imagine what it would be like. By realizing that conscious presence is the basis and foundation of experience, we recognize that consciousness is indestructible. The objective content of experience cannot divide consciousness. No one has experienced a fragmented consciousness, because it is not affected by its content in any way.

> קֹדֶם כֹּל נֶאֱצָל הָיָה אֵין־סוֹף לְבַדּוֹ וְהוּא הוּא כָּל הַמְּצִיאוּת, וְגַם אַחַר שֶׁהִמְצִיא הַנִּמְצָאִים – אֵין בִּלְתּוֹ. וְאֵין לְךָ דָּבָר שֶׁיִּהְיֶה מִבַּלְעָדָיו חַס־וְחָלִילָה, שֶׁאֵין שׁוּם נִמְצָא שֶׁלֹּא יִהְיֶה כֹּחַ הָאֱלוֹהַּ בּוֹ, שֶׁאִם לֹא כֵּן, אַתָּה נוֹתֵן לוֹ גְּבוּל וּשְׁנִיּוּת חָס וְחָלִילָה. אֶלָּא הָאֱלוֹהַּ כָּל נִמְצָא, וְאֵין כָּל נִמְצָא הָאֱלוֹהַּ, בְּעִנְיָן שֶׁסֵּדֶר הַמְּצִיאוּת הוּא עַל הַסֵּדֶר הַזֶּה, כָּל מָה שֶׁהוּא בִּמְצִיאוּת הוּא הָאֱלוֹהַּ, שֶׁהֲרֵי הוּא כָּל הַמְּצִיאוּת, וְכֵן בְּכָל הַנִּבְרָא וְכֵן בְּכָל הַנּוֹצָר, וְכֵן בְּכָל הַנַּעֲשֶׂה, הוּא נִמְצָא בְּהַכֹּל, וְהַכֹּל נִמְצָא מֵאִתּוֹ, וְאֵין דָּבָר רֵיק מֵאֱלֹהוּתוֹ חָס־וְחָלִילָה, הַכֹּל בּוֹ וְהוּא בַּכֹּל וְחוּץ הַכֹּל וְאֵין מִבַּלְעָדָיו.
>
> (רבי משה קורדוברו, אילימה, מעין א', תמר ד', פרק א')
>
> Prior to all emanations, there was only the *Ein Sof* (the Infinite) alone, and He, indeed, is the entire existence. Even after He gave existence to all that exists, there is nothing but Him, and you cannot find anything that exists besides Him, God forbid, for there is nothing that exists without God's power within it. For if there were, it would imply that God has limits and duality, God forbid. But God is everything that exists, while no existing entity is God. This is the order of existence: All that exists is God because He is all that exists. And so it is with all that is created, made, or done; He is in everything and everything gets its existence from Him. There is nothing vacant from His divinity, God forbid. Everything is in Him, and He is in everything, both inside and outside of everything, and there is nothing besides Him.
>
> (Rabbi Moses Kordovero, *Eilimah*, spring 1, palm 4, chapter 1)

All experiences, whether mental, emotional, or perceptual, arise from and in consciousness. It is strange that, despite being so obvious, humans insist on placing the objective content as the foundation of experience. We continue with the inherited habit of believing that objective reality is independent and it is perceived by our senses, to such an extent that many great scientists consider consciousness to be a product of the brain. However, this interpretation is completely foreign to our experience.

> אַתָּה הוּא עַד שֶׁלֹּא נִבְרָא הָעוֹלָם, אַתָּה הוּא מִשֶּׁנִּבְרָא הָעוֹלָם, אַתָּה הוּא בָּעוֹלָם הַזֶּה וְאַתָּה הוּא לָעוֹלָם הַבָּא.
> (סידור התפילה, תפילת שחרית, ברכות השחר)
>
> You existed before the world was created. You exist [in the same way] now that the world has been created. You exist in this world, and You will exist in the World-to-Come.
> (*Siddur*, Morning Prayer, Morning Blessings)

Consciousness precedes any perception arising in and from it. According to our experience, consciousness is prior to space, time, and every thought that is generated in it. Therefore, space, time, and thoughts can only be consciousness.

Consciousness has no objective properties. Since thoughts and perceptions possess qualities, they might be considered different from it. They appear to be hanging in the infinite space of consciousness, like stars in the sky. Such mental or perceivable experiences seem to possess their own existence separate from their source and exist in their own right. However, when we perceive an object, we only know our perception of it. Perceptions of the texture, shape, and colors of the tree do not remain in the tree but arise in and from consciousness and are known to it. Both thoughts and perceptions are consciousness, because consciousness is all that is.

The Lurianic Kabbalah tells us that creation is the product of a contraction of consciousness, or *tzimtzum*. It is a self-withdrawal of consciousness to free space from itself to allow for creation. The only way to create a space free of consciousness is through disengagement.

> וַיֹּאמֶר אֵלַי הֲרָאִיתָ בֶן־אָדָם אֲשֶׁר זִקְנֵי בֵית־יִשְׂרָאֵל עֹשִׂים בַּחֹשֶׁךְ אִישׁ בְּחַדְרֵי מַשְׂכִּיתוֹ כִּי אֹמְרִים אֵין ה' רֹאֶה אֹתָנוּ עָזַב ה' אֶת־הָאָרֶץ:
> (יחזקאל ח', י"ב)

> And He said to me, "Have you seen, son of man, what the elders of the house of Israel are doing in the darkness, each one in his paved chambers? For they say, 'The Lord does not see us; the Lord has forsaken the land'."
>
> (Ezekiel, 8:12)

A space devoid of consciousness has been created through voluntary self-forgetfulness. In this space, all mental objects seem to have their own existence. The independent existence of every mental, emotional, and perceptual object is only possible by disengaging from the medium in which they arise. Consequently, all things arise from and within consciousness, borrowing their existence from it, much like a spoon whose existence entirely depends on the metal from which it is made. Although the spoon may bend, break, or be melted down, the metal retains the capacity to be reused and shaped into new forms or objects. The spoon is an ephemeral manifestation, subject to a beginning and an end; however, the metal, as a raw material, remains and can be recycled indefinitely. Similarly, though we perceive a wide variety of objects that seem to exist, their beingness is taken from consciousness.

In a film, we see the image of a ship; however, even though the ship appears to have an independent existence, its true nature lies in the screen. To engage with the story, one must abstract from the screen itself and focus on the variety of ships, sailors, and ports that appear on the scene. Only through this focus can the plot be fully experienced. Yet, upon interacting with the screen to verify the "reality" of these elements, it becomes evident that they are nothing more than projections of the same screen. All characters and objects derive their existence from this screen on which they manifest. Although the elements presented seem to be separate and autonomous entities, the screen remains unchanging, singular, and undivided in its essence. From the sailor's perspective, a plurality of ships and ports is perceived. However, he too is part of the screen, though he is unaware of it, as his perception is confined within the film, unable to transcend it. The sailor assumes that everything he observes has its own spatial existence, without recognizing that even the space itself is a projection emerging from the screen, which gives reality to everything that appears. If the existence of a screen were mentioned, he would attempt to find it within the film itself; but no matter how hard he tries, it would be impossible for him to locate it, for his search is confined to the realm of representation and does not transcend to the origin of his own manifestation.

The only way to explain to the characters what a screen is would be to place a small television within the film. Similarly, a finite and limited mind can only access the background of existence through a personal god who is "someone." That background of reality is their true nature, but they cannot know it. When consciousness assumes the form of thought and perception, an apparent universe is created that is never independent of it. If consciousness were no longer completely ignored, the objective reality would revert to its natural state of non-existence. If even for an instant the oblivion ceased, the multiplicity of objects would lose its meaning.

In creation, the negative powers of withdrawal or contraction (*tzimtzum*) operate, creating a space hypothetically devoid of divinity. The manifestation (*yesh*) out of nothing (*ain*) requires a power to maintain it constantly. Without this, it would be impossible for *yesh* to be sustained without returning to its origin as *ain*. Just as an aircraft needs constant force to stay in the air and prevent it from falling, *yesh* needs constant power to prevent it from returning to its original null condition. Such power is the voluntary disengagement from the divine presence, which allows the creation of that which is (*yesh*) out of voidness (*ain*). God or consciousness, is the only absolute reality. The objective world lacks substance. The empirical reality is a divine expression.

בָּרוּךְ שֶׁאָמַר וְהָיָה הָעוֹלָם. בָּרוּךְ הוּא.
(סידור התפילה, תפילת שחרית, פסוקי דזמרה)

Blessed is He Who spoke, and the world came into being, Blessed is He.

(*Siddur*, Morning prayer, *Psukei DeZimrah*)

In Hebrew, the name of God is written י-ה-ו-ה, and the last three letters (הוה) mean *havayah*, or "manifestation," that is to say, the Absolute *mehaveh*, or "manifests" the universe. The letter *yod* (י), in Hebrew grammar, emphasizes the continuity of a verb. We can see this, for example, in a verse from the book of Job:

וַיְהִי כִּי הִקִּיפוּ יְמֵי הַמִּשְׁתֶּה וַיִּשְׁלַח אִיּוֹב וַיְקַדְּשֵׁם וְהִשְׁכִּים בַּבֹּקֶר וְהֶעֱלָה עֹלוֹת מִסְפַּר כֻּלָּם כִּי אָמַר אִיּוֹב אוּלַי חָטְאוּ בָנַי וּבֵרְכוּ אֱלֹהִים בִּלְבָבָם כָּכָה יַעֲשֶׂה אִיּוֹב כָּל הַיָּמִים.

(איוב א', ה')

And it was so, when the period of feasting had run its course, Job would send and invite them and he would rise early in the morning and would sacrifice a burnt offering for each of them, thinking, "Perhaps my children have sinned and blasphemed God in their hearts." This was Job wont to do all the days.

(Job, 1:5)

As we see in the verse, the letter *yod* (י) in front of the verb *to do* indicates constant activity: "did continually" (יעשה). Therefore, י-ה-ו-ה means "That which is constantly manifesting and vivifying the universe." In the preamble of the beginning, from the depths of consciousness, its different modulations were expressed as letters.

אֵלּוּ עֶשְׂרִים וּשְׁתַּיִם אוֹתִיּוֹת שֶׁבָּהֶם יָסַד הקב"ה, י-ה, י-ה-ו-ה צְבָאוֹת אֱלֹהִים חַיִּים אֱלֹהֵי יִשְׂרָאֵל רָם וְנִשָּׂא שֹׁכֵן עַד וְקָדוֹשׁ שְׁמוֹ מָרוֹם וְקָדוֹשׁ הוּא.

(ספר יצירה, פרק ה', משנה ד')

These are the twenty-two letters from which the Holy One, Blessed be He, Y-H, Yud-Hei-Vav-Hei The lord of the Hosts, the God who is Life, the God of Israel, exalted and sublime, the Dweller in eternity, formed and established all things; High and Holy is His Name.

(*Sefer Yetzirah*, 5.4)

בְּרֵאשִׁית בָּרָא אֱלֹהִים אֵת הַשָּׁמַיִם וְאֵת הָאָרֶץ:
(בראשית א', א')

In the beginning God created the heaven and the earth.
(Genesis, 1:1)

As we mentioned earlier, the Hebrew word *et* (את) is written with an *alef* (א), the first letter of the alphabet, and the last one, which is *tav* (ת). *Et* is a superfluous word with no literal translation, and yet, it appears twice in the first line of the Torah. The *magid* of Mezritch explains that this is because the letters of the alphabet from *alef* to *tav* were created before heaven and earth. These letters would be metaphorical luminous bricks with which thinking would take the form of the mind, feeling that of the body, and perceiving the universe. That is to say, they are the vessels of light with which the One formed the divine dream.

The first word of the book of Genesis is *bereshit*, which begins with the second letter *bet* (ב). Creation is possible only from duality, and *bet* was the right letter, because with the first letter *alef*, or the One, no manifestation is possible.

God's name י-ה-ו-ה is written, but not pronounced because it is indefinable and indescribable. The separate "I" cannot name it. From silence and the deepest intimacy, the consonants of his name emerge without vowels. They represent the boundary between silence and what can be named.

The *Tanya* says that Hebrew letters "give life (*meḥayot*) and existence (*mehavot*) to inanimate matter so that it might arise out of the naught and nothingness." All that is created is composed of two different elements: *ḥayut* (vitality) and *havayah* (manifestation). *Havayah* is the general transformation from nullity to existence, meaning, and the substantiality of the cosmos. *Ḥayut* is the individual aspect that gives life to each created element. After manifestation, vitality expresses diversity as *domem* (inert), *tsomeaḥ* (vegetable), *ḥai* (animal), and *medaber* (speaking). General expressions manifest what exists from nothingness. Individual expressions vivify each and every created thing.

However, we have an enigma: there is a wide variety of created objects, seemingly inanimate like stones or metals, but their names do not appear in the ten expressions of Genesis. It is understood that upon possessing an individual *ḥayut*, the name of every living entity has to be found in the Torah. In this regard, the Alter Rebbe explains that they too receive their individual vitality from the ten original expressions, but through combinations (*tserufim*) and exchanges (*ḥilufim*) of Hebrew letters.

In the beginning of Genesis, we read that Adam, the first man, gave names to all the livestock, the birds in the sky, and all the wild animals. Adam names and identifies the different entities he perceives around him. It is the man who names and defines what is objective. He does not refer to experience, but its content, which comes from the mind.

There is no division between what is created and the Creator; rather, the Creator *is* the created. Everything is a constant divine manifestation. It is important to note that this includes all seemingly static objects, such as stones, water, and mountains. There is nothing that has an existence independent from Divinity. God is the very existence of everything and everyone. It is said in the scripture *Pirkei Avot*:

בַּעֲשָׂרָה מַאֲמָרוֹת נִבְרָא הָעוֹלָם.

(פרקי אבות ה', א')

The world was created with ten utterances.

(*Pirkei Avot*, 5.1)

We read in Genesis that God first creates the heavens and the earth. Subsequently, he creates with ten expressions: first he manifests (*mehaveh*) and then he vivifies (*meḥayeh*). Obviously, God does not need ten expressions to create: one should have been quite enough. The reason is that the manifestation is general, but the vivification happens at the individual level. These are two aspects of the divine expression: with the *mehaveh* power God creates the manifestation (*etzem hahithavut*) and with the *meḥayeh* power, God bestows individual qualities (*hatchunot hapratiot*) on every object, animal, plant, and person.

For example, water manifests (*mithaveh*) from non-existence (*ain*) to an existent state (*yesh*). The specific characteristics of water come from *ḥesed* or "goodness, kindness, grace, or mercy," and *atzilut*, or "emanation."

Like *ḥesed* (grace), water flows from high to low. The element of fire also manifests from *ain* to *yesh*, and it is *gvura* (might) that gives it individual characteristics (*tchunot pratiot*) or individual vitality (*ḥayut pratit*).

The reason the Alter Rebbe uses the terms *mehavot* (manifest) and *meḥayot* (vivify) is that even seemingly static objects possess the aspect of *hithavut* (creation from *ain* to *yesh*) and *ḥayut pratit* (individual vitality). From here we can understand that each and every created thing is mentioned within the Torah. If there were only *hithavut*, this would not be necessary, but because we have the aspect of the *ḥayut pratit*, the mention of each created thing within the Torah becomes indispensable.

For example, let us take the case of a fruit. The fruit itself is manifested from *sovev kol almin* (the aspect of Divinity that surrounds all worlds), whereas its individual qualities come from *memale kol almin* (the aspect of Divinity that fills all worlds). Similarly, the individual qualities of each created thing also come from God at any given moment, in such a way that each created thing has a place within the Torah, because it is the origin of its individual qualities. Likewise, all human beings have their own individual qualities that make up their individuality. The *ḥayut pratit* is the individuality of the human being. It should not be confused with the *yetzer hara*, or "ego," which is a type of idolatry, as the *Babylonian Talmud* explains:

> אָמַר רַבִּי אָבִין: "מַאי קְרָאָה: 'לֹא יִהְיֶה בְךָ אֵל זָר וְלֹא תִשְׁתַּחֲוֶה לְאֵל נֵכָר' (תהילים פ"א, י')? אֵיזֶהוּ אֵל זָר שֶׁיֵּשׁ בְּגוּפוֹ שֶׁל אָדָם? הֱוֵי אוֹמֵר, זֶה יֵצֶר הָרָע".
> (תלמוד בבלי, שבת, ק"ה, ב')

Rabbi Avin observed: "What verse indicates this? 'There shall be no strange god among you, nor shall you worship

> any foreign god.' (Psalms, 81:10) Who is the strange god that resides in man himself? Indeed, it is The Tempter (*yetzer hara*)!"
>
> (*Babylonian Talmud*, "*Shabbat*," 105b)

The ego, or the "I," is to put ourselves in the center of everything and to be interested in whatever is personal. The egoic phenomenon is expressed as personality. Individuality, on the other hand, is manifested as service of the part to the Whole. The ego, *ahaṅkāra* in Sanskrit, is a mechanical product of society and the culture that raised and educated us. Individuality is a flower that is born or expressed from the depths of consciousness.

The first to give us these teachings was the Arizal, who explained that among inanimate things there is also a *nefesh*, or "soul," and *ḥayut*, or "individual qualities."

Many confuse individuality with personality. Although they seem similar, they refer to completely different phenomena. Personality is a product of the mind; it is an illusory phenomenon that is supported by habits and behavioral patterns. Without mental foundations, personality would simply disappear. Individuality, on the other hand, is a state that transcends the mind. Authentic and real individuals do not compare themselves with anyone because they are aware that each one is unique. They do not suffer from inferiority or superiority complexes, since they do not feel inferior or superior to anyone. They are free of selfishness, desires, and ambitions, because they experience the joy of being what they are. They live in constant celebration of their own selfhood and are happy to simply be themselves as they are.

The term individuality emerges from Latin as *individuus*, referring to "that which cannot be divided." The word is formed from the negative prefix *in* and the adjective *dividuus*, from the verb *divide* as *dividěre*. This is because individuality is organic, whereas personality is mechanical. It is organic in the sense that it blossoms harmoniously in an orderly manner from the depths of existence. Living creatures are organic, like a baby, a flower, or a butterfly. The power that causes organic creatures to evolve is called *meḥayeh* in Hebrew, that is, "vivifies." On the other hand, that which is mechanical is made from the outside, and assembled with different parts, such as a watch or a computer. Personality comprises an accumulation of opinions and behaviors acquired from very different people. Personality continues to develop and at all times depends on the opinions, ideas, and behaviors of others. It can be obstinate, stubborn, or opinionated in order to survive, out of fear of being mistreated. So-called strong personalities sustain themselves through their stubbornness and aggressiveness. They know that they can be transformed into slaves of others' opinions.

Personality is very solid and inflexible and is always on the defensive. It is a mental structure that can only be a source of suffering. Individuality, on the other hand, lacks fixed routes and is highly adaptable to the situations that life presents. Personality is egoic and illusionary. Its origin is not divine; it comes from society. Individuality comes from deep within and expresses itself in actions, while personality comes from outside and affects your inner world. Personality is a disguise; individuality is your authenticity. Personality is what the world imposes on you; individuality is what comes with you into the world. The more developed our personality, the less possibility our individuality has to express itself. Personality can occupy all your space and possess you until it suffocates your individuality. As long as we do not empty ourselves of personality and renounce it, there is no room for the development of what is individual. Personality is only egoism, and therefore, it is dominant and political. Individuality, on the other hand, lacks "I" and selfishness, and is therefore compassionate and religious. Personality is your own; individuality is not yours because it comes from God. You do not acquire it; existence fills you with it. Acquiring individuality means emptying ourselves and allowing existence to manifest itself according to its will. Emptying oneself means getting rid of the personality and all that it implies, in order to let individuality develop.

We still need to clarify why the following verse uses the phrase "in the heavens above and upon the earth below." That is, why it mentions the heavens, which is the most subtle, and the earth, which is the grossest.

וְיָדַעְתָּ הַיּוֹם וַהֲשֵׁבֹתָ אֶל־לְבָבֶךָ כִּי ה' הוּא הָאֱלֹהִים בַּשָּׁמַיִם מִמַּעַל וְעַל־הָאָרֶץ מִתָּחַת אֵין עוֹד:

(דברים ד', ל"ט)

Acknowledge this day and take to heart that the Lord, He is God (*Havayah is Elohim*) in the heavens above and on the earth below. There is nothing else.

(Deuteronomy, 4:39)

To clarify this point, we will quote a *midrash* which reads as follows:

"כִּי ה' הוּא הָאֱלֹהִים". רַבָּנָן אַמְרֵי: "יִתְרוֹ נָתַן מַמָּשׁ בַּעֲבוֹדַת כּוֹכָבִים, שֶׁנֶּאֱמַר: 'עַתָּה יָדַעְתִּי כִּי גָדוֹל ה' מִכָּל הָאֱלֹהִים' (שמות י"ח, י"א). נַעֲמָן הוֹדָה בְּמִקְצָת מִמֶּנָּה, שֶׁנֶּאֱמַר: 'הִנֵּה נָא יָדַעְתִּי כִּי אֵין אֱלֹהִים בְּכָל הָאָרֶץ כִּי אִם בְּיִשְׂרָאֵל' (מלכים ב' ה', ט"ו). רָחָב שַׂמְתָּהוּ בַּשָּׁמַיִם וּבָאָרֶץ, שֶׁנֶּאֱמַר: 'כִּי ה' אֱלֹהֵיכֶם הוּא אֱלֹהִים בַּשָּׁמַיִם מִמַּעַל וְעַל הָאָרֶץ מִתָּחַת' (יהושע ב', י"א). מֹשֶׁה שָׂמוֹ אַף בַּחֲלָלוֹ שֶׁל עוֹלָם, שֶׁנֶּאֱמַר: 'כִּי ה' הוּא הָאֱלֹהִים בַּשָּׁמַיִם מִמַּעַל וְעַל הָאָרֶץ מִתָּחַת אֵין עוֹד' (דברים ד', ל"ט). מַהוּ אֵין עוֹד? אֲפִלּוּ בַּחֲלָלוֹ שֶׁל עוֹלָם".

(דברים רבה, ואתחנן, פרשה ב')

"That the Lord, He is God." Our Rabbies said: "Jethro considered idolatry as real, as it is written (Exodus 18:11): 'Now I know that the Lord is greater than all other gods'; Na'aman recognized some of this, as it is written (II Kings 5:15): 'Now I know that there is no God in all the world except in Israel'; Rahab placed Him in the heavens and earth, as it is written (Joshua, 2:11): "for the Lord your God, He is God in heaven above, and on the earth below"; Moses placed him even in the space of the world, as it is written (Deuteronomy, 4:39): 'That the Lord, He is God, in the heavens above and on the earth below, there is nothing else.' What does 'there is nothing else' mean? Even in the space of the world."

(*Dvarim Rabbah*, "*Va'etḥanan*," 2)

The *Midrash Rabbah* recognizes that God resides in the heavens and on earth. Popular religiosity says that God is in the heavens and human beings are on earth, as if the two were totally disconnected. This idea comes from the ancient conceptual horizon based on motion. From this perspective, objects are destined to an inevitable end: everything that is born dies, everything that has a beginning has an end, everything that starts finishes. Obviously, humans are part of this mutability, both individually and socially. Greek thought oriented its conception of cosmic movement toward "generation." Proof of this is that the ancient Greek term *gígnomai* (γίγνομαι) means "to come into being" and contains both the idea "to be born of people" (generation) and "to take place" (event). In ancient thought, this conception of motion as generation is the boundary of the basic scheme of the universe. The earth is where we find all that is mutable, transient, and finite, while the immortal gods reside in the heights (Ouranos), where objects are incorruptible and immutable.

We have grown up with a dualistic heaven–earth conception. The ancient Greeks had heaven and earth; modern religions have the soul and the body; most people today think of things and humans. We have been taught that the spirit and the body are two separate phenomena. Likewise, God and the world, spiritual and material, divine and human are presented to us as completely disconnected realities. Therefore, we are told that to find God we must discard, abandon, and renounce the world. But I say rejecting earth or going to heaven is unnecessary. In order to find God, we should delve into the depths of our being. *Yeridah letsorech aliyah*, because it is "by going down that we rise": not by flying but by digging down, digging into the heavens. Because deep within us lies the entrance to the here, where every experience happens. Being aware of divine presence, both in heaven and on earth, is the recognition of consciousness. The entire universe is consciousness

Materialists focus on the earth since they believe it is all that exists. Some live their whole lives striving to possess and accumulate earthly things. Escaping from the fear of poverty and loneliness, they become attached to the earth. If they bore of pursuing earthly things, they reject them and seek heavenly things.

On the other hand, many religious people, running from the fear of insecurity and death, seek above and chase heavenly achievements.

They do not notice that they lack authentic inner transformation. Although they seek spiritual objects, they remain prisoners of their desires and ambitions. They are just living life on autopilot. They perceive reality from a robotic perspective and, instead of living, they just function.

However, for seekers of Truth, what is tangible is not everything; it is only a means to access another dimension through observation. Therefore, they focus on observing themselves: eating, walking, talking, listening, working, and sitting in silence. As observation grows in our lives, we will spread our wings and effortlessly be lifted into the heavens. Humans are fusions of earth and sky, of body and soul. If you find what is real, true, and eternal in you, wherever you look, you will no longer see earth or heavens, but God, who is the essence of both.

לְפִי שֶׁאֵין פְּרָטֵי הַנִּבְרָאִים יְכוֹלִים לְקַבֵּל חַיּוּתָם מֵעֲשָׂרָה מַאֲמָרוֹת עַצְמָן שֶׁבַּתּוֹרָה, שֶׁהַחַיּוּת הַנִּמְשָׁךְ מֵהֶן עַצְמָן – גָּדוֹל מְאֹד מִבְּחִינַת הַנִּבְרָאִים פְּרָטִיִּים, וְאֵין כֹּחַ בָּהֶם לְקַבֵּל הַחַיּוּת, אֶלָּא עַל יְדֵי שֶׁיּוֹרֵד הַחַיּוּת וּמִשְׁתַּלְשֵׁל מִמַּדְרֵגָה לְמַדְרֵגָה פְּחוּתָה מִמֶּנָּה, עַל יְדֵי חִילּוּפִים וּתְמוּרוֹת הָאוֹתִיּוֹת, וְגִימַטְרִיָּאוֹת שֶׁהֵן חֶשְׁבּוֹן הָאוֹתִיּוֹת, עַד שֶׁיּוּכַל לְהִתְצַמְצֵם וּלְהִתְלַבֵּשׁ וּלְהִתְהַוּוֹת מִמֶּנּוּ נִבְרָא פְּרָטִי.
וְזֶה שְׁמוֹ אֲשֶׁר יִקְרְאוּ לוֹ בִּלְשׁוֹן הַקֹּדֶשׁ, הוּא כְּלִי לַחַיּוּת הַמְצוּמְצָם בְּאוֹתִיּוֹת שֵׁם זֶה, שֶׁנִּשְׁתַּלְשֵׁל מֵעֲשָׂרָה מַאֲמָרוֹת שֶׁבַּתּוֹרָה, שֶׁיֵּשׁ בָּהֶם כֹּחַ וְחַיּוּת לִבְרוֹא יֵשׁ מֵאַיִן, וּלְהַחֲיוֹתוֹ לְעוֹלָם, דְּ"אוֹרַיְיתָא וְקוּדְשָׁא בְּרִיךְ הוּא כּוּלָּא חַד":

[This descent is necessary] because individual creatures are not capable of receiving their life-force directly from the Ten Utterances of the Torah, for the life-force issuing directly from them is far greater than the capacity of the individual creatures. They can receive the life-force only when it descends and is progressively diminished, degree by degree, by means of substitutions and transpositions of the letters and by *gematriot*, their numerical values, until the life-force can be condensed and enclothed and there can be brought forth from it a particular creature. And the name by which it is called in the

Holy Tongue is a vessel for the life-force condensed into the letters of that name which has descended from the Ten Utterances in the Torah that have power and vitality to create being *ex nihilo* and give it life forever. For the Torah and the Holy One, Blessed is He, are one.

(***Tanya***, **"*The portal of unity and faith,*" chapter 1**)

Creation is a process of concealment of what is. Consciousness is objectified as mind, body, and universe through the word. We call mind to the objectified thoughts; body to the objectified sensations and universe to the objectified perceptions. The word is the skin that covers what we consider our inner self; letters are its clothing. Those of us who enjoy writing know that our job is to design the appropriate lexical clothing for ideas and thoughts. Although words and letters are symbols of mental or emotional objects, they are also linguistic objects in their own right. We might know that sexual interaction through language is possible, and perhaps we have even experienced linguistic caresses and embraces that have brought us to the brink of orgasm. But it is also possible that many of us carry invisible bruises and scars left by verbal blows, whose painful consequences can last for years or even a lifetime.

אָמַר רַבִּי אַחָא: "בְּשָׁעָה שֶׁבָּא הַקָּדוֹשׁ־בָּרוּךְ־הוּא לִבְרֹאת אֶת הָאָדָם, נִמְלַךְ בְּמַלְאֲכֵי הַשָּׁרֵת. אָמַר לָהֶן: 'נַעֲשֶׂה אָדָם' (בראשית א, כ"ו). אָמְרוּ לוֹ: 'אָדָם זֶה מַה טִיבוֹ?' אָמַר לָהֶן: 'חָכְמָתוֹ מְרֻבָּה מִשֶּׁלָּכֶם'. הֵבִיא לִפְנֵיהֶם אֶת הַבְּהֵמָה וְאֶת הַחַיָּה וְאֶת הָעוֹף, אָמַר לָהֶם: 'זֶה מַה שְּׁמוֹ?' וְלֹא הָיוּ יוֹדְעִין. הֶעֱבִירָן לִפְנֵי אָדָם, אָמַר לוֹ: 'זֶה מַה שְּׁמוֹ?' אָמַר: 'זֶה שׁוֹר, זֶה חֲמוֹר, זֶה סוּס וְזֶה גָּמָל'. 'וְאַתָּה מַה שְּׁמְךָ?' אָמַר לוֹ: 'אֲנִי נָאֶה לְהִקָּרֵא אָדָם שֶׁנִּבְרֵאתִי מִן הָאֲדָמָה'. 'וַאֲנִי מַה שְּׁמִי?' אָמַר לוֹ: 'לְךָ נָאֶה לְהִקָּרְאוֹת אֲדֹנָי, שֶׁאַתָּה אָדוֹן לְכָל בְּרִיּוֹתֶיךָ'".

(בראשית רבה, בראשית, פרשה י"ז)

Rabbi Aḥa said: "When the Holy One Blessed be He came to create man, He consulted with the ministering angels. He said to them: 'Let us make mankind' (Genesis, 1:26). They said to Him: 'This man, what is his nature?' He said to them: 'His wisdom is greater than yours.' He brought the animals, the beasts, and the birds before them and said to them: 'What is the name of this one?' And they did not know. He passed them before Adam and said to him: 'What is the name of this one?' He said: 'This is a *shor* (ox); this is a *ḥamor* (donkey); this is a *sus* (horse); this is a *gamal* (camel).' He [God] then asked: 'And you, what is your name?' He said to Him: 'It is appropriate that I be called Adam, as I was created from the ground (*adama*).' He [God] asked further: 'And I, what is My name?' He said to Him: 'It is appropriate to call you Adonai, as You are the Lord (*adon*) over all your creatures'."

(*Bereshit Rabbah*, "*Bereshit*," 17)

Relative or dual reality is just a dream. You are God, just asleep. This entire multiplicity consists of modulations of thought. Each living entity receives individuality, or is objectified, through its name. As this section says: **"...from the Ten Utterances in the Torah that have power and vitality to create being *ex nihilo* and give it life forever. For the Torah and the Holy One, Blessed is He, are one."**

Objective diversity is materializing consciousness. The only reason for our relative existence as parts or entities is to live in the service of the Whole.

וַאֲנִי נִבְרֵאתִי לְשַׁמֵּשׁ אֶת קוֹנִי.

(תלמוד בבלי, קידושין, פ"ב, ב')

I was created to serve the one who formed me.

(*Babylonian Talmud*, "*Kiddushin*," 82b)

God is not another "someone"; He does not exist, but He is existence itself.

וַיִּטַּע אֶשֶׁל בִּבְאֵר שָׁבַע וַיִּקְרָא־שָׁם בְּשֵׁם ה' אֵל עוֹלָם:

(בראשית, פרשת וירא, כ"א, ל"ג)

> And he [Abraham] planted an orchard in Beersheba, and there he called out the name of the Lord, the God-World.
>
> (Genesis, 21:33, The "*VaYera*" Torah portion)

In *Parashat Va'Yera*, Abraham calls the Almighty *El 'Olam*, which means "God World." If he had referred to God as "something" or "somebody" who is the creator of the universe, it would have been logical to call him *El Ha'Olam* (אל העולם), or "God of the World." However, the term used is *El 'Olam* or "God-World" (אל עולם). Abraham refers to God as the universe itself and not as its creator. God is consciousness or all that exists.

This understanding is reflected in the commentary on this verse by the Malbim, Rabbi Meir Leibush ben Yeḥiel Michel Wisser.

> "וַיִּקְרָא שָׁם בְּשֵׁם ה' אֵל עוֹלָם", כִּי אַחַר הַמִּילָה הִשִּׂיג יוֹתֵר שֶׁ"אֵין עוֹד מִלְּבַדּוֹ" וְשֶׁאֵין שׁוּם כֹּחַ מוֹשֵׁל בָּעוֹלָם – רַק ה' לְבַדּוֹ, וְזֶה קָרָא וּפִרְסֵם לָרַבִּים.
>
> (מלבי"ם, בראשית כ"א, ל"ג)

> "There he called out the name of the Lord, the God-World." For after his circumcision, he realized even more that "There is nothing but Him" and that there is no power that is ruling in the world, but The Lord alone. And this was what he called out and propagated.
>
> (Malbim on Genesis, 21:33)

The disappearance of our cause threatens the very foundations of our reality. However, the Divine does not proceed from any cause; therefore, only God is truly independent. Consciousness has no cause because it has no objective qualities. From the perspective of thought, consciousness is nothing. It is not something or someone in need of a creator or a principle: it was, it is, and it will be.

> וְהוּא הָיָה, וְהוּא הֹוֶה, וְהוּא יִהְיֶה, בְּתִפְאָרָה.
>
> (סידור התפילה, פיוט "אדון עולם")

And He was, He is, and He will be—in splendor.
(*Siddur*, *Adon ʻOlam Piyyut*)

אֲשֶׁר בֶּאֱמֶת עִקַּר הַהַשָּׂגָה הוּא בְּדַעַת הַמְחַבֵּר הַמֹּחַ וְהַלֵּב בְּהַרְגָּשַׁת הָאַיִן [...] כִּי בֶּאֱמֶת הַכֹּל כְּאַיִן וְאֶפֶס [...] רַק מֵחֲמַת הַהֶרְגֵּל שֶׁהֻרְגַּל בְּזֶה הָעוֹלָם כִּי לֹא יַבִּיט רַק עַל גֶּשֶׁם הָעָב וְלֹא יוּכַל לְהַבִּיט רַק עַל חָמְרִיּוּת הַדְּבָרִים הַמַּסְתִּירִים וּמְכַסִּים וּמַכְחִישִׁים הָאֱמֶת אֲשֶׁר מֵחֲמַת הַסְתָּרַת אֱלֹקוּתוֹ יִדְמֶה לוֹ הַיֵּשׁ. וְכָל עִקַּר הָעֲבוֹדָה לִהְיוֹת נֶעְתָּק מִמְּקוֹמוֹ הַשָּׂגָה חוּשִׁית אֱנוֹשִׁית רַק לְהַשִּׂיג דְּבַר הָאֱמֶת שֶׁאֵינוֹ מְלֻבָּשׁ [...] דְּהַיְנוּ לְהַרְגִּיל עַצְמוֹ וּלְהִתְבּוֹנֵן בְּרוּחָנִיּוּת הַמְחַיָּה [...] וְעִקַּר הַשָּׂגָה הוּא [...] שֶׁכָּל הַמְּצִיאוּת וְהַשָּׂגוֹת שֶׁלָּהּ הוּא הָאַיִן, וְזֶהוּ הַתְחָלַת כָּל עֲבוֹדָה. אֲבָל מָה אֶעֱשֶׂה לָכֶם שֶׁאִי אֶפְשָׁר שֶׁאַרְאֶה לָכֶם אֵיךְ הוּא הַשָּׂגַת הָאַיִן [...] וְהָאֱמֶת לֹא הֻרְגַּלְתֶּם בָּזֶה בְּהַשָּׂגָה כָּזוֹ, רַק הַשָּׂגָה הָאֱנוֹשִׁית אֲשֶׁר תּוּכַל לְמַשֵּׁשׁ בַּחוּשִׁים הַגַּשְׁמִיִּים [...] וְזֶה בֶּאֱמֶת תַּאֲמִינוּ לִי כִּי זֶהוּ הַתְחָלַת הָעֲבוֹדָה לִהְיוֹת נֶעְתָּק מִמְּקוֹמוֹ, אַךְ מַה אֶעֱשֶׂה כִּי לֹא הֻרְגַּלְתֶּם לְהַבִּיט הַשָּׁמַיְמָה רַק שֶׁמִּתַּחַת לָאָרֶץ, וְכָל הָעִקָּר הוּא הַהִתְבּוֹנְנוּת וְכָל מָה שֶׁתּוֹסִיפוּ בָּזֶה הַתְמָדָה יִוָּלֵד מִזֶּה יוֹתֵר דַּעַת וְהַשָּׂגָה [...] אֲבָל הָעִקָּר לִבָּטֵל מִמְּקוֹמוֹ [...]

(האדמו"ר הזקן, רבי שניאור זלמן מליאדי, "איגרת עיקר ההשגה")

[…] In reality, the essence of knowing is in *da'at*, which bridges between the brain and the heart with the feeling of *ayin* (nothingness) […] For in fact, everything is null and void […] It is just because of the habit that the world has become accustomed to, of only paying attention to the gross matter, and to pay attention only to the material aspect of things, which is concealing and denying the Truth and because the things' Divinity is concealed, they appear to be *yesh*, to exist. The essence of the work is shifting from one's habitual place, and taking a new perspective; removing the human sensual perception and perceiving only the unclothed Truth. […] That is, creating a habit of observing the life-giving spirituality […] and the essence of realization is […] that all existence and its comprehensions is nothingness. And this is the beginning of any work. But what can I do, that I cannot show you how it is to realize nothingness. […] And the fact is that you did not get used to such realization, but only to human perception, which can only sense with material senses. […] And believe me, this is really the beginning of the work: shifting from one's habitual place, but what can I do that you are not accustomed to looking to the heavens but only to what is under the earth? […] and the essence of everything is watchfulness, and the more you stick with it, it will give birth to more knowledge and realization […] but the main thing is to nullify oneself from one's place. […]

(The Alter Rebbe, Rabbi Shneor Zalman of Liadi, *Epistle of the Essence of Realization*)

The world has not been created by adding what is missing, but concealing what truly is, the Self. Consciousness achieves objectification through self-concealment or voluntary withdrawal. God hides Himself in you, as you.

הוּא יִתְבָּרֵךְ הַיֵּשׁ הָאֲמִתִּי וְכֻלָּא קַמֵּהּ כְּלָא חֲשִׁיב וְאַיִן וָאֶפֶס מַמָּשׁ.
(האדמו"ר הזקן, רבי שניאור זלמן מליאדי, לקוטי תורה, "מטות", פ"ו)

He, Blessed be He, is the real *yesh* (existence), and in front of him everything is considered as nothing, and completely null and void.

(The Alter Rebbe, Rabbi Shneor Zalman of Liadi, *Likutei Torah*, "*Matot*," 86)

The later evolution of this concealment process is the cognitive modulation of letters:

כָּל הָאוֹרוֹת הָעֶלְיוֹנִים עַד שֶׁיַּגִּיעוּ לְהֵעָשׂוֹת מֵהֶם פְּעֻלָּה בְּמַעֲשֶׂה, צָרִיךְ שֶׁיָּבֹאוּ לְסוֹד הָאוֹתִיּוֹת. וְהֵם מְצִיאוּת סֵדֶר אֶחָד הָעוֹמֵד לְהוֹצִיא כָּל הַדְּבָרִים לַפֹּעַל, וְהוּא סוֹד "בִּדְבַר ה' שָׁמַיִם נַעֲשׂוּ" (תהילים ל"ג, ו'). כִּי אֵין מְצִיאוּת לַדִּבּוּר אֶלָּא בָּאוֹתִיּוֹת.
(רמח"ל, קל"ח פתחי חכמה, י"ח, י')

In order to become an act in the world of actions, all the divine lights must become fit to the secret of letters. The letters constitute a complete order that exists to bring all

> things into actual being. This is the meaning of the verse: "By the word of the Lord the heavens were made" (Psalms, 33:6). For speech exists only by the virtue of the letters.
>
> (Ramḥal, *Kla"ḥ Pitḥei Ḥochma*, 18.10)

Letters are a metaphor for a crucial stage in the universal process of cognitive evolution. They are the cognitive bricks of multiplicity, with which consciousness objectifies itself.

> עֶשְׂרִים וּשְׁתַּיִם אוֹתִיּוֹת חֲקָקָן חֲצָבָן שְׁקָלָן וֶהֱמִירָן צְרָפָן וְצָר בָּהֶם נֶפֶשׁ כָּל הַיְּצוּר וְנֶפֶשׁ כָּל הֶעָתִיד לָצוּר.
>
> (ספר יצירה, פרק ב', משנה ב')
>
> Twenty-two letters: He engraved and carved them, weighed and transmuted them, combined them and formed with them the soul of everything—of all that had been created and everything that will be created in the future.
>
> (*Sefer Yetzirah*, 2.2)

Most people base their existence on a belief in two apparent factors: the experiential subject and the surrounding objects. Average individuals erroneously postulate that they exist as an autonomous "I," rooted in a corporeality that witnesses an objective reality detached from their own individual consciousness. By only talking to others with the same vision, the subject's conclusion is temporarily validated, and then the issue at hand can be explored from this outlook. Such dialectical exchanges seek to build bridges of communication with those who hold this conception, avoiding the temptation to seclude ourselves in the more abstract and sublime spheres of ontological reality.

The retroprogressive process of *teshuvah*

Until now, we have explained how the *Tanya* describes creation as a process of concealment of what is. In the opposite direction, the discovery of consciousness is a return to the source, which I call the retroprogressive process of *teshuvah*. In order to deeply understand its nature, it is essential to break down and thoroughly examine each of its four phases.

The first phase involves a transition from "being someone," or the perception of oneself as a defined being, to the notion of "being no one." At this point, I recognize that personality does not constitute a solid entity or a tangible object; rather, what is considered "I" is nothing but a void, since objects are merely experiences without independent existence. In this initial stage, I realize that I am neither a concrete entity nor an object. I am not someone because people do not exist; there are only experiences. We can say that at this stage, the experience consists in being nobody. However, this step is not the final phase because we still recognize ourselves as nobody, a form of non-being that still has presence. This perception implies that, although we recognize our emptiness, we maintain a minimal form of being. As we deepen our investigation of experience, it is revealed that the knower of the experience is the observation that transcends the observed. However, this revelation is not conclusive because it maintains a presumed subjective observer who still perceives hypothetical objective elements such as the mind, the body, and the cosmos.

In the second stage, this notion of "being nobody" transforms into "being everything." Here, a realization occurs that the totality of experiences is my very self. This stage involves the recognition of the experiencer, the experienced, and the space where these experiences occur, emphasizing an indivisible unity of experience. "I am everything" because I am all experiences. But this phase is not the final one because, considering ourselves to be this "everything," attention does not rest in the transcendental core. Although I do not consider myself to be neither "someone" nor "nobody," I perceive myself as being an objective "everything," which has thingness.

The third phase of the return marks a transition from "being everything" to "being nothing." In this stage, the notion of reality dissolves into the realization that everything is ephemeral. Only experiences exist, and therefore, there is no "thing" or "object" in reality; I am just nothing. But this phase is not final because if nothingness "is," it loses its essential quality of non-existence.

"Nothingness is," therefore, is a "relative nothingness" that has two components: "nothing" and "being." By existing, this nothingness becomes an object of analysis, discussion, and description.

Finally, in the last stage, from "being nothing" one moves to "not being nothing." It is a transition from a "relative nothingness" that still is, to an "absolute nothingness" that lacks both being and non-being, which we call pure consciousness, God, or the One. The One is transcendental, the source and origin of all Being. "Absolute nothingness" is a condition in which no existence is possible. It is identified with the concept of the One, in which all duality and distinction completely dissolve. Let us not forget that the One cannot be considered existent in conventional terms, because its existence would imply determination and, thereby, it would lose its quality of absolute. If the One were determined, it would become a specific entity and, being something particular, a duality would be established between the One and that specific entity. This duality would compromise the absolute unity of the One, since it would imply the presence of a distinction within what must be absolutely indivisible. Consequently, to preserve its essence of absolute unity, the One cannot be understood as a determined or particular existence. This absolute One is neither something nor someone; in reality, it is nothing at all. Precisely because of its nature of being nothing, it becomes the foundation of Being. Heidegger refers to this One that is nothing as "the original nothing," which is the foundation of being, and being, in turn, is the foundation of the entity. Therefore, the final phase of awakening must be the acceptance of a nothingness that transcends all forms of existence, reaching a state of absolute inexistence. It is recognized that there is no reality beyond consciousness. This phase marks the culmination of the Path of Retroprogressive Alignment, with the realization that there is nothing outside of God.

We will discuss each phase in greater detail.

Stage 1: From being someone to being nobody

The first retroprogressive stage is a step from being someone to being nobody. Under the prism of a relative and dual reality, discernment emerges between the "I" that presumably resides in our bodily form and the presumed "not I" that is the objective cosmos. From this paradigm, we perceive ourselves as an entity or subject, an apparent witness of a vast objectual universe.

The knower of the experience

Perceptions we illusorily attribute to the supposed subject are called "sensations." On the other hand, sensations that we mistakenly connect to the object of our observation are called "perceptions." Contrary to this belief, our physical structure is not merely a solid and concrete object, but a conglomeration of sensations. The presumed possession and development of a form or body, in reality, consists of an embodiment or ontification of sensory and perceptual activity.

Similarly, the intellect is not an object or tangible entity but the objectification of cognitive activity. The premise of an objective reality is erroneous, since what we hypothetically regard as the universe is actually an objectification of the perceptual act. Although the cosmos exists, it lacks autonomous reality because its existence constitutes the ontification of perception.

From the absolute perspective, pure and unaltered consciousness is reified corporeally, mentally, and universally to become perceptions, thoughts, and sensations, respectively. Pure consciousness modulates sensations and manifests a form. It catalyzes thinking and emulates a mind. It processes perceptions and creates a universe. Breaking down this premise dismantles the belief in a mind–body diptych as an active observing subject in experience and a cosmos as an observed object entity. The objective value of the body, mind, and universe is firmly established within the framework of experience.

Attempting to evaluate the knower of experience, we encounter an intriguing reality: whatever lies beyond the boundaries of mind, body, and cosmos lacks definable attributes. If the knower of experience possessed inherent qualities, it would clearly be confined to the objective dimension and categorized in the manifested realm that is observable within the context of experience. From a conceptual perspective, yet, if the knower of experience lacks definable properties, it is not considered an existent entity.

However, this revelation is not conclusive because it retains the dual conception of subject–object. This dichotomy continues despite a more sophisticated understanding than the preconceived one, according to which mind and body were regarded as the subjective core and the cosmos as the object. Here, the fracture of consciousness still prevails, which remains segmented into an apparent observing entity and that which is supposedly observed.

Knowingness of experience

In this interstitial phase of our retroprogressive pilgrimage toward Truth, an unquestioned principle becomes clear: knowingness of experience is not merely an additional entity, but our own genuine reality. Likewise, it is evident that the basic and fundamental pillar for any experience to manifest lies in the previous presence of consciousness. At this point, the understanding arises that knowingness stands as the fundamental support for all experiential phenomena. In the absence of such primordial consciousness, the very conception of body, mind, and cosmos would be untenable.

Within the empirical realm, there is nothing that suggests that knowingness is subordinate to exogenous entities or indications that consciousness is conditioned by anything external. At this point, it can be asserted with full confidence that consciousness is inherently autarkic, self-sufficient, uncoercible, and autonomous.

It is imperative to clarify that knowingness does not sprout, emerge, emanate, appear, or diffuse from a substratum, since every manifestation would insinuate the presence of a primordial cause. Accepting an origin previous to consciousness would mean allowing the prior presence of something that transcends consciousness itself. If so, knowingness would not be the One without a second.

Consciousness is one

Consciousness is the One without a second, eternal and unlimited. It is neither born nor dies; begins nor ends; starts nor ceases. It is unique, indivisible, and has no counterpart. Being immutable in the course of time, consciousness is alien to the cycles of birth or death, and lacks temporal and spatial confines. It is established as perennial and infinite.

> "אָנֹכִי ה' אֱלֹהֶיךָ". לָמָּה נֶאֱמַר? [...] שֶׁלֹּא לִתֵּן פִּתְחוֹן פֶּה לְאֻמּוֹת הָעוֹלָם לוֹמַר: שְׁתֵּי רָשֻׁיּוֹת הֵן. אֶלָּא "אָנֹכִי ה' אֱלֹהֶיךָ"; אֲנִי בְּמִצְרַיִם, אֲנִי עַל הַיָּם, אֲנִי בְּסִינַי, אֲנִי לְשֶׁעָבַר, אֲנִי לֶעָתִיד לָבֹא, אֲנִי בָעוֹלָם הַזֶּה, אֲנִי לָעוֹלָם הַבָּא, שֶׁנֶּאֱמַר: "רְאוּ עַתָּה כִּי אֲנִי אֲנִי הוּא" (דברים ל"ב, ל"ט) [...]
>
> (מכילתא דרבי ישמעאל, מסכתא דבחודש, ה')

> "I am the Lord your God" What is the intent of this? [...] So as not to provide an opening for the nations of the world to say that there are two Powers, [He said] "I am the Lord your God." It was I in Egypt, I at the [Red] Sea, it is I at Sinai. It was I in the past and it will be I in time to come. I in this world and I in the world to come. As it is written, "See now that I myself am He!" (Deuteronomy, 32:39).
>
> (*Mechilta DeRabbi Yishma'el*, Tractate "*Baḥodesh*," 5)

Therefore, consciousness cannot become extinct or perish. If it could, then consciousness would fade away into an entity that is separate from itself, whose existence would operate autonomously in the absence of consciousness. An entity capable of absorbing the disappearance of consciousness would have to be intrinsically larger to encompass it. These considerations would conceptualize consciousness as an objectual, finite, circumscribed, and transitory phenomenon.

At this first stage, I realize that I am not a concrete entity or an object. I am not something or someone. I understand that I am nobody because no objects exist, only experiences.

Stage 2: From being nobody to being everything

The second stage is a step from being nobody to being everything. Only knowingness or the knower of experience can recognize consciousness.

The unity of the experiencer and the experience

Clearly, only consciousness is capable of self-recognition, self-perception, or self-awareness. Its main obstacle lies in the formation of a self-conception that is presented as if it were dissimilar to itself. It is arduous and complicated to recognize ourselves as knowingness of experience because our essence has been profusely impregnated with an assortment of emotions, ideas, imaginations, and conjectures. The superimposition of mental and emotional components on pure knowingness hinders the recognition of consciousness as our genuine authenticity.

In the domain of contingent, relative, and dichotomous reality, an objective plurality is postulated that seems to unfold before an evaluating subject. The latter, confined within a specific form, believes to discern the existence of separate mental, emotional, and sensory entities. However, a rigorous inquiry reveals an exceptional finding: the separation that we noted between the presumed evaluating subject and the evaluated hypothetical entities is unreal. It is impossible to discern a space or distance between the experiencing subject and the object of that experience. Within the experience itself, we fail to identify a point of intersection between the evaluator and the evaluated.

It is elusive to determine where the apparent witness ends and the alleged observed object begins. We cannot delineate a threshold at which our essence as an individual perceiving consciousness ceases and the perceivable cosmos emerges. This is because objective plurality does not unfold before consciousness, but is donated inherently from its core, as Jean-Luc Marion asserts.

In analyzing the dynamics of experience, it becomes evident that entities do not emerge at a distance before the prism of consciousness.

Instead, they unfold from and in its very essence. This leads to the realization that the existential becoming and its events do not present themselves externally to our being, but are intrinsically donated in our intimacy. As *Midrash Rabbah* says:

> מִפְּנֵי מָה מְכַנִּין שְׁמוֹ שֶׁל הַקָּדוֹשׁ בָּרוּךְ הוּא וְקוֹרְאִין אוֹתוֹ מָקוֹם? שֶׁהוּא מְקוֹמוֹ שֶׁל עוֹלָם וְאֵין עוֹלָמוֹ מְקוֹמוֹ.
>
> (בראשית רבה, ס"ח)
>
> Why do they change the name of the Holy One, Blessed be He, and call Him 'The Place'? It is because He is the place of the world, and His world is not His place.
>
> (*Bereshit Rabbah*, 68)

Infinitude includes finitude

Consciousness is like an unlimited receptacle where empirical reality resides, an oceanic domain in which phenomena such as mind, body, cosmos, and galaxies emerge and dilute.

Hegel wrote two monumental works: *The Phenomenology of Spirit* in 1807 and *The Science of Logic* in 1810. In the latter, Hegel argues that, logically, the finite and the infinite cannot be opposed. If the infinite did not also include the finite, it would lose its infinitude. For the infinite to maintain its unlimited nature, it must encompass everything, including the finite. The existence of the finite outside the infinite would compromise the infinitude of the infinite. The mere presence of the finite would be an obstacle to the true infinitude of the infinite. For the infinite to retain its unlimited nature, it cannot be conditioned by the finite. Hegel's philosophical strategy is to integrate the finite within the infinite.

According to Hegel, the infinite is identified with Being, Spirit, or Absolute Consciousness, while the finite refers to the human being and their history. Hegel argues that the finite and the infinite are not completely separate entities; the finite is an internal manifestation of the infinite. This allows the infinite to encompass everything, including the limitations and contingencies of the finite, without losing its infinitude. For consciousness to be truly absolute, it is fundamental that the individual consciousness of humans and their history be integrated into it. This means that all beings and events must be contained within absolute consciousness and that all historical development must occur within it, not outside of it.

In this way, Hegel overcomes the traditional dichotomy between the finite and the infinite, proposing that absolute reality, or Absolute Consciousness, is a dialectical process in which the finite and the infinite are in a relationship of interdependence and mutual inclusion. Hegel's philosophy posits that true infinitude must integrate the finite within itself without being limited by it. According to Hegel, Absolute Consciousness encompasses all reality, including history and human experience, and its infinitude lies precisely in its capacity to contain everything without being restricted by any finite limitation.

Consciousness can be envisioned as an unlimited receptacle that houses the entirety of empirical reality. It is a vast, profound oceanic expanse in which various phenomena arise and disappear, such as the mind, the body, the cosmos, and galaxies. This metaphorical space has no defined boundaries, allowing all these elements to exist simultaneously and interrelate within its infinite extension. Thus, consciousness manifests as an integral realm where the material and the immaterial seamlessly coexist.

A notable transformation in this cognitive stage is the rise of experiential depth and intimacy. Previously, we postulated that consciousness positioned itself before an objective reality while maintaining a discernible distance. Up to this level, we assumed that consciousness was a mere spectator facing a distant objective reality. Thus, we lived our lives believing that genuinely intimate experiences were confined to the spheres of thought and emotion.

However, from this phase on, any semblance of separation evaporates and each experience is internalized with an unusual depth. The experience from this dimension is characterized by an amplitude that intensifies existence. Phenomena as diverse as flowers, clouds, the moon, smiles, or life caress and touch us deeply. These experiences resonate with poignant depth. Despite the magnitude of this high level, it remains anchored in the dual and relative plane. This space of consciousness persists in its subjective role as observer, while that which is observed, though integrated, persists within it. In this sphere, the perceived fragmentation of consciousness remains, as the conscious space is positioned as the subject and its content stands as the objective reality. We continue to operate at a level where an apparent distinction is maintained between the observer entity and the observed entity, the knower and the known.

The essence of experience

To continue on the Path of Retroprogressive Alignment, we must evaluate the essence of experience. This leads us to a meticulous study of both the substantial component and the fundamental nature inherent in the presumed observing subject. Such endeavor involves a detailed scrutiny of both the subjective and the objective dimensions in the matrix of experience. This observation or analysis clearly demonstrates that our mind emerges from the act of thinking, the body emerges from sensations, and the universe is born from our perception. The substance of thinking, feeling and perceiving coincides exactly with that of consciousness.

Just as waves, vortices, bubbles, and foam are expressions of water, all that is known in our reality can be reduced to knowing, which is simply consciousness. Every element of our perceptual field of reality is focused solely on the act of recognition, which is intrinsically conscious. Although we believe we know a mind, a body, and an ontic or objective universe, in reality, we only know knowing itself. Ultimately, consciousness is only conscious of itself.

Consciousness is everything and everyone

In this phase of realization, consciousness is unmistakably experienced as the fundamental and omnipresent pillar. It is clearly revealed that consciousness is everything and everyone. As the *Tanya* explains, through different cognitive modulations or letters, the One becomes an objectual and tangible diversity. Succinctly, it is consciousness that metamorphoses into cognitive manifestations such as language, expressed as alphabetical characters, configuring itself in the form of mind.

> וְהוּא סוֹד, "בִּדְבַר ה' שָׁמַיִם נַעֲשׂוּ" (תהילים ל"ג, ו'), וְהַיְנוּ כִּי בַּתְּחִלָּה יֵשׁ הַמַּחְשָׁבָה – אָדָם קַדְמוֹן, וְהִיא נֶעֱלֶמֶת, וּגְלוּיָה עַל יְדֵי הַדִּבּוּר בָּאוֹתִיּוֹת. וְהִנֵּה נִמְצָא שֶׁכָּל מָה שֶׁנֶּעֱלַם בַּמַּחְשָׁבָה – צָרִיךְ לָצֵאת עַל יְדֵי הַדִּבּוּר. וְהִנֵּה אֵין חֶלְקֵי וְסִדְרֵי הַמַּחְשָׁבָה שָׁוִים לְסִדְרֵי הַדִּבּוּר כְּלָל, כִּי הַמַּחְשָׁבָה תַּחֲשֹׁב הָעִנְיָן, וְהַדִּבּוּר יוֹצִיא הַמִּלּוֹת בְּאוֹתִיּוֹת, וְאַף עַל פִּי כֵן צָרִיךְ שֶׁמָּה שֶׁצִּיְּרָה הַמַּחְשָׁבָה – יִשְׁתַּעְבֵּד לְסִדְרֵי הַדִּבּוּר לָצֵאת עַל יְדֵיהֶם. כָּךְ הוּא לְמַעְלָה, סֵדֶר רִאשׁוֹן – הוּא הַמַּחְשָׁבָה, וְהַגִּלּוּי שֶׁלָּהּ - הוּא הַדִּבּוּר. וּמָה שֶׁנִּצְטַיֵּר בַּמַּחְשָׁבָה לְפִי סִדְרָהּ – צָרִיךְ שֶׁיֵּצֵא בְּדִבּוּר לְפִי סְדָרָיו, וְהֵם סִדְרֵי הָאוֹתִיּוֹת כְּדִלְקַמָּן.
> (רמח"ל, קל"ח פתחי חכמה, י"ח, ט")

> This is the secret meaning of the verse: "By the word of the Lord the heavens were made" (Psalms, 33:6). For initially there is the thought, or *Adam Kadmon* (The primordial person), but it is concealed and is revealed through speech, which consists of letters. You will find that whatever is concealed in thought must become speech in order to be revealed. However, the component parts and organizing principles of thought are by no means identical to those of speech. A thought is in the mind, whereas in speech, we express our thoughts in words with the help of letters. In order to be communicated, whatever is conceived in thoughts must be submitted to the rules of language so as to be cast in the form of letters and words. The same applies in the upper worlds. The first in order is the thought, and its revelation comes about through speech. What is conceived in the mind within the parameters of thought can come forth only within the parameters of speech, namely, letters.
>
> (Ramḥal, *Kla"ḥ Pitḥei Ḥochma*, 18.9)

Despite awakening to the substantial congruence between the objective and the consciousness, we continue to be self-absorbed in the objective realm. These objects, which have substantial identity with consciousness, lead us to conclude that by being omnipresent, God is everything. This "everything" refers to an objective reality that has been recognized as substantially congruent with consciousness. Even after having realized that God, being omnipresent, is everything and everyone, we are continually diverted by the ontic presence of "everything." Our attention does not rest in the bosom of the transcendent but remains fascinated by entities and bewitched by objects. Therefore, the realization that "divinity is everything and is in everyone" obviously cannot be the ultimate and definitive reality.

Stage 3: From being everything to being nothing

At the third stage of the retroprogressive process, it is clearly established that consciousness is the foundation of experience, relegating the objective to a secondary consideration. The nature of ultimate reality, the One (*unum* in Latin), is inclusive, holistic, and encompasses all facets of reality. As the One without a second, absolute consciousness must encompass all the various relative realities, incorporating both the cognizing agent and the cognized object. Given its oneness, the supreme reality embraces both the observer and the observed. However, our tendency to perceive and operate in tangible terms, rather than in the pure essence of reality or consciousness, prevents its full understanding. As its very essence, reality itself is the foundation of the objective platform. Both the observer and the observed are intrinsic components of the irrefutable reality.

Reality is not of an ontic nature

Earlier, we alluded to the rabbinic framework known as *pardes* as a heuristic tool for categorizing the layers of consciousness through which Truth can be discerned. In its elementary stages, such a framework conforms to the most rudimentary degrees of understanding. At its apex is the esoteric wisdom reserved for the pinnacle of revelation. As we saw earlier, this scheme is not unique to Judaism. In fact, it applies to various religious traditions and even human existential dynamics.

It is interesting to note that discrepancies between different religions tend to occur only among believers who are at the most elementary levels of consciousness. However, as we move closer to the *sod*, or "secret," the multiplicity of beliefs transcends individual identities denominations to converge in the one, universal religion. We transcend religions to know religion, in the depths of which lies the secret: behind the veil of apparent heterogeneity there is a primordial and indivisible reality. This one reality, not being ontic in nature, escapes all definition, since it is only from this fundamental reality that every entity can be defined.

Reality is neither this nor that

Different masters have resorted to negative approaches when alluding to transcendental reality. They have articulated their postulates by emphasizing absence rather than inherent presence, stressing what is not rather than what is. As we have already mentioned, the "principle of exclusion" of Saint Thomas Aquinas, also known as "the method of negative selection," is a philosophical and theological strategy that consists of discarding the false to arrive at the truth. Saint Thomas employed this principle as a logical tool to clarify concepts and reach true conclusions by systematically eliminating incorrect or contradictory propositions. The process begins with the identification of various propositions or hypotheses related to a specific topic. Each proposition is subjected to exhaustive critical analysis, evaluating its internal coherence and consistency with observed reality and other accepted knowledge. Propositions found to be false, contradictory, or inconsistent are discarded. This process of elimination purifies the set of assertions, retaining only those that endure rigorous scrutiny. Through this method of elimination, it is hoped to achieve a truer and more precise understanding of the subject in question. The elimination of the false allows the truth to stand out more clearly. In his work, Saint

Thomas Aquinas often employed this principle to refute heresies and doctrinal errors. For example, in the *Summa theologiae*, when discussing the nature of God, he analyzed various propositions about God and, through a process of exclusion, rejected those that are contradictory or incompatible with Christian doctrine. This process allows him to formulate a more precise and orthodox understanding of the divine nature.

In the search for a vital explanation, beyond a mere theoretical framework, adjectives and characterization are avoided. It is preferable to address indirectly that which escapes definition and understanding. Attempting to transcend mere speculation and achieve profound understanding, it has been chosen to avoid assigning definitive characteristics by omitting qualities of the undefinable and inexplicable. As we mentioned before, this principle is known in Advaita Vedanta as *neti-neti*, which means "neither this nor that."

Such a strategy avoids creating mental representations or analogies that limit and reduce the ineffable to the constraints of thought and the narrow confines of conceptualization. It is a precaution against degrading transcendental truths into mere conceptual idolatry. The essence lies in the recognition of consciousness and the endeavor to align existence with such recognition. Thus, we realize that only reality is. The mere insinuation of an alternative existence would imply a duality in reality, which would contradict its singular and unique nature.

Reality is indivisible

Ultimate reality, in its purest essence, is exclusively self-referential; it is self-sufficient and, therefore, unalterable in its essence. It contains only itself so that any perception of division or fragmentation is but the result of a circumscribed and limited observation. If its content and constitution is itself, fragmentation would be as incongruous as a watery barrier in the middle of the ocean, or a barrier made of space in the firmament. The characteristic of being unlimited derives from its self-referential nature: it harbors nothing beyond itself.

Establishing a boundary would imply a dichotomy between what is and what is not, which is contradictory, since the introduction of a non-conscious entity would mean it coexists with something beyond primordial unity. By harboring nothing except of itself, establishing a boundary would imply recognizing a counterpoint between what exists and what does not exist. Following this logic, the emergence of something external to consciousness would imply the coexistence of an additional element beyond the One without a second.

> אַחֵר קִיצֵּץ בִּנְטִיעוֹת, עָלָיו הַכָּתוּב אוֹמֵר: "אַל תִּתֵּן אֶת פִּיךָ לַחֲטִיא אֶת בְּשָׂרֶךָ" (קהלת ה', ה'). מַאי הִיא? חֲזָא מִיטַטְרוֹן דְּאִתְיְהִיבָא לֵיהּ רְשׁוּתָא לְמֵיתַב לְמִיכְתַּב זַכְוָתָא דְיִשְׂרָאֵל, אֲמַר: "גְּמִירִי דִּלְמַעְלָה לָא הָוֵי לֹא יְשִׁיבָה וְלֹא תַּחֲרוּת, וְלֹא עֹרֶף וְלֹא עִפּוּי. שֶׁמָּא, חַס וְשָׁלוֹם, שְׁתֵּי רָשׁוּיוֹת הֵן".
>
> (תלמוד בבלי, חגיגה, ט"ו, א')
>
> [Rabbi Elisha ben Avuya who is named] "Aḥer" (The other) chopped down the plants [i.e. became a heretic]. The following verse is speaking about him: "Do not allow your mouth to bring sin upon your flesh" (Ecclesiastes, 5:5). What is it about? He saw [the angel] Mitatron, who had permission to sit and write the merits of Israel. He said, "There is a tradition: Above [i.e., in heaven], there is no sitting, no competition, no turning one's back, and no fatigue [among the angels, yet Mitatron was sitting]. Maybe, heaven forbid, there are two powers."
>
> (*Babylonian Talmud*, "*Ḥagigah*," 15a)

With respect to our spatial understanding, the cognitive pinnacle we can access holds that consciousness is omnipresent and permeates all corners of existence. Such a conceptual reach is the highest degree that human reasoning can attain. An intermediate and conciliatory proposal with the separate "I" could establish that there is no experience or spatial coordinate devoid of consciousness. The retroprogressive process erodes conceptual solidity. What is clear becomes ambiguous, what is evident becomes enigmatic, and what is obvious becomes doubtful. But, in turn, what is ethereal becomes tangibile. Ultimate reality shows itself as everything: good and bad, beautiful and ugly, pleasure and suffering, attachment and hatred. Dichotomies only appear on the dual stage projected and sustained by a fragmented "I," but they dissolve within pure and immaculate consciousness.

The ego: a contraction in consciousness

The concept of the "I," understood as an autonomous entity, is a contraction in consciousness, a mechanism by which consciousness is confined and localized. It is evident that the experience of an apparently independent "I" is one of deficiency. This egoic phenomenon manifests itself in daily life as a feeling of chronic discontent and unfathomable dissatisfaction. Each egoic entity visualizes itself as a fragment, which inevitably culminates in feelings of imperfection, deficiency, and incompleteness.

Thus arises the incessant struggle of the ego to reach a state of fullness, or to cease being a part, aspiring to be integrated into something or someone that completes it. However, the desire is not for objects, events, individuals, or interactions, rather it wants to transcend its perceived limitations. The real desire behind its attempts to integrate with external phenomena is to remove limitations and return to its original state of primordial unity. However, it is a mistake to try to solve an inherently subjective problem with an objective solution.

Reality is undefinable

Attributing characteristics to something such as unlimitedness and indivisibility leads directly to its consideration as infinitude. However, infinitude presupposes a comparison with another finite factor. Such a comparison is unfeasible, since in reality there are no bounded elements. In other words, it is an impossible comparison because reality does not include elements of a finite nature. Therefore, it is an error to refer to ultimate reality or consciousness as unlimited and infinite, because it presupposes limited and finite components. This conception of reality as infinite, unlimited, and indivisible belongs to an intermediate stage. This stage's purpose is to overcome the opposing notion of reality as finite, limited, and divisible. Only when we overcome these presuppositions can we reject conceptual categorizations of an unlimited, infinite, and indivisible reality.

If reality is undefinable, we could say that reality is "nothing." However, by existing, this "nothingness" becomes an object of analysis, debate, and description. Therefore, this stage is not definitive, because a nothing that "is" is "relative nothing," since it includes two elements, "nothing" and "being," it loses its quality of inexistence.

Stage 4: From being "nothing" to "not being nothing"

The Retroprogressive Path of *teshuvah* returns us to the origin that was never abandoned. To elucidate our return to the primordial source, we must unravel the circumstances that brought us to where we are now and discern the initial deviation. Let us examine how pure consciousness, the One without a second, adopted an ontic human character. Adopting the vehicle of thought, it manifests as mind and with it, arise concepts, definitions, comparisons, analogies, and memorization, or as the *Tanya* allegorically describes it, sacred letters. Manifesting itself in the domain of sensation, it configures itself as form or corporeal entity. Lastly, in its perceptive ability, it reveals itself as the cosmos. This is the quintessence of cosmic creation. The totality of human experience is reduced to thoughts, sensations, and perceptions. Everything we have experienced or will experience is circumscribed to thoughts, sensations, and perceptions.

In the last stage, it is essential to understand that consciousness, in this whole process, never metamorphoses into something other than itself. Creation is thoughts, emotions, sensations, and perceptions; however, consciousness remains ever immutable. Only upon reaching this level is it revealed that consciousness encompasses the totality of reality. In this specific phase of the reverse process of *teshuvah*, the complete revelation of the omnipresence of consciousness is accessed. Divinity permeates all, it is everything in everyone, as the following verse says:

וְיָדַעְתָּ הַיּוֹם וַהֲשֵׁבֹתָ אֶל־לְבָבֶךָ כִּי ה' הוּא הָאֱלֹהִים בַּשָּׁמַיִם מִמַּעַל וְעַל־הָאָרֶץ מִתָּחַת אֵין עוֹד:

(דברים ד', ל"ט)

Acknowledge this day, and take it to heart, that the Lord is God in heaven above and on the earth below. There is nothing else.

(Deuteronomy, 4:39)

The verse does not suggest that consciousness encompasses the multiplicity of "everything and everyone," since epistemologically speaking, there are no concrete objects that can be perceived as "everything and everyone." The text rises to the peak of the retroprogressive process of *teshuvah* to clearly exclaim that "there is none other [besides God]." The assertion that God is everything could erroneously lead us to think of a multiplicity of concrete entities coexisting in a definite universe. This would erroneously imply that this divinity is an aggregation of objects that, in essence, have no real existence. The central argument lies on a more transcendental plane: consciousness is not reducible to discernible objects or finite entities. In reality, there are no objects that consciousness observes.

In its total and absolute solitude, this nothingness does not even share the presence of "being." It remains eternally in a state of complete nonexistence, as a nothingness that lacks existence, without being, or simply is not.

וְנִקְרָא יָחִיד. כַּיָּדוּעַ וּמְבֹאָר בְּכַמָּה דֻּכְתִּין דִּזְעֵיר אַנְפִּין נִקְרָא "אֶחָד הָאֱמֶת וְיֵשׁ זוּלָתוֹ" וְאַבָּא חָכְמָה הוּא בְּחִינַת "אֶחָד הָאֱמֶת אֵין זוּלָתוֹ" שֶׁבִּבְחִינָתוֹ הוּא בִּטּוּל הָעוֹלָמוֹת בְּיֵשׁוּתָן אֶל הָאַיִן וְהַיִּחוּד. אֲבָל בְּחִינַת יָחִיד הוּא שֶׁאֵין הָעוֹלָמוֹת עוֹלִין בְּשֵׁם כְּלָל לוֹמַר עֲלֵיהֶם שֶׁהֵן בְּטֵלִים בִּמְקוֹרָן, אֶלָּא הוּא לְבַדּוֹ הוּא הַנִּמְצָא בְּכָל צְפִיָּתוֹ שֶׁצּוֹפֶה וּמַבִּיט עַד סוֹף כָּל הַדּוֹרוֹת.

(רבי יצחק אייזיק הלוי אפשטיין מהומיל, חנה אריאל, בראשית, דף 217)

And [*Atik Yomin*, or "The ancient of days" which is the uppermost aspect or countenance of the Divine in '*Olam*

Ha'atzilut, or "The world of emanation"] is called *Yaḥid*, or "solitary." As it is known and explained in a few places, that *Ze'er Anpin*, (Lesser Countenance) [a lower countenance of the Divine in '*Olam Ha'atzilut*, which is closer to the human level] is called "The True One and presence of other," and *Aba Ḥochma* [a third countenance of the Divine, which is higher than *Ze'er Anpin* but below *Atik Yomin*] is called "The True One and absence of other" for in this level the worlds' "isness" is nullified in the face of nothingness and the unity. But the aspect of *Yaḥid* (solitary) is that in which the worlds would not even appear in thought, or called by name, so you could say that they are nullified, but He, alone is; in His complete watchfulness, He watches all the way through, to the end of times.

(Rabbi Yitzchak Isaac Halevi Epstein of Hamil, *Ḥanah Ari'el*, "*Genesis*," page 217)

Here, the One is broken down into three distinct approaches. The first is called *Eḥad veyesh zulato*, translated as "One and presence of otherness." This aspect acknowledges the One that is. The second approach is called *Eḥad ve'ein zulato*, or "One and absence of being or a One that is not," referring to the non-existent One. Finally, the third aspect is *yaḥid*, meaning "Alone or solitary," meaning solitude, or *levad*, in which nothing has ever happened, nor has anyone truly existed. This is a nothingness not in the sense of emptiness but of inaccessibility to the mind.

כְּתִיב "כִּי אֵל דֵּעוֹת ה'" (שמואל א' ב',ג'), וְיָדוּעַ הַפֵּרוּשׁ שֶׁשֵּׁם הוי"ה דִּזְעֵיר אַנְפִּין ב"ה יֵשׁ לוֹ שְׁנֵי דֵּעוֹת. דֵּעָה אַחַת הִיא שֶׁבּוֹרֵא הָעוֹלָם מֵאַיִן לְיֵשׁ: שֶׁלְּמַעְלָה הוּא הָאַיִן. כְּלוֹמַר, שֶׁכָּל שֹׁרֶשׁ הָעוֹלָמוֹת הַתַּחְתּוֹנִים הוּא אַיִן וָאֶפֶס בִּסְפִירוֹת עֶלְיוֹנוֹת די"ה הוי' צוּר עוֹלָמִים [...] וְזֶה כֹּחוֹ וּגְבוּרָתוֹ שֶׁל יוֹצֵר הַכֹּל ב"ה, שֶׁעוֹשֶׂה אֶת מָה שֶׁהִיא אַיִן – שֶׁיִּהְיֶה מְצִיאוּת, יֵשׁוּת גָּמוּר [...] עִנְיַן דֵּעָה תַּחְתּוֹנָה דִּזְעֵיר אַנְפִּין מֵאַיִן לְיֵשׁ. וְיֵשׁ עוֹד דֵּעָה עֶלְיוֹנָה בִּזְעֵיר אַנְפִּין וְהוּא: שֶׁלְּמַעְלָה דַּוְקָא הוּא הַיֵּשׁ וּלְמַטָּה הוּא הָאַיִן. כְּלוֹמַר גַּם בִּבְחִינַת יֵשׁוּתוֹ שֶׁנִּבְרָא – אֵין זֶה הַיֵּשׁוּת הַגָּלוּי בַּבְּרִיאָה עוֹלֶה בְּשֵׁם כְּלָל, אֶלָּא לְמַעְלָה הוּא יֵשׁוּתוֹ שֶׁל זֶה הַנִּבְרָא.

(רבי יצחק אייזיק הלוי אפשטיין מהומיל, חנה אריאל, בראשית, דף 217)

> It is written: "*ki el de'ot HaShem*," or "For the Lord is a God of knowledge(s)" (I Samuel, 2:3). [The verse uses the word *de'ot*, which means "knowledges," the plural of the word *da'at*, or "knowing or knowledge"]. A well-known explanation says that it is because there are two ways to know the divine manifestation of the name Yud-Hei-Vav-Hei (ה-ו-ה-י) as *Ze'eir Anpin*, (the "Lesser Countenance"); [a lower countenance of the Divine in '*Olam Ha'atzilut*, which is closer to the human level] Blessed be He. The first way to know Him, is that He is creating the world from *ain* to *yesh* (from nothingness into beingness, or from nothing to something). In this point of view, the *ain* (nothingness)," is above, which means that the very root of all the lower worlds [which is in the higher *sefirot* of Divinity], is seen in fact as naught and complete nothingness [...] and it is the power of the Creator of all, Blessed be He, that He transforms that which is nothingness (*ain*) into reality, or a complete something (*yesh*) [...] This knowledge of *Ze'er Anpin* is from the point of view of the lower. From nothingness into existence. The second way of knowing *Ze'er Anpin* is from the point of view of the high. In this point of view, the *yesh* (the real "existence"), is in fact, in the higher realms, and the *ain*, (the nothingness), is in the lower realms. This suggests that the existence of the manifested creation is not considered "existence," or *yesh*, at all but, in fact, the real existence [or beingness] of anything created is in the higher realms.
>
> (Rabbi Yitzḥak Isaac Halevi Epstein of Hamil, *Hanah Ariel*, "*Genesis*," page 217)

The One cannot be because by affirming that "the One is," a duality is immediately introduced: being and one. Therefore, the One is a non-existent One. The concept of *Ain*, representing the non-existent One, is the basis of Being and existence itself, bestowing even what it does not possess in an act of kindness and mercy. This form of generosity is the most authentic, for it is not about giving what one has in abundance, but about offering even what is not possessed.

וַיִּקְרָא אֱלֹהִים לַיַּבָּשָׁה אֶרֶץ וּלְמִקְוֵה הַמַּיִם קָרָא יַמִּים וַיַּרְא אֱלֹהִים כִּי טוֹב:
וַתּוֹצֵא הָאָרֶץ דֶּשֶׁא עֵשֶׂב מַזְרִיעַ זֶרַע לְמִינֵהוּ וְעֵץ עֹשֶׂה פְּרִי אֲשֶׁר זַרְעוֹ בוֹ
לְמִינֵהוּ וַיַּרְא אֱלֹהִים כִּי טוֹב:
וַיַּעַשׂ אֱלֹהִים אֶת שְׁנֵי הַמְּאֹרֹת הַגְּדֹלִים אֶת הַמָּאוֹר הַגָּדֹל לְמֶמְשֶׁלֶת הַיּוֹם וְאֶת
הַמָּאוֹר הַקָּטֹן לְמֶמְשֶׁלֶת הַלַּיְלָה וְאֵת הַכּוֹכָבִים:
וַיִּתֵּן אֹתָם אֱלֹהִים בִּרְקִיעַ הַשָּׁמָיִם לְהָאִיר עַל הָאָרֶץ:
וְלִמְשֹׁל בַּיּוֹם וּבַלַּיְלָה וּלֲהַבְדִּיל בֵּין הָאוֹר וּבֵין הַחֹשֶׁךְ וַיַּרְא אֱלֹהִים כִּי טוֹב:
וַיִּבְרָא אֱלֹהִים אֶת הַתַּנִּינִם הַגְּדֹלִים וְאֵת כָּל נֶפֶשׁ הַחַיָּה הָרֹמֶשֶׂת אֲשֶׁר שָׁרְצוּ
הַמַּיִם לְמִינֵהֶם וְאֵת כָּל עוֹף כָּנָף לְמִינֵהוּ וַיַּרְא אֱלֹהִים כִּי טוֹב:
וַיַּעַשׂ אֱלֹהִים אֶת חַיַּת הָאָרֶץ לְמִינָהּ וְאֶת הַבְּהֵמָה לְמִינָהּ וְאֵת כָּל רֶמֶשׂ הָאֲדָמָה
לְמִינֵהוּ וַיַּרְא אֱלֹהִים כִּי טוֹב:

(בראשית א', י', י"ב, ט"ז–י"ח, כ"א, כ"ה)

And God called the dry ground "land," and the gathered waters he called "seas." And God saw that it was good.
And the land produced vegetation: plants bearing seed according to their kinds and trees bearing fruit with seed in it according to their kinds. And God saw that it was good.
And God made the two great luminaries, the great luminary to govern the day and the small luminary to govern the night, and the stars.
And God set them in the firmament of the heavens to illuminate the earth.
And to govern the day and the night, and to separate light from darkness. And God saw that it was good.
And God created the leviathans, and every living creature that creeps, which the waters brought forth abundantly, after their kind, and every winged bird after its kind: and God saw that it was good.
And God created the animals of the land, after their kind, and all the insects of the land, after their kind. And God saw that it was good.

(Genesis, 1:10, 12, 16–18, 21, 25)

In the retroprogressive itinerary of *teshuvah*, we move from the notion of a distinct, separate personal identity to the recognition of our ontic unreality. From this void, the realization of being an entity part of an ontic whole emerges. Then there is access to the realization that there is no reality separate from the primordial essence, to ultimately awake to the authentic reality that there is no other than God or the One without being. Only God is.

אַתָּה הָרְאֵתָ לָדַעַת כִּי ה' הוּא הָאֱלֹהִים אֵין עוֹד מִלְּבַדּוֹ:
(דברים ד', ל"ה)

You have been shown to know that the Lord, He is God;
there is no more than only Him.
(Deuteronomy, 4:35)

In reality, there is nothing here, absolutely nothing, other than God...

Appendixes

Prabhuji

H.H. Avadhūta Bhaktivedānta Yogācārya
Śrī Ramakrishnananda Bābājī Mahārāja

About Prabhuji

Prabhuji is a faithful official member of Hinduism, as well as a universalist *Advaita* mystic. He combines his deep religious commitment with a remarkable artistic work as a writer and abstract painter. He is recognized by his line of disciplic succession as a realized master. As an *avadhūta*, a title conferred upon him in recognition of his state of realization, he has developed the Path of Retroprogressive Alignment, an original contribution rooted in the inclusive principles of *Sanātana-dharma* (the Hindu religion).

His solid training includes a doctorate in *Vaiṣṇava* philosophy, awarded by the prestigious Jiva Institute of Vedic Studies in Vrindavan, India, and a doctorate in Yogic philosophy earned at Yoga-Samskrutham University. These doctorates reaffirm his commitment to traditional teachings and his connection to the spiritual roots of the Hindu religion.

In 2011, with the blessings of his Gurudeva, he adopted the path of a secluded *bhajanānandī* and withdrew from society to lead the contemplative life of a hermit. Since then, he has been living as an independent Christian-Marian Hindu religious hermit. His days have been spent in solitude, praying, writing, painting, and meditating in silence and contemplation.

Prabhuji is the sole disciple of H.D.G. Avadhūta Śrī Brahmānanda Bābājī Mahārāja, who in turn is one of the closest and most intimate disciples of H.D.G. Avadhūta Śrī Mastarāma Bābājī Mahārāja.

Prabhuji was appointed as the successor of the lineage by his master, who conferred upon him the responsibility of continuing the sacred *paramparā* of *avadhūtas*, officially appointing him as guru and ordering him to serve as Ācārya successor under the name H.H. Avadhūta Bhaktivedānta Yogācārya Śrī Ramakrishnananda Bābājī Mahārāja.

Prabhuji is also a disciple of H.D.G. Bhakti-kavi Atulānanda Ācārya Mahārāja, who is a direct disciple of H.D.G. A.C. Bhaktivedānta Swami Prabhupāda. We could say that Gurudeva Atulānanda affectionately assumed the role of guide during his initial stage of learning, and because he was Prabhuji's first guru, he is considered the grandfather of Prabhuji Mission. For his part, Guru Mahārāja was Prabhuji's second and last guru and provided him with guidance during his advanced stage. Gurudeva acted as the primary educator at the dawn of his spiritual development, while Guru Mahārāja exercised with great diligence the role of master at the highest level, accompanying him until his realization.

Prabhuji's Hinduism is so broad, universal, and pluralistic that at times, while living up to his title of *avadhūta*, his lively and fresh teachings transcend the boundaries of all philosophies and religions, even his own. His teachings promote critical thinking and lead us to question statements that are usually accepted as true. They do not defend absolute truths but invite us to evaluate and question our own convictions. The essence of his syncretic vision, the Path of Retroprogressive Alignment, is self-awareness and the recognition of consciousness. For him, awakening at the level of consciousness, or the transcendence of the egoic phenomenon, is the next step in humanity's evolution.

Prabhuji was born on March 21, 1958, in Santiago, the capital of the Republic of Chile. When he was eight years old, he had a mystical experience that motivated his search for the Truth, or the Ultimate Reality. This transformed his life into an authentic inner and outer pilgrimage.

In his youth (18 years old), Prabhuji embraced the monastic discipline through long stays in various ashrams of different Hindu currents (*Gauḍīya* Vaishnavas, Advaita Vedanta, etc.) in Chile, Israel, and India. There, he underwent rigorous training within the Hindu religion. Immersed in the strict observance of religious life, he received a systematic education, following traditional methods of monastic teaching. His training included the in-depth study of sacred scriptures, the practice of austerities, the fulfillment of strict vows, and participation in prescribed rituals, all under the guidance of masters or gurus. Through this intensive discipline, he internalized the fundamental principles of Hindu monastic life, adopting its values, codes of conduct, and contemplative practices. This allowed him to learn the theory and also to incorporate the ideals that characterize the spirituality of Hinduism.

He has completely devoted his life to deepening the early transformative experience that marked the beginning of his process of retroevolution. He has dedicated more than fifty years to the exploration and practice of different religions, philosophies, paths of liberation, and spiritual disciplines. He has absorbed the teachings of great masters, shamans, priests, machis, shifus, roshis, shaykhs, daoshis, yogis, pastors, swamis, rabbis, kabbalists, monks, gurus, philosophers, sages, and saints whom he personally visited during his years of searching. He has lived in many places and traveled the world thirsting for Truth.

From an early age, Prabhuji noticed that the educational system prevented him from devoting himself to what was really important: learning about himself. He recognized that in the Western educational system of elementary schools, high schools, and universities he would not find what he wanted to learn. At the age of 11, he decided to stop attending conventional school and dedicated himself to autodidactic learning. Over time, he would become a serious critic of the current educational system.

Prabhuji is a recognized authority on Eastern wisdom. He is known for his erudition on the *Vaidika* and *Tāntrika* aspects of Hinduism and all branches of yoga (*jñāna*, *karma*, *bhakti*, *haṭha*, *rāja*, *kuṇḍalinī*, *tantra*, *mantra*, and others). He has an inclusive attitude toward all religions and is intimately familiar with Judaism, Christianity, Buddhism, Islam, Sufism, Taoism, Sikhism, Jainism, Shintoism, Bahaism, Shamanism, and the Mapuche religion, among others.

During his stay in the Middle East, his esteemed friend and scholar, Kamil Shchadi, imparted profound knowledge about the Druze faith to him. He also benefited from his closeness to another illustrious acquaintance, the revered and wise Salach Abbas, who helped him to reach a thorough understanding of Islam and Sufism. He studied Theravada Buddhism personally from the Venerable W.

Medhananda Thero of Sri Lanka. He studied Christian theology in depth with H.H. Monsignor Iván Larraín Eyzaguirre at the Veracruz Church in Santiago de Chile and with Mr. Héctor Luis Muñoz, who holds a degree in theology from the Universidad Católica de la Santísima Concepción, Chile.

His curiosity for Western thought led him to venture into the field of philosophy in all its different branches. He specialized in Transcendental Phenomenology and the Phenomenology of Religion. He had the privilege of studying intensively for several years with his uncle Jorge Balazs, philosopher, researcher, and author, who wrote *The world upside-down* under his pen name Gyuri Akos. He studied privately for many years with Dr. Jonathan Ramos, a renowned philosopher, historian, and university professor graduated from the Universidad Católica de Salta, Argentina. He also studied with Dr. Alejandro Cavallazzi Sánchez, who holds an undergraduate degree in philosophy from the Universidad Panamericana, a master's degree in philosophy from the Universidad Iberoamericana, and a doctorate in philosophy from the Universidad Nacional Autónoma de México (UNAM). He also studied privately with Santiago Sánchez Borboa, who holds a PhD in Philosophy from the University of Arizona, USA.

His profound studies, his masters' blessings, his research into the sacred scriptures, and his vast teaching experience have earned him international recognition in the field of religion and spirituality.

Prabhuji's spiritual quest led him to study with masters from different traditions and to travel far from his native Chile, to places as distant as Israel, Brazil, India, and the United States. He is fluent in Spanish, Hebrew, Portuguese, and English. During his stay in Israel, he furthered his Hebrew and Aramaic studies in order to broaden his knowledge of the sacred scriptures. He studied other languages intensively, such as Sanskrit with Dr. Naga Kanya Kumari Garipathi, from Osmania University in Hyderabad (India); Pali at the Oxford Center for Buddhist Studies; and Latin and Ancient Greek with Professor Ariel Lazcano and later with Javier Alvarez, who holds a degree in Classical Philology from the University of Seville.

Prabhuji's paternal grandfather was a prominent senior police sergeant in Chile, who raised his son, Yosef Har-Zion ZT "L, under strict discipline. Affected by that upbringing, Yosef decided to raise his own children in an environment characterized by complete freedom and unconditional love.

In this context, Prabhuji grew up without experiencing any external pressure. From an early age, his father manifested constant love, independent of academic performance or external achievements. When Prabhuji decided to leave school to pursue his inner quest, his family responded with deep respect and acceptance. Yosef fully supported his son's interests, encouraging him in every step of his search for Truth.

From the age of ten, Yosef shared with Prabhuji wisdom from Hebrew spirituality and Western philosophy, fostering an environment conducive to daily discussions that often lasted late into the night. In essence, Prabhuji embodied the ideal of freedom and unconditional love that his father had striven to cultivate within the family.

At an early age and on his own initiative, Prabhuji began to practice karate and study philosophy and religion. During his adolescence, no one interfered with his decisions. At the age of 15, he established a deep, intimate, and long friendship with the famous Uruguayan writer and poet Blanca Luz Brum, who was his neighbor on Merced Street in Santiago, Chile. He traveled throughout Chile in search of wise and interesting people to learn from. In southern Chile, he met machis who taught him about the rich Mapuche spirituality and shamanism.

In June 1975, at the young age of 17, he earned his first certification as a Yoga Teacher under H.H. Śrī Brahmānanda Sarasvatī (Rāmamurti S. Mishra, M.D.), the founder of the World Yoga University, the Yoga Society of New York, and the Ananda Ashram.

Two great masters contributed to Prabhuji's retroprogressive process. In 1976, he met his first guru, H.D.G Bhakti-kavi Atulānanda Ācārya Swami, whom he called Gurudeva. In those days, Gurudeva was a young *brahmacārī* who held the position of president of the ISKCON temple at Eyzaguirre 2404, Puente Alto, Santiago, Chile. Years later, he gave Prabhuji his first initiation,

Brahminical initiation, and finally, Prabhuji formally accepted the sacraments of the holy order of *sannyāsa*, becoming a monk of the Brahma Gauḍīya Saṁpradāya. Gurudeva connected him to the devotion to Kṛṣṇa. He imparted to him the wisdom of bhakti yoga and instructed him in the practice of the *māhā-mantra* and the study of the holy scriptures.

In 1980, Prabhuji received the blessings of H.G. Mother Krishnabai, the famous disciple of S.D.G. Swami Rāmdās. In 1984, he learned and began to practice Maharishi Mahesh Yogi's Transcendental Meditation technique. In 1988, he took the *kriyā-yoga* course on Paramahaṁsa Yogānanda. After two years, he was officially initiated into the technique of *kriyā-yoga* by the Self-Realization Fellowship. In 1982 he received *dikṣā* from H.H. Kīrtanānanda Swami, disciple of Śrīla Prabhupāda, who also gave him his second initiation in 1991 and *sannyāsa* initiation in 1993.

Prabhuji wanted to confirm the sacraments of the holy order of *sannyāsa* also within the Advaita Vedanta lineage. His *sannyāsa-dīkṣā*, or sacraments, were confirmed on August 11, 1995, by H.H. Swami Jyotirmayānanda Sarasvatī, founder of the Yoga Research Foundation and disciple of H.H. Swami Śivānanda Sarasvatī of Rishikesh.

In 1996, Prabhuji met his second guru, H.D.G. Avadhūta Śrī Brahmānanda Bābājī Mahārāja, in Rishikesh, India. Guru Mahārāja, as Prabhuji would call him, revealed that his own master, H.D.G. Avadhūta Śrī Mastarāma Bābājī Mahārāja, had told him years before he died that a person would come from the West and request to be his disciple. He commanded him to accept only that particular seeker. When he asked how he would identify this person, Mastarāma Bābājī replied, "You will recognize him by his eyes. You must accept him because he will be the continuation of the lineage." From his first meeting with young Prabhuji, Guru Mahārāja recognized him and officially initiated him as his disciple. For Prabhuji, this initiation marked the beginning of the most intense and mature stage of his retroprogressive process. Under the guidance of Guru Mahārāja, he studied Advaita Vedanta and deepened his meditation. Since his guru was a great devotee of Śrī Rāmakṛṣṇa Paramahaṁsa and Śāradā Devī, Prabhuji desired to be initiated into this disciplic lineage. He sought initiation from Swami Swahananda (1921–2012), minister and spiritual leader of the Vedanta Society of Southern California from 1976 to 2012. Swami Swahananda was a disciple of Swami Vijñānānanda, a direct disciple of Rāmakṛṣṇa. In 2008, Swami Swahananda initiated him, granting him both *dīkṣā* and the blessings of Śrī Rāmakṛṣṇa and the Divine Mother.

Guru Mahārāja guided Prabhuji until he officially bestowed upon him the sacraments of the sacred order of *avadhūtas*. In March 2011, H.D.G. Avadhūta Śrī Brahmānanda Bābājī Mahārāja ordered Prabhuji, on behalf of his own master, to accept the responsibility of continuing the lineage of *avadhūtas*. With this title, Prabhuji is the official representative of the line of this disciplic succession for the present generation.

Besides his *dikṣā-gurus*, Prabhuji studied with important spiritual and religious personalities, such as H.H. Swami Yajñavālkyānanda, H.H. Swami Dayānanda Sarasvatī, H.H. Swami Viṣṇu Devānanda Sarasvatī, H.H. Swami Jyotirmayānanda Sarasvatī, H.H. Swami Kṛṣṇānanda Sarasvatī from the Divine Life Society, H.H. Ma Yoga Śakti, H.H. Swami Pratyagbodhānanda, H.H. Swami Mahādevānanda, H.H. Swami Swahānanda of the Ramakrishna Mission, H.H. Swami Adhyātmānanda, H.H. Swami Svarūpananda, and H.H. Swami Viditātmānanda of the Arsha Vidya Gurukulam, while the wisdom of tantra was awakened in Prabhuji by H.G. Mātājī Rīnā Śarmā in India.

In Vrindavan, he studied the bhakti yoga path in depth with H.H. Narahari Dāsa Bābājī Mahārāja, disciple of H.H. Nityānanda Dāsa Bābājī Mahārāja of Vraja. He also studied bhakti yoga with various disciples of His Divine Grace A.C. Bhaktivedānta Swami Prabhupāda: H.H. Kapīndra Swami, H.H. Paramadvaiti Mahārāja, H.H. Jagajīvana Dāsa, H.H. Tamāla Kṛṣṇa Gosvāmī, H.H. Bhagavān Dāsa Mahārāja, H.H. Kīrtanānanda Swami, among others.

Prabhuji has been honored with various titles and diplomas by many leaders of prestigious religious and spiritual institutions in India. He was given the honorable title Kṛṣṇa Bhakta by H.H. Swami Viṣṇu Devānanda (the only title of Bhakti Yoga given by Swami Viṣṇu), disciple of H.H. Swami Śivānanda Sarasvatī and the founder of the Sivananda Organization. He was given the title Bhaktivedānta by H.H. B.A. Paramadvaiti Mahārāja, the founder of Vrinda. He was given the title Yogācārya by H.H. Swami Viṣṇu Devānanda, the Paramanand Institute of Yoga Sciences and Research of Indore, India, the International Yoga Federation, the Indian Association of Yoga, and the Śrī Shankarananda Yogashram of Mysore, India. He received the respectable title Śrī Śrī Rādhā Śyam Sunder Pāda-Padma Bhakta Śiromaṇi directly from H.H. Satyanārāyaṇa Dāsa Bābājī Mahant of the Chatu Vaiṣṇava Saṁpradāya.

Prabhuji dedicated more than forty years to studying hatha yoga with prestigious masters of classical and traditional yoga, such as H.H. Bapuji, H.H. Swami Viṣṇu Devānanda Sarasvatī, H.H. Swami Jyotirmayānanda Sarasvatī, H.H. Swami Satchidānanda Sarasvatī, H.H. Swami Vignānānanda Sarasvatī, and Śrī Madana-mohana.

He attended several systematic hatha yoga teacher training courses at prestigious institutions until he achieved the level of Master Ācārya. He has completed studies at the following institutions: World Yoga University, the Sivananda Yoga Vedanta, the Ananda Ashram, the Yoga Research Foundation, the Integral Yoga Academy, the Patanjala Yoga Kendra, the Ma Yoga Shakti International Mission, the Prana Yoga Organization, the Rishikesh Yoga Peeth, the Swami Sivananda Yoga Research Center, and the Swami Sivananda Yogasana Research Center.

Prabhuji is a member of the Indian Association of Yoga, Yoga Alliance ERYT 500 and YACEP, the International Association of Yoga Therapists, and the International Yoga Federation. In 2014, the International Yoga Federation honored him with the position of Honorary Member of the World Yoga Council.

His interest in the complex anatomy of the human body led him to study chiropractic at the prestigious Institute of Health of the Back and Extremities in Tel Aviv, Israel. In 1993, he received a diploma from Dr. Sheinerman, the founder and director of the institute. Later, he earned a massage therapy diploma at the Academy of Western Galilee. The knowledge he acquired in this field deepened his understanding of hatha yoga and contributed to the creation of his own method.

Retroprogressive Yoga is the result of Prabhuji's efforts to improve his practice and teaching methods. It is a system based especially on the teachings of his gurus and the sacred scriptures. Prabhuji has systematized various traditional yoga techniques to create a methodology suitable for Western audiences. Retroprogressive Yoga aspires to the experience of our authentic nature, promoting balance, health, and flexibility through proper diet, cleansing techniques, preparations (*āyojanas*), sequences (*vinyāsas*), postures (*āsanas*), breathing exercises (*prāṇayama*), relaxation (*śavāsana*), meditation (*dhyāna*), and exercises with locks (*bandhas*) and seals (*mudras*) to direct and empower *prāṇa*.

Since his childhood and throughout his life, Prabhuji has been an enthusiastic admirer, student, and practitioner of classic karate-do. From the age of 13, he studied different styles in Chile, such as kenpo with Sensei Arturo Petit and kung-fu, but specialized in the most traditional Japanese style of shotokan. He received the rank of black belt (third dan) from Shihan Kenneth Funakoshi (ninth dan). He also learned from Sensei Takahashi (seventh dan) and Sensei Masataka Mori (ninth dan). Additionally, he practiced shorin ryu style with Sensei Enrique Daniel Welcher (seventh dan), who granted him the rank of black belt (second dan). Through karate-do, he delved into Buddhism and gained additional knowledge about the physics of motion. He is a member of Funakoshi's Shotokan Karate Association.

Prabhuji grew up in an artistic environment and his love of painting began to develop in his childhood. His father, the renowned Chilean painter Yosef Har-Zion ZT"L, motivated him to devote himself to art. He learned with the famous Chilean painter Marcelo Cuevas. Prabhuji's abstract paintings reflect the depths of the spirit.

Since he was a young boy, Prabhuji has been especially drawn to postal stamps, postcards, mailboxes, postal transportation systems, and all mail-related activities. He has taken every opportunity to visit post offices in different cities and countries. He has delved into the study of philately, the field of collecting, sorting, and studying postage stamps. This passion led him to become a professional philatelist, a stamp distributor authorized by the American Philatelic Society, and a member of the following societies: the Royal Philatelic Society London, the Royal Philatelic Society of Victoria, the United States Stamp Society, the Great Britain Philatelic Society, the American Philatelic Society, the Society of Israel Philatelists, the Society for Hungarian Philately, the National Philatelic Society UK, the Fort Orange Stamp Club, the American Stamp Dealers Association, the US Philatelic Classics Society, Filabras - Associação dos Filatelistas Brasileiros, and the Collectors Club of NYC.

Based on his extensive knowledge of philately, theology, and Eastern philosophy, Prabhuji created "Meditative Philately" or "Philatelic Yoga," a spiritual practice that uses philately as the basis for practicing attention, concentration, observation, and meditation. It is inspired by the ancient Hindu mandala meditation and it can lead the practitioner to elevated states of consciousness, deep relaxation, and concentration that fosters the recognition of consciousness. Prabhuji wrote his thesis on this new type of yoga, "Meditative Philately," attracting the interest of the Indian academic community due to its innovative way of connecting meditation with different hobbies and activities. For this thesis, he was honored with a PhD in Yogic Philosophy from Yoga-Samskrutham University.

For more than 20 years, Prabhuji lived in Israel, where he furthered his studies of Judaism. One of his main teachers and sources of inspiration was Rabbi Shalom Dov Lifshitz ZT"L, whom he met in 1997. This great saint guided him for several years along the intricate paths of the Torah and Hassidism. He personally taught him Tanakh, Talmud, Midrash, Shulchan Aruch, Mishneh Torah, Tanya, Kabbalah and Zohar. The two developed a very close relationship. Prabhuji also studied the Talmud with Rabbi Raphael Rapaport Shlit"a (Ponovich), Hassidism with Rabbi Israel Lifshitz Shlit"a, and the Torah with Rabbi Daniel Sandler Shlit"a. Prabhuji is a great devotee of Rabbi Mordechai Eliyahu ZT"L, who personally blessed him.

Prabhuji visited the United States in 2000 and during his stay in New York, he realized that it was the most appropriate place to found a religious organization. He was particularly attracted by the pluralism and respectful attitude of American society toward freedom of religion. He was impressed by the deep respect of both the public and the government for religious minorities. After consulting his masters and requesting their blessings, Prabhuji relocated to the United States. In 2003, the Prabhuji Mission was born, a Hindu church aimed at preserving Prabhuji's universal and pluralistic vision of Hinduism and his Path of Retroprogressive Alignment.

Although he did not seek to attract followers, for 15 years (1995–2010), Prabhuji considered the requests of a few people who approached him asking to become his monastic disciples. Those who chose to see Prabhuji as their spiritual master voluntarily accepted vows of poverty and life-long dedication to spiritual practice (*sadhāna*), religious devotion (bhakti), and selfless service (*seva*). Although Prabhuji no longer accepts new disciples, he continues to guide the small group of monastic disciples of the contemplative Ramakrishnananda Monastic Order that he founded.

According to Prabhuji, the quest for the Self is individual, solitary, personal, private, and intimate. It is not a collective endeavor to be undertaken through organized, institutional, or communitarian religiosity. Since 2011, Prabhuji has disagreed with spirituality practiced in a social, communal, or collective manner. Therefore, he does not proselytize or preach, nor does he try to persuade, convince, or make anyone change their perspective, philosophy, or religion. His message does not promote collective spirituality, but individual inner search.

In 2011, Prabhuji founded the Avadhutashram (monastery) in the Catskills Mountains in upstate New York, USA. The Avadhutashram is his hermitage, the residence of the monastic disciples of the Ramakrishnananda Order, and the headquarters of the Prabhuji Mission and the Academy of Retroprogressive Yoga, in which Prabhuji personally teaches his method of yoga to disciples and students, without departing from his hermit life. The ashram organizes humanitarian projects such as the Prabhuji Food Distribution Program and the Prabhuji Toy Distribution Program. Prabhuji operates various humanitarian projects, inspired in his experience that serving the part is serving the Whole.

Prabhuji has delegated the choice to his disciples between keeping his teachings exclusively within the monastic order or spreading his message for the public benefit. Upon the explicit request of his disciples, Prabhuji has agreed to have his books published and his lectures disseminated, as long as this does not compromise his privacy and his life as a hermit.

In 2022, Prabhuji founded the Institute of Retroprogressive Alignment. Here, his most senior disciples can systematically share his teachings and message through video conferences. The institute offers support and help for a deeper understanding of Prabhuji's teachings.

Prabhuji is a respected member of the American Philosophical Association, the American Association of Philosophy Teachers, the American Association of University Professors, the Southwestern Philosophical Society, the Authors Guild, the National Writers Union, PEN America, the International Writers Association, the National Association of Independent Writers and Editors, the National Writers Association, the Alliance Independent Authors, and the Independent Book Publishers Association.

Prabhuji's vast literary contribution includes books in Spanish, English, and Hebrew, such as *Kundalini Yoga: The Power is in you, What is, as it is, Bhakti-Yoga: The Path of Love, Tantra: Liberation in the World, Experimenting with the Truth, Advaita Vedanta: Be the Self, Yoga: union with reality,* commentaries on the *Īśāvāsya Upanishad and the Diamond Sūtra, I am that I am, The Symbolic turn, Being, Questioning your answers: Philosophy as a question, Beyond answers: Philosophy in the eternal quest, Phenomenology of the sacred: Foundations for a Retroprogressive Phenomenology, and Discovering the Last God.*

The term prabhuji

by H.G. Swami Ramananda

Several years ago, some disciples, followers and friends of His Holiness Avadhūta Bhaktivedānta Yogācārya Śrī Ramakrishnananda Bābājī Mahārāja, opted to refer to him as Prabhuji. In this article, I would like to clarify the deep meaning of this Sanskrit term. The word *prabhu* in Sanskrit means "a master, lord or a king" and it is applied in the scriptures to God and to the Guru.

Like many words in the Sanskrit language, the word is actually made of some components, and understanding its etymology will lead us to discover its various meanings. The word *prabhu* is a combination of the root *bhu* which means "to become, to exist, to be, to live" and the prefix *pra*, which can mean "forth, or forward" and which then, when attached to *bhu* would mean "one who causes to exist, who gives life, from whom life emanates, that which sustains or maintains."

The prefix *pra* can also mean "very much, or supremacy," and then when attached to the root *bhu* would mean "to be the master, to rule over."

The suffix *jī* is an honorific title in Hindi and other Indian languages. It is added after the names of Gods and esteemed personalities to show respect and reverence.

As manifestations of the Divine, great *ṛṣis,* or 'seers' and gurus are also called as *prabhus*. For example, the sage Nārada is addressing the *ṛṣi* Vyasadeva as prabhu:

जिज्ञासितमधीतं च ब्रह्म यत्तत्सनातनम् ।
तथापि शोचस्यात्मानमकृतार्थ इव प्रभो ॥

jijñāsitam adhītaṁ ca
brahma yat tat sanātanam
tathāpi śocasy ātmānam
akṛtārtha iva prabho

You have fully delineated the subject of impersonal Brahman as well as the knowledge derived therefrom. Why should you be despondent in spite of all this, thinking that you are undone, my dear master (*prabhu*)?

(*Bhāgavata Purana*, 1.5.4)

Mahārāja Parīkṣit addresses Śukadeva as *prabhu* when he approaches the sage to seek spiritual guidance, thus accepting him as his guru.

यच्छ्रोतव्यमथो जप्यं यत्कर्तव्यं नृभिः प्रभो ।
स्मर्तव्यं भजनीयं वा ब्रूहि यद्वा विपर्ययम् ॥

yac chrotavyam atho japyaṁ
yat kartavyaṁ nṛbhiḥ prabho
smartavyaṁ bhajanīyaṁ vā
brūhi yad vā viparyayam

O prabhu, please let me know what a man should hear, chant, remember and worship, and also what he should not do. Please explain all this to me.

(*Bhāgavata Purana*, 1.19.38)

THE TERM *AVADHŪTA*

This is an excerpt from the book *Sannyāsa Darśana* by Swami Niranjanānanda Sarasvatī, a disciple of Paramahaṁsa Swami Satyānanda.

Stages of *sannyāsāvadhūta*

"The *avadhūta* represents the pinnacle of spiritual evolution; none is superior to him. *Avadhūta* means 'one who is immortal' (*akṣara*) and who has totally discarded worldly ties. He is really Brahman itself. He has realized he is pure intelligence and is not concerned about the six frailties of human birth, namely: sorrow, delusion, old age, death, hunger, and thirst. He has shaken off all bondage of the experimental world and roams freely like a child, a madman or one possessed by spirits.

He may be with or without clothes. He wears no distinctive emblem of any order. He has no desire to sleep, beg, or bathe. He views his body as a corpse and subsists on the food that comes to him from all classes. He does not interpret the *śāstras* or the Vedas. For him, nothing is righteous or unrighteous, holy or unholy.

He is free from karma. The karmas of this life and past lives are all burned out, and due to the absence of *kartṛtva* (the doer) and *bhoktṛtva* (the desire for enjoyment), no future karmas are created. Only the *prārabdha-karmas* (unalterable) that have already begun to operate will affect his body, helping to sustain it, but his mind will remain unaffected. He will live in this world until the *prārabdha-karmas* are extinguished, and then his body will fall. Then he is said to attain *videhamukti* (the state beyond body consciousness).

Such a liberated soul never returns to the embodied state. He is not born again; he is immortal. He has achieved the final aim of being born in this world."

The *Bṛhad-avadhūta Upanishad* reads as follows: "The *avadhūta* is so called because he is immortal; he is the greatest; he has discarded worldly ties, and he is alluded to in the meaning of the sentence 'Thou art That'."

His Divine Grace Śrīla Bhakti Ballabh Tīrtha Mahārāja in his article entitled "Pariṣads: Śrīla Vamśi das Bābājī" wrote: "He was a *Paramahaṁsa Vaiṣṇava* who acted in the manner of an *avadhūta.* The word *avadhūta* refers to one who has shaken off from himself all worldly feelings and obligations. He does not care for social conventions, especially the *varṇāśrama-dharma*, that is, he is quite eccentric in his behavior. Nityānanda Prabhu is often characterized as an *avadhūta*."

From the foreword to Dattātreya's *Avadhūta-gītā*, translated and annotated by Swami Aśokānanda: "The *Avadhūta-gītā* is a Vedanta text representing extreme Advaita or non-dualism. It is attributed to Dattātreya, who is looked upon as an Incarnation of God. Unfortunately, we possess no historical data concerning when or where he was born, how long he lived, or how he arrived at the knowledge disclosed in the text.

Avadhūta means a liberated soul, one who has 'passed away from' or 'shaken off' all worldly attachments and cares and has attained a spiritual state equivalent to the existence of God. Although *avadhūta* naturally implies renunciation, it includes an additional and even higher state that is neither attachment nor detachment, but is beyond both. An *avadhūta* feels no need to observe any rules, whether secular or religious. He seeks nothing and avoids nothing. He has neither knowledge nor ignorance. Having realized that he is the infinite Self, he lives in that vivid realization."

Swami Vivekānanda, one of the greatest advaitins of all times, often quoted this *Gītā*. He once said, "Men like the one who wrote this song keep religion alive. They have experienced. They care for nothing, and feel nothing done to the body; they don't care for heat, cold, danger, or anything else. They sit still, enjoying the bliss of the Ātman, and even if embers burn their bodies, they do not feel them."

The *Avadhūta Upanishad* is number 79 in the *Muktikā* canon of Upanishads. It is a *Sannyāsa Upanishad* associated with the Black (Kṛṣṇa) Yajur-veda: "One who has transcended the *varṇāśrama* system and has always established in himself, that yogi, who is above the *varṇāśrama* divisions, is called *avadhūta*." (*Avadhūta Upanishad*, 2).

The *Brahma-nirvāṇa Tantra* book describes how to identify *avadhūtas* of the following types:

Bramhāvadhūta: An *avadhūta* by birth, who appears in any cast of society and is completely indifferent to the world or worldly matters.

Śaivāvadhūta: *Avadhūtas* who have taken to the renounced order of life or *sannyāsa*, often with long matted hair (*jaṭa*), or who dress in the manner of Shaivites and spend almost all of their time in trance *samādhi*, or meditation.

Virāvadhūta: This person looks like a *sadhū* who has put red-colored sandal paste on his body and wears saffron-colored clothes. His hair is very well grown and is normally furling in the wind. They wear around their necks a *rudrākṣa-mālā* or a chain of bones. They carry a wooden stick, or *daṇḍa*, in their hand, and additionally always carry an axe (*paraśu*) or an *ḍamaru* (small drum) with them.

Kulāvadhūta: These people are supposed to have taken the Kaul *Saṁpradāya* initiation. It is very difficult to recognize these people as they do not wear any outward signs that can identify them from others. The specialty of these people is that they stay and live like normal people. They may show themselves in the form of kings or family men.

The *Nātha Saṁpradāya* is a form of *Avadhūta-pantha* (sect). In this *Saṁpradāya*, Guru and yoga are of extreme importance. Therefore, the most important book of this *Saṁpradāya* is the *Avadhūta-gītā*. Śrī Gorakṣanāth is considered the highest form of the *avadhūta* state.

The nature of *avadhūta* is the subject of the *Avadhūta-gītā*, traditionally attributed to Dattātreya.

According to Bipin Joshi, the main characteristics of an *avadhūta* are: "He who is a sinless philosopher and has cast off the shackles of ignorance (*ajñāna*). He who lives in a stateless state and relishes the experience all the time. He revels in this blissful state, unperturbed by the material world. In this unique state, the *avadhūta* is neither awake nor in deep sleep; there is no sign of life or death. It is a state defying all descriptions. It is the state of infinite bliss, which a finite language is incapable of describing. It can only be intuited purely by our intellect. A state that is neither truth nor non-truth, neither existence nor nonexistence. He who has realized his identity with the imperishable, who possesses incomparable excellence, who has shaken off the bonds of *saṁsāra* and never deviates from his goal. That thou art (*tat tvam asi*), and other upanishadic statements, are ever present in the mind of such an enlightened soul. That sage who is rooted in the plenary experience of 'Verily, I am Brahman (*ahaṁ Brahmāsmi*)', 'All this is Brahman (*sarvaṁ khalvidaṁ brahma*)', and that '…there is no plurality, I and God are one and the same…', etc. Supported by the personal experience of such Vedic statements, he moves freely in a state of total bliss. Such a person is a renunciant, liberated, *avadhūta*, yogi, paramahamsa, *brāhmaṇa*."

From Wikipedia, the free encyclopedia:

Avadhūta is a Sanskrit term used in Indian religions to refer to mystics or antinomian saints who are beyond ego-consciousness, duality, and common worldly concerns, and act without consideration of standard social etiquette. Such personalities "roam free as a child on the face of the Earth." An *avadhūta* does not identify with his mind or body or 'names and forms' (Sanskrit: *nāma-rūpa*). Such a person is considered pure consciousness (Sanskrit: *caitanya*) in human form.

Avadhūtas play a significant role in the history, origins, and rejuvenation of a number of traditions such as yoga, Advaita Vedanta, Buddhist, and bhakti *paraṁparās* even as they are released from standard observances. *Avadhūtas* are the voice of the *avadhūti*, the channel that resolves the dichotomy of *Vāmācāra* and *Dakṣiṇācāra* or "left and right-handed traditions." An *avadhūta* may or may not continue to practice religious rites as long as they are free from sectarian ritual observance and affiliation.

The Monier Williams Sanskrit dictionary defines the term *avadhūta* as follows: "अवधूत / अव-धूत – one who has shaken off from himself worldly feelings and obligations."

From *Hinduism, an alphabetical guide* by Roshen Dalal

Avadhūta

A term for a liberated soul, one who has renounced the world. Totally beyond all that is, an *avadhūta* follows no rules, no fixed practices, and has no need to follow conventional norms. There are several texts dealing with the life and nature of an *avadhūta*. In the *Avadhūta Upanishad*, the Ṛṣi Dattātreya describes the nature of the *avadhūta*. Such a person is immortal, has discarded all worldly ties, and is always full of bliss. One of its verses states: "Let thought contemplate Viṣṇu, or let it be dissolved in the bliss of Brahman. I, the witness, do nothing, nor do I cause anything to be done." (v.28)

The *Turīyātīta Avadhūta Upanishad* contains a description of the *avadhūta* who has reached the state of consciousness beyond the *turīya*. In this state, a person is pure, detached and totally free. An *avadhūta* who has reached this level does not chant mantras or practice rituals, wears no caste marks, and is finished with all religious and secular duties. He wears no clothes and eats whatever comes his way. He wanders alone, observing silence, and is totally absorbed in non-duality. The *Avadhūta-gītā* has similar descriptions.

The *Uddhava-gītā*, which is part of the *Bhāgavata Purāṇa*, describes an *avadhūta* who learned from all aspects of life and was at home anywhere in the world. The term *avadhūta* can be applied to any liberated person, but it also refers specifically to a *sannyāsa* sect.

Avadhūta Upanishad

Avadhūta Upanishad is a small Upanishad consisting of about 32 mantras. It falls under the category of the *Sannyāsa Upanishads* and is a part of Kṛṣṇa Yajurveda. The *Avadhūta Upanishad* takes the form of a dialogue between Dattātreya and Ṛṣi Saṁkṛti.

One day Ṛṣi Saṁkṛti asks Dattātreya the following questions: "Who is an *avadhūta*?; What is his state?; What are the signs of the *avadhūta*?; How does he live?"

The following are the answers given by the compassionate Dattātreya.

Who is an *avadhūta*?

The *avadhūta* is so called because he is beyond any decay; he lives freely according to his will, he destroys the bondage of worldly desires, and his only goal is That thou Art (*tat tvam asi*).

The *avadhūta* goes far beyond all the castes (such as *brāhmaṇa*, *vaiśya*, *kṣatrya*, and *śūdra*) and *Āśramas* (such as *brāmhacaryā*, *gṛhastha*, *vānaprastha*, and *sannyāsa*). He is the highest Yogi who is established in a constant state of self-realization.

What is his state?

An *avadhūta* always enjoys supreme bliss. The divine joy represents his head, happiness is his right wing, ecstasy represents his left wing, and bliss is his very nature. The life of an *avadhūta* shows extreme detachment.

What are the signs of *avadhūta*? How does he live?

An *avadhūta* lives according to his own will. He may wear clothes or go naked. For him, there is no difference between *dharma* or *adharma*, sacrifice or non-sacrifice, because he is beyond these aspects. He performs inner sacrifice and that forms their *aśvamedha-yajña*. He is a great yogi who remains unaffected even when engaged in worldly objects. He remains pure.

The ocean accepts water from all the rivers but remains unchanged. Similarly, an *avadhūta* is unaffected by worldly objects. He is always at peace and (like the ocean), all his desires are absorbed in this supreme peace.

For an *avadhūta* there is no birth or death, no bondage or liberation. He may have performed various actions for the sake of liberation, but they become history once he becomes an *avadhūta*. He is always satisfied. Others wander to fulfill their desires. But an *avadhūta*, being already satisfied, does not run after any desire. Others perform various rituals for the sake of heaven, but an *avadhūta* is already established in the omnipresent state and hence needs no rituals.

Other qualified teachers spend time teaching the scriptures (Vedas) but *avadhūta* goes beyond those activities, because he has no actions. He doesn't have any desire to sleep, beg (*bhikṣa*), bathe, or clean.

An *avadhūta* is always free from doubt, and since he is always in union with the supreme reality, he does not even need to meditate. Meditation is for those people who are not yet one with God, but an *avadhūta* is always in the state of union and therefore does not need to meditate.

Those who are after *karmas* (actions) are filled with *vāsanās*. These *vāsanās* haunt them even when they finish their *prārabdha-karma*. Ordinary men meditate because they wish to fulfill their desires. However, an *avadhūta* always stays away from that trap. His mind is beyond mental destruction and *samādhi*. Mental destruction as well as *samādhi* are possibly modifications of the mind. The *avadhūta* is already eternal and hence, there is nothing to attain for him.

Following worldly duties is like an arrow released from a bow, i.e. it cannot be stopped from giving good or bad fruits causing a cycle of action–reaction. However, an *avadhūta* is not a doer at any level and is not engaged in any action.

Having attained such a stage of detachment, an *avadhūta* remains unaffected even if he follows a way of life as prescribed by the scriptures. Even if he engages in *actions* such as worshipping God, bathing, begging, etc., he remains unattached to them. He lives as a witness and therefore does not perform any action.

An *avadhūta* can clearly see Brahman before his eyes. He is free from ignorance or *māyā*. He has no actions left to be performed and nothing left to achieve. He is totally satisfied and there is no one else with whom he can be compared.

नलिनी नालिनी नासे गन्धः सौरभ उच्यते ।
घ्राणोऽवधूतो मुख्यास्यं विपणो वाग्रसविद्रसः ॥

nalinī nālinī nāse
gandhaḥ saurabha ucyate
ghrāṇo 'vadhūto mukhyāsyaṁ
vipaṇo vāg rasavid rasaḥ

The two doors called Nalinī and Nālinī are to be known as the two nostrils, and the city named Saurabha represents the aroma. The companion spoken of as *avadhūta* is the sense of smell. The door called *mukhyā* is the mouth, and *vipaṇa* is the faculty of speech. *Rasajña* is the sense of taste.

(*Bhāgavata Purana*, 4.29.11)

Purport of H.D.G. Bhaktivedanta Swami Prabhupada:

The word *avadhūta* means "most free." A person is not under the rules and regulations of any injunction when he has attained the stage of *avadhūta*. In other words, he can act as he likes. This stage of *avadhūta* is exactly like air, which does not care for any obstruction. In the Bhagavad Gita (6.34) it is said:

चञ्चलं हि मनः कृष्ण प्रमाथि बलवद्दृढम् ।
तस्याहं निग्रहं मन्ये वायोरिव सुदुष्करम् ॥

cañcalaṁ hi manaḥ kṛṣṇa
pramāthi balavad dṛḍham
tasyāhaṁ nigrahaṁ manye
vāyor iva suduṣkaram

"The mind is restless, turbulent, obstinate, and very strong, O Kṛṣṇa, and to subdue it is, it seems to me, more difficult than controlling the wind."

(Bhagavad Gita, 6.34)

Just as air or wind cannot be stopped by anyone, the two nostrils, situated in one place, enjoy the sense of smell without impediment. With the tongue, the mouth continuously tastes all kinds of tasty foods.

अक्षरत्वाद्वरेण्यत्वाद्धूतसंसारबन्धनात् ।
तत्त्वमस्यर्थसिद्धत्वात् अवधूतोऽभिधीयते ॥

akṣaratvād vareṇyatvād
dhūta-saṁsāra-bandhanāt
tat tvam asy-artha siddhatvāt
avadhūto 'bhidhīyate

Since he is immutable (*akṣara*), the most excellent (*varenya*), since he has removed the worldly attachments (*dhūta-samsāra-bandanāt*) and he has realized the meaning of *tat tvam asi* (That thou art), he is called *avadhūta*.

(*Kulārṇava Tantra*, 17.24)

From Yogapedia:

What does *avadhūta* mean?

Avadhūta is a Sanskrit term used to refer to a person who has reached a stage in their spiritual development in which they are beyond worldly concerns. People who have reached the stage of *avadhūta* may act without considering common social etiquette or their own ego. This term is often used in the cases of mystics or saints.

Advanced yoga practitioners may find inspiration in the idea of reaching this stage through further sustained meditation and asana practice. *Avadhūta* is often associated with some sort of eccentric and spontaneous behavior from a holy person. This comes partly from the fact that mystics who have achieved this level of spiritual enlightenment may forget wearing clothes or other normal social behavior.

About the Prabhuji Mission

Prabhuji Mission is a Hindu religious, spiritual, and charitable organization founded by H.H. Avadhūta Bhaktivedānta Yogācārya Śrī Ramakrishnananda Bābājī Mahārāja. Its purpose is to preserve the "Path of Retroprogressive Alignment," which reflects Prabhuji's vision of *Sanātana-dharma* and advocates for the global awakening of consciousness as the radical solution to humanity's problems.

Apart from imparting religious and spiritual teachings, the organization carries out extensive philanthropic work in the USA, based on the principles of karma yoga, selfless work performed with dedication to God.

Prabhuji Mission was established in 2003 in the USA as a Hindu church aimed at preserving its founder's universal and pluralistic vision of Hinduism.

The Prabhuji Mission operates a Hindu temple called Śrī Śrī Bhagavān Yeshua Jagat Jananī Miriam Premānanda Mandir, which offers worship and religious ceremonies to parishioners.

The extensive library of the Institute of Retroprogressive Alignment provides its teachers with abundant study materials to research the various theologies and philosophies explored by Prabhuji in his books and lectures. The Avadhutashram monastery educates monastic disciples on various aspects of Prabhuji's approach to Hinduism and offers them the opportunity to express devotion to God through devotional service by selflessly contributing their skills and training to the Mission's programs.

The Mission publishes and distributes Prabhuji's books and lectures and operates humanitarian projects such as the "Prabhuji Food Distribution Program," a weekly event in which dozens of families in need from Upstate New York receive fresh and nutritious food and the "Prabhuji Toy Distribution Program," which provides the less privileged kids with abundance of Christmas gifts.

Avadhutashram
Round Top, New York, United States

About the Avadhutashram

The Avadhutashram (monastery) was founded by Prabhuji. It is the headquarters of the Prabhuji Mission and the hermitage of H.H. Avadhūta Bhaktivedānta Yogācārya Śrī Ramakrishnananda Bābājī Mahārāja and his monastic disciples of the Ramakrishnananda Contemplative Monastic Order.

The ideals of the Avadhutashram are love and selfless service, based on the universal vision that God is in everything and everyone. Its mission is to distribute spiritual books and organize humanitarian projects such as the Prabhuji Food Distribution Program and the Prabhuji Toy Distribution Program.

The Avadhutashram is not commercial and operates without soliciting donations. Its activities are funded by Prabhuji's Gifts, a non-profit company founded by Prabhuji, which sells esoteric items from different traditions that he himself has used for spiritual practices during his evolutionary process. Its mission is to preserve and disseminate traditional religious, mystical, and ancestral crafts.

The Path of Retroprogressive Alignment

The Path of Retroprogressive Alignment does not require you to be part of a group or a member of an organization, institution, society, congregation, club, or exclusive community. Living in a temple, monastery, or *āśram* is not mandatory, because it is not about a change of residence, but of consciousness. It does not urge you to believe, but to doubt. It does not demand you to accept something, but to explore, investigate, examine, inquire, and question everything. It does not suggest being what you should be but being what you really are.

The Path of Retroprogressive Alignment supports freedom of expression but not proselytizing. This route does not promise answers to our questions but induces us to question our answers. It does not promise to be what we are not or to attain what we have not already achieved. It is a retro-evolutionary path of self-discovery that leads us from what we think we are to what we really are. It is not the only way, nor the best, the simplest, or the most direct. It is an involutionary process par excellence that shows what is obvious and undeniable but usually goes unnoticed: that which is simple, innocent, and natural. It is a path that begins and ends in you.

The Path of Retroprogressive Alignment is a continuous revelation that expands eternally. It delves into consciousness from an ontological perspective, transcending all religion and spiritual paths. It is the discovery of diversity as a unique and inclusive reality. It is the encounter of consciousness with itself, aware of itself and its own reality. In fact, this path is a simple invitation to dance in the now, to love the present moment, and to celebrate our authenticity. It is an unconditional proposal to stop living as a victim of circumstance and to live as a passionate adventurer. It is a call to return to the place we have never left, without offering us anything we do not already possess or teaching us anything we do not already know. It is a call for an inner revolution and to enter the fire of life that only consumes dreams, illusions, and fantasies but does not touch what we are. It does not help us reach our desired goal, but instead prepares us for the unexpected miracle.

This path was nurtured over a lifetime dedicated to the search for Truth. It is a grateful offering to existence for what I have received. But remember, do not look for me. Look for yourself. It is not me you need, because you are the only one who really matters. This life is just a wonderful parenthesis in eternity to know and love. What you yearn for lies in you, here and now, as what you really are.

Your unconditional well-wisher,
Prabhuji

Prabhuji today

Prabhuji has retired from public life

Prabhuji is the sole disciple of H.D.G. Avadhūta Śrī Brahmānanda Bābājī Mahārāja, who is himself one of the closest and most intimate disciples of H.D.G. Avadhūta Śrī Mastarāma Bābājī Mahārāja.

Guru Mahārāja guided Prabhuji until he officially bestowed upon him the sacraments of the sacred order of *avadhūtas*. Prabhuji was appointed as the successor of the lineage by his master, who conferred upon him the responsibility of continuing the line of disciplic succession of *avadhūtas*, or the sacred *paramparā*, officially designating him as guru and commanding him to serve as the successor Ācārya under the name H.H. Avadhūta Bhaktivedānta Yogācārya Śrī Ramakrishnananda Bābājī Mahārāja. Prabhuji is also a disciple of H.D.G. Bhakti-kavi Atulānanda Ācārya Mahārāja, who is a direct disciple of H.D.G. A.C. Bhaktivedānta Swami Prabhupāda.

In 2011, with the blessings of his Gurudeva, he adopted the path of a secluded *bhajanānandī* and withdrew from society to lead the contemplative life of a hermit. Since then, he has been living as an independent Christian-Marian Hindu religious hermit. His days have been spent in solitude, praying, writing, painting, and meditating in silence and contemplation.

He no longer participates in *sat-saṅgs*, lectures, gatherings, meetings, retreats, seminars, study groups, or courses. We ask everyone to respect his privacy and do not try to contact him by any means for gatherings, meetings, interviews, blessings, *śaktipāta*, initiations, or personal visits.

Prabhuji's teachings

As an *avadhūta* and a realized Master, Prabhuji has always appreciated the essence and wisdom of a wide variety of religious practices from around the world. Although many see him as an enlightened being, Prabhuji has no intention of presenting himself as a public figure, preacher, propagator of beliefs, promoter of philosophies, guide, coach, content creator, influencer, preceptor, mentor, counselor, consultant, monitor, tutor, teacher, instructor, educator, enlightener, pedagogue, evangelist, rabbi, *posek halacha*, healer, therapist, satsangist, pointer, psychic, leader, medium, savior, New Age guru, or authority of any kind, whether spiritual or material. According to Prabhuji, the quest for the Self is individual, solitary, personal, private, and intimate. It is not a collective endeavor to be undertaken through organized, institutional, or community religiosity. Since 2011, Prabhuji has disagreed with spirituality practiced in a social, communal, or collective manner. Therefore, he does not proselytize or preach, nor does he try to persuade, convince, or make anyone change their perspective, philosophy, or religion. Many may find his insights valuable and apply them partially or fully to their own development, but Prabhuji's teachings should not be interpreted as personal advice, direction, counseling, instruction, guidance, tutoring, self-help methods, or techniques for spiritual, physical, emotional, or psychological development. The proposed teachings do not aspire to be definitive solutions for life's spiritual, material, financial, psychological, emotional, romantic, family, social, or physical problems. Prabhuji does not promise miracles, mystical experiences, astral journeys, healings of any kind, connections with spirits, angels or extraterrestrials, astral travel to other planets, supernatural powers, or spiritual salvation.

Service and glorification of the guru are fundamental spiritual principles in Hinduism. The Prabhuji Mission, as a traditional Hindu church, practices the millenary *guru-bhakti* tradition of reverence to the master.

Prabhuji has delegated the choice to his disciples between keeping his teachings exclusively within the monastic order or spreading his message for the public benefit. Upon the explicit request of his disciples, Prabhuji has agreed to have his books published and his lectures disseminated, as long as this does not compromise his privacy and his life as a hermit. Some disciples and friends of the Prabhuji Mission, on their own initiative, help to preserve Prabhuji's legacy and his interfaith teachings for future generations by disseminating his books, videos of his internal talks, and websites.

The Sacred Way

Some time ago, on the sacred journey toward transcendence, Prabhuji reaffirmed his resolve not to disturb those who showed no interest in joining him on this path. This decision is not simple detachment, but instead, a deliberate choice to preserve the essence of this migratory route: a commitment to authenticity and deepening self-inquiry. Such a decision, far from being an abandonment, is a respectful recognition of individual autonomy and divergent destinies and aspirations. On this journey, choosing fellow travelers is not a mere whim, but an exercise in critical discernment and alignment with those whose vision intertwines with his own in the search for our home within our own house.

Public services

Even though the monastery does not accept new residents, volunteers, donations, collaborations, or sponsorships, the public is invited to participate in daily religious services and devotional festivals at the Śrī Śrī Bhagavān Yeshua Jagat Jananī Miriam Premānanda Mandir.

Titles by Prabhuji

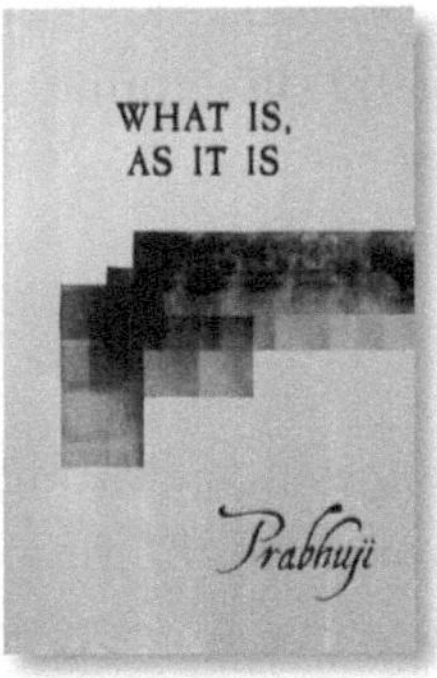

What is, as it is: Satsangs with Prabhuji (English)
ISBN-13: 978-1-945894-26-8

Lo que es, tal como es: Satsangas con Prabhuji (Spanish)
ISBN-13: 978-1-945894-27-5

Russian: ISBN-13: 978-1-945894-18-3

Kundalini yoga: The power is in you (English)
ISBN-13: 978-1-945894-30-5

Kundalini yoga: El poder está en ti (Spanish)
ISBN-13: 978-1-945894-31-2

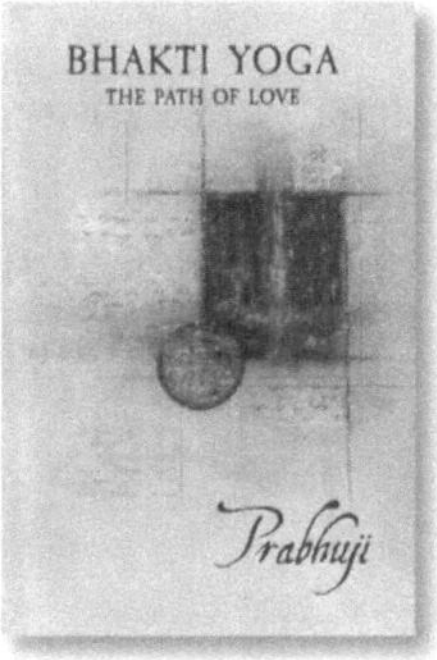

Bhakti yoga: The path of love (English)
ISBN-13: 978-1-945894-28-2

Bhakti-yoga: El sendero del amor (Spanish)
ISBN-13: 978-1-945894-29-9

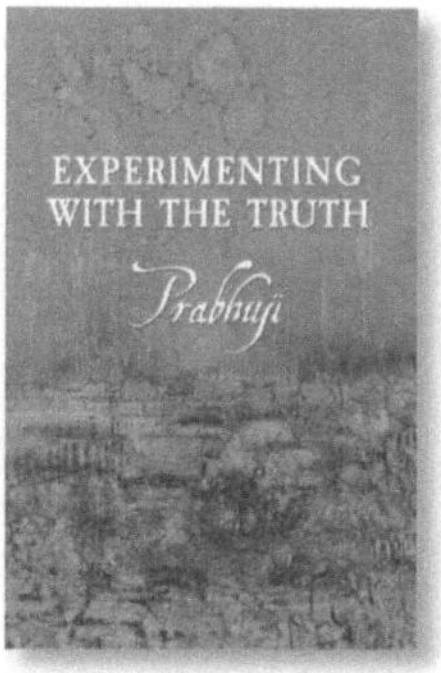

Experimenting with the Truth (English)
ISBN-13: 978-1-945894-32-9
Experimentando con la Verdad (Spanish)
ISBN-13: 978-1-945894-33-6
Experimenting with the Truth (Hebrew)
ISBN-13: 978-1-945894-93-0

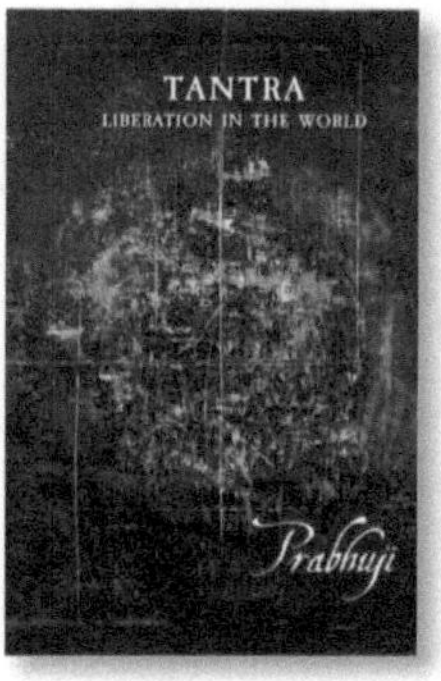

Tantra: Liberation in the world (English)
ISBN-13: 978-1-945894-36-7

Tantra: La liberación en el mundo (Spanish)
ISBN-13: 978-1-945894-37-4

Advaita Vedanta: Being the Self (English)
ISBN-13: 978-1-945894-34-3

***Advaita Vedānta*: Ser el Ser (Spanish)**
ISBN-13: 978-1-945894-35-0

Beyond Answers: Philosophy in the Eternal (English)
ISBN-13: 978-1-945894-91-6

Más allá de las respuestas: La filosofía en la búsqueda eterna (Spanish)
ISBN-13: 978-1-945894-88-6

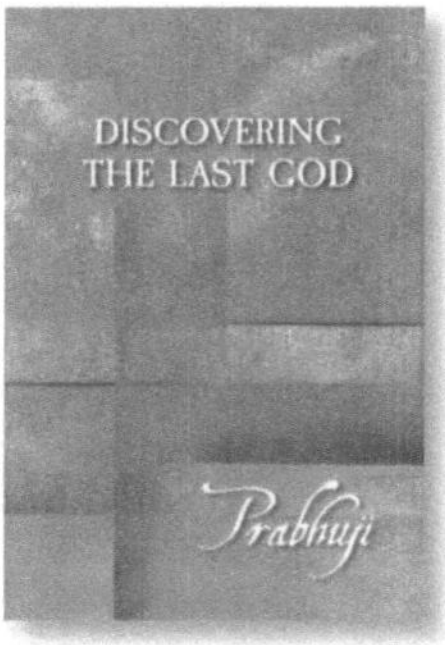

Discovering the last God (English)
ISBN-13: 978-1-945894-75-6

Descubriendo al último Dios (Spanish)
ISBN-13: 978-1-945894-81-7

Questioning your answers: Philosophy as a question (English)
ISBN-13: 978-1-945894-80-0

Cuestionando tus respuestas: La filosofía como pregunta (Spanish)
ISBN-13: 978-1-945894-77-0

Īśāvāsya Upanishad
commented by Prabhuji
(English)
ISBN-13: 978-1-945894-38-1

Īśāvāsya Upaniṣad
comentado por Prabhuji
(Spanish)
ISBN-13: 978-1-945894-40-4

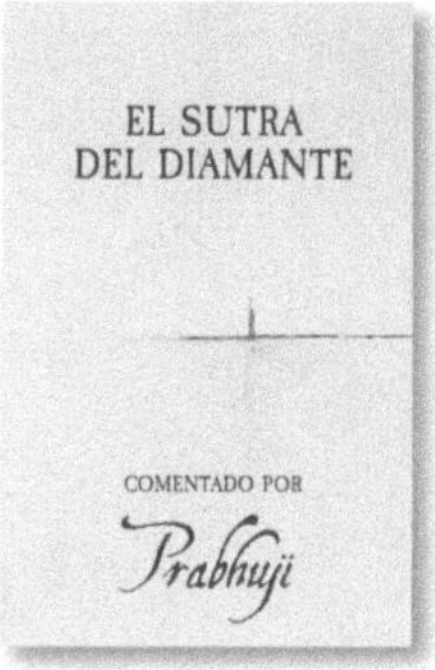

The Diamond Sūtra
commented by Prabhuji
(English)
ISBN-13: 978-1-945894-51-0

El Sūtra del Diamante
comentado por Prabhuji
(Spanish)
ISBN-13: 978-1-945894-54-1

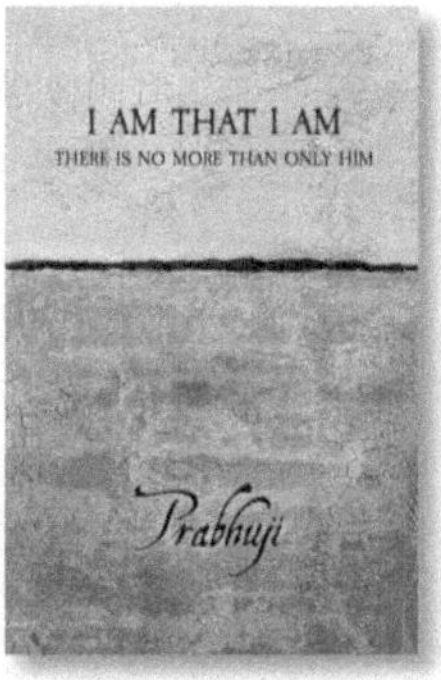

I am that I am
(English)
ISBN-13: 978-1-945894-45-9

Soy el que soy
(Spanish)
ISBN-13: 978-1-945894-48-0

Being - Volumen I and II (English)
ISBN-13: 978-1-945894-73-2
ISBN-13: 978-1-945894-80-0

Ser - Volumen I y II (Spanish)
ISBN-13: 978-1-945894-70-1
ISBN-13: 978-1-945894-94-7

Symbolic turn (English)
ISBN-13: 978-1-945894-61-9

El giro simbólico (Spanish)
ISBN-13: 978-1-945894-58-9

Phenomenology of the sacred (English)
ISBN-13: 978-1-945894-67-1

La fenomenología de lo sagrado (Spanish)
ISBN-13: 978-1-945894-64-0

www.ingramcontent.com/pod-product-compliance
Lightning Source LLC
Chambersburg PA
CBHW052102280426
43673CB00069B/24
* 9 7 8 1 9 4 5 8 9 4 7 8 7 *